EUROPEAN MENNONITES
AND THE HOLOCAUST

During the Second World War, Mennonites in the Netherlands, Germany, occupied Poland, and Ukraine lived in communities with Jews and close to various Nazi camps and killing sites. As a result of this proximity, Mennonites were neighbours to and witnessed the destruction of European Jews. In some cases they were beneficiaries or even enablers of the Holocaust. Much of this history was forgotten after the war, as Mennonites sought to rebuild or find new homes as refugees. The result was a myth of Mennonite innocence and ignorance that connected their own suffering during the 1930s and 1940s with earlier centuries of persecution and marginalization.

European Mennonites and the Holocaust identifies a significant number of Mennonite perpetrators, along with a smaller number of Mennonites who helped Jews survive, examining the context in which they acted. In some cases, theology led them to accept or reject Nazi ideals. In others, Mennonites chose a closer embrace of German identity as a strategy to improve their standing with Germans or for material benefit.

A powerful and unflinching examination of a difficult history, *European Mennonites and the Holocaust* uncovers a more complete picture of Mennonite life in these years, underscoring actions that were not always innocent.

MARK JANTZEN is a professor of history and chair of the Department of History and Conflict Studies at Bethel College.

JOHN D. THIESEN is an archivist and co-director of libraries at Bethel College.

Transnational Mennonite Studies
General Editor: Aileen Friesen

European Mennonites
and the Holocaust

EDITED BY MARK JANTZEN
AND JOHN D. THIESEN

UNIVERSITY OF TORONTO PRESS
Toronto Buffalo London

PUBLISHED IN ASSOCIATION WITH THE
UNITED STATES HOLOCAUST MEMORIAL MUSEUM

© University of Toronto Press 2020
Toronto Buffalo London
utorontopress.com

ISBN 978-1-4875-0795-4 (cloth) ISBN 978-1-4875-3725-8 (EPUB)
ISBN 978-1-4875-2554-5 (paper) ISBN 978-1-4875-3724-1 (PDF)

Transnational Mennonite Studies

Library and Archives Canada Cataloguing in Publication

Title: European Mennonites and the Holocaust / edited by Mark Jantzen and John D. Thiesen.
Names: Jantzen, Mark, 1963– editor. | Thiesen, John D., editor.
Description: Series statement: Transnational Mennonite studies | Includes bibliographical references and index.
Identifiers: Canadiana (print) 20200308122 | Canadiana (ebook) 20200308300 | ISBN 9781487525545 (softcover) | ISBN 9781487507954 (hardcover) | ISBN 9781487537258 (EPUB) | ISBN 9781487537241 (PDF)
Subjects: LCSH: Mennonites – Europe – History – 20th century. | LCSH: Mennonites – Europe – Social conditions – 20th century. | LCSH: Holocaust, Jewish (1939–1945) | LCSH: World War, 1939–1945 – Collaborationists – Europe. | LCSH: World War, 1939–1945 – Underground movements – Europe. | LCSH: World War, 1939–1945.
Classification: LCC D810.C665 E97 2020 | DDC 940.53/180882897 – dc23

The assertions, arguments, and conclusions contained herein are those of the author or other contributors. They do not necessarily reflect the opinions of the United States Holocaust Memorial Museum.

University of Toronto Press acknowledges the financial assistance to its publishing program of the Canada Council for the Arts and the Ontario Arts Council, an agency of the Government of Ontario.

When you spread out your hands in prayer,
I hide my eyes from you;
even when you offer many prayers,
I am not listening.
Your hands are full of blood!

Isaiah 1:15

Then he will say to those on his left, "Depart from me, you who are cursed, into the eternal fire prepared for the devil and his angels. For I was hungry and you gave me nothing to eat, I was thirsty and you gave me nothing to drink, I was a stranger and you did not invite me in, I needed clothes and you did not clothe me, I was sick and in prison and you did not look after me."

They also will answer, "Lord, when did we see you hungry or thirsty or a stranger or needing clothes or sick or in prison, and did not help you?"

He will reply, "Truly I tell you, whatever you did not do for one of the least of these, you did not do for me."

Matthew 25:41–45

The solitariness of grief is so heavy.
Who alone can bear it?
The cavern is without light.
Who can roll the stone from your mouth?

Connie T. Braun
"Remember"

Contents

List of Illustrations ix

Acknowledgments xi

Introduction – Neighbours, Killers, Enablers, Witnesses:
The Many Roles of Mennonites in the Holocaust 3
DORIS L. BERGEN, MARK JANTZEN, AND JOHN D. THIESEN

Introduction to Chapter 1 – Mennonites and Nazi Crimes:
Gerhard Rempel's Call for Historical Reckoning 35
DORIS L. BERGEN

1 Mennonites, War Crimes, and the Holocaust 41
GERHARD REMPEL, EDITED BY DORIS L. BERGEN
WITH JOHN D. THIESEN

2 Enjoying the Entitlements of German Freedom: German
Mennonites and Nazi Church-State Policy 72
JAMES IRVIN LICHTI

3 Antisemitism and the Concept of *Volk*: The Mennonite
Youth Circular Community at the Beginning of the Nazi
Dictatorship 104
IMANUEL BAUMANN

4 German Mennonite Theology in the Era of National
Socialism 125
ARNOLD NEUFELDT-FAST

5 Dutch Mennonite Theologians and Nazism   153
PIETER POST

6 Mennonite Collaboration with Nazism: A Case Study of the Responses of Mennonites in Deutsch Wymyschle, Poland, to the Plight of Local Jews during the Early Nazi Occupation Period (1939–1942)   172
COLIN P. NEUFELDT

7 Mennonites in Ukraine before, during, and Immediately after the Second World War   202
DMYTRO MYESHKOV

8 A Portrait of Khortytsya/Zaporizhzhia under Occupation   229
AILEEN FRIESEN

9 Dutch Mennonites and Yad Vashem Recognition   250
ALLE G. HOEKEMA

10 Identity and Complicity: The Post–Second World War Emigration of Chortitza Mennonites   269
ERIKA WEIDEMANN

11 A Usable Past: Soviet Mennonite Memories of the Holocaust   290
HANS WERNER

12 Selective Memory: Danziger Mennonite Reflections on the Nazi Era, 1945–1950   307
STEVEN SCHROEDER

List of Contributors   319

Index   323

Illustrations

Maps

1   Mennonites in Europe during the Second World War   7
2   Gąbin and Surrounding area   175
3   Chortitza/Zaporizhzhia area   207
4   Molotschna/Molochans'k area   209

Illustrations

1.1   Kiev killing scene   49
1.2   Heinrich Wiens   58
5.1   Cornelis B. Hylkema   160
5.2   Frits Kuiper   161
6.1   Frieda and Peter Ratzlaff with daughter Ella, circa 1940   173
6.2   The wedding of Agnes Pauls to Gustav Ratzlaff, Peter's brother, 6 March 1942   174
6.3   Minna and Peter Pauls   184

Figures

2.1   Sect, Free Church, Provincial Church Properties   75

Acknowledgments

The subject of European Mennonites and the Holocaust remains a contentious and emotional issue for many whose relatives and co-religionists were involved as neighbours, killers, accomplices, or witnesses. We thus asked for and received assistance that was more wide-ranging and notably more personal than might be typical for such a book, in that a number of contributors have written about their own family or community history. Since this volume builds on work done in March 2018 at the "Mennonites and the Holocaust" conference held at Bethel College, North Newton, Kansas, our thanks will start there.

In addition to the volume editors, John Sharp of Hesston College, Hesston, Kansas, was on the conference organizing committee. Our first phone call was to Doris Bergen, whose quick acceptance of the role of keynote speaker lent impetus to the conference and whose advice at many stages has shaped this book, including especially in her contribution to the introduction. Important support before and, crucially, at the conference was provided by Bethel College's President Jon Gering and Vice-President of Academic Affairs Robert Milliman as well as by Rachel Pannabecker, Renae Stucky, Alec Loganbill, and William Eash, along with the students in Mark Jantzen's spring 2018 History of the Holocaust course.

Important financial support for the conference came from the Marpeck Fund, the Fransen Family Foundation, and the Schowalter Foundation, with additional support from Bethel College and Hesston College, as well as the Mennonite Library and Archives and the Mennonite Polish Studies Association, both housed at Bethel College. The more than two hundred attendees at the conference helped create a dynamic and intense environment that demonstrated the high level of interest in this topic. A special thanks to all the presenters, some of whom became contributors to this volume. Coming from many countries on both sides of the Atlantic, those who presented new archival work and engaged one another in discussion made it possible for the larger audience to experience research in action. Others shaped more reflective contributions via literature and theatre that helped listeners better understand and process the trauma. One of these presentations was by the Canadian poet Connie T. Braun, who wrote the poem "Remember" soon afterwards to reflect on the conference and on her parents' trauma as Mennonite children in Poland and Ukraine. That poem is part of a larger project soon to be published. We are grateful for her permission to use a small excerpt in the preface of this volume.

To hear English, Dutch, German, Ukrainian, and Russian mixing together during breaks and from the podium during the questions that followed the presentations was an unusual aural sensation on the Great Plains of today; it was also an important reminder of the international dimensions of both Mennonite life and the Holocaust. Our thanks to those who helped translate at the conference in both formal and informal settings, particularly Johannes Dyck for his assistance with Russian.

The book benefited greatly from early interest shown by Richard Ratzlaff and the later support of Stephen Shapiro of the University of Toronto Press. Hadas Binyamini, formerly at the University of Toronto, and currently a PhD student at New York University, gave valuable assistance in initial editorial and formatting work on several chapters. Michael J. Fisher created our maps. The latter two aspects were funded by an Insight Grant from the Social Science and Humanities Research Council of Canada and Doris Bergen's Wolfe Chair in Holocaust Studies.

In addition to the strong support of the University of Toronto Press and its excellent staff, one Jewish and one Mennonite institution each provided generous publishing support. Our thanks to the Anne Tanenbaum Centre for Jewish Studies at the University of Toronto and its director, Anna Shternshis, and to the Centre for Transnational Mennonite Studies at the University of Winnipeg and its co-director Royden Loewen. In addition, Aileen Friesen, also co-director at the latter centre and a contributor to this volume, offered this volume a home as the inaugural text for her new Transnational Mennonite Studies series with the University of Toronto Press. We were delighted to accept that offer and look forward to seeing much additional scholarship being published here.

Finally, a note about place names, which occur in a variety of languages in our sources and changed often between different languages during and after the Second World War. We have decided to use current names, most notably for Polish and Ukrainian place names, when available and possible, and older German names if current names are not readily available. The main exception is our retention of German regional names for Mennonite areas of settlement in Ukraine, known as colonies, most prominently Chortitza and Molotschna, since those area names are not currently part of Ukrainian administrative nomenclature. For those readers who are accustomed to reading all German place names this may require some adjustment. For readers who are newer to this literature, this approach makes it easier to find the locations named on current maps. We ask that readers accept the remaining inconsistencies with an understanding of the complexities involved since it was not always clear how best to implement this goal.

EUROPEAN MENNONITES
AND THE HOLOCAUST

Introduction

Neighbours, Killers, Enablers, Witnesses: The Many Roles of Mennonites in the Holocaust

DORIS L. BERGEN, MARK JANTZEN,
AND JOHN D. THIESEN

By August 1942, the Holocaust had passed a terrible milestone: half of its Jewish victims were now dead. Those still alive anywhere in Europe were fighting for survival. That same month, SS Captain (*Hauptstürmführer*) Heinrich Wiens was leading a subunit of Mobile Killing Squad D (*Einsatzgruppe* D).[1] Four such squads, lettered A to D, with about 500 men in each, were primarily responsible for the murder of 1.5 million Jews on German-occupied Soviet territory.[2] Wiens's unit, D-10a, was stationed at that time in Pyatigorsk and Kislovodsk in the northern Caucasus, registering Jews and planning their murders, which he and his men carried out in the beginning of September. The "glass factory" massacre of 1,800 Jews from Kislovodsk was carried out under Wiens's command and involved driving groups of fifty people in the back of a gas van that asphyxiated them with carbon monoxide. Wiens personally scouted and selected the tank trap near a glass factory on the edge of Mineralnye Vody for this killing spree.[3]

Wiens was born to Mennonite parents in 1906 near Molochans'k/Halbstadt, the main city of the former Mennonite colony of Molotschna. He left, most likely in 1930, for Danzig, where there was a large Mennonite settlement, joined the Nazi Party and the SS in 1931, and served as a Nazi Party bureaucrat until the war started. In the fall of 1941 he was back in his home town, where his squad assisted in murdering Jews, Roma, and Soviet activists in the Molotschna area before moving on to commit other crimes in Crimea and the Caucasus.[4]

Also in August 1942, across the continent in Zaandam, the Netherlands, Geertje Pel, a Mennonite woman, was asked if she would keep a promise made in 1940 at the start of the German occupation to help a Jewish family. Although her husband had died since they made that promise together, after Nazi transports of Jews to killing centres in the East began in the spring of 1942, she agreed to take in a newborn baby, Marion Swaab. Geertje said that a Mennonite should abide by Jesus's teaching in Matthew 5:37: "But let your 'yes' be 'yes,' and your 'no' 'no.'" Even as a widow she would therefore keep her word. Marion's parents were able to escape the country; her grandparents and most of the rest of her family were killed in Auschwitz or Sobibor. In 1944 a neighbour who was a policeman betrayed Marion and Geertje. Ordered to report to Amsterdam with the baby, Geertje complied for herself, so as to spare others in the family interrogation, arrest, and imprisonment, but she left Marion with her twenty-one-year-old daughter Trijnie. Geertje was sent to a camp and eventually murdered in the gas chambers of Ravensbrück early in 1945.[5] Trijnie and Marion survived the war.[6]

These two Mennonites, Heinrich Wiens and Geertje Pel, played radically different roles in the Holocaust. This volume recounts their stories and others and explores what binds them together, along with many other Mennonite actions, ideas, and memories. Two general arguments emerge. The first relates to variety: Mennonites varied widely in location, beliefs, and actions. The second is about a pattern: Mennonites landed on the end of a spectrum tilted toward enabling, participating in, and benefiting from Nazi German rule, which included the genocide of Jews. The evidence presented in this book suggests that most Mennonites under Nazi rule, collectively and individually, sometimes consciously, in many cases unawares, through their actions and often their inaction, accepted and supported the Nazis. To put it simply, the killer Heinrich Wiens and the rescuer Geertje Pel were both exceptions, but Pel may have been even more exceptional than Wiens.

Who Were the Mennonites?

"Mennonite" refers to a number of Christian groups who developed out of the sixteenth-century Anabaptist movement and who shared commitments to adult baptism, a decentralized organizational structure that left final decisions to congregations, and an impulse to form networks and conferences to foster mutual support, to promote projects that could not be undertaken by congregations alone (such as mission work and education), and to appeal to governments and other institutions. Mennonites in the Netherlands had been together in a single conference since 1811. Mennonites in Germany in the early twentieth century were mostly split between a larger, northern, more liberal and nationalist Alliance (*Vereinigung*) and a smaller, southern, pietist-leaning Federation (*Verband*).

One cannot accurately describe Mennonites in Europe at the time of the Holocaust as non-resistant or as rejecting the use of violence in any circumstance, a tenet developed by Anabaptists but lost in Europe over time. Mennonites in Russia (later, the Soviet Union) were the last group to hold to the historical doctrine of rejecting all forms of military service, as a decreasing number of them won exemptions from the Soviet army through service in a labour force in the 1920s with the support of Tolstoyans. This opportunity ended in the 1930s after work with youth was forbidden all churches in 1929; in that decade many pastors were shot and churches closed. After 1935 the Red Army rejected all requests from Mennonites to serve in the army's labour force or as non-combatants. Dutch Mennonites had begun serving in the military at the time of the French Revolution, and German Mennonites accepted military service in the 1870s, although initially as non-combatants. By the end of the First World War, however, the vast majority were serving as regular German soldiers.[7]

Nonetheless, most Mennonites retained a sense of being different from the majority national culture. Those elements of Mennonite life that stand out as exotic in North American media culture related to the lifestyles of Amish, plain Mennonites, and Hutterites were, however, never a feature of twentieth-century Mennonite life in Europe. The Hutterites and Amish emigrated in the latter half of the nineteenth century since Europe would no longer tolerate them, and "horse-and-buggy" Mennonites developed only in the Americas.

What did Mennonites have to do with the Holocaust? One simple answer to that question involves proximity. Important Mennonite communities and colonies were located near key sites of the Holocaust: in Germany itself, in the German borderlands and contested regions of Alsace and western Poland, in the Netherlands, and, most fatefully, in the southern part of Soviet Ukraine. The area around Gdańsk/Danzig, site of the major concentration camp complex of Stutthof, was also home to the largest Mennonite population in Germany. In short, virtually all Mennonites in Europe were neighbours to Jews: Mennonites and Jews encountered each other in the marketplace and on the street, in schools and in military training; some even intermarried.[8] The chapters by Gerhard Rempel and Hans Werner in this book each cite an example of Jewish–Mennonite intermarriage.

There were somewhat fewer than 185,000 Mennonites in Europe in 1939, although statistics from the Soviet Union are so unreliable that it is best not to trust them entirely. In addition, some statistics count only church members (adults), whereas others count the community (*Seelenzahl*). The largest group (120,000) was in the Soviet Union, where

Mennonites would have constituted roughly 10 per cent of the German speakers registered in the 1926 Soviet census. Of these, 75,000 lived in Soviet Ukraine and 45,000 in Soviet Russia, mostly in settlements in Siberia. These numbers were collected after roughly 25,000 Mennonites emigrated in the early and mid-1920s, mostly to Canada. Between 1929 and 1938, between 5 and 15 per cent of Ukraine's Mennonites were banished as part of Stalin's collectivization drive, or they were shot during purges, decreasing the total number accordingly.

The German invasion of the Soviet Union in June 1941 and the occupation that followed brought roughly 35,000 of Ukraine's Mennonites under German rule, a bit less than one third of all Mennonites in the Soviet Union. Others had been evacuated or expelled ahead of the German advance. Those who remained inhabited a killing area in the Holocaust and were involved as perpetrators, beneficiaries, and witnesses of crimes against Jews. This subgroup of 35,000 Mennonites retreated with the Germans, mostly to the Poznań/Posen/Wartheland region of German-occupied Poland in 1943. Of these, some 12,000 managed to stay in the West after the war, with the largest group emigrating to Canada. The majority were transported back to the Soviet Union.[9]

Given that most Soviet Mennonites never came under German rule, Dutch Mennonites were the largest group confronted with the Holocaust, albeit at some remove from most sites of mass killing. In 1940 there were 44,234 Mennonites listed in the *Doopsgezinde Jaarboekje* (Mennonite Yearbook).[10] A smaller group that also found themselves under German occupation were the 2,000 Mennonites of France, most of them located in Alsace and Lorraine.[11] Their story is unfortunately not included in this volume.

Particularly important during the Holocaust were the responses and attitudes of the roughly 17,000 Mennonites in Germany itself. This number includes Mennonites of the Free City of Danzig and those in Poland who had been part of the German empire until 1918. An additional 1,000 Mennonites lived on the former territory of Russian Poland in Mazovia, west of Warsaw along the Vistula River, and west of Lviv in Galicia in what had been Austrian Poland. The latter group had been shifting from German to Polish language use in the early twentieth century. Within the German empire, Mennonites were concentrated in the Vistula delta around Gdańsk – about 10,600 people; in the Palatinate – 2,800; and in urban congregations of the northwest, predominantly Krefeld and Hamburg – 2,000; with the balance of 1,700 Mennonites scattered across the three southern German states of Baden, Württemberg, and Bavaria, and associated together as the Federation (*Verband*).[12]

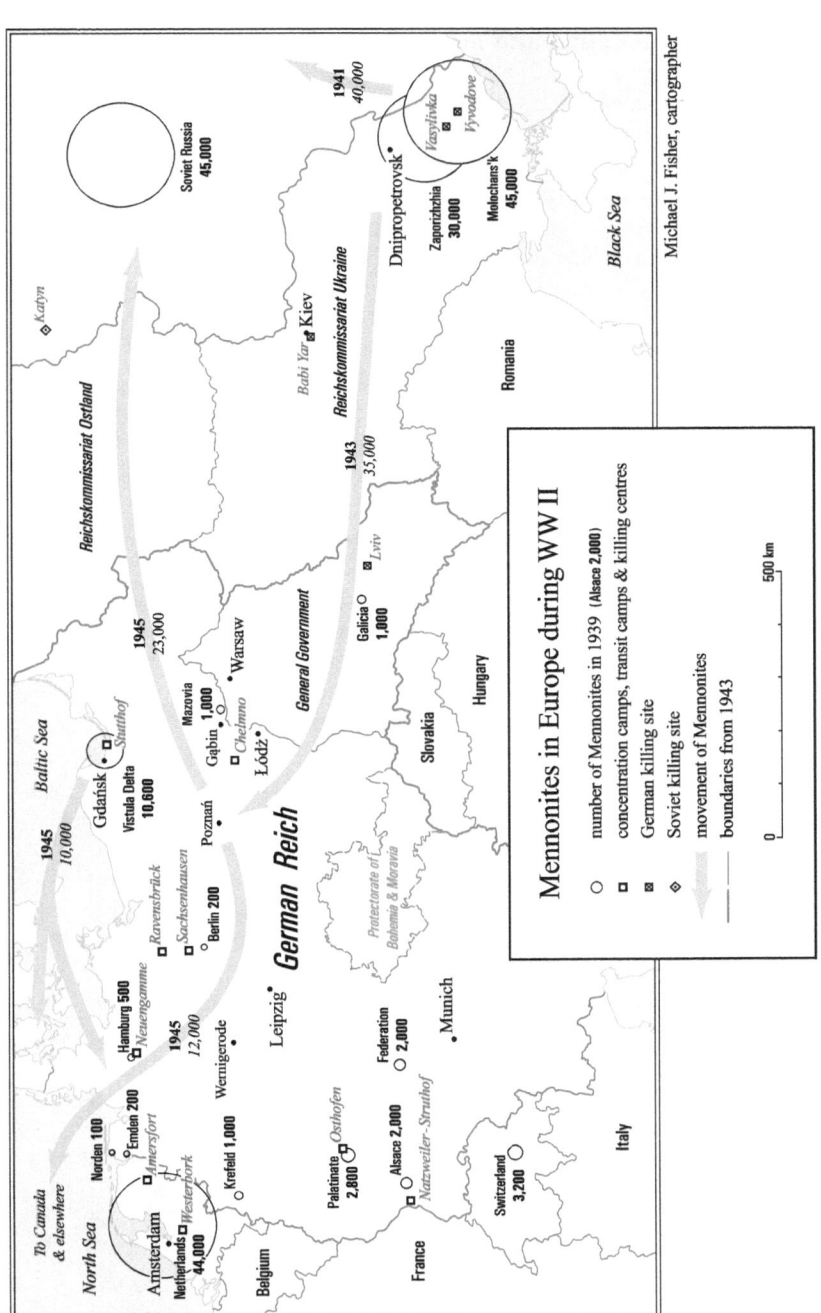

European Mennonites lived in proximity to Nazi German concentration camps and sites of mass killing of Jews and other victims, including Roma, Soviet POWs, Poles, and political opponents. Many such camps and sites of mass killing existed; this map shows some of those located near Mennonite communities.

Why Bother with Mennonites and the Holocaust?

Given the small number of Mennonites and their relative unimportance, what is the point of looking at Mennonites and the Holocaust? The answer is twofold. For "insiders" – that is, for Mennonites themselves – the subject is linked to identity, a sense of community, and the pursuit of truth. In Mennonite circles, even within families, topics related to the Second World War, the Holocaust, and antisemitism are often sites of disagreement, distortion, shame, and above all, silence.[13] Scholarship can be a powerful way to open up blocked conversations about the past and its significance in the present. For anyone interested in the Holocaust, be they Mennonite or not, research on this specific aspect produces a fuller historical picture, sheds light on the dynamics of extreme violence and the role of Christianity and Christian minorities in the destruction of Jewish lives and communities, and reveals the transnational dimensions of the Nazi German empire and its aftermath.

In the decades since the Second World War, some Mennonites in North America have asked whether there was a particular connection between Mennonites and Nazism. Were Mennonites more accepting of Nazism than their contemporaries? More resistant? Or pretty much the same? Were their responses similar to those of members of other small Christian groups?[14] If there is some particular connection one way or the other, then why is that? Are there lessons or guidelines in this history for preventing future atrocities and failures?

Mennonites have often written their history in a Menno-centric way that ignores important patterns related to being part of a larger group – of ethnic Germans in Russia, for example – or being aligned with particular social movements or political parties. "Mennonite exceptionalism" appeals to those who would like Mennonites to be either unusually good or unusually bad or perhaps unusually influential. But in the broader history of Nazism, Mennonites are rather insignificant and almost invisible. Hitler did not mention them in *Mein Kampf* or in any public speeches. They do not appear in the indices of major biographies of Heinrich Himmler, although Himmler was responsible for much of the operational activity of the Holocaust and for many policies imposed on the occupied Soviet Union.[15] Mennonites do not even show up in the indices of standard works on the German occupation of Ukraine, by Karel Berkhoff and Wendy Lower.[16] Some Mennonite writers boast about or lament occasional Mennonite encounters with Nazi leaders, but history does not revolve around Mennonites![17]

Perhaps a better approach would be to think about Mennonite *particularity*, rather than exceptionalism. The Mennonite interaction with

Nazism is a *particular* story that is not the same as anyone else's, but it need not carry the moral baggage that Mennonites were exceptionally good, exceptionally bad, or exceptionally significant. Readers will draw their own conclusions, but one interpretation of the chapters in this volume is that they offer little evidence of Mennonite exceptionalism. For people inside and outside Mennonite circles, the subject of Mennonites and the Holocaust offers a particular window onto interactions among ethnic, religious, and national groups in the midst of extreme violence. It provides a transnational case study of how a small religious group with historical and theological ties across several continents responded to the force of German nationalism and Nazi racism, and how those actions and decisions affected members of the group, their neighbours, and their descendants.

Scholarship focused on Mennonites in the 1930s and '40s pays some attention to the Holocaust, although Mennonites' own suffering has received considerably more attention.[18] Mennonites barely register in the general scholarship on Nazi Germany, the Second World War, the Holocaust, Jewish history, the Soviet Union, or Ukraine. This absence is not just because Mennonites were few in number; it is also because they were often illegible to others. For instance, in the vast collection of the USC Shoah Foundation Visual History Archive, with its more than 52,000 testimonies by survivors and witnesses of the Holocaust, a search for the term "Mennonites" produces only five hits, none of them related to interviews with Jews.[19] Almost certainly, many of the Jewish survivors interviewed encountered Mennonites, but why would they differentiate them from other ethnic Germans in German-occupied Ukraine or Poland or from other Dutch, Alsatian, or German Protestants?

This book seeks to bridge the gap between scholarship and discussions within Mennonite circles and research on the Holocaust in general. Unearthing what we can about what happened, telling the truth about this painful past, and making that knowledge more widely known is an important step both for Mennonites better to know their own history and for understanding the Holocaust. Many of the contributions in this volume were first presented at the "Mennonites and the Holocaust" conference held in March 2018 at Bethel College in North Newton, Kansas.[20] The impetus for the conference came from Mennonite Church USA. In September 2016, Andre Gingerich Stoner, at the time Director of Interchurch Relations, suggested to a number of Mennonite academics that Mennonite Church USA was interested in supporting three conferences: one on Mennonites and the Holocaust, one on "Reading the Bible after the Holocaust,"[21] and one on "the Jewish and Mennonite Experiences of Trauma." Mark Jantzen, Professor of

History at Bethel College; John D. Thiesen, Archivist at the Mennonite Library and Archives at Bethel; and John Sharp, Professor of History at Hesston College in Kansas, decided to accept this offer and planned the conference that dealt with the history portion of these issues. The Bethel conference took place in the context of two others on Mennonites and the Holocaust: one in Germany in 2015 that resulted in a book publication,[22] and one in Paraguay in 2017, with some of the resulting papers published in *Mennonite Quarterly Review*.[23]

It may seem that scholars have only recently begun to examine the role of Mennonites in the Holocaust, but the broader connections have long been an area of research. In many ways the current generation of English-language historiography on Mennonites and Nazism began with John Thiesen's 1999 book *Mennonite and Nazi?* and his 1992 article on US Mennonites and Nazism.[24] Thiesen was particularly interested in ideological affinities, and he traced the "American Mennonite Encounter with National Socialism" and analysed "Attitudes among Mennonite Colonists in Latin America, 1933–1945." Others picked up on Thiesen's themes and added questions of their own. James Urry's extensive scholarship on Mennonites deserves particular mention here.[25]

German Mennonites began their own public debates in the 1970s, and Canadian Mennonites were confronted with their own pro-Nazi sympathies by 1965 as a result of Frank Epp's dissertation, which remained unpublished.[26] In the wake of Thiesen's publications, broader attention to Mennonites and the Holocaust, especially in the new millennium, has had a variety of causes, including scholarly attention from Mennonites and non-Mennonites (notably Marlene Epp's path-breaking publications[27] and Eric Steinhart's 2009 article on Jack Reimer);[28] growing awareness of deportation cases in Canada and the United States against accused Nazi war criminals who belong to Mennonite congregations or have a Mennonite background; and increased engagement by Mennonites with public policy and the Israel/Palestine conflict. Mennonites as a whole, and institutions like the Mennonite Central Committee (MCC) and Mennonite Church USA, remain perplexed, divided, and uncertain as to how this history relates to their current activities and policies in Israel/Palestine. Meanwhile, Benjamin Goossen has done significant work to publicize the topic beyond Mennonite circles,[29] and the issue of Mennonites and the Holocaust dovetails with wider developments in the field of Holocaust studies, including increased attention to the Soviet Union and Soviet Jews during the Second World War.[30]

Themes: Actions/Agency, Definitions/Identities, Memory/Myth

Three major themes are woven into this volume. We have labelled them actions/agency, definitions/identities, and memory/myth. To some extent, all are present in each chapter.

Mennonite Actions, Mennonite Agency

A major achievement of the researchers whose work is presented in this volume has been to document the fact that some Mennonites were actively involved in the killing of Jews, disabled people, and others in countries under Nazi rule. Mennonites assisted the German occupiers in promoting antisemitism and removing Jews and Jewish influence from public life; they also served as administrators and translators for a vast colonial enterprise in the east, even helping set up a ghetto in one documented case. And they helped normalize genocide by accepting what most knew to be the stolen property, houses, and clothing of recently murdered Jews.

Using the recently opened KGB Archive in Kiev, Dmytro Myeshkov provides chilling accounts of Mennonite collaborators. For example, Ivan Klassen, a physician in the service of the SS, examined disabled patients in a hospital in the Mennonite Molotschna settlement. A killing squad followed up by shooting more than 100 children, women, and men whom Klassen had deemed unable to work. Aileen Friesen describes a massacre of Jews in Zaporizhzhia in southern Ukraine in 1942, just miles from a church where Mennonites from the Chortitza colony had gathered to celebrate Easter. Among the local police who did the killing were two Mennonite brothers. Erika Weidemann's chapter analyses the experiences of two Chortitza Mennonite women. One of them, an informant for the SS killing squad *Einsatzgruppe* C, used her language skills to inform on potentially subversive forced labourers.

Not all forms of involvement appear at first glance so dramatic. Several contributors draw attention to translation work, which opened the way to collaboration for many Mennonites, and to policing, the main role in which Mennonites participated in the killing of Jews. Colin Neufeldt's chapter, on Mennonites in the Mazovian voivodeship, shifts attention to German-occupied Poland and notes that at least twenty Mennonites, including Neufeldt's grandparents, left their village of Nowe Wymyśle/Deutsch Wymyschle to take over properties in nearby Gąbin from which Jews had been expelled. The chapters by Arnold Neufeldt-Fast and Pieter Post identify Mennonite theologians in

Germany and the Netherlands who embraced and propagated National Socialist ideology. In a publication outside this volume, Joachim Wieler quotes a letter by his father, a Wehrmacht officer, who in 1941 exulted from France, "The Lord is visibly on our side."[31]

Most challenging is the evidence that Mennonites were directly involved in the Holocaust as killers. This volume stakes out that far end of the spectrum. An important impetus in this direction came from Gerhard Rempel, a professor of German history and an outsider to the field of Mennonite studies. Late in his career Rempel began to research the context of his Mennonite family's wartime history. Shocked by what he found, he decided to write a book on Mennonites and the Holocaust, but he died before he was able to finish it. Rempel was the first to point out that Heinrich Wiens, the killing squad leader described at the beginning of this introduction, who was responsible for the murder of thousands of Jews, came from a Mennonite community in southern Ukraine.

Identities and Definitions

A central problem in this volume has to do with defining "Mennonite." When the stakes are so high, it is tempting to argue about definitions to the point of distraction. Rather than attempting to pin the category down with precision, we offer some considerations on approaches to defining Mennonites and analyse their implications. The muddled nature of Mennonite identity has been a major challenge in investigating Mennonites and Nazism. People find it hard to explain their rationale on whom to include or even to ask the question, "Who counts as a Mennonite?" There are at least five overlapping possibilities, all of them present in some form in this volume: familial, social, cultural, imposed, or theological. Researchers and readers alike need to be alert to the interplay among these categorizations. Since most individual Mennonites share several of these forms, our authors have not tried to parse Mennonite identity. It is clear that Mennonites differ regarding what being Mennonite means to them.[32]

A simplistic approach is to assume that a Mennonite is someone with a "Mennonite name" who comes from a "Mennonite family." An example might be Gerhard Rempel's discussion of the war criminal Jack Reimer.[33] Rempel asserts that Reimer was a Mennonite, without explanation or discussion. Doing so arguably sets up a contrast to an image of twenty-first-century North American, socially progressive Mennonites, or else an image of nineteenth-century or current North American Mennonite non-conformity to the world, and then applies that notion to a Soviet youth who would have had little if any experience of Mennonite community or church life. Historically, it might seem meaningless to describe Reimer as a Mennonite. But for Rempel, himself a Mennonite seeking traces of Mennonites in the past, Reimer's "Mennonite name" and family background, coupled with his Nazi ties, raised troubling questions.

Yet the category "Mennonite" cannot be defined simply on the basis of family background. Mennonite identity is in part a social network identity, not an individual one – a crucial point often forgotten. Rather than seeking a precise definition, it is worthwhile to consider how linguistic categories work. Labels like "Mennonite" or "Anabaptist" are more like the descriptors "tall" or "cold." Is a particular person "tall"? Well, compared to whom or what? Is it "cold" outside? Not if you ask a Manitoban. Are Jack Reimer or Walter Quiring or the Epp family or the perennials John Denver or Dwight Eisenhower "Mennonites?"[34] The answer is not a simple "yes" or "no" but "well, sort of," or "a little," or "not really," or "in this way, but not in other ways."

Look, for example, at the journalist and German propagandist Walter/Jacob Quiring. Here is someone who explicitly renounced his Mennonite religious beliefs and changed his name from the "Jewish-sounding" biblical name "Jacob" to the Germanic "Walter." Quiring may never have actually been a church member. During the Nazi era he listed himself as a "believer in God" (*gottgläubig*). Nazis used this term to explicitly repudiate a connection with the established churches and Christianity. This label might be loosely translated as "theistic," though it implied neopaganism. A bilingual person raised in Russia, but who left for Germany in 1921, and an early and ardent Nazi supporter, Quiring worked for a time on the Eastern Front as a Waffen SS intelligence officer. In that capacity he led interrogations of captured Soviet soldiers during which at least a score and perhaps many more were tortured to death.[35] Yet Quiring interacted constantly with the broader Mennonite community for most of his life, including during the Nazi era.[36] Later he was the long-time editor of *Der Bote*, an important Canadian Mennonite newspaper. To exclude him from the category "Mennonite" would be ridiculous.

Hans Harder, an author of novels set among Mennonites and ethnic Germans in Russia, is a similar case – someone who, at least in the 1930s, rejected his Mennonite affiliation and family background but continued to interact socially with Mennonites.[37] Harder features prominently in Rempel's analysis of Mennonites who witnessed and recorded the murder of Jews. Hajo Schroeder, a Nazi publicist and speaker also analysed by Rempel, is yet another, perhaps more extreme example.[38]

Or consider the case of an Epp family in the Danzig region, members of a Mennonite congregation who rarely attended, some of whom were ardent Nazi functionaries, and one of whom was imprisoned at Stutthof for leftist activities.[39]

For some Mennonites and for some outsiders observing them, being Mennonite was a cultural, even ethnic identity. One might call this group "non-religious Mennonites." Mennonites had a long history of marrying other Mennonites, and where this practice persisted over centuries and into the twentieth century, as it largely did in Germany and to an even greater extent in Russia, the sense of belonging to a distinct culture was not one that could be dropped as easily as rejecting church membership or disappearing into a new social group. Thus, certain names, customs, and foods, and in Soviet Ukraine the Low German language, were identified both by insiders and outsiders as "Mennonite."

A cultural approach casts a wide enough net to include those whose grandparents and parents were Mennonite, even if the person in question never entered a Mennonite church. It is also a wider net than that of a social network, since people raised in that culture who turned their back on it nonetheless might take its influence with them in unconscious ways. It is doubtful that Heinrich Wiens, the killing squad leader, had much exposure to Mennonite theology, or that he cultivated Mennonite social ties, although his widow and children became part of a Mennonite community after they arrived in Kansas in 1950.[40] Wiens seems at the very least to have been a product of Mennonite culture. He was also an ethnic German who escaped the Soviet Union in the 1920s, and an SS and Nazi Party member who murdered Jews. In the end Wiens was all these things.

As Doris L. Bergen highlights in her introduction to Gerhard Rempel's chapter, the cultural case to be made that Helmut Oberlander was a Mennonite is even more controversial. In the absence of any known family ties, is the identification of a person as Mennonite by some inside the community and some outside the community enough to include a person as Rempel does? This case highlights the multivalent nature of Mennonite identity and exposes the significance of determining who is inside and who outside the category.

Mennonites have often tried to impose order on their unruly social networks, and other times outsiders have tried to do it for them or to them. John Eicher, in his 2015 dissertation, described what might be called "Mennonite category hegemony" (not his term) in the early twentieth century, where some Mennonites (H.S. Bender) attempted to claim other Mennonites for their universal Mennonite category, even though those people did not want to be so claimed.[41] When we use the term "Mennonite," are we squeezing people of the past into an ideological system against their will or imposing expectations on them that they would not recognize? Does that matter? Is the historian's job to talk about people in the past the way they would want to be spoken of? If so, it would be difficult to analyse perpetrators. One reader of this chapter posed the question more broadly: what are the obligations of scholars toward the living?

Equally fraught are attempts to claim Mennonites for a specific nationality. This matter was especially contested in Ukraine, where Russian imperial law identified Mennonites first as foreign colonists, then specifically during the First World War as Germans aligned with a foreign enemy power whose land should be expropriated. The Soviet government kept the "German" label for Mennonites and added the class label "kulak" to many of them.[42] Because these labels carried serious threats to life, property, and the survival of Mennonite communities as distinct entities, Mennonites there, as Adolf Ehrt noted in the late 1920s, out of a combination of expediency and loyal commitment, adopted four different national identities: German, Russian, Mennonite, and indifferent.[43] As Mark Jantzen has observed, Mennonites in the nineteenth and twentieth centuries proved remarkably adaptable.[44]

In the pressure cooker of twentieth-century European wars and nationalism, many forces tried to morph Mennonite identity into something different. In Ukraine during the First World War and the disruptions that followed, most people who did not identify with any nation were forced to do so by the violence. Polish, Jewish, Ukrainian, Russian, and German national identities were claimed by and assigned to people who previously had mostly local, social, ethnic, or imperial identities.[45] Myeshkov's use of NKVD files from the 1930s reveals further twists to the story. A number of Mennonites and individuals with Mennonite connections show up in the records as agents first for the Soviets and later for the Germans. Was active collaboration one way that people suddenly living under German rule tried to counter potentially compromising pasts?[46]

After the Second World War, the issue of who is a Mennonite was complicated but also simplified by actions of the Mennonite Central Committee (MCC), a widely respected relief organization that provided help to people they considered part of Mennonite communities. In the process they sheltered some criminals and, sometimes knowingly, probably more often inadvertently, helped conceal wartime activities, including the killing of Jews. A case in point is Jacob Luitjens, who collaborated with Nazi Germans against Jews in the Netherlands and was tried and convicted of war crimes in that country, having been stripped of his Canadian citizenship in 1992. In the upheaval at the end of the war, Luitjens, a Dutch Mennonite, passed himself off as a Mennonite from the Danzig area, adopted the name Gerhard Harder, and emigrated with other Mennonites and MCC assistance to Paraguay. There he reverted to his real identity; he later went to Canada. For decades, he was an active member of a Mennonite church in Vancouver.[47] Although it is easy to point to thin claims to Mennonitism among many individuals from the Soviet Union who changed sides, names, and biographies – often more than once – in the tumultuous period of the 1930s and '40s, it is hard to exclude individuals who were welcomed into the fold by Mennonite organizations themselves.

Nazi ideology and practice subsumed Mennonites in the East under the label "ethnic German," a category that was the flipside of the target group "Jews."[48] The same SS agencies assigned to annihilate Jews in the former Soviet Union also coordinated the identification, protection, and promotion of ethnic Germans there. As Jews were expelled, ethnic Germans moved into their houses. As Jews were forced out of jobs, ethnic Germans took over their positions. As Jews were given starvation rations, ethnic Germans received extra food. Clothing taken from Jews who were killed was given to ethnic Germans. Ethnic Germans, who until 1943 could not be drafted into the German military as noncitizens, signed up for SS agencies, including auxiliary police, so-called self-defence units, the Waffen SS, and mobile killing squads. Indeed, part of the official rationale for "removing" Jews from society was to make room for ethnic Germans.[49] The 1935 movie *Friesennot* (*Frisians in Distress*) showed how Mennonites, real and imagined, were mobilized for Nazi purposes. The film does not explicitly refer to "Mennonites" or "Jews." Nonetheless, antisemitic canards about Jews/Bolsheviks as the lascivious, blasphemous, brutal foe of pure and noble "Aryans"/Christians/Germans/Mennonites are embedded in the story.[50]

Yet ethnic Germans were often considered second-class Germans who had to earn their place, as a display case in the Schindler Factory Museum in Krakow shows. A 1940 poster celebrating the seventh anniversary of the Nazi seizure of power on 30 January invited German citizens to the main program at the principal theatre and ethnic Germans to a different, smaller program in the old theatre. For Nazis, all Mennonites had the potential to fit the category of ethnic German, unless their behaviour did not conform to expectations. Thus, Nazis forced Mennonites both to accept an identity they might not otherwise have adopted and to prove themselves worthy of it or face dire consequences.[51]

Finally, some Mennonites claimed a primarily theological identity.[52] Rarely is this tendency as clearly documented as in the case of Geertje Pel, who cited a Bible verse, Matthew 5:37, that was key for Anabaptists in the sixteenth century and remains important to theological Mennonite identity even today. Often, however, it was theological variability rather than consistency that characterized Mennonites. In his chapter, James Lichti is careful to point out the range of Mennonite positions, public and private, on everything from the Hebrew Bible to antisemitism and Nazi racial policies. At the same time, he observes that the lack of centralized structures made it almost impossible to develop a coherent Mennonite voice of opposition. Alle Hoekema's discussion of Dutch Mennonites recognized by Yad Vashem as "Righteous Among the Nations" confirms this point. The forty individuals identified are, as Hoekema put it, not insignificant, but they are few. Nor do their accounts on the whole highlight Mennonite identity or beliefs as key factors. Instead they emphasize their networks, commitment to humanity, or even socialist leanings as what motivated them to help Jews.

Memory and Myth

Exploring the roles Mennonites played in the Holocaust unsettles the myth of Mennonite innocence, and this demythologizing is an important contribution of this volume. This collection of research about the Holocaust, mostly by Mennonites (by various definitions), inevitably raises the question of why Mennonites and other scholars are only now, seventy-five years after the fact, turning to this subject. An important framework for understanding this phenomenon involves collective memory, an idea developed by the French sociologist Maurice Halbwachs.[53] Other equivalent terms might be *popular* or *public* memory. All of these terms refer to a shared and widely accepted explanation for a historical event – for example, the American Revolution was about freedom. Collective memories, that is, how people explain particular events, can develop and change over time depending on circumstances, giving memory an unexpected (and self-fulfilling) element of choice. As Peter Novick noted, "we choose to center certain memories because they seem to us to express what is central to our collective identity."[54] This propensity to develop collective myths was especially active in postwar Europe: many nations that experienced messy histories of complicity settled on simplistic stories of victimhood and heroism.[55] Mennonites set up a particular myth of their history, but it was right in tune with the fashion of the day.

What is it about Mennonite collective memory that has shaped how Mennonites remember the Holocaust? As chapters by Erika Weidemann, Hans Werner, and Steven Schroeder show, Mennonites' initial Holocaust memories were forged in the crucible of postwar rebuilding. Their identity as German citizens or ethnic Germans or "Dutch" refugees from the East was connected to the matter of making a future after displacement and massive disruption. As Post and Hoekema demonstrate, identifying Dutch collaborators or resisters gave way to re-creating a Dutch and a *Doopsgezinde* community.

This path to highlighting Mennonite suffering fit well and easily into the larger collective memory of Mennonites as a persecuted people. Of course, the Nazis and the Soviets had made life difficult for Mennonites, but collective memory cast them as more extreme versions of the government oppression that Mennonites had faced for centuries. In the Soviet case this assumption was true, making the elision with the Nazi case come easily. A related and even more common practice was to recount Soviet crimes at length while treating the Nazi era, the war, and the Holocaust, at least in public, with almost total silence.[56]

For North American Mennonites, their own shifting collective memory set up a particularly jarring collision course on the topic of Mennonites and the Holocaust. The intense pressure on Mennonites, who had emigrated in part to preserve their exemption from military service, now to serve in the US and Canadian armed forces during the two world wars fostered an institutional commitment to achieving alternatives to the draft and then implementing them. This achievement – Civilian Public Service in the United States and various Alternative Service options in Canada – became the postwar collective memory of Mennonites even though a significant minority, and in some subgroups a majority, of Mennonite men became soldiers.

With the end of compulsory military service in both the United States and Canada, by the twenty-first century, progressive Mennonites had shifted from rejecting military service as the key component of a collective identity to seeing Mennonites as proponents of peace and justice claims on behalf of downtrodden minorities; this view encouraged them to understand themselves as a people always on the "right" side of history.[57] This centring of progressive Mennonite identity has made the conversation about Mennonite complicity in the Holocaust particularly painful. The biblical epigrams at the beginning of this book refer to Mennonites who collectively have blood on their hands but cannot fit that image into their self-understanding. We see ourselves as sheep doing good in the name of Christ, not as goats deserving judgment. Meanwhile, those with older, unreconstructed memories of

Mennonites as "good" Germans reject the need to revisit this period in history.

The dynamics of the Soviet context during the Nazi German war of annihilation deserve some attention. Mennonite particularity meant that although Mennonites were part of a shared history of occupation, devastation, and dislocation, they also played certain roles within that setting. Karel Berkhoff analysed how the brutality of Soviet policies in the wake of the 1932 famine broke down communal solidarity and norms and made the region susceptible to the Germans' divide-and-rule methods.[58] Diana Dumitru's observation, based on her study of Transnistria, that Soviet policies against antisemitism could have a long-term impact and lessen the vulnerability of Jews, is relevant in the way it was negated in Mennonite mythology, which erased traces of its ties to the Soviet system.[59] Myeshkov, Friesen, and Weidemann all note the disastrous impact of the Soviet experience on Mennonite communities in Ukraine. But those who had been victimized by Stalin were not the only Mennonites who joined the Nazi cause. Colin Neufeldt's chapter on Jewish–Mennonite relations in the Mazovian voivodeship shifts attention to German-occupied Poland, where Mennonites likewise also proved willing participants.

Familiar narratives about Mennonite suffering and survival can serve to conceal negative assumptions about Jews and Judaism. In some historical writing by Mennonites, the desire to defend the Mennonite community comes across as stronger than the desire to talk about the Holocaust. Mennonites seem to need a narrative to shield them from the Soviet past and the ways they participated in that system as well as from the Nazi past. Some Mennonite spokespersons have insisted that Mennonites were severely persecuted in a way comparable to what Jews faced. This notion of Mennonites as somehow akin to Jews easily elides knowledge and memory of Jewish suffering and Mennonite involvement in inflicting it and replaces it with an image of Mennonites as the true victims. Cultural expressions have encouraged reflection on issues that tend to be neglected or repressed in the harsh light of scholarship. Connie Braun's poetry and prose invite listeners to contemplate "the missing pieces of our narratives": Mennonite prejudices and the suffering and losses experienced by others.[60]

Many of the scholars in this volume have a personal involvement with their subjects, though not all have chosen to discuss those ties. Such connections both enrich this work and point to the fraught nature of our topic. These qualities are foregrounded in Colin Neufeldt's chapter on Mennonites in Nowe Wymyśle and the plight of local Jews in occupied Poland. In the very first sentence, Neufeldt introduces readers to "my Mennonite grandparents," Peter and Frieda Ratzlaff. Mennonites in Nowe Wymyśle benefited from German policies of "Aryanization" to gain everything from businesses and homes to wedding rings. The only resister Neufeldt's research turned up in Nowe Wymyśle was not a Mennonite but one of the few Lutherans in town. Steven Schroeder also worked with his own community, including close relatives, for interviews and research. Hans Werner examines Mennonite memoir literature from the standpoint of someone who has interrogated his own father's past in this regard. Jim Lichti, as a gay Mennonite, brings the perspective of someone who could have been targeted by the Nazis. All our authors combine profound engagement in this project, be it based on familial, moral, theological, professional, or activist commitments, with scholarly discipline and balance. We hope this approach creates an opening to confront and explore very difficult issues.

Chapter Outline

A portion of Gerhard Rempel's unfinished manuscript, titled "Mennonites, War Crimes, and the Holocaust," constitutes the first chapter of this book. We have placed it at the beginning because it articulates some core issues of our project. Most significantly, Rempel establishes that some Mennonites, or people with links to Mennonite families and communities, were killers. In the process, directly and indirectly, he reveals a series of problems and challenges that connect the chapters to follow. If "perpetrator" was a role some Mennonites played in the Holocaust, it is essential to examine how those individuals fit into or fell out of broader patterns, not only within Mennonite communities in occupied Ukraine and other sites of Nazi killing but also inside Germany and across the Mennonite diaspora. The matter of definition becomes urgent as the stakes for who counts as "Mennonite" rise.

Also instructive for our volume are the methodological problems evident in Rempel's piece. Unlike Rempel's 2010 article, which appeared in a Mennonite periodical, the chapter included here was directed at a general audience and intended for a university press. But Rempel's efforts to situate Mennonites in a wider history of the Holocaust, for instance by connecting them to the ethnic Germans whom Nazi Germans recruited as partners and beneficiaries of violence, are disrupted by his recurring slides back into a narrow perspective that expresses shock at Mennonites' supposed deviation from some imagined ideal. His goal of exposing Mennonite crimes against Jews largely erases Jews from the narrative and leaves little room for Jewish agency or Jewish perspectives. Indeed, he risks reproducing some of the anti-Jewish positions of his sources by leaving them uninterrogated. For instance, Rempel's key informants, even when they speak directly about Jews they knew, never provide their names, nor does Rempel draw attention to this absence. An integrated approach, by contrast, would try to see Jews as living parts of the story, not just as corpses.

Yet Rempel's piece is valuable, because it reveals the significance of this volume and of the ongoing discussions about Mennonites and the Holocaust. If some Mennonites were killers, others were their relatives, witnesses, enablers, partners, beneficiaries, and protectors. Only a very few opposed the killing or tried to help victimized Jews. What accounts for this pattern? The chapters that follow offer explanations.

Chapters 2, 3, and 4, by James Lichti, Imanuel Baumann, and Arnold Neufeldt-Fast, address prewar patterns among Mennonites in Germany and identify social structures and theologies that were predisposed toward National Socialism. Lichti argues that for Mennonites in Germany, their status as a "free church" was an important factor in generating acceptance of the Nazi system. Denominationalism, Lichti shows, proved remarkably compatible with Hitler's church-state policy, and German Mennonites easily joined forces with "positive Christianity" in the assault against "Jewish materialism." Lichti compared Mennonites with other "free" churches, notably Quakers and Seventh-day Adventists.

In Germany, most Mennonites were either farmers, business people, or professionals, all social groups that in general welcomed the new regime. Imanuel Baumann focuses on the prewar years in Hitler's Germany. His analysis identifies intense "racial thinking" among young Mennonites, which "created a blindspot for Nazi crimes." The Mennonite youths he studies were strongly attached to the concept of "community." Mennonites had come to think of themselves as part of the German "community" and viewing that now as a "racial" category bound them more tightly to the Nazi state. Such ideas justified political involvement, pro-Nazi of course, and legitimated military service.

For Arnold Neufeldt-Fast, theology is the main issue, but it is theology entwined with social engineering. Within Germany, both theologically conservative and liberally disposed Mennonites accepted and in fact welcomed exclusion of Jews. In occupied Ukraine, the categories of "German nationality" and "blood and destiny" mapped all too neatly onto Mennonite notions of superiority vis-à-vis Ukrainians, Bolsheviks, and Jews.

The next set of chapters – by Pieter Post, Colin Neufeldt, Dmytro Myeshkov, Aileen Friesen, and Alle Hoekema – reveal additional factors by moving geographically and chronologically beyond Germany.

The Nazi system provided benefits to Mennonites outside German borders and protected them from some of the ravages of war. Claiming Germanness gave them an advantage or an option to join the system. Jews did not have that option, and neither did most ethnic Poles. The Mennonite embrace of the Nazi version of being German was not inevitable. Mennonites did not all act the same way; that said, those who pushed against the tide were exceptions.

With the invasion of Poland in 1939 and of the Low Countries and France a year later, additional Mennonite populations found themselves living under Nazi German rule, a situation that created myriad opportunities for those favoured by the occupiers at the same time as it devastated the lives and livelihoods of the unwanted. Post's contribution extends the focus on theology by examining two Dutch Mennonite contemporaries, one of whom (Cornelis Hylkema) avidly supported National Socialism, even before the war, and one (Frits Kuiper) who remained a pacifist and social democrat. In a rather different context, Post, quoting Elisabeth Brussee-van der Zee, echoes Lichti's finding that the Mennonite emphasis on freedom of the church provided minimal guidance as to the place of the congregation in the world. Members of the Dutch National Socialist Movement sat in the pews undeterred. Still, Kuiper and a few others were involved in resistance and relief efforts, and Kuiper helped hide Jews. Unsurprisingly, Kuiper was honoured after the war, while the Mennonite community kept quiet about Hylkema.

Colin Neufeldt uses extensive research in German and Polish sources, and interviews with members of his extended family, to provide a detailed analysis of Mennonite participation in the appropriation of Jewish property, exclusion of Jews, and destruction of Jewish lives and communities. If the question posed is, "How could Mennonites be part of the Holocaust?," Neufeldt's answer is both nuanced and clear. Hitler Germany's aggression fuelled Polish violence against ethnic Germans before the war, and memories of arrests and beatings in turn justified attacks on Jewish and non-Jewish Poles once the invasion gave permission to ethnic Germans, among them Mennonites, to deal with their neighbours as they pleased. In 1939 and 1940, during the period of the Molotov–Ribbentrop pact, Germany and the Soviet Union cooperated in the destruction of Poland. As Neufeldt's analysis proves, anti-Communism was not necessary for Mennonites to turn on Jews. Other factors sufficed: greed, disruption of previous norms, antisemitism, and a sense of impunity.

Dmytro Myeshkov's chapter moves us to the setting introduced by Rempel and touched on by Arnold Neufeldt-Fast: Soviet Ukraine. Here

Mennonites and Jews lived in close proximity, and here Mennonites enacted their most brutal roles in the Holocaust. Also significant is the importance of women in Myeshkov's narrative. First, the Soviet Union depended on informers to infiltrate tight-knit communities, and some Mennonite women obliged. Then, when the Germans arrived, they too needed local contacts and translators. Again, Mennonite women, some of them the same individuals, fit the bill. Like Rempel, Myeshkov describes individual Mennonites who were active killers – among them Heinrich Wiens – and he also provides extensive evidence of the key role a Mennonite doctor played in the massacre of 100 elderly people and children from a home for the disabled in the Molotschna colony. Myeshkov's use of NKVD records raises its own set of methodological challenges, but he makes a thoughtful and compelling case for their utility, and they provide a valuable counterpoint to the Mennonite memoirs and other internal sources often used by "insider" scholars.[61]

Aileen Friesen, too, reaches beyond Mennonite records to add depth and detail to the picture in Ukraine. Hers is the first chapter in the book to consider Jewish sources as relevant and indeed indispensable for particular subjects, notably regarding rescuers and helpers. Also important to note is the small number of Mennonites, mostly in the Netherlands, who took immense risks to aid Jews. Aileen Friesen describes a few cases of Ukrainians from Zaporizhzhia who helped Jews and were recognized after the war as Righteous Among the Nations. However, she finds no confirmed examples of rescue or assistance by Mennonites for persecuted Jews and only one complicated, unconfirmed account that may refer to a child who may have had a Jewish background. Friesen's discussion of rescue throws into relief the disputes around defining Mennonites. When tempted to dismiss a perpetrator as not really Mennonite, one might conduct a thought experiment: if an individual with that same biography were depicted as a rescuer of Jews, a hero, or a martyr, would that person still be dismissed as not Mennonite enough to count?

The subject of Mennonites who helped Jews is the central focus of Alle Hoekema's chapter, though here the setting is the Netherlands under German occupation. Not surprisingly, given the large number of Dutch "Righteous Among the Nations," some Mennonites from the Netherlands are represented in that group. As Hoekema shows, their individual stories are fascinating and inspiring, but they were few in number, and only in one or two cases did their being Mennonite appear to have played a role. Perhaps as well, the free nature of Mennonite congregations worked against solidarity on the side of helping Jews, as it did against developing a coherent position against Nazism.

The final three chapters, by Erika Weidemann, Hans Werner, and Steven Schroeder, bridge the war and postwar eras by examining issues of justice, retribution, memory, and responsibility as they affect Mennonites and would-be Mennonites. Weidemann analyses the postwar testimonies of two Chortitza women, Franziska Reimers and Adina Epp. Both were implicated in Nazi crimes. Reimers, who had been a spy for the Soviets, went over to the Germans in 1941 and worked for Mobile Killing Squad C at a time when its men murdered tens of thousands of Jews. After the war she fled into the British Zone of Occupation, and rumour has it that she may have made it to Canada, perhaps with the help of the Mennonite Central Committee. Epp worked as a teacher in German-occupied Poland, where, like the many women studied by Elizabeth Harvey,[62] she enjoyed career opportunities and adventures she would not have had without a war that put her on the side of racial privilege. Those Chortitza Mennonites who succeeded in reinventing themselves after the war as Dutch, often thanks to MCC efforts, were able to qualify as displaced persons and gain refugee assistance.

Hans Werner approaches many of the same themes as Weidemann but from a self-conscious position as an insider, "a second generation descendent of Mennonites from the former Soviet Union who experienced the Second World War as adults." His father was a soldier, first for the Red Army and then for the Wehrmacht, and his mother was working on a collective farm when the Germans invaded.[63] Werner analyses passages from a number of memoirs by Mennonites and people no longer connected to a Mennonite identity and draws attention to narrative patterns that equate annihilation of Jews with experiences of their own communities under Stalin. Steve Stern's concept of "memory as salvation" gives Werner a way to describe Mennonite accounts that balance the offence of killing innocent Jews with Hitler's supposed saving of Soviet Mennonites from "godless Communism."[64] For example, Werner analyses how Mennonites frame their memories to produce "usable" versions of the past by writing only about the Soviet years or by balancing sadness about the Holocaust with joy at the Nazi German "liberation" of Christianity.

Steven Schroeder's chapter, the last in the book, brings together the themes of personal involvement with those of collective or communal memory and its gaps and failures.[65] Schroeder, whose great-grandfather was a Mennonite preacher in a small village in the Gdańsk region, learned from records found by Gerhard Rempel that his family used forced labourers from Stutthof concentration camp. At least judging from the names on the records, Mennonites were deeply involved in the day-to-day operation of Stutthof.[66]

Drawing on interviews he conducted in Germany and Canada, Schroeder presents the Danziger Mennonites' embrace of National Socialism alongside their strategies for avoiding confronting their involvement in the crimes of Hitler's Germany. Here too, narratives that situate Mennonites as "Jews" function to distract from Mennonite complicity; those same narratives claim for Mennonites the status of chosen people and the moral high ground of victimization. In Schroeder's assessment, there are barriers but also hopeful signs. He lays out what is at stake for the past, present, and future: "Unexamined – or worse, embraced – the Mennonite encounter with Nazism remains as a lingering problematic case full of injustice, particularly as Nazism harbours contempt and violence." Schroeder calls on readers to recognize the colonial enterprises in which we participate, if we are settlers or the beneficiaries of settlers, and to take the steps of truth telling and "listening to those who have been harmed – yes, including those who have been harmed by us."

As Schroeder and the other contributors to this volume demonstrate, the history of Mennonites and the Holocaust is not a sealed-off chapter from a bygone era but a challenge, a warning, and a reflection of the world around us. Thinking critically about history does not imply that I would do better. But it might open possibilities to listen, understand, and care.

NOTES

1 On Einsatzgruppe D, see Andrej Angrick, *Besatzungspolitik und Massenmord. Die Einsatzgruppe D in der südlichen Sowjetunion 1941–1943* (Hamburg: Hamburger Edition, 2003).
2 Regarding the Einsatzgruppen in general, see Hilary Earl, *The Nuremberg SS-Einsatzgruppen Trial, 1945–1958: Atrocity, Law, and History* (New York: Cambridge University Press, 2009); Yitzhak Arad, Shmuel Krakowski, Shmuel Spector, and Stella Schossberger, eds., *The Einsatzgruppen Reports: Selections from the Dispatches of the Nazi Death Squads' Campaign against the Jews, July 1941–January 1943*, trans. Schlossberger (New York: Holocaust Library, 1989); and Helmut Krausnick, *Hitlers Einsatzgruppen. Die Truppe des Weltanschauungskrieges 1938–1942* (Frankfurt am Main: Fischer Taschenbuch, 1985).
3 Gerhard Rempel, "Mennonites and the Holocaust: From Collaboration to Perpetration," *Mennonite Quarterly Review* 84 (October 2010): 540–47.
4 Kiril Feferman, *The Holocaust in the Crimea and the North Caucasus* (Jerusalem: Yad Vashem, 2016).

5 For context, see Rochelle Saidel, *The Jewish Women of the Ravensbrück Concentration Camp* (Madison: University of Wisconsin Press, 2004); Germaine Tillion, *Ravensbrück* (Garden City: Anchor Press, 1975).
6 On rescuers and the Righteous, see Mordecai Paldiel, *The Righteous Among the Nations: Rescuers of Jews during the Holocaust* (New York: Harper, 2007); Bob Moore, *Survivors: Jewish Self-Help and Rescue in Nazi-Occupied Western Europe* (New York: Oxford University Press, 2010); Bert Jan Flim, *Saving the Children: History of the Organized Effort to Rescue Jewish Children in the Netherlands, 1942–1945* (Bethesda, MD: CDL, 2005).
7 The best current overview of Mennonites in Europe is John A. Lapp and C. Arnold Snyder, eds., *Testing Faith and Tradition*, Global Mennonite History Series: Europe (Intercourse: Good Books, 2006.) See also Diether Götz Lichdi, *Die Mennoniten in Geschichte und Gegenwart. Von der Täuferbewegung zur weltweiten Freikirche*, ([Weisenheim]: Agape Verlag, 2004); and Mark Jantzen and John D. Thiesen, eds., *European Mennonites and the Challenges of Modernity* (North Newton: Bethel College, 2016). On Soviet Mennonite resistance to the draft see Lawrence Klippenstein, *Peace and War: Mennonite Conscientious Objectors in Tsarist Russia and the Soviet Union before World War II, and other COs in Eastern Europe* (Winnipeg: Mennonite Heritage Centre, 2016); Hans Rempel, *Waffen der Waffenlosen: Ersatzdienst der Mennoniten in der UdSSR* (Winnipeg: Canadian Mennonite Bible College, 1980). On German Mennonites' switch to military service, see Mark Jantzen, *Mennonite German Soldiers: Nation, Religion, and Family in the Prussian East, 1772–1880* (Notre Dame: University of Notre Dame Press, 2010).
8 For example, see interview with Anna Braun, 20 September 1946, in David P. Boder, "Topical Autobiographies of Displaced People," Bound Section IV, ch. 16, 28–9, in United States Holocaust Memorial Museum archives, Washington, D.C.; also, more generally, Helen Stoltzfus and Albert Greenberg's 1989 play, *Heart of the World*, raised the topic of intermarriage as a way to explore what divides and connects Mennonites and Jews: for an excerpt and current introduction, see *Mennonite Life* 72 (2018), https://mla.bethelks.edu/ml-archive/2018/excerpt-heart-of-the-world.php (accessed 27 November 2019).
9 Cornelius J. Dyck, *An Introduction to Mennonite History*, 3rd ed. (Scottdale: Herald, 1993), 182, 190; Adolf Ehrt, *Das Mennonitentum in Rußland von seiner Einwanderung bis zur Gegenwart* (Berlin: Julius Beltz, 1932), 151–3; John B. Toews, *Czars, Soviets, and Mennonites* (Newton: Faith and Life, 1982), 167; Terry Martin, "The Russian Mennonite Encounter with the Soviet State, 1917–1955," *Conrad Grebel Review* 20, no. 1 (Winter 2002): 5–59.
10 Nanne van der Zijpp and C. F. Brüsewitz, "Netherlands," *Global Anabaptist Mennonite Encyclopedia Online*, February 2011 (accessed 26 July 2018),

https://gameo.org/index.php?title=Netherlands&oldid=145932#Membership_Statistics.
11 *Christlicher Gemeinde-Kalender* 42 (1933): 153–5.
12 Lichdi, *Die Mennoniten in Geschichte und Gegenwart*, 432. On Galician Mennonites, who are otherwise not covered here, see James Regier, "Utopia of Ash: Galician Mennonites and the Second Polish Republic," in *European Mennonites and the Challenge of Modernity over Five Centuries: Contributors, Detractors, and Adapters*, ed. Mark Jantzen and John D. Thiesen (North Newton: Bethel College, 2016): 347–65.
13 Relevant to these issues is a review essay by James C. Juhnke, "Ingrid Rimland, the Mennonites, and the Demon Doctor," *Mennonite Life* 60, no. 1 (March 2005), https://mla.bethelks.edu/ml-archive/2005Mar/juhnke%20essay.php (accessed 27 November 2019).
14 See Daniel Heinz, ed., *Freikirchen und Juden im "Dritten Reich," Instrumentalisierte Heilsgeschichte, Antisemitische Vorurteile und Verdrängte Schuld* (Göttingen: Vandenhoeck & Ruprecht, 2011); also Rebecca Carter-Chand, "Doing Good in Bad Times: The Salvation Army in Germany, 1886–1946, PhD diss., University of Toronto, 2016.
15 Peter Longerich. *Heinrich Himmler* (Oxford, UK: Oxford University Press, 2012); Richard Breitman, *The Architect of Genocide: Himmler and the Final Solution* (New York: Alfred A. Knopf, 1991).
16 Karel C. Berkhoff, *Harvest of Despair: Life and Death in Ukraine under Nazi Rule* (Cambridge: Belknap Press of Harvard University Press, 2004); Wendy Lower, *Nazi Empire-Building and the Holocaust in Ukraine* (Chapel Hill: University of North Carolina Press, 2005). Mennonites do show up briefly in Martin Dean, "Soviet Ethnic Germans and the Holocaust in the Reich Commissariat Ukraine, 1941–1944," in *The Shoah in Ukraine: History, Testimony, Memorialization,* ed. Ray Brandon and Wendy Lower (Bloomington: Indiana University Press, 2011): 252–54.
17 Horst Gerlach, "Mennonites, the Molotschna, and the Volksdeutsche Mittelstelle in the Second World War," *Mennonite Life* 41, no. 3 (September 1986): 6; Heinrich B. Unruh, *Fügungen und Führungen. Benjamin Heinrich Unruh 1881–1959. Ein Leben im Geiste christlicher Humanität und im Dienste der Nächstenliebe* (Detmold: Verein zur Erforschung und Pflege des Russlanddeutschen Mennonitentums, 2009), 332–4; Benjamin W. Goossen, *Chosen Nation: Mennonites and Germany in a Global Era* (Princeton: Princeton University Press, 2017), 149–161.
18 For example: Peter Letkemann, *A Book of Remembrance: Mennonites in Arkadak and Zentral, 1908–1941* (Winnipeg: Old Oak, 2016); Frank H. Epp, *Mennonite Exodus: The Rescue and Resettlement of the Russian Mennonites since the Communist Revolution* (Altona: D.W. Friesen and Sons, 1962). A memoir with scholarly apparatus is Jacob A. Neufeld, *Path of Thorns: Soviet Mennonite*

28   Doris L. Bergen, Mark Jantzen, and John D. Thiesen

Life under Communist and Nazi Rule, ed. and intro. by Harvey L. Dyck, trans. Sarah Dyck (Toronto: University of Toronto Press, 2014).

19   The five interviews indicated give scant information about Mennonites. For instance, Peter Pintus, born to Jewish parents in 1927 in Berlin, was baptized Lutheran in 1935. After the war, he and his parents came to the United States under the sponsorship of the Mennonite church, which sent them to live for a year on a farm in western Kansas. Pintus, interview 15886, tape 4, 5–5:20. *Visual History Archive,* USC Shoah Foundation, 1996. Accessed 17 January 2018. Albertina Brink, born in 1932 in Amsterdam, describes how her mother hid Jews in a small room in their house for short periods of time. Only in passing does Brink mention that she, her mother, and her sisters attended a Mennonite (*doopsgezinde*) church. Brink, interview 55078, tape 4, 26:25. *VHA,* USC Shoah Foundation, 1995. Accessed 17 January 2018. Thanks to Camila Collins Araiza for research assistance.

20   Joel H. Nofziger, Ben Goossen, Aileen Friesen, and Jason Kauffman prepared thoughtful summaries of all the sessions for the "Anabaptist Historians" blog. Those are available at https://anabaptisthistorians.org/tag/mennonites-and-the-holocaust-conference/page/1.

21   This conference is tentatively scheduled to take place at Anabaptist Mennonite Biblical Seminary, Elkhart, Indiana, although the final decision on dates has not yet been taken.

22   Marion Kobelt-Groch and Astrid von Schlachta, eds. *Mennoniten in der NS-Zeit. Stimmen, Lebenssituationen, Erfahrungen* (Bolanden-Weierhof: Mennonitischer Geschichtsverein, 2017).

23   *Mennonite Quarterly Review* 92, no. 2 (April 2018).

24   John D. Thiesen, *Mennonite and Nazi? Attitudes among Mennonite Colonists in Latin America, 1933–1945* (Kitchener: Pandora Press, 1999); Thiesen, "The American Mennonite Encounter with National Socialism," *Yearbook of German-American Studies* 27 (1992): 127–58. Notwithstanding the date, this publication actually appeared in January 1994.

25   See, most recently, James Urry, "Mennonites in Ukraine during World War II: Thoughts and Questions," *Mennonite Quarterly Review* 93 (Jan 2019): 81–111; for an earlier overview, Urry, *Mennonites, Politics, and Peoplehood: Europe – Russia – Canada* (Winnipeg: University of Manitoba Press, 2006).

26   The German Mennonite historiography is outlined in this volume in ch. 3 by Imanuel Baumann; see also Hans-Jürgen Goertz, Gerhard Rempel, and Alfred Neufeld Friesen, "Drittes Reich," *Mennonitisches Lexikon V,* http://www.mennlex.de/doku.php?id=top:drittes_reich. Frank H. Epp, "An Analysis of Germanism and National Socialism in the Immigrant Newspaper of a Canadian Minority Group: The Mennonites, in the 1930s," PhD diss., University of Minnesota, 1965. The newspaper analysed was

Der Bote. He did publish a brief summary outlining many Canadian Mennonites' support for Nazis in the 1930s in *Mennonite Exodus*, 319–28.

27 Marlene Epp, *Women without Men: Mennonite Refugees of the Second World War* (Toronto: University of Toronto Press, 2000); see also Epp, "The Memory of Violence: Soviet and East European Mennonite Refugees and Rape in the Second World War," *Journal of Women's History* 9, no. 1 (1997): 58–87.

28 Eric Steinhart, "The Chameleon of Trawniki: Jack Reimer, Soviet *Volksdeutsche*, and the Holocaust," *Holocaust and Genocide Studies* 23, no. 2 (Fall 2009): 239–62; idem, "Policing the Boundaries of 'Germandom' in the East: SS Ethnic German Policy and Odessa's 'Volksdeutsche,' 1941–1944," *Central European History* 43, no. 1 (2010): 85–116; idem, *The Holocaust and the Germanization of Ukraine* (New York: Cambridge University Press in association with the United States Holocaust Memorial Museum, 2015). See also Viktor K. Klets, "Caught between Two Poles: Ukrainian Mennonites during World War Two," in *Minority Report: Mennonite Identities in Imperial Russia and Soviet Ukraine, 1789–1945*, ed. Leonard G. Friesen (Toronto: University of Toronto Press, 2018): 287–317. Access to previously closed archives in the old East Bloc is another significant factor. For a masterful demonstration of the possibilities such records afford historians of the period, see Lynne Viola, *Stalinist Perpetrators on Trial: Scenes from the Great Terror in Soviet Ukraine* (New York: Oxford University Press, 2017).

29 Goossen, *Chosen Nation*, esp. ch. 6, "Fatherland: War and Genocide in the Mennonite East," 147–73; Goossen, "Measuring Mennonitism: Racial Categorization in Nazi Germany and Beyond," *Journal of Mennonite Studies* 34 (January 2016): 225–46.

30 For an overview, Omer Bartov, "Eastern Europe as the Site of Genocide," *The Journal of Modern History* 80, no. 3 (2008): 557–93; on Mennonites, Aileen Friesen, "Soviet Mennonites, the Holocaust and Nazism," *Anabaptist Historians* (25 April 2017), https://anabaptisthistorians.org/2017/04/25/soviet-mennonites-the-holocaust-nazism-part-1; on Soviet Jews, Anna Shternshis, *When Sonia Met Boris: An Oral History of Jewish Life under Stalin* (New York: Oxford University Press, 2017).

31 Joachim Wieler, "Family Responses to the 1930s and 1940s in West Prussia," *Mennonite Life* 72 (2018), https://mla.bethelks.edu/ml-archive/2018/family-responses-to-the-1930s-and-1940s-in-west-pr.php (accessed 27 November 2019). For the German version, see Joachim Wieler, "Das ist kein Schatzkästchen, doch es blieb gut behütet!," in *Mennoniten in der NS-Zeit. Stimmen, Lebenssituationen, Erfahrungen*, ed. Marion Kobelt-Groch and Astrid von Schlachta (Bolanden-Weierhof: Mennonitscher Geschichtsverein, 2017), 244–64. Wieler presented at both the 2018 Mennonites and the Holocaust conference in North Newton, Kansas, and the 2015 conference in Münster, Germany.

32 Marlene Epp has surveyed the problems of trying to define a Mennonite identity, noted the obsession this search became for Mennonite academics from the 1970s to early 2000s, and concluded that the task is elusive at best and may, in fact, be "useless." "Cookbook as Metaphor for a People of Diversity: Canadian Mennonites after 1970," *Journal of Mennonite Studies* 37 (2019): 11–27 at 12.
33 Rempel, "Mennonites and the Holocaust," 535–40. See also ch. 1.
34 For those who are not Mennonite insiders, it should be explained that a frequent Mennonite pastime is to speculate about the Mennonite linkages of certain celebrities and prominent personalities. So, for example, the singer John Denver and US president Eisenhower both had relatives who were members of Mennonite-related denominations.
35 Ted Regehr, "Walter Quiring: Mennonite Historian and German Propagandist," in *Shepherds, Servants and Prophets: Leadership among the Russian Mennonites (ca. 1880–1960)*, ed. Harry Loewen (Kitchener: Pandora, 2003), 324.
36 See Jonathan F. Wagner, *Brothers beyond the Sea: National Socialism in Canada* (Waterloo: Wilfrid Laurier University Press, 1981), 49, 107.
37 In his application for membership in the *Reichsschrifttumskammer*, Harder listed himself as Protestant (*evangelisch*) rather than Mennonite. A copy of the application is at the Mennonite Library and Archives in MS 416, box 7, John D. Thiesen papers. The original comes from the former "Berlin Document Center" collection now housed at the German Bundesarchiv in Berlin-Lichterfelde, with microfilm copies available at the US National Archives, microfilm publication A3339 series RKK. For a general biographical sketch of Harder, see Al Reimer, "Harder, Johannes 'Hans' (1903–1987)." *Global Anabaptist Mennonite Encyclopedia Online* http://gameo.org/index.php?title=Harder,_Johannes_%22Hans%22_(1903–1987)&oldid=141151 (accessed 8 February 2019).
38 Gerhard Rempel, "Heinrich Hajo Schroeder: The Allure of Race and Space in Hitler's Empire," *Journal of Mennonite Studies* 29 (2011): 227–54.
39 Christiana Epp Duschinsky, "Mennonite Responses to Nazi Human Rights Abuses: A Family in Prussia/Danzig," *Journal of Mennonite Studies* 32 (2014): 81–96.
40 In 1936 Wiens was not listed as a member in any of the Mennonite congregations around Danzig: *Mennonitisches Adreßbuch 1936* (Karlsruhe: Heinrich Schneider, 1936). His widow apparently connected with Kansas Mennonites after receiving an aid package that included the address of the sender, *Mennonite Weekly Review* 28, no. 25 (22 June 1950), 4.
41 John Phillip Robb Eicher, "Now Too Much for Us: German and Mennonite Transnationalisms, 1874–1944," PhD diss., University of Iowa, 2015.
42 See Lynne Viola, *Unknown Gulag: The Lost World of Stalin's Special Settlements* (Oxford: Oxford University Press, 2009). On Mennonites

specifically, see Colin Neufeldt, "Separating the Sheep from the Goats: The Role of Mennonites and Non-Mennonites in the Dekulakization of Khortitsa, Ukraine (1928–1930)," *Mennonite Quarterly Review* 83 (April 2009): 221–91.
43 Ehrt, *Das Mennonitentum in Rußland*, 109; see also Tara Zahra, "Imagined Noncommunities: National Indifference as a Category of Analysis," *Slavic Review* 69, no. 2 (Spring 2010): 93–119. In addition, Russian and Soviet Mennonites at times claimed a Dutch identity. For the First World War–era Dutch claims, see Abraham Friesen, *In Defense of Privilege: Russian Mennonites and the State before and during World War I* (Winnipeg: Kindred Productions, 2006). An uncritical account of the Mennonite Central Committee's role in recognizing Mennonite refugees from Ukraine as Dutch is in Peter and Elfrieda Dyck, *Up from the Rubble: The Epic Rescue of Thousands of War-Ravaged Mennonite Refugees* (Scottdale: Herald Press, 1991), 81–131.
44 Jantzen, *Mennonite German Soldiers*.
45 George O. Liber, *Total Wars and the Making of Modern Ukraine, 1914–1954* (Toronto: University of Toronto Press, 2016), esp. 48–54. The importance of violence in creating new identities in this time period is documented by Max Bergholz, *Violence as a Generative Force: Identity, Nationalism, and Memory in a Balkan Community* (Ithaca: Cornell University Press, 2016). See also Doris L. Bergen, "The Nazi Concept of 'Volksdeutsche' and the Exacerbation of Anti-Semitism in Eastern Europe," *Journal of Contemporary History* 29 (1994): 569–82.
46 The claim that NKVD informants quickly switched to being active Nazi supporters is central to Jan Gross's explanation for the killing of Jews by local Poles in early July 1941 in Jedwabne: Jan T. Gross, *Neighbors: The Destruction of the Jewish Community in Jedwabne, Poland* (Princeton: Princeton University Press, 2001).
47 The Dutch historian David Barnouw's research on Jacob Luitjens, "From War Criminal in the Netherlands to Mennonite Abroad and Back, to Prison in the Netherlands," presented at the March 2018 conference at Bethel College, documented how Luitjens used his Mennonite ties to gain refuge. On the Luitjens case, see Thiesen, *Mennonite and Nazi*, 206–7; and Henriette Boas, "Dutch Court Dismisses Appeal by Nazi Collaborator Luitjens," *Jewish Telegraphic Agency*, 30 December 1992, 2, https://www.jta.org/1992/12/30/archive/dutch-court-dismisses-appeal-by-nazi-collaborator-luitjens (accessed 26 October 2018).
48 Doris L. Bergen, "Tenuousness and Tenacity: The Volksdeutsche of Eastern Europe, World War II, and the Holocaust," in *The Heimat Abroad: Boundaries of Germanness*, ed. Krista O'Donnell, Renate Bridenthal, and Nancy Reagin (Ann Arbor: University of Michigan Press, 2005): 267–86.

49 See Alexa Stiller, *Völkische Politik. Praktiken der Exklusion und Inklusion in polnischen, französischen und slowenischen Annexionsgebieten 1939–1945* (Göttingen: Wallstein, 2019); Gerhard Wolf, *Ideologie und Herrschaftsrationalität. Nationalsozialistische Germanisierungspolitik in Polen* (Hamburg: Hamburger Edition, 2012); Isabel Heinemann, *"Rasse, Siedlung, deutsches Blut." Das Rasse- und Siedlungshauptamt der SS und die rassenpolitische Neuordnung Europas* (Göttingen: Wallstein, 2003); Götz Aly, *"Final Solution": Nazi Population Policy and the Murder of the European Jews*, trans. Belinda Cooper and Allison Brown (London: Arnold, 1999); Valdis Lumans, *Hitler's Auxiliaries: The Volksdeutsche Mittelstelle and the German National Minorities of Europe* (Chapel Hill: University of North Carolina Press, 1993); Robert L. Koehl, *RKFDV: German Resettlement and Population Policy, 1939–1945* (Cambridge, MA: Harvard University Press, 1957).

50 Paul Hanebrink, *A Specter Haunting Europe: The Myth of Judeo-Bolshevism* (Cambridge, MA: Belknap Press, 2018).

51 For an analogous example, see Mirna Zakic, *Ethnic Germans and National Socialism in Yugoslavia in World War II* (New York: Cambridge University Press, 2017).

52 For a cogent critique of this approach as taken by some Mennonite theologians since the 1940s, see Paul Martens, "How Mennonite Theology Became Superfluous in Three Easy Steps: Bender, Yoder, Weaver," *Journal of Mennonite Studies* 33 (2015): 149–66.

53 Maurice Halbwachs, *On Collective Memory*, ed. and trans. Lewis A. Coser (Chicago: University of Chicago Press, 1992); see also Patrick H. Hutton, *History as an Art of Memory* (Hanover: University Press of New England, 1993); Aleida Assmann, *Der lange Schatten der Vergangenheit. Erinnerungskultur und Geschichtspolitik* (Munich: Beck, 2006); and the very helpful presentation in Assmann, "Europe: A Community of Memory?" and "Response to Peter Novick," in *GHI Bulletin*, No. 40 (Spring 2007): 11–25 and 33–8.

54 Peter Novick, *The Holocaust in American Life* (Boston: Houghton Mifflin, 1999), 1–15 at 7. For this process at work in a wide range of European contexts, see John-Paul Himka and Joanna Beata Michlic, eds., *Bringing the Dark Past to Light: The Reception of the Holocaust in Post-Communist Europe* (Lincoln: University of Nebraska Press, 2013); also relevant is John-Paul Himka, *Ukrainians, Jews, and the Holocaust: Divergent Memories* (Saskatoon: Heritage, 2009).

55 Keith Lowe, *Savage Continent: Europe in the Aftermath of World War II* (New York: St Martin's Press, 2012), 371–78.

56 The tendency to talk about Soviet but not Nazi terror is on display in Theodor Schieder, ed., *Documents on the Expulsion of the Germans from*

Eastern-Central Europe, vol. 1: *The Expulsion of the German Population from the Territories East of the Oder-Neisse Line* (Bonn: Federal Ministry for Expellees, Refugees and War Victims, 1958). On the widespread and persistent proclivity to hide Holocaust participation behind being victims of Soviet crimes, see Hanebrink, *Specter Haunting Europe*, ch. 8, "Between History and Memory," 237–73; for German context, see Robert G. Moeller, *War Stories: The Search for a Usable Past in the Federal Republic of Germany* (Berkeley: University of California Press, 2001); and Elizabeth Heineman, "Gender, Sexuality, and Coming to Terms with the Nazi Past," *Central European History* 38, no. 1 (2005): 41–74.

57 Leo Driedger and Donald B. Kraybill, *Mennonite Peacemaking: From Quietism to Activism* (Scottdale: Herald Press, 1994); Ervin Stutzman, *From Nonresistance to Justice: The Transformation of Mennonite Church Peace Rhetoric 1908–2008* (Scottdale: Herald Press, 2011).

58 Berkhoff, *Harvest of Despair*.

59 Diana Dumitru, *The State, Antisemitism, and Collaboration in the Holocaust: The Borderlands of Romania and the Soviet Union* (New York: Cambridge University Press in association with the United States Holocaust Memorial Museum, 2016).

60 Connie Braun, *Reflections on Unspoken: An Inheritance of Words* (Vancouver: Fern Hill, 2016), idem, *The Steppes Are the Colour of Sepia* (Vancouver: Ronsdale, 2008), idem, *Silentium and Other Reflections on Memory, Sorrow, Place, and the Sacred* (Eugene: Resource Publications, 2017). Note the difference between the earlier and later works. See also Christina Guenther and Beth A. Griech-Polelle, eds., *Trajectories of Memory: Intergenerational Representation of the Holocaust in History and the Arts* (Newcastle upon Tyne: Cambridge Scholars Publishing, 2008).

61 See Alexander Prusin, "'Fascist Criminals to the Gallows!': The Holocaust and Soviet War Crimes Trials, December 1945–February 1946," *Holocaust and Genocide Studies* 17, no. 1 (2003): 1–30; Tanja Penter, "Local Collaborators on Trial: Soviet War Crimes Trials under Stalin (1943–1953)," *Cahiers du Monde Russe* 49/2–3 (2008): 341–64; Oleksandr Melnyk, "Stalinist Justice as a Site of Memory: Anti-Jewish Violence in Kyiv's Podil District in September 1941 through the Prism of Soviet Investigation Documents," *Jahrbücher für Geschichte Osteuropas* 61 (2013): 223–48.

62 Elizabeth Harvey, *Women in the Nazi East: Agents and Witnesses of Germanization* (New Haven: Yale University Press, 2003). On Mennonite women in the East, see Marlene Epp, *Women without Men*; Marlene Epp, "Memory of Violence."

63 On Werner's parents, see Hans Werner, *The Constructed Mennonite: History, Memory and the Second World War* (Winnipeg: University of Manitoba Press, 2013).

64 On memory as salvation, see Steve J. Stern, *Battling for Hearts and Minds: Memory Struggles in Pinochet's Chile, 1973–1988* (Durham: Duke University Press, 2006).
65 See also Steven M. Schroeder, *To Forget It All and Begin Anew: Reconciliation in Occupied Germany, 1944–1954* (Toronto: University of Toronto Press, 2013).
66 On Stutthof, see Hermann Kuhn, ed., *Stutthof. Ein Konzentrationslager vor den Toren Danzigs*, 2nd ed. (Bremen: Edition Temmen, 2004); Wolfgang Benz and Barbara Distel, eds., *Der Ort des Terrors. Geschichte der nationalsozialistischen Konzentrationslager*, vol. 6: *Natzweiler, Groß-Rosen, Stutthof* (Munich: Beck, 2007).

Introduction to Chapter One

Mennonites and Nazi Crimes: Gerhard Rempel's Call for Historical Reckoning

DORIS L. BERGEN

In the early 2000s, a university press asked me to evaluate a manuscript titled "Dove and Swastika: Russian Mennonites under Nazi Occupation, 1939–1945."[1] It was by Gerhard Rempel, a historian I had not met but knew as the author of a well-regarded study of the Hitler Youth.[2] Presumably the editor asked me because I had published on a related subject: the *Volksdeutschen*, ethnic Germans in Eastern Europe, during the Second World War. That research, plus the fact that my parents were born in Mennonite villages in Soviet Ukraine, made me curious about Rempel's manuscript (if dismayed by its title). So I agreed to read it and have been thinking about it ever since.

Some of Rempel's findings were familiar to me: I knew that Heinrich Himmler considered the Mennonites in Ukraine to be loyal guardians of "German blood," and I had seen evidence of Mennonites who served in the SS.[3] Anecdotally, I had heard of individuals who collaborated with Nazi Germany, came to Canada after the war as displaced persons, and found homes in Mennonite communities. But Rempel linked these and many other scattered pieces of information into a vivid and coherent narrative, and the effect was explosive. Moreover, his text was not a memoir, an apology, or an accusation – all genres that are easy to dismiss as special pleading – but a historical analysis. And he had submitted it to a major university press with the goal of reaching a wide audience, not only Mennonites.

The pattern Rempel revealed stunned me, as it had him: Mennonites in and from the Soviet Union were involved directly and in multiple ways with the Nazi regime and its crimes, including the murder of Jews, and their cumulative impact was overwhelmingly pro-Nazi – before, during, and after the war. Mennonites had ideological affinities with National Socialism, and some held important offices during the German occupation. They cultivated close, even intimate ties with the occupiers, some of whom lived in Mennonite homes. They accepted stolen Jewish property and even stole it themselves. Most shocking, some were active killers, and in individual cases, they spearheaded massacres of Jewish children, women, and men. Rempel recounted, at length and in painstaking detail, the case of Heinrich Wiens, a Mennonite who led a mobile killing squad (*Einsatzkommando*) that slaughtered thousands, perhaps tens of thousands, of Jews.

Gerhard Rempel published his key findings in a 2010 article in *Mennonite Quarterly Review*,[4] but he died in 2014, without being able to finish his book. The readers, including me, had been enthusiastic, and the press was keen, but everyone agreed the manuscript needed work. It was too long, the analysis was uneven, and many references remained incomplete. Rempel's historical rigour notwithstanding, he came across as defensive at times and accusatory at others, in part because he did not always clearly delineate his interpretation from positions articulated in his sources. Yet Rempel's contribution is essential to any study of Mennonites and the Holocaust. His research continues to be the starting point for everyone who ventures into this area, and even its imperfections serve as potent reminders of the challenges of the topic.

What follows is a portion of chapter 10 from Rempel's book manuscript. It has been edited by me for brevity and clarity. John D. Thiesen reviewed the text, checked every footnote, corrected errors, filled in missing information, and added citations based on his own extensive research in various archival holdings. I updated some references to include scholarship that appeared too late for Rempel to consider.

Three aspects of Rempel's contribution merit particular attention. The first is his groundbreaking exploration of the subject of Mennonites as killers. Much of the literature on Mennonites during the Holocaust, and indeed on all Christian individuals and groups, is dominated by the notion of "silence," that is, the accusation that failure consisted of not "speaking out" or "doing enough" to help Hitler's victims. More difficult to face is the evidence that Mennonites played active roles, as hands-on killers of Jews, and also Roma, Soviet prisoners of war, and people with disabilities. Rempel's chapter shows individual Mennonites as killers of people in the first three of those categories. (Dmytro Myeshkov's chapter in this volume adds examples of Mennonites as killers of people with disabilities.)

Rempel comes at the topic of Mennonite killers from a number of different perspectives, presented in order of intensity, from witnesses to accomplices to perpetrators. He begins by examining Mennonites who revealed knowledge of Mennonite involvement in Nazi atrocities in their postwar accounts. His most important sources here are

Anna Sudermann, Alexander Rempel, and Hans Harder – a teacher, an obsessive researcher, and a novelist – and he quotes extensively from all of them. Of the three, Alexander Rempel is both the most explicit and the most complicated, and Gerhard Rempel struggles to convince readers, and perhaps himself, of Alexander's credibility while recognizing the unconventional and even bizarre nature of the records he produced.

To my reading, these somewhat contorted passages reflect Gerhard Rempel's own experience discovering, assessing, coming to terms with, and trying to communicate the reality of Mennonite perpetrators. The image of the "madman" or "lunatic" who conveys the truth about the genocide of Jews, applied here to Alexander Rempel, occurs in many works of Holocaust studies, most famously in Elie Wiesel's *Night*. In this chapter, an idiosyncratic footnote to his own unpublished text, "Odessa sticks in my craw," provides a fleeting glimpse of Gerhard Rempel's emotional engagement with his subject.[5] He does not mention here a detail he provided in the 2010 article in *Mennonite Quarterly Review* that placed his own family in occupied Ukraine among the beneficiaries of genocide. It involved, as was often the case, property:

> In 1942, the mayor of Osterwick, my hometown, reported to German authorities a fellow townsman who happened to be a Jew married to a Mennonite woman. This Jew, who had spent his whole life with Mennonites and even spoke Plautdietsch [Low German], was arrested and killed. For a few months my own family lived in the house of this family. It was known as the *Judenhaus*.[6]

That recollection, he noted, gave him an ominous feeling: "How much guilt and condemnation is shared by those Mennonites who witnessed and observed or benefited from the Holocaust in their midst?"[7]

The second point I want to emphasize has to do with defining "Mennonite." In fact, Rempel does not engage this matter directly, and he might be faulted (and has been, by John Thiesen, among others) for making assumptions based on such flimsy evidence as names. For people who grew up in North American Mennonite communities that included many immigrants from the Soviet Union, or who attended a Mennonite school, as I did, it is second nature and a kind of game to spot "Mennonite names." Wiens, Reimer, Kroeker, Wiebe, Rempel, Jantzen, and Thiesen are obvious suspects; so are Neufeld, Friesen, Schroeder, Loewen, Penner, Epp, and Toews; other strong contenders include Dyck/Dueck, Fast, Klassen, and Bergen. You will see most of these names in Rempel's chapter (and all of them in this volume).

Rempel's method is not scientific, and no doubt it missed some people and led to false positives in other cases. But it implies a practical approach that, in my assessment, turns out to be the most historically sound way to deal with the challenge of defining who counts as a Mennonite for purposes of studying "Mennonites and the Holocaust." In Rempel's analysis, a "Mennonite" is anyone who at any point presented him or herself as Mennonite or was accepted and treated as Mennonite by Mennonite agencies and communities. This functional definition does not depend on subjective "identity" or theological belief, both of which are unstable and probably impossible for historians to measure. Rather the question is who belongs in a discussion of Mennonites and the Holocaust, and someone perceived to have ties to Mennonites is definitely relevant.

Rempel's treatment of the case of Helmut Oberlander, charged in Canada with concealing his SS past, illustrates this functional definition of "Mennonite." Rempel's assumption that Oberlander had a "Mennonite connection" appears to rest on circumstantial evidence only. And as John Thiesen found, records of the Nazi German Central Bureau for Immigration (*Einwandererzentralstelle*) list Oberlander only as "Protestant" (*evangelisch*).[8] It was the Canadian Minister of Immigration, building on documents prepared by the US Office of Special Investigations, who presented Oberlander as originating from a "German Mennonite community" in southern Ukraine. Was this a mistake? Did Oberlander himself, his lawyers, or his Mennonite friends in Kitchener-Waterloo encourage this perception in the hope that it might get him a more sympathetic hearing? Either way, his case was discussed in public as if he had a tie to Mennonites and it was followed very closely by Mennonites in Canada. On this basis alone, Oberlander belongs in an analysis of Mennonites and the Holocaust.

The third issue is methodological. Rempel's chapter draws on an eclectic and rather unconventional source base: memoirs, German records, unpublished correspondence, private conversations, newspapers, and fiction all appear in his footnotes. This method leaves Rempel open to criticism, and there is no question that he extrapolates more in some cases than sceptical readers will accept. But his multifaceted approach also models a way forward in treating a topic so deep in the shadows. In Raul Hilberg's words, as a researcher of the Holocaust, "you cannot skip anything: you cannot omit any place or organization."[9] Rempel shared that view, as is evident from his correspondence with historians and friends all over the world as he energetically followed every possible lead. Research of this nature is an endless process, and it continues to produce surprises.

One surprise emerged as we prepared this chapter. Rempel was unable to uncover the postwar fate of Heinrich Wiens, the man responsible for the 1942 massacre of Jews at the glass factory. Those who insist on a clear-cut definition would disqualify Wiens as a Mennonite: by the early 1930s he had officially renounced Christianity and left the church. But others, at least one congregation, continued to honour Wiens's Mennonite connection and to deal with his family accordingly. On 22 June 1950, exactly nine years after Germany invaded the Soviet Union, the following notice appeared in a Kansas Mennonite newspaper:

> Mrs. Margaret Wiens and three children, a refugee family from Germany, arrived several weeks ago and are now at home … in a house provided by the … church. The family's transportation to this country was provided by J.H. Schroeder, who made their acquaintance through a gift package sent them some time ago. The … congregation, which has now assumed the family's support, held a shower and reception for them some time ago at which Mrs. Wiens related some of their experiences as refugees.[10]

In his scholarship, Gerhard Rempel did not take a position as to what Mennonites after the fact should or should not do about the legacies of the Nazi past. But as a historian he was committed to doing what he could to make sure those difficult questions could be raised from a position that was both honest and informed.

NOTES

1. Thank you to Lise Rempel Hoy for allowing and encouraging this publication of her father's work. For feedback on Gerhard Rempel's manuscript, thanks to the 2017 workshop group: Rebecca Carter-Chand, Diana Dumitru, Aileen Friesen, Mark Jantzen, Robert Nelson, Richard Ratzlaff, and Robert Teigrob. Thanks to Hadas Binyamini for editorial help; to John D. Thiesen for his invaluable input; and to Conrad Stoesz, James Urry, Gail Niles Stucky, Peter Letkemann, Arnold Neufeldt-Fast, Renae Stucky, and Richard Thiessen for their expert assistance. This project has been supported by an Insight Grant from the Social Science and Humanities Research Council of Canada.
2. Gerhard Rempel, *Hitler's Children: The Hitler Youth and the SS* (Chapel Hill: University of North Carolina Press, 1989).
3. See Doris L. Bergen, "The 'Volksdeutschen' of Eastern Europe, World War II, and the Holocaust: Constructed Ethnicity, Real Genocide," in *Germany and Eastern Europe: Cultural Identities and Cultural Differences*,

ed. Keith Bullivant, Geoffrey Giles, and Walter Pape; *Yearbook of European Studies* 13 (Amsterdam: Rodopi, 1999): 70–93; and Bergen, "Mourning, Mass Death, and the Gray Zone: The Ethnic Germans of Eastern Europe and the Second World War," in *Symbolic Loss: The Ambiguity of Mourning and Memory at Century's End*, ed. Peter Homans (Charlottesville: University of Virginia Press, 2000): 171–93.

4 Gerhard Rempel, "Mennonites and the Holocaust: From Collaboration to Perpetration," *Mennonite Quarterly Review* 84, no. 4 (Oct. 2010): 507–49. Thank you to *Mennonite Quarterly Review* and its editor, John D. Roth, for generously agreeing to this publication, parts of which first appeared in *MQR*.

5 Other scholars who touch on personal and family connections to Holocaust perpetrators and enablers include Katharina von Kellenbach, *The Mark of Cain: Guilt and Denial in the Post-War Lives of Nazi Perpetrators* (New York: Oxford University Press, 2013); Mary Fulbrook, *A Small Town Near Auschwitz: Ordinary Nazis and the Holocaust* (New York: Oxford University Press, 2013); and Doris L. Bergen, "Protestants, Catholics, Mennonites, and Jews: Identities and Institutions in Holocaust Studies," in *Holocaust Scholarship: Personal Trajectories and Professional Interpretations*, ed. Christopher R. Browning et al. (New York: Palgrave Macmillan, 2015): 142–56.

6 Rempel, "Mennonites and the Holocaust," 549, "the Jews' house."

7 Ibid.

8 US National Archives microfilm publication A3342, "Documents Generated in Connection with Activities of the Einwandererzentralstelle," roll G005, frame 1934ff.

9 Hilberg, "The Development of Holocaust Research – A Personal Overview," in *Holocaust Historiography in Context: Emergence, Challenges, Polemics, and Achievements*, ed. David Bankier and Dan Michman (Jerusalem and New York, Berghahn Books, 2008), 25–36 at 29.

10 *Mennonite Weekly Review* 28, no. 25 (22 June 1950), 4. Thanks to Alec Loganbill for research assistance.

Chapter One

Mennonites, War Crimes, and the Holocaust

GERHARD REMPEL, adapted from his
unfinished book manuscript,
edited by DORIS L. BERGEN with JOHN D. THIESEN

The purpose of this chapter is to demonstrate a painful truth, that the Mennonite German minority showed a willing and at times eager collaboration with Hitler's military and the Nazi regime during their occupation of Ukraine. Several Mennonite memoir writers and more than one non-Mennonite historian have documented their assertion that individuals of Mennonite background were part of Himmler's machinery of death, including the mobile killing squads (*Einsatzgruppen*) that murdered Jews in Ukraine and elsewhere in the occupied Soviet Union.[1] In the 1990s, a number of Mennonites were accused of war crimes, or of lying on their applications for immigration, and were prosecuted by the US Justice Department Office of Special Investigations and its Canadian counterpart.

Our discussion begins with three Mennonites in a Leipzig beer hall. In April 1944, John Kroeker, son of the Mennonite Brethren writer and theologian Jakob Kroeker, was meeting Heinrich Janzen of the SS and Peter Dietrich Wiebe. They had just returned from Łódź/Litzmannstadt in Poznań/Posen/Wartheland. Janzen had served "under the death head" – in the Waffen SS – and had a story to tell. Starting behind Zaporizhzhia and all the way west to Poznań, he and his SS fellows had made a three-month journey. Their job was to "clean out" Soviet partisans from Ukrainian localities near the front. The SS men entered homes at 5:00 a.m. and ordered everyone out by 8:00 a.m. Many people froze "when they saw the sign of the death head on the uniforms." If anyone resisted, the SS had standing orders to shoot ("give them the bullet").[2]

West of Nikopol', Janzen went on, the roads were clogged with ethnic Germans (*Volksdeutsche*), who were endangered by partisans. According to Janzen, those "desperadoes" attacked the ethnic German refugees and blew up bridges so people could not escape. The SS units chased the bandits and shot as many as they could. In the process, Kroeker noted later in his diary, they destroyed entire villages and everything in them: the water supply, the trees, "cut down, thrown on a pile and burned," and "the people who resisted."[3] To what degree Kroeker's informants themselves participated in murder is unclear. Janzen certainly made no effort to distance himself from the perpetrators.

Over the next months, Kroeker picked up additional reports. A manager, presumably Mennonite, in the office of a district commissar in Poznań, told Kroeker he had been drafted by the Red Army in Zaporizhzhia only to be taken POW by the Germans. He saw Soviet prisoners clubbed to death or shot when they could no longer walk. In the German prison camp, he said, "untold numbers died every day."[4] In the town of Plotha, near Leipzig, Kroeker heard a horrifying story from a woman named Maria Penner. As she and other Mennonites fled westward, they encountered a death march:

> Herds of Jews, mothers, old people, women and girls were driven along the road. A few soldiers were employed as drivers. They clearly were attempting to escape from the Wartheland. Other soldiers marching toward the front spoke to them and said that it must be difficult to serve as drivers for these people. They replied that they would rather drive cattle than these people. The marching soldiers then asked what was being done with these people. The reply was: "they are driven into granaries and shot."

Kroeker relayed Penner's account in vivid detail:

> The poor Jews looked awful. It was at the end of January and snow was everywhere; the road was muddy, the clothing amounted to rags and bits of cloth; a few had some dirty blankets hung over their shoulders. No one had normal clothes. Shoes were torn; many walked barefoot, covered with mud. It was a pitiful sight. Haggard, tired and weak, they were completely exhausted. They sat down on the side of the road to rest; they could not go on …

Perhaps Kroeker put his own questions into his informant's mouth:

> What can one say about this? Moving, appalling, painful. And who, one asks oneself, is responsible? Is the guilt immediate or of long duration, or is it tooth for tooth? Revenge for revenge? Can we expect more evil deeds to follow?[5]

Nearly all Mennonite memoirists of the Second World War mention treatment of Jews, and some describe atrocities they heard about

Mennonites, War Crimes, and the Holocaust   43

or observed. The teacher Anna Sudermann had pleasant memories of meeting her father's Jewish business associates on their estate, and she attended a secondary school of commerce, where, she said, most of her classmates were young Jewish women. But in Sudermann's telling, not all her experiences with Jews had been positive. When she was under Soviet police surveillance, following her brother's arrest, the informant and interrogators were Jews, she claimed.[6]

Sudermann reported how, during the war, she observed Jews being rounded up and marched out of town to be murdered. She knew their fate from neighbours and friends. The reader will get a better idea from her own words:

> Shortly before Christmas 1941 four men of the field constabulary were quartered in our home. They took over Liese's room. We had gotten used to such shrinkage of our living space and took it quietly in stride in exchange for liberation from fear of the GPU [Soviet intelligence service and secret police]. ... At the time, we were unsure in our judgment of Germans, since our basic attitude towards everything and everyone that came from Germany was openly receptive. ...
>
> It did not take long for the Jewish problem "to be solved." Today, the more I think about those times, the more a feeling of guilt overcomes me. How disturbing my judgment was at that time with regard to the treatment of Jews by the National Socialists![7]

Sudermann's remarks revealed the close proximity of Mennonites and Jews in the region:

> We sensed a great uneasiness in reference to Jews since the very first day of the occupation. On the second day we discovered that the pharmacist Vogel and his wife had poisoned themselves before the occupation of Chortitza. He died but his wife survived. Many Jews had fled, but the pharmacy couple had apparently missed an opportunity to flee. Many longtime Jewish residents, who had always lived among Mennonites, who were never unfriendly toward us during Soviet times or revealed any discriminatory behavior, remained in their Chortitza homes, as did the old shoemaker Aaron with his wife, hoping that nothing would happen to them. But all Jews lived in great fear ...

Sudermann made it clear that she had first-hand knowledge of mass murder:

> One day we saw how Jews, about 50 men, women and children, were marched down the street. They were all shot outside the village, including

half-Jews. A Russian mother with her half-Jewish child is supposed to have gone along with the child to her death. The rural constabulary was ordered to carry out these actions.

She concluded with a declaration of guilt that blurred into a rationalization:

> With horror I write these lines today. This event was a heavy burden for all of us to bear. Inconceivable it is today and will never be understood by people who did not experience these times with us how we could accept these inhuman deeds without open protest. I would like to mention the following facts, not to make excuses, but only to make understanding of our behavior possible: under the Soviet regime we lived through a great deal of inhumanity, and also were aware of the prominence of Jews in the economic and political life of the country. At the top of the GPU we noticed many Jews and the interrogating judges were also Jews. Millions of people disappeared and died in the "silent camps." We knew what life was like in a totalitarian state. Our concepts of law and justice had been confused. In Germany we saw the opposite of Soviet Russia, that is to say something better. At that time we still revered Hitler. If he had decided upon such a solution of the Jewish question, then the Jews apparently were endangering the political security of Germany. In this manner I tried to justify the inhuman treatment of Jews. In this lies my great guilt, which cannot be expiated by any means. I can only hope for forgiving mercy.[8]

Sudermann's nephew, Alexander Rempel, the son of a prominent Mennonite elder, Jakob Aron Rempel (1883–1943), who disappeared in Stalin's Gulag, provided another revealing account.[9] For more than forty years Alexander carried a secret about an event that took place one spring night in Einlage, now encompassed by Nove Zaporizhzhia, near Zaporizhzhia in occupied Ukraine. The few Mennonite leaders he shared this secret with rejected it out of hand. It was too awful to contemplate, and besides, Alexander, known as "Sasha" to his friends, was said to be mentally unstable. He revealed what he called the "Massacre of Zaporizhzhia," with Mennonites as perpetrators, to the archivists at the Mennonite Heritage Center in 1984, the year before his death. His exposition came in the form of a jumbled letter, presented as a research article, that charged Mennonite leaders with a conspiracy of silence.

The massacre occurred in the region of Chortitza, the Mennonite capital of the Old Colony on the Dnieper River. After spending time with his exiled father, Alexander had escaped GPU surveillance and crossed the front line somewhere near Kiev, spent time as translator for a German divisional staff, and then made his way to Einlage. Thus, he observed events in the Chortitza area during October 1941. The Wehrmacht occupied Zaporizhzhia on 3 October, ending seven weeks of bombardment, during which Mobile Killing Commando (MKC) 6, a subunit of Mobile Killing Squad C assigned to Army Group South, completed its work. According to Alexander Rempel, MKC 6

> had won the cooperation of some young Mennonites and a Lutheran man, altogether about one to two dozen persons, mostly from Chortitza and Rosenthal, to voluntarily join the commando. They had marched across the Dnieper on 3–4 October 1941, added 50 to 60 Russian and Ukrainian volunteers to their ranks and were then given control, under the leadership of the men of MKC 6, over the city administration and the area around the city.[10]

MKC 6, commanded by Dr E. Kroeger, was headquartered at Kryvyi Rih in August and September 1941. From there Kroeger sent an advance commando to Chortitza, part of the large area in the Dnieper bend incorporating the cities of Dnipro (Dnipropetrovsk), Kamianske/Dniprodzerzhynsk, Zaporizhzhia, and Nikopol'. The men of MKC 6 "processed" all the Jews they could get their hands on, to use the mendacious language of these killing squads. The small MKC teams were enlarged by recruiting local men who wore the SD uniform and were willing to help in the gruesome work.[11] At the end of November, Robert Mohr replaced Kroeger and moved his staff to Zaporizhzhia. There he carried out what Rempel called the "Massacre of Zaporizhzhia."[12]

The Wehrmacht appointed a temporary mayor for Zaporizhzhia, a Mennonite named Heinrich Wiebe.[13] As for the Mennonite identity of the auxiliary policemen who participated in the massacre south of the village of Schönwiese/Oleksandrivs'k, Rempel makes a plausible argument. They had to come from the Chortitza villages, he reasoned, because there were no available ethnic Germans on the eastern bank.[14] The Mennonite villages of Schönwiese and Hochfeld and the Lutheran village of Katharinendorf had been "evacuated" to Siberia. Rempel goes on to say:

> I was acquainted with some of these individuals since childhood. In the spring of 1942, I sat with four of them during a whole evening as they celebrated the completion of the extermination of Jews for the region of Zaporizhzhia. My recollection of the killing of Jews in this district coincides with the German documents in the case.[15]

Unnoted by Rempel, MKC 12 of Mobile Killing Squad D was also active around Zaporizhzhia. It "cleaned up" the area west of the line

Melitopol'–Vasylivka to the Dnieper bend south of Zaporizhzhia. Activity reports from this unit state repeatedly that they had "made the area assigned to the commando free of Jews." In the second half of September alone, they reported killing 22,467 people, so that by 30 September 1941, a total of 35,782 "Jews and Communists had been shot by Mobile Killing Squad D."[16]

Rempel said nothing about how he had made his way back to the Mennonite village of Einlage under German occupation. Casual acquaintances might have thought he was hiding something, and his belated research report of 1971 hints at activity not normally associated with Mennonite sons of the clergy. Rempel's many research projects included two military histories, one on the "9th Panzer Division of the German Wehrmacht and the Russian-Germans," and the other about the "Panzer Group Kleist" and its relationship to the German minority in the Soviet Union. In a detailed outline he refers to "the liberation of all German colonies from Bolshevik troops and officials on this stretch of land from Kryvyi Rih to Zaporizhzhia." When referring to the battle for Kiev he notes in parentheses that "he was liberated from Bolshevism near the city of Lubny." Later, in a prelude to the tank battle of Kursk, he states, "The Orthodox churches were returned to the archdiocese of Kursk at my suggestion."[17] Somehow Rempel landed in the confusion created by the initial German thrust toward Orel and became involved as a translator or some sort of consultant to the military command of the 9th Panzer Division. Another young Mennonite was also involved in these operations as a combat reporter for the Germans. His name was Gerhard Fast (1894–1974), son of the pastor Gerhard Fast, who surveyed the Mennonite villages of Chortitza for the Reich Ministry for the Eastern Occupied Territories (*Ostministerium*).[18]

It must have been fairly easy for Rempel to make his way from Kursk to his family in Einlage – he had apparently received permission from the German command. But then he left again for Berlin to embark on a course of study without any visible means of support. He was twenty-six years old. In Berlin, Rempel was taken in by the Crous family. Supported by them and the Mennonite congregation, he seemed to acquire a sense of direction. When the Prussian State Library was transferred to Göttingen to save its treasures from Allied bombing, Dr Crous and Rempel went with the books. There he began an ambitious career of historical investigations of the Mennonite church worldwide. In a report from 1971, he noted some forty-three individual topics of research, though none were anywhere near completion.[19]

The reasoning in Rempel's works is frequently laboured and redundant, indicating that he was preoccupied for years with anxieties and suspicions related to secret services, Cold War government tactics, emigration policies, and Mennonite unwillingness to face the truth of his allegations. Key pieces of evidence are missing from his presentation – for example, the investigative commission in the Zaporizhzhia region[20] is not even cited. He never explains how he concluded that between one and two dozen Mennonites were recruited for the MKCs. Did he glean this from acquaintances who bragged about their killing sprees? He can give only three Mennonite names for certain – which appear to come from the investigations of the Extraordinary Commission created for the city of Zaporizhzhia in 1944 – but he does not reveal how he came by that report. It took Rempel a very long time to go from initial conversations with friends to the final delineation of his case on paper. Having finally done so, he sent his missive to an unsuspecting archivist instead of to Mennonite authorities or a state's attorney.

Several other Mennonite leaders served as witnesses to the Holocaust in occupied Ukraine, although these men did not point to Mennonite perpetrators. One of them, Hans Rempel (1909–1990), is unusual in that he worked for the notorious ethnic German activist Georg Leibbrandt, who represented his boss, Alfred Rosenberg, at the Wannsee Conference.[21] Also unusual is that Hans Rempel worked at the German Armed Forces High Command during the early months of the war. That position afforded him a top-down perspective that no other Mennonite had. That Hans Rempel heard about SS atrocities but did not report or oppose them probably makes him representative of a number of Mennonites who witnessed the Holocaust:

> Leibbrandt, who continued his publications about the life and history of the German colonists in the East even during the war, enabled me to make an official trip to the German settlement areas in the Ukraine. During my train trip I fell into conversation with a German army corporal who sat across from me in the compartment; what he said disturbed me beyond measure and opened my eyes to what the National Socialist subhuman policies meant in practice. The corporal must have been in his mid-thirties: he looked sickly.
>
> "I was mustered as capable for garrison duty on the home front only and served in a barracks until I was transferred to an SS unit in the Ukraine where I served as driver. The SS Special Unit [*Sonderkommando*] bivouacked on the eastern bank of the Dnister River, which was the demarcation line between German and Romanian troops. One day a trek of Gypsies came to us. The group had about 150 persons in it. They were bound for Romania but were stopped at the Dnister by Romanian soldiers who prevented them from crossing and sent them to the SS headquarters.

They complained bitterly about the Romanians. Our office told them they would receive food and then be led further on their journey; meanwhile they were to arrange themselves in groups of four and form a line for the reception of food."

"I received the order," my trip companion told me, "to take the children to the back of the garden. There I found two large rectangular holes in the ground. In front of both sides of the holes stood men with machine pistols in shallow ditches. In front of the two holes two men in uniform stood guard. When I approached the rim of a hole with the children they were kicked in the back and fell into the hole, with shots immediately following." At this point my trip companion halted and then continued with tear-choked voice. "I cannot forget this picture; even today I still see those children, four, five, six years old, in front of me, how they in their bare feet, carefully hobbled over the stony roadway with painful expressions in their faces – as children will do." Again there was a long pause. "I had to think about my own children."

My hand resists as I try to write this down. We are dealing here with one of those abhorrent crimes committed in the German name, which have befouled our honour in an atrocious way. The historian cannot keep silent on this subject.[22]

Another witness, Hans Harder, was a Mennonite novelist of distinction.[23] He offered only mild objection to the atrocities he observed while serving in the German military and Waffen SS. Sometime in 1942, Harder arrived in Odessa with the Special Unit Russia (*Sonderkommando Russland*). He roomed with a young Communist from Magdeburg, who had volunteered for the SS in order to stave off hunger, he said, and a fatuous Protestant parson of the "German Christian" persuasion.[24] According to Harder, aside from a former prewar associate in the Confessing Church and some women working in ethnic German villages, his main contacts during two years in Odessa were young Russians who worked delivering propaganda to the occupied populations, and ethnic Germans before their evacuation. Some of them must have been present in the city when the single largest Jewish massacre took place, and you would expect it to have been a subject for discussion, but by Harder's account it was not.[25]

In his memoirs Harder mentions Easter 1941, when he received an order to report for mustering by the German military. When his knowledge of Slavic languages became known, he was dispatched to a company of translators in Berlin and subsequently sent to Galicia in July. The unit remained for several weeks in Lviv/Lemberg, where Harder found SS and regular German soldiers murdering Jewish civilians.[26]

Mennonites, War Crimes, and the Holocaust   49

He saw "Jewish women pulled from streetcars and a wild hunt for children and old men":

> I remember that one night there was continuous shooting so that the air literally throbbed all the way to the edge of town. My neighbour did not return until the morning. With a face white as chalk, he told me with nearly paralysed tongue about the bloodbath in the cellars of our city quarter, where drunken enlisted men and non-commissioned officers fired with their pistols into heaps of Jews lying on the floor. The remaining shreds of life were extinguished by kicking soldiers' boots, as the victims crawled along the floor. The next morning I reported this scandal to my captain. But he wanted to hold back a report to the general, in deference to the "responsible party," until the Security Service, which arrived in the meantime, could take over. When I threatened to bypass the chain of command and report directly to the general, he overcame his hesitation. The finding and result: transfer of those who took part in the pogrom to a penal unit. I thought to myself, he who believes this and sells his fur coat will freeze this Christmas.[27]

The weeks passed in "disgust and idleness" until Harder's unit finally moved on toward Kiev.[28] Along the way Harder made contact

1.1. Kiev killing scene. Photograph taken or acquired by Harder showing civilians who had just been shot, most likely by an SS unit

with Soviets, including a young woman teacher, with whom he discussed Russian literature, and an Orthodox priest, with whom he discoursed on theology. Near Zhitomir he helped ethnic German villagers restore church services.[29] He seems to have done little translating, but spent time recovering from dysentery and, in his account, tricking the military intelligence officers in his unit into making him spy on the local clergy so that he could enjoy Orthodox services. (A *"Führer* order" forbade German soldiers from worshiping with the local population, but it was not always obeyed.)[30] When they got to Kiev shortly after it fell to the Germans, he recalled helping a group of nuns restore their ancient convent and paying a visit to a hermit holy man named Antonius.

Harder had another encounter with the murder of Jews when the captain took him and a group of colleagues to inspect a local sugar factory. "One morning in September," Harder wrote, as they drove south of Kiev over muddy field roads, they picked up a young lieutenant who had lost his unit. Suddenly the vehicle began to jump as if they had hit a roadway paved with logs:

> The driver stopped. We looked for the cause of our discomfort below the vehicle and recognized – corpse after corpse – prisoners of war! – The captain spoke about the long battle known as the "Kiev cauldron." We understood. Naturally! But what good are explanations, when primordial fear grips your throat? The little lieutenant suddenly turned white and tried to throw up through the window. "Damn it," he groaned, "on the frontline – that is something else – but here …!" We ground our teeth and struggled to restrain our anger. "We will soon enter a partisan wood," our driver predicted. He was trying to divert our attention. When we discovered our factory in the middle of the night, after long study of the maps and relentless searching, our tongues loosened. At the samovar placed on the table by an old woman from the factory staff who had remained behind, the urge to speak with one another returned. Yet, no one dared to begin properly. What we had experienced confused our feelings and made every word difficult. Then someone tried to explain the "hell in the mud," as our driver called it: prisoners of war, without question. But what kind of people could these have been, who had been buried in the morass and driven deeper into the ground by our vehicle? A couple of times, we remembered, a head had been seen in the sludge. Jews? Armenians? Or some other type of "Orientals?" … I reminded everyone of the visit of our general in Kiev, which was still in our minds. Our soldiers had ambushed some Karaims, an oriental ethnic group, under the assumption that they were members of a synagogue in the neighbourhood. Therefore, it is clear, they were Jews! No defence of the most fearful among us helped; finally

experts were requested from Berlin, who knew that an "Aryan tribe" was in question here, a tribe which had been converted to the Jewish faith in the Ukraine during the eighteenth century. That was it.[31]

Mennonites and War Crimes Investigations in the United States and Canada

Another category of Mennonites connected to war crimes received sensational publicity long after the war. These were men who had come to North America after the Second World War after suppressing their service with various SS units and now were being charged with war crimes by justice officials in Canada and the United States. Most notorious was Helmut Oberlander (Oberländer), not an active Mennonite but possibly Mennonite by background.

In 2002 the Office of Special Investigations (OSI) of the US Department of Justice arrested Oberlander in Florida, where the Ontario homebuilder had fled when Canadian authorities initiated proceedings against him in an effort to revoke his citizenship. The OSI had discovered documents proving that Oberlander had been a member of MKC 10a of Mobile Killing Squad D, "a mobile killing unit of the Nazi SS that murdered tens of thousands of Jews and other civilians in southern Ukraine and the Caucasus." He had immigrated to Canada from Germany in 1954 and become a Canadian citizen in 1960. OSI documents established that Oberlander was an ethnic German from the vicinity of Zaporizhzhia and had served with Himmler's *Sicherheitsdienst* (Security Service; SD) from 1941 to 1944. MKC 10a comprised more than one hundred men

> responsible for annihilating all persons in its areas of operation who were considered "undesirable" by the Nazi regime, particularly the Jewish and Sinti and Roma (so-called Gypsy) inhabitants. ... In one report to Berlin, Mobile Killing Squad D declared that "the Jewish problem has been solved" in the area in which Commando 10a was then operating. In January 1943, Oberländer was awarded the War Meritorious Service Cross Second Class for his service in Commando 10a.[32]

Canada's immigration minister presented enormous detail in the Oberlander case, much of it collected by the US Department of Justice. Thus the court knew that "Mr. Oberländer was born in 1924 and raised in the town of Halbstadt [Molochans'k], as it was known before the Second World War to the local community of *Volksdeutsche*, that is, persons of German descent, in southeastern Ukraine. His forebears had lived there for more than 250 years, having originally come to settle there as members of a German Mennonite community."[33] It was deemed relevant that the Molochans'k residents, including the Oberlander family, endured severe hardships in the 1920s and '30s due to "Sovietization." Oberlander's father, a physician, had died when Helmut was quite young, and he was raised by his mother, a nurse, and his sister and grandmother. By the time of the German invasion in 1941, he had completed tenth grade and acquired sufficient mastery of three languages to make him attractive as an interpreter to the occupation forces.

Oberlander described the Soviet evacuation of most males from the Molotschna region and the arrival of German troops. The Germans discovered his facility with languages and asked him to assist in registering all remaining inhabitants once the front line had moved farther east. Thus, by his account, he slipped into service for German troops almost by accident. The court considered him a volunteer though he insisted that "a local authority, whom he believes was a policeman, came to his house" in early 1942 and "ordered that he report in two hours to the town hall to serve with the German troops as an interpreter. His mother was very upset." Helmut reported as directed, and the same day "was taken by vehicle, with two or three other, older ethnic Germans, to Melitopol'."

John Huebert, from the Mennonite village of Ladekopp, today part of the city of Tokmak, a few kilometres from Molochans'k, provided evidence in the case. Seven years older than Oberlander, Huebert had served the Red Army as a driver but managed to switch sides and become a driver for MKC 10a. Despite discrepancies between Oberlander's and Huebert's accounts, the court concluded that they had known each other well and taken a joint leave, travelling by motorcycle and sidecar from Taganrog back to Halbstadt.

· Another witness, Nikolai Siderenko from Taganrog and Donets'k, had deserted the Red Army and become an auxiliary policeman for MKC 10a. Both Huebert and the Ukrainian Siderenko recalled details that Oberlander denied regarding the nature of MKC 10a work: "killing activities." Huebert "witnessed some executions, by shooting, first at Taganrog. Later at Krasnodar he saw people forced into a gassing van operated by MKC 10a as an execution chamber." He also admitted to driving German officers when they interrogated civilians and later shot them point blank. Siderenko had observed Jews being summoned to meet and then being marched or trucked away, and from reports of others, he learned that the Jews had been killed. He also witnessed the massacre of civilians, by German troops serving in his unit, in a Belarusian village in 1943, in the course of anti-partisan operations.

Oberlander, however, claimed "not to have witnessed any of these killing activities and not to have been involved in any," although he did acknowledge that "while serving with EK 10a he was aware of its execution of civilians."[34]

The court then called on the historian Manfred Messerschmidt. He traced the trajectory of MKC 10a through southern Ukraine to the Caucasus and then back through the Crimea and the Kerch Peninsula to Belarus. Oberlander was with MKC 10a in all those places, including during the anti-partisan massacres around the Pripet Marshes. Even after MKC 10a was partly dismantled, he served other SS and army units in German-occupied Poland. In Łódź he joined his family for naturalization procedures in April 1944. Messerschmidt left little doubt that Oberlander had been deeply involved with the crimes committed by MKC 10a, whether his hand had actually been on a murder weapon or not. The deadly cause he served has subsequently been confirmed by Andrej Angrick's study of Mobile Killing Squad D's staggering crimes in occupied Ukraine.[35]

Another expert witness, David Marwell, demolished Oberlander's claims that he did mainly menial jobs for MKC 10a, such as translating, guarding, and household chores. The fact that Oberlander wore the SD uniform and was armed with rifle, pistol, and submachine gun made him a full-fledged policeman and SS/SD man. He was therefore condemned as a war criminal by virtue of the Nuremberg trials, which had defined MKC 10a and all SS organizations as criminal.

The prosecutor summed up as follows:

> In his testimony Mr. Oberlander denied that he was ever a member of the SS, that he ever participated in execution of civilians or anyone, or that he assisted in such activity or that he was even present at executions or deportations. Yet Mr. Oberlander, by his testimony, acknowledges that he served as an interpreter with the SD, that the police unit was referred to as SD, and that after serving for some time he did know of its executions of civilians and others. He knew also its "resettlement" practice for Jews, though he professes not to have understood the meaning of the latter as executions, until later at Krasnodar. In all the circumstances, it is not plausible that he remained ignorant of the executions of Jews and others, as a major activity of the men with whom he served, until he was in Krasnodar.[36]

Above all the legal back-and-forth loomed the starkest evidence of all – the number of dead human beings in places where Oberlander had been present with the murderers of MKC 10a: Melitopol' – 2,000;

Berdyans'k – 1,000; Mariupol' 8,000; Taganrog 1,500; and Rostov – 2,000.[37] That many people could not have been killed in a few days without everyone in a unit of fewer than one hundred men knowing what was happening.[38]

In May 2000 the Canadian government won a round in one of the oldest war crimes deportation cases, against Jacob Fast of St Catharines. Federal judge Francois Lemieux ruled that the case against the accused Nazi collaborator could continue despite his age, ill health, and inability to pay the costs of his defence, estimated at $750,000.[39] According to documents presented in court:

> Mr. Fast was an ethnic German born in a Mennonite community on the Dnieper River, next to the city of Zaporozhye in Ukraine. He was 31 when Nazi Germany invaded Russia in June 1941. By October of that year, German forces occupied Zaporozhye. ... Fast became an auxiliary member of the German Security Police, the infamous Sicherheitspolizei, or Sipo.[40]

Fast worked for the Security Police from October 1941 through 1944, under his brother Ivan, who headed the Zaporizhzhia Security Police. The government charged that Jacob Fast "was personally responsible for the arrest and mistreatment of prisoners, some of whom were later deported to concentration camps." Evacuated with the rest of the Mennonite population to German-occupied Poland in 1944, he succeeded in obtaining German citizenship. He managed to immigrate to Canada when his wife's uncle sponsored the family for settlement in July 1947. The prosecutor alleged that Fast lied to officials about his past and should therefore be deported.[41] Fast appealed, and the case, like so many others, got lost in litigation.[42]

An earlier case, brought in August 1998, against Jack Reimer of Carmel, New York, also had to do with dishonesty about wartime activities.[43] The nature of his actual offence was more precisely determined than in the Fast case in Canada:

> He [Reimer] was captured by the Germans in the summer of 1941 and kept in a prisoner of war camp where at least a truckload of soldiers a day died from the cold or starvation. Being of German descent, he was transferred to the SS Training Camp at Trawniki, in occupied Poland, where he allegedly helped to train men whose job it was to assist the SS in killing European Jews.[44]

While at Trawniki in the winter of 1941–42, Reimer was "accused of having taken part in the mass murder of a group of Jewish prisoners in the woods near the camp. He is also accused of taking part in the deportation of Jews from ghettos in Częstochowa and Lublin in 1942 and Warsaw in 1943." Reimer's defence attorney, none other than former US Attorney General Ramsey Clark, maintained that Reimer was an ordinary POW and had nothing to do with the crimes. But Reimer had earlier conceded to the OSI that he lied to immigration officials in 1952 about his actions at Trawniki. In 1992 he told justice officials that another man had brought him to the site where Jews were being killed. There he "shot toward a man in the pit full of murdered Jews after the man pointed to his head in what Reimer said was a request for a mercy killing."[45]

This was likely the same Jacob Reimer who showed up at John J. Kroeker's refugee station in Berlin after the war. Neither the court nor the OSI knew that the Mennonite Central Committee in the person of Kroeker and Dutch MCC representative Hylkema had likely been instrumental in providing Reimer with a "Menno Pass" that facilitated his escape into the Netherlands and eventually the United States under the Displaced Persons Act.[46] Whether Kroeker, Hylkema, or any MCC official was aware of Reimer's past is uncertain. We do know Kroeker realized that many Mennonites had been in the SS, because he complained about it to Benjamin Unruh.[47]

For decades rumours had circulated about Mennonite complicity in harbouring war criminals, including Adolf Eichmann.[48] The *New York Times* followed the Reimer case carefully and published thirteen major articles on it over as many years. The final piece, by reporter Dan Barry, is titled "A Face Seen and Unseen on the Subway." Barry described how the "unassuming, unremarkable" Jack Reimer escaped deportation to Germany at the last minute by having the temerity to die a natural death.[49] Probably the most damning bit of late-arriving testimony was that of a Soviet witness coming in out of the cold to tell OSI investigators about remembering Reimer leading a brutal squad of SS men during the "clearing" of several ghettos and also at the training camp in occupied Poland.[50] Had this evidence entered the proceedings earlier Reimer might actually have been deported. As it was, he was found to have misrepresented his past, and Judge McKenna of the Federal District Court in Manhattan revoked his citizenship in September 2002.[51] Newspaper stories at the time did not specify where he was to be deported to: it could have been Ukraine, Germany, or Poland.[52]

In May 1995 the Canadian Minister of Citizenship and Immigration alleged that Johann Dueck had been a member of the district police organization in the town of Selydove/Selidovka, Ukraine, during the

German occupation between 1941 and 1943. At times he had used the Russian version of his name, Ivan Ivanovich Dik. According to the ministry, "the Selidovka police force was a voluntary organization composed of local collaborators," and "the respondent served either as the deputy chief of police, chief of police or assistant to the chief of police and ... as required, he also acted as an interpreter for members of the German occupying forces." Dueck was charged with "participating in the arrests and executions of civilians, including Jews, and members of the Red Army who were prisoners-of-war."

A specific case of murder was attributed to Dueck. He was said to have visited the home of a Jewish family called Kovalevsky, and shortly thereafter members of the family, including women and children, were arrested and "executed" by a detachment of policemen including Johann Dueck. Later Dueck and his police murdered fifteen more people at the same location: "the trenches behind the former military registration office in the old centre of Selidovka." The names of three victims were registered in the charges.

Another slaughter by the policemen and soldiers during the late fall of 1941 occurred at a collective farm on the outskirts of town. There the victims were seven people wearing the uniform of the Red Army: "The Respondent was one of the senior policemen present and acting as the interpreter for the Germans at the site of the execution." The indictment also placed Dueck at the murder of nine Soviet soldiers, including two women, at the Yekaterinovskaya mineshaft. On yet another occasion in the fall of 1942, the accused was present at the execution site on a different collective farm where ten prisoners were killed, with Dueck "personally ordering members of the police where to stand in the encirclement of the site." Moreover the respondent was the senior policeman in charge of a detachment holding thirty civilian hostages in the winter of 1942–43, when the Soviet army temporarily broke through the front at Selydove. Villagers who tried to bring food to the hostages were beaten with rifle butts.[53]

Dueck kept all of these incidents from the immigration officials who approved his application for a visa. His membership in the Selydove police department was only discovered many years later, when the Canadian and US governments created special investigative units within their respective justice departments to hunt for Nazi war criminals. Most of these alleged war criminals got off rather easily, with inconclusive legal resolution or lesser charges. Those who actually received punishment escaped with minor penalties or a few months of detention.[54]

Heinrich Wiens and the Massacre at the Glass Factory

Research reveals proof of war crimes committed by the son of a Mennonite farmer and merchant from Muntau/Yablunivka (after 1938 part of Molochans'k). Heinrich Wiens was born on 22 March 1906 in the prosperous village of Yablunivka, located just to the south of the capital Molochans'k in the Molotschna Mennonite Settlement of South Ukraine. In Mennonite circles Yablunivka was known mainly for its excellent hospital and the legendary Dr Tavonius, who resided in the town, along with other professionals and wealthy merchants.[55]

Heinrich's father Hermann Wiens was a landowner and merchant. During the First World War, Heinrich was interned with his parents because all were still German citizens, suggesting a late resettlement from the Danzig region or Prussia.[56] He completed the village elementary school, graduated from an agricultural secondary school, and finished a one-year pedagogical seminar. Between 1926 and 1930 he appears to have been trained and employed as some sort of dairy inspector in various localities in Ukraine, leaving for Danzig in 1930 with the object of starting his own "association of dairy inspectors."[57]

Within a year Wiens joined the Nazi Party in Danzig and received a fairly low membership number (633222), dated 1 October 1931, the year after the first NSDAP electoral success in the Reichstag and in various provinces. On 12 January 1931 he also joined the SS (membership number 22914); this was followed by a fairly rapid rise in rank from staff sergeant (*Scharführer*) in 1933 to captain (*Hauptsturmführer*) in April 1939.

From the start Wiens appears to have been meticulous in complying with SS personnel policy in that he declared his Mennonite heritage but described himself as *gottgläubig* (believer in God but not a church member), the classification Himmler allowed for those who wanted to signal some element of personal religiosity outside Christianity.[58] At some point after 1931, he left the Mennonite church or told the SS he had cancelled his membership. A sign of confidence in Wiens's commitment to the SS cause, he was transferred in 1937 from his regional SS unit, the 71st General SS Standarte of SS Abschnitt XXVI, to the elite SD, Reinhard Heydrich's special internal party intelligence agency and external spy service.[59]

Wiens served in the personnel department of the civilian SS unit in the Danzig district and became its full-time personnel director in 1939, when he received his first medal for good service and a recommendation for promotion. Serving in Security Service units in the occupied eastern territories as soon as the war began, he received the Eastern Front

1.2. Heinrich Wiens

Medal (*Ostmedaille*) in 1941 and several war-related medals in subsequent years. An otherwise spotless record was slightly blemished by an internal field mail service court, which punished him for losing a secret courier package he had been tasked with carrying from the police commander in Kiev to the police commander in Simferopol'. The judgment was not made until 1944, but the incident appears to have occurred in 1942 and may have had something to do with Wiens's transfer to MKC 12 of Mobile Killing Squad D, headquartered at the time in Simferopol'. That is what Wiens's record in Berlin Document Center files indicates, but Angrick's research found him active as deputy commander of EK 10a in Simferopol as early as November 1941. So his entire career in the East may have transpired within the Mobile Killing Squads rather than as a Security Service officer in Kiev and other cities.

After the German retreat began, following the defeat at Stalingrad, Wiens was transferred to the 14th Galician SS Division as Ic officer and was entrusted with the political monitoring of the Ukrainians serving in this Waffen SS division.[60] The records suggest that his service was indispensable and that the division "could not have functioned without him."[61]

In November 1941, about the same time that Mennonites were recruited to serve as auxiliary policemen for Special Unit 6 of Mobile Killing Squad C in the villages of Chortitza, SS Captain Heinrich Wiens appeared on the scene in Simferopol' leading a section of MKC 10a for Mobile Killing Squad D. He was sent to the Crimean capital by the commander of MKC 10a, Kurt Christmann, a major perpetrator of genocide in German-occupied Ukraine, to arrange for a new headquarters for Mobile Killing Squad D, which was about to move from Mykolaiv to Simferopol'. The military situation in the Crimea had been stabilized, and the time had come for Otto Ohlendorf to move his staff deep into the eastern front-line region; from there he would be able to send out his murdering teams known as action commandos right behind the Wehrmacht.[62]

With MKC 10a, Wiens searched through the building formerly occupied by the Soviet secret police in Simferopol'. He sequestered a comfortable set of rooms for his chief, gathered propaganda material about German POWs who had been killed by the Soviets, and recruited all the necessary technical personnel to establish a functioning headquarters for Ohlendorf's Mobile Killing Squad D. Wiens had been entrusted with an important task, since the capital of the Crimea was soon to become a major administrative centre for the German military formations on the Southern Front as well as a strongpoint for the SS.

Wiens appears to have been still with MKC 10a under Christmann in early 1942, probably at Krasnodar since his name (Winz) is mentioned in Krasnodar trial records.[63] When Alexander Rempel made reference to this trial and to a Mennonite being involved he was on the right trail. Krasnodar was one of the cities cited in the Oberlander court records, and MKC 10a perpetrated a major atrocity there. Thus, the question arises whether MKC 10a and MKC 12 were operating in Krasnodar at the same time or different times.

At some point in the summer of 1942, Wiens was transferred to another subunit of Mobile Killing Squad D and given more leeway in organizing his own killing operations. This was MKC 12, commanded by Dr Erich Müller between February and October 1942. As the main German military force advanced on Stalingrad, MKC 12 moved rapidly into the Caucasus region, setting up headquarters in Pyatigorsk at the end of August 1942. One of several resort towns in the northern Caucasus, Pyatigorsk had hardly been touched by the war, and most of its cultural institutions and its food supply had been left intact, along with the essential infrastructure, when the Red Army withdrew. Shops remained open, and opera and theatre performances continued on schedule. Yet large numbers of GPU prisoners were languishing in the cellars of the prisons. Wehrmacht officers were eager to isolate these people, whom they described as carriers of syphilis and scabies, so that they would not infect German soldiers.[64]

Soon after their arrival in late August 1942, MKC 12 dealt with the Jewish population of Pyatigorsk and neighbouring towns in the "established manner." SS Colonel (*Standartenführer*) Müller left the planning and implementation of the anti-Jewish measures to his deputy Heinrich Wiens, who had a record of efficiency in this grisly business. Müller may also have been intent on enjoying his advantages as lord in a wealthy and unscathed resort region. For his task Wiens had the use of "gas vans," newly arrived from the manufacturer in Berlin.

As in all massacres by the Mobile Killing Squads, there was a period of "registering" the Jews in the area, which took eight days in this case and was followed by the command to start the killing. A deadline of 5 September 1942 was set for all Jews to report to the cavalry barracks in Pyatigorsk from the city itself and the surrounding localities of Goryachevodsky, Svobody and Novopyatigorsk. From the barracks the eight hundred to one thousand Jews who had reported were taken to a remote area, having been told they would be resettled. Half an hour later the trucks arrived at a gravel pit guarded by members of MKC 12, along with a battalion of "Caucasians" commanded by a Wehrmacht officer named Kehrer. As each truckload of Jews arrived they were ordered to get out, deposit their valuables on blankets, and remove all their clothes. They were forced to climb into the gas van, which drove back and forth and finally stopped at the edge of the pit. There a small number of Jewish prisoners had to remove the bodies from the truck and throw them into the pit.

According to an eyewitness account, at least one zealous sergeant, Kurt Wenzel, singled out individual Jews for extra torment. He ordered a young, blond woman who was already completely undressed to lie down on the ground with her knees pulled up. He proceeded to torture her with a stick, meanwhile screaming that she was hiding gold and jewellery in her body cavities. She denied it vociferously and spat at Wenzel when he forced her into the gas van.[65] None of the victims survived. Pyatigorsk was now "Judenrein" (cleansed of Jews), the term the Reich Security Main Office activity reports used euphemistically when referring to these massacres. But Dr Müller was not satisfied. He told his fellow *Einsatzgruppen* commanders during a social at the officers' casino that he preferred shooting Jews to the cumbersome method of gas van killings.[66]

While Müller deliberated over killing techniques, his subordinates in MKC 12 began to destroy the Jewish population in the neighbouring resort towns. For Heinrich Wiens, Kislovodsk was the next target. A Mennonite settlement called Tempelhof was in the immediate vicinity,[67] although probably few Mennonites remained there, after emigration and Soviet deportations. The people of Kislovodsk appear to have received the men of MKC 12 with open arms, an ominous sign for the Jews, many of whom had fled to this town in the hills from the Crimea, the Donbas, and Rostov, and had no personal contacts in Kislovodsk.

The town's German commandant and two subsquad leaders of MKC 12, Wiens and Strohschneider, ordered the formation of a Jewish Committee, led by Dr Moses Belinsch, which had to follow the instructions of the German administration. This committee was ordered to arrange for the registration and identification of all Jews starting on 18 August 1942, and to immediately confiscate all valuables held by Jews. The stolen treasure was estimated to be worth five million rubles. MKC 12 used the Jews as forced labour for several weeks until on 7 September 1942 they announced by placards and radio that all Jews were to assemble early in the morning at the railway freight depot for immediate "resettlement in sparsely populated areas of Ukraine." The order signed by "the city commandant's office No. 12" was clearly the work of the Wiens/Strohschneider team.

Early in the morning of 7 September some 1,800 Jews appeared and were separated into groups in front of twenty freight cars. Around noon, once everyone was loaded, the train, guarded by the men of MKC 12, moved off in a northeasterly direction. It passed the resort town of Mineralnye Vody, where several German military units were headquartered, and came to a halt in an open field. The MKC 12 guards, under the command of Heinrich Wiens, surveyed the field with binoculars but found the area inadequate for the scale of the killing planned. They returned the train to Mineralnye Vody, where it stopped on a siding near a glass factory.

Roughly a kilometre away there was a large tank trap, which SS Captain Wiens personally selected as the appropriate place for the massacre. Soviet sources suggest that the place was intended all along to be the killing site for the Jews of Kislovodsk, as it had been for the Jews of Pyatigorsk, and that the train had been stopped because the guards needed to orient themselves in the region.[68] Certainly the method of killing was the same. Guards forced fifty Jews at a time into a gas van, which was driven around the field until all the people had been asphyxiated by the carbon monoxide piped in.[69] The van then stopped on the edge of the tank trap, and Jewish prisoners were compelled to pull the bodies out and throw them into the hole.[70]

The genocidal act was not secret. Administrative staff from the 17th German Army and the 1st Panzer Army came to observe. When one of the Jews escaped from the train, German soldiers captured him and returned him to Wiens's MKC 12 team. That team did not limit itself to the Jews of Kislovodsk; it extended its murderous activities to the Jewish population of Essentuki and other towns as well. The German military commandant of Essentuki, Lieutenant Colonel von Beck, had anticipated the work of MKC 12 by forming a "Jewish Committee" on 11 August 1942, and he used it to register the Jews and rob them of their possessions. Thus 1,500 Jews from Essentuki joined the Jews of Kislovodsk in a mass grave at the glass factory. A similar fate awaited the Jews of Georgiyevsk, who were driven to the place of execution by a detachment of Caucasian auxiliaries employed by MKC 12.

A Soviet investigative commission for the war crimes trials conducted after the area had been reconquered by Red Army troops claimed to have disinterred some 6,300 people at the glass factory near Mineralnye Vody. Although the number may be exaggerated, designed to impress the Soviet people at the trial at Krasnodar, the huge grave remains forever associated with the name of Wiens. An atrocity had been committed by the son of Mennonites near the former Mennonite settlements of Templehof, Suvorovka, Olgino, and Terek. Jewish life and the presence of Jewish culture in the foothills of the Caucasus had been wiped out,[71] and the deed had been done by a Mennonite from Yablunivka named Heinrich Wiens.

NOTES

1 Some relevant memoirs by Mennonites include: Helen Wiens Franz, *My Memoirs* (Abbotsford: Memoirs Publishing, 1996), 15; Wilhelm Janzen, "A Refugee Travels from Russia through Germany over Paraguay to Canada," unpublished memoir (Winnipeg: Mennonite Heritage Centre, n.d.), 52–4; and Anna Sudermann, *Lebenserinnerungen: 1893–1970* (Winnipeg: Mennonite Heritage Centre, 1970). For scholarship by non-Mennonites, see James Urry, "Mennonites in Ukraine during World War II: Thoughts and Questions," *Mennonite Quarterly Review* 93 (January 2019): 81–111, which includes an extensive discussion of Gerhard Rempel's research; Martin Dean, "Soviet Ethnic Germans and the Holocaust in the Reich Commissariat Ukraine," in *The Shoah in Ukraine: History, Testimony, Memorialization*, ed. Ray Brandon and Wendy Lower (Bloomington: Indiana University Press in association with the United States Holocaust Memorial Museum, 2010): 248–71; Andrej Angrick, *Besatzungspolitik und Massenmord. Die Einsatzgruppe D in der*

Mennonites, War Crimes, and the Holocaust 63

südlichen Sowjetunion 1941–1943 (Hamburg: Hamburger Edition, 2003). Also of interest: Karel C. Berkhoff, "Was There a Religious Revival in Soviet Ukraine under the Nazi Regime?" *The Slavonic and East European Review* 78, no. 3 (July 2000): 536–67. An important article on a perpetrator with Mennonite connections appeared after Rempel wrote this text: Eric C. Steinhart, "The Chameleon of Trawniki: Jack Reimer, Soviet Volksdeutsche, and the Holocaust," *Holocaust and Genocide Studies* 23, no. 2 (2009): 239–62.

2 John J. Kroeker, diary fragment, 4 April 1944, folder "Berlin-diary 1944," box 33, John J. Kroeker Papers, MS 501, Mennonite Library and Archives, North Newton, Kansas.
3 Kroeker, diary fragment, 10 April 1944.
4 Kroeker, diary fragment from Tschiemanowsky, 21 December 1944.
5 Maria Penner story in Kroeker diary fragment, 10 September 1945. For context see Daniel Blatman, *The Death Marches: The Final Phase of Nazi Genocide* (Cambridge, MA: Harvard University Press, 2011).
6 Sudermann did not explain how she would have known whether the informant and interrogators were Jews.
7 Anna Sudermann fonds, vol. 3770, Mennonite Heritage Archives, Winnipeg. Sudermann uses the terms "Feldgendarmerie" and "Gendarmerie" interchangeably, though they could have been distinct police units. Martin Dean, *Collaboration in the Holocaust: Crimes of the Local Police in Belorussia and Ukraine, 1941–44* (New York: St Martin's Press, 2000), 63, delineates these units and describes their role in the destruction of Jews of southern Ukraine. On the nexus between policing, soldiering, and genocide, see Edward B. Westermann, *Hitler's Police Battalions: Enforcing Racial War in the East* (Lawrence: University Press of Kansas, 2005), esp. ch. 6, "The Face of Occupation."
8 Sudermann, *Lebenserinnerungen*, 349–52. Sudermann's account of the "half-Jewish child" is echoed in Harry Loewen, ed., *Road to Freedom: Mennonites Escape the Land of Suffering* (Kitchener: Pandora, 2000), 61–2; and in John Sawatzky, *One Out of Three: How My Family and I Survived Russian Communism* (Mountain Lake, MN: John Sawatzky, 1996). See also Susanna Toews, *Trek to Freedom: The Escape of Two Sisters from South Russia during World War II* (Winkler, MB: Heritage Valley, 1976): "We observed the Germans in Russia, and saw their treatment of the Jews. They shot thousands upon thousands. It seemed incredible to us. We were forbidden to help any Jews. In the village of Nickolaidorf, a Jewish girl had managed to escape execution. We thought, surely, this girl would be spared. She was not. The S.S. commander came to investigate. 'There's a Jewess left somewhere in this area.' She was soon apprehended. After a brief release, she was again taken. She was brought to a trench on the outskirts of the village. There she was shot to death, her body tumbling into the trench. Though she had

been pleading that her life be spared, she was shown no pity. We were terribly upset by this incident. How we grieved for this girl, who grew up among us, and was now so brutally murdered. Many met the same fate. Could such a system survive and be blessed? Germany did fall. Unbelief reigns in Germany" (20).

9 Alexander Rempel and Amalie Enns, *Hope Is Our Deliverance: Aeltester Jakob Aron Rempel: The Tragic Experience of a Mennonite Leader and His Family in Stalin's Russia* (Kitchener: Pandora, 2005). For context, see Anne Applebaum, *Gulag: A History* (New York: Doubleday, 2003).

10 Alexander Rempel, "Ein Protest gegen die Judenvernichtung: Untersuchungen zur Frage nach der Beteiligung von Volksdeutschen aus dem Schwarzmeergebiet in der Ukraine an der Judenvernichtung während des II-ten Weltkriegs" (Winnipeg: Mennonite Heritage Centre, 1984), MHC, vol. 3440:3. Today Rosenthal is part of Zaporizhzhia.

11 Helmut Krausnick, *Hitler's Einsatzgruppen: Die Truppen des Weltanschauungskrieges 1938–1942* (Frankfurt: Fischer Taschenbuch, 1985), 166–7. See also Yuri Radchenko, "Ukrainian Historiography of the Holocaust through the Prism of Modern Discourse on Collaboration on the Territory of Ukraine," *Dapim: Studies on the Holocaust* 31, no. 3 (2017): 313–21.

12 SD, "Ereignismeldung UdSSR Nr. 143 vom 8. Dezember 1941," file 17, vol. 3781, Alexander Rempel fonds. The collection contains numerous such reports. An overview is in Michael Gesin, "Holocaust: The Reality of Genocide in Southern Ukraine" (PhD diss., Brandeis University, 2003), 259–60: "When in October 1941, the Germans occupied the city of Zaporozhe itself, they immediately ordered the Jews to form their own government of ten German-speaking people to whom they would transfer all future orders. The next day, the registration of all Jews in the city began. … [At the] beginning of 1942, 150 Jews were ordered to gather in the center of town to be transported to their new workplace. On January 3, 1942, they were all killed. … On March 29, 1942, all the remaining Jews were ordered to stay home and await further instructions. They were told to take clothing and food to last for three weeks for their resettlement in Melitopol. … On April 1, they were all transferred to the outskirts of the city and shot. … The killings continued until the autumn of 1943. In all, more than 44,000 Jews were murdered in the Zaporozhe oblast." See also Gesin, *The Destruction of the Ukrainian Jewry during World War II* (Lewiston, ME: Edwin Mellen, 2006). The Melitopol killing site has been confirmed by interviews with witnesses conducted by Patrick Desbois, *The Holocaust by Bullets: A Priest's Journey to Uncover the Truth behind the Murder of 1.5 Million Jews* (New York: Palgrave Macmillan, 2008), 75ff.

13 Dr. Kieling, Field Command 676, "Report about the Inspection of the Administration in Zaporozhye," 2 November 1941, reel 92, RG-11.001M,

Osobyi Archive (Moscow) records 1932–1945, US Holocaust Memorial Museum Archives, Washington, DC (hereafter USHMMA).
14 In the research files of Frank H. Epp, James Urry found photocopies of three records from the Einwandererzentralstelle (EWZ). One is a good example of a self-identified Russian Mennonite who joined the SS. It identifies a Jakob Ediger, born 29 May 1917 at Millerovo. He listed himself as "Mechaniker" by trade and gave the date of his naturalization by EWZ, 13 April 1944. "From November 1941 to 1943 he was with the Sicherheitspolizei und Sicherheitsdienst Saporoshje as a Hilfspolizist, and from 1943 to March 1944 with the Einsatzkommando 6B as an SS Mann. Picture available, (Einwanderer Zentrale)." Mennonite Exodus research ch. 26, Frank H. Epp papers, Hist. Mss. 2.26.7, Conrad Grebel College Archive, University of Waterloo, Waterloo. Copy of the Ediger EWZ file also at the MLA (US National Archives microfilm publication A3342, "Documents Generated in Connection with Activities of the Einwandererzentralstelle," roll B034, frame 1214 ff.). On the EWZ, see Andreas Strippel, "Race, Regional Identity and *Volksgemeinschaft*: Naturalization of Ethnic German Resettlers by the Einwandererzentralstelle / Central Immigration Office of the SS," in Claus-Christian W. Szejnmann and Maiken Umbach, eds., *Heimat, Region and Empire: Spatial Identities under National Socialism* (Houndsmills: Palgrave Macmillan, 2012): 185–98.
15 Rempel, "Ein Protest gegen die Judenvernichtung."
16 Krausnick, *Hitlers Einsatzgruppen*, 175.
17 Rempel, "Ein Forschungsbericht," 43–4. On church openings, see Johannes Due Enstad, "Prayers and Patriotism in Nazi-Occupied Russia: The Pskov Orthodox Mission and Religious Revival, 1941–1944," *Slavonic and East European Review* 94, no 3 (2016): 468–96. To trace the course of the panzer units, see Dennis Showalter, *Hitler's Panzers: The Lightning Attacks that Revolutionized Warfare* (New York: Berkley Caliber, 2009).
18 Gerhard Fast, *Das Ende von Chortitza* (Winnipeg, Man.: Regehr's Printers, 1973): 9–10, 46, 70–71, and elsewhere.
19 Rempel, "Ein Forschungsbericht," 10.
20 Extraordinary State Commission to Investigate German-Fascist Crimes Committed on Soviet Territory from the USSR, 1941–1945: 7021–61. Ukraine, Zaporozhskaya (Zaporozhe) *oblast*. These materials are now available on microfilm RG-22.002M at the USHMMA.
21 Eric J. Schmaltz and Samuel D. Sinner, "The Nazi Ethnographic Research of Georg Leibbrandt and Karl Stumpp in Ukraine and Its North American Legacy," *Holocaust and Genocide Studies* 14, no. 1 (March 2000): 28–64.
22 Autobiography of Dr Hans Rempel, formerly of Kiel, Germany, *Der Bote*, nos. 22–5, (27 May–17 June 1992), ed. Gerhard Ens, instalments 26–9. This text was published in the Canadian Mennonite periodical *Der Bote* in

fifty instalments, beginning with the 20 November 1991 issue (68/44), 9. The first instalment had no overall title; it started with a photo of Hans Rempel and his name and address, with no clear indication that it was an autobiography. The text started with a subheading "Orenburg am Ural." The second instalment, in the 27 November issue, clarified that it constituted excerpts from Hans Rempel's autobiography. The book was subsequently published: Johannes Rempel, *Mit Gott über die Mauer springen: Vom mennonitischen Bauernjungen am Ural zum Kieler Pastor* (Husum: Matthiessen, 2013).

23 Johannes Harder, *Aufbruch ohne Ende: Geschichten meines Lebens* (Wuppertal: Brockhaus, 1992).

24 See Doris L. Bergen, *Twisted Cross: The German Christian Movement in the Third Reich* (Chapel Hill: University of North Carolina Press, 1996).

25 Cf. Gerhard Rempel, "Odessa sticks in my craw …" Rempel described his text as follows: "This is an unpleasant and unpublished reflection, penned on the spur of the moment. It reveals impatience with Harder's sarcasm when it comes to Mennonite leaders he depicts as Nazi fellow travelers yet his inability to come to terms with his own collaboration with Nazi bigshots and SS benefactors." On the 1941 wave of pogroms, including massacres of Jews in Lviv, see Jeffrey S. Kopstein and Jason Wittenberg, *Intimate Violence: Anti-Jewish Pogroms on the Eve of the Holocaust* (Ithaca: Cornell University Press, 2018).

26 Harder's own admission notwithstanding, some sources argue improbably that he did not know about the Holocaust. See Al Reimer, "Johannes (Hans) Harder," in *Shepherds, Servants, and Prophets: Leadership among the Russian Mennonites (ca. 1880–1960)*, ed. Harry Loewen (Kitchener: Pandora, 2003), 154. Compare with John D. Thiesen's review of *Shepherds, Servants, and Prophets* in *Mennonite Life* 60, no. 2 (June 2005), https://mla.bethelks.edu/ml-archive/2005June/reviews.php#loewen (accessed 27 November 2019). As Thiesen points out, "Harder signed some of his letters during the 1930s and 40s with the formulaic 'Heil Hitler,'" and "Harder's willing acceptance of a position with the SS in Russia meant that he had almost no way to avoid knowing what the SS was doing in the extermination of Jews and others there."

27 Harder, *Aufbruch Ohne Ende*, 117. Harder is undoubtedly referring to the "Einsatzgruppen der Sicherheitspolizei und des SD." See Krausnick, *Hitlers Einsatzgruppen*, 143,145, 162f. Elements of Einsatzgruppe C arrived in Lviv on the day it fell to the German army.

28 Harder, on duty with a Wehrmacht unit in Kiev, took or acquired the picture showing civilians in Kiev having just been shot, most likely by an SS unit. Source: MLA, https://mla.bethelks.edu/archives/numbered-photos/pholist2.php?num=2004-0036 (accessed 2 Nov 2018). Presumably Harder sent it to his friend Cornelius Krahn.

29 Zhytomyr was the seat of Himmler's experiment in racist demographics, known as the Hegewald project. It was well under way by the time Harder arrived, but he did not write about it. See Wendy Lower, *Nazi Empire-Building and the Holocaust in Ukraine* (Chapel Hill: University of North Carolina Press, 2005), ch. 7.
30 In early August 1941, Hitler issued a decree (*Erlaß*) ordering the Wehrmacht neither to promote nor to hinder local religious practice in occupied territories. Nor were German soldiers and officers to worship alongside the local populations. See complaint about the prohibition in Georg Werthmann, Catholic military bishop to Army High Command, 9 July 1943, p. 5, BA-MA Freiburg, RH 15/280, 123.
31 Harder, *Aufbruch ohne Ende*, 126–8. On Karaims, also known as Karaites, see Raul Hilberg, *The Destruction of the European Jews* (Chicago: Quadrangle Books, 1967), 240. According to German records, Wiebe, the Mennonite mayor of Zaporizhzhia, informed military commanders that the city had its own Karaite community and persuaded them to make an exception so that its members did not have to wear an armband identifying them as Jews. The prevailing argument was that Karaites were converts to Judaism but not really Jews in the racial sense. Perhaps these Karaites found by Harder's party had been seized in Zaporizhzhia and murdered before Wiebe became mayor. Kieling, "Report about the Inspection." For context, see Mikhail Kizilov, "Social Adaptation and Manipulation of Self-Identity: Karaites in Eastern Europe in Modern Times," in *Karaites in the Last Generations*, ed. Dan Shapira and Daniel Lasker (Jerusalem: Ben Zvi Institute, 2011), 130–53.
32 "Accused Nazi Murderer Is Expelled from the United States," press release no. 261, 9 May 1995, Office of Public Affairs, US Department of Justice, https://www.justice.gov/archive/opa/pr/Pre_96/May95/261.txt.html (accessed 15 October 2018).
33 *Canada (Minister of Citizenship and Immigration) v. Helmut Oberlander*, Docket: T-866–95, 28 February 2000, http://www.telusplanet.net/public/mozuz/d-d/oberlander20000228.html (accessed 16 October 2018). The part about Oberlander's family having been in Russia for 250 years reflects a typically garbled version of Mennonite history.
34 Canada (Minister of Citizenship and Immigration) v. Helmut Oberlander.
35 Angrick, *Besatzungspolitik und Massenmord*, 564.
36 *Oberlander*, Docket T866–95, end of Marwell testimony.
37 Ibid., fn26. Cf. Angrick, *Besatzungspolitik und Massenmord*, 307ff.
38 For reactions see David Matas, "Global Justice," *Jewish Tribune*, 29 September 2005, https://web.archive.org/web/20060111011013/http://jewishtribune.ca:80/tribune/jt-050929-09.html (accessed 2 November 2018); also Paul Lungen, "Two New War Crimes Cases Launched," *Canadian Jewish News*, 29 January 2004, 1, 19.

39 *Canada (Minister of Citizenship and Immigration) v. Fast*, (2001) 217 F.T.R. 166 (TD), https://ca.vlex.com/vid/can-m-c-i-680734205 (accessed 20 October 2018).
40 Andrew Duffy, "Government wins a round in deportation case," *Ottawa Citizen*, 22 May 2000, A6, https://www.newspapers.com/newspage/466509809/ (accessed 20 October 2018).
41 Ibid.
42 The controversial course of Canadian war crimes litigation is outlined in Peter Worthington, "Making all citizens equal," *Toronto Sun*, 23 June 2005, 48. Also of interest is an extensive report prepared by a Government of Canada commission in the mid-1980s, headed by Jules Deschênes: *Commission of Inquiry on War Criminals*, 1986, http://publications.gc.ca/site/eng/471452/publication.html.
43 See Steinhart, "The Chameleon of Trawniki." Reimer's EWZ indicates some ambiguity about his Mennonite identity. In one document outlining his ancestry, he identified his religion as "Mennonit"; in another, dated the same day, he identified himself as "evangelisch." EWZ microfilm, roll G063, frame 1966ff.
44 See Peter Black, "Foot Soldiers of the Final Solution: The Trawniki Training Camp and Operation Reinhard," *Holocaust and Genocide Studies* 25, no. 1 (Spring 2011): 1–99.
45 Gail Appleson, "Accused Nazi collaborator testifies that war is evil," http://www.nizkor.org/ftp.cgi/people/r/ftp.cgi?people/r//reimer.jack/press/war-is-evil.980812 (accessed 20 October 2018). This text seems originally to have been a Reuters news article.
46 In a letter to Pastor Hylkema, Kroeker enclosed a draft for approval. The pass was to help those who could not come to Berlin but somehow managed to get to the West to cross over the border into the Netherlands. The text attested that "Mr. Jacob Reimer, born October 24th in Halbstadt, is a Mennonite of Dutch origin." It included places for the signature of Hylkema and the commander of the Dutch Frontier Guard. The bearer would be delivered to one of the Mennonite refugee camps and prepared for emigration to Canada or the United States. Kroeker to Hylkema, 7 March 1946, folder "Berlin – Correspondence 1946 January-May," box 33, Kroeker Papers. It is not certain, however, that Kroeker's Jacob Reimer is the same as the Carmel, NY, Jack Reimer. The 24 October birthday does not include a year and does not match the birthdate of the Carmel, NY, Jack Reimer, nor does the birthplace Halbstadt match that of the Carmel, NY, Jack Reimer. On the Reimer case, see US Department of Justice press release, "Government Moves to Deport New York City Area Man for Involvement in Nazi Mass Murder of Jews," 2 May 2005, https://www.justice.gov/archive/opa/pr/2005/May/05_crm_234.htm (accessed 22 October 2018); e-mail James Urry to Gerhard Rempel, "Reimer," 20 March 2006.

47 "The American CIC (Secret Police) puts everyone through a rigorous sieve. They put me in prison for two days, because I violated military law by dragging 192 people to Berlin. We are always under observation in the camp. We do have in our midst several people who were drafted into the Wehrmacht and SS and this costs us a lot of problems about why and how." Kroeker to Benjamin H. Unruh, "Lieber Onkel Benny," 11 April 1946, folder "Berlin – Correspondence 1946 January–May," box 33, Kroeker Papers. See also Heinrich B. Unruh, *Fügungen und Führungen: Benjamin Heinrich Unruh, 1881–1959. Ein Leben im Geiste christlicher Humanität und im Dienste der Nächstenliebe* (Detmold: Verein zur Erforschung und Pflege des Russlanddeutschen Mennonitentums, 2009). Gerhard Rempel's review of this biography noted that it skirts past "serious questions concerning Unruh's collaboration with the Nazis." *Conrad Grebel Review* 20 (Winter 2002): 37–9.
48 The Eichmann connection comes up in another Mennonite context. A Canadian author and raconteur recalls seeing correspondence between Walter Jakob Quiring and Eichmann in an archive in Germany. Confidential email from Harry Loewen, 24 August 2006. Loewen is not the raconteur in question. John D. Thiesen has also heard the story that Simon Wiesenthal accused Mennonites of harbouring Eichmann but has not seen that accusation in print. Nor did his research find evidence that Mennonites in Paraguay or Brazil "harboured" any well-known war criminals, although there is evidence that Mengele visited the Paraguayan colonies as a farm implement salesman. See also Daniel Stahl, "How the Fernheimers Learned to Speak about the Nazi Era: The Long Historical Echo of a Conflict," *Mennonite Quarterly Review* 92 (April 2018): 285–98, esp. 290–1.
49 Dan Barry, "A Face Seen and Unseen on the Subway," *New York Times*, 17 September 2005.
50 Colin Miner, "Onetime Nazi Guard Who Settled in Brooklyn Misses Court Date," *New York Sun*, 14 June 2005. "From the Soviets, the OSI also received transcripts of interviews conducted by the KGB in 1964 with two Soviets who had been taken prisoner by the Nazis and forced to work at Trawniki. Both said they knew Reimer. One of them, Nikolaj Leontev, said he was in a unit commanded by Reimer to 'empty a town in Czechoslovakia of its Jews and execute them in a forest'" (2).
51 Ronald Sullivan, "U.S. Moves against Man It Links to Death Camp," *New York Times*, 25 June 1992, B7. See also subsequent articles in *New York Times*: Sullivan, "Charging War Crimes, U.S. Seeks to Revoke Citizenship," 10 July 1993; Benjamin Weiser, "Man Accused of Nazi Role Faces Trial," 2 August 1998; Benjamin Weiser, "U.S. Seeks to Expel Man Accused of Role as SS Leader," 4 August 1998, B3; Benjamin Weiser, "Reporter's Notebook: Former Attorney General Defending a Brooklyn Man in Nazi War Crimes," 9 August 1998; Susan Sachs, "Holocaust Survivors Tell of Horrors at Trial

of Accused Guard," 11 August 1998, B4; Benjamin Weiser, "Suspect in Nazi War Crimes Claims Ignorance of Killings," 13 August 1998, B6; Benjamin Weiser, "Man Weeps as He Relates Killing of Jews," 14 August 1998, B7; Susan Sachs, "Man Says He Never Hid His Nazi Past," 18 August 1998, B3; Susan Sachs, "In Testimony, Man Denies War Crimes at Nazi Camp," 19 August 1998, B3; Susan Sachs, "Trial Is Over for a Man Accused in War Crimes," 20 August 1998, B6. It was established that Reimer was present at Trawniki, but what he actually did there remained in doubt.

52 US Court of Appeals, Second Circuit, United States of America, Plaintiff-Appellee, v. Jack REIMER, a/k/a Jakob Reimer, Defendant-Appellant, Docket No. 02–6286. Decided: 27 January 2004, http://caselaw.lp.findlaw.com/data2/circs/2nd/026286p.pdf (accessed 20 October 2018).

53 Docket: T-938–95, *Canada (Minister of Citizenship and Immigration) v. Dueck*, (1998) 155 F.T.R. 1 (TD), https://app.vlex.com/#vid/can-m-c-i-681538585 (accessed 20 October 2018).

54 John D. Thiesen, *Mennonite and Nazi? Attitudes among Mennonite Colonists in Latin America, 1933–1945* (Kitchener: Pandora, 1999), 206–7.

55 James Urry email to Gerhard Rempel, 20 March 2005.

56 On internment and late nineteenth-century migrations from Prussia, see Johannes Harder, *Das sibirische Tor. Vier Jahre Orenburger Zivilgefangenschaft. 1914–1918* (Stuttgart: Steinkopf, 1938).

57 I am grateful to George C. Browder for providing me with his notes on Heinrich Wiens from a 1990 research trip to Berlin, taken from the Berlin Document Center/Bundesarchiv Berlin-Lichterfelde SSO (SS Officer) and RS (Rasse und Siedlungs Hauptamt) files on Wiens. See Browder, *Hitler's Enforcers: The Gestapo and the SS Security Service in the Nazi Revolution* (Oxford: Oxford University Press, 1996). Source of portrait of Heinrich Wiens: Angrick, *Besatzungspolitik und Massenmord*, 614. (The former Berlin Document Center collections are now in the Bundesarchiv Berlin-Lichterfelde and are also available on microfilm from the US National Archives.) Wiens is also discussed in chapter 7.

58 Church membership was never categorically forbidden to members of the SS. See Richard Steigmann-Gall, *The Holy Reich: Nazi Conceptions of Christianity, 1919–1945* (New York: Cambridge University Press, 2003).

59 Browder cites Bundesarchiv RS.

60 Ic in a Wehrmacht unit stands for the third general staff officer in charge of enemy intelligence and defense.

61 Browder notes; Angrick, *Besatzungspolitik und Massenmord*, 324. Angrick did not use the BDC material on Wiens in his book but provided information based on the latter's *Lebensläufe*. There is, however, no information about Wiens's life after his transfer to the 14th Waffen SS Division in January 1945.

62 On Ohlendorf, see Hilary Earl, *The Nuremberg SS-Einsatzgruppen Trial, 1945–1958: Atrocity, Law, and History* (New York: Cambridge University Press, 2009).
63 *The People's Verdict: A Full Report of the Proceedings at the Krasnodar and Kharkov German Atrocity Trials* (London and New York: Hutchinson, 1944). The first trial was held 14–17 July 1943 before the military tribunal of the North Caucasian Front. The defendants were I.F. Kladov, I.F. Kotomtsev, and others. The second trial was held 15–18 December 1943 before the military tribunal of the 4th Ukrainian Front. Defendants were Reinhard Retzlaff, Wilhelm Langheld, and others. The only Mennonite name mentioned in the document is "Winz," which almost certainly refers to Heinrich Wiens. "Retzlaff" may also have been a Mennonite, although no further evidence supports that surmise. Alexander Rempel appears to have seen this book. The relevant passage reads as follows: "The Sonderkommando SS-10a was a punitive unit of the Gestapo, numbering about 200 men. The head of this Sonderkommando was Colonel Christmann, a German, Chief of the Gestapo. His immediate assistants in the work of exterminating Soviet citizens were the German officers: Rabbe, Boss, Sargo, Salge, Hahn, Erich Meier, Paschen, Winz and Hans Münster, the German Army Surgeons in the prison and the Gestapo, Herz and Schuster and also officials of the Gestapo, the interpreters Jakob Eicks and Scherterlan" (8). For analysis of Soviet trials see Alexander Victor Prusin, "'Fascist Criminals to the Gallows!': The Holocaust and Soviet War Crimes Trials, December 1945–February 1946," *Holocaust and Genocide Studies* 17/1 (Spring 2003): 1–30.
64 Angrick, *Besatzungspolitik und Massenmord*, 613.
65 Wassili Grossmann and Ilja Ehrenburg, eds., *Das Schwarzbuch: Der Genozid an den sowjetischen Juden* (Reinbek bei Hamburg: Rowohlt, 1994), 426; in English, Ilya Ehrenburg and Vasily Grossman, *The Complete Black Book of Russian Jewry* (New York: Routledge, 2017). See also Ilya Altman and Joshua Rubenstein, eds., *The Unknown Black Book: The Holocaust in the German-Occupied Soviet Territories* (Bloomington: Indiana University Press in association with the United States Holocaust Memorial Museum, 2010).
66 Angrick, *Besatzungspolitik und Massenmord*, 614–15.
67 William Schroeder and Helmut T. Huebert, *Mennonite Historical Atlas*, 2nd ed. (Winnipeg: Springfield, 1996), 119.
68 See Munich court records cited in Angrick, *Besatzungspolitik und Massenmord*, 614–15.
69 There is a technical yet gruesome description of the gas van in *The Peoples' Verdict*, 8–9.
70 Angrick, *Besatzungspolitik und Massenmord*, 617–18.
71 Ibid., 619–20.

Chapter Two

Enjoying the Entitlements of German Freedom: German Mennonites and Nazi Church-State Policy

JAMES IRVIN LICHTI

When Hitler became chancellor in 1933, the vast majority of the German population belonged to one of the state-supported provincial churches. Other Christian communities, including German Mennonites, tended to be dismissed as "sects." But this label did not really fit German Mennonites; for some time, their theology, outlook, and practice had been growing closer to the German Protestant mainstream. Yet this proximity did not quiet challenges from within the provincial churches: if German Mennonites were not a sect, then why did they persist in setting themselves apart? What distinctions in Mennonite teachings justified their separate existence?

This question led to soul-searching among German Mennonite leaders, who knew all too well that those distinctions had dwindled. Teachings on non-resistance and the refusal to swear oaths had been losing ground among the laity for some time.[1] Increasingly, the German Protestant mainstream seemed to have a point: had German Mennonites assimilated to the point that a separate institutional existence was no longer justified?[2]

This question of whether German Mennonites constituted a sect took on greater urgency once Hitler became chancellor. The secular Weimar Republic had made room for sects, but the Nazi regime was intent on eliminating all forms of Christianity that conflicted in any way with the ideology of the new "racial state." By the mid-1930s the regime was outlawing one sect after another, sending thousands of sectarians to jails and concentration camps. Earlier, German Mennonites had responded to the sectarian label as a kind of insult; now it could threaten their very existence.[3]

But sect and provincial church were not the only possible categories of Christian community in Germany. Since the mid-nineteenth century the idea of a "free church" had gained in both currency and legitimacy.

In its most basic definition, a free church enjoys the societal respectability of a "church" while remaining "free" of the ties to the state that characterize the provincial church.⁴ This status included, for example, many Anglo-American denominations that had taken root in Germany, such as Methodists, Baptists, Seventh-day Adventists, and Quakers. To be sure, the average German might still label any of these denominations a "sect," but what really mattered was the label selected by the new Nazi state.

Free church status thus served German Mennonites in two ways. Since the Nazi regime recognized German Mennonites as a free church, this status shielded them from the sectarian label. But the free church concept also justified an ecclesiastical existence beyond the provincial churches. German Mennonite leaders expanded this self-justification beyond a one-dimensional definition of the free church as free of state influence. They further characterized their denomination as Germany's oldest free church, praising the Anabaptist shift from infant to adult baptism as a "flight from magic into the God-given light of reason and obedience to truthfulness."⁵ In addition, their Anabaptist forbearers had banished all "coercion of conscience," removed all "authoritative levels of [clerical] mediation," and embraced pluralism. The list of freedoms enjoyed by German Mennonites was diverse, multidimensional, and distinctive, contrasting so vividly with the anachronisms of the provincial churches that the free church might more accurately be called an "anti-church."⁶

This self-characterization reminded me of the liberal General Conference congregation of my childhood. In my memory, these same freedoms set our congregation apart from other denominations in that rural California town. And these freedoms were taking on a new importance in my life: they permitted me to dare hope that I might one day find a home for myself as a gay man in some corner of a "liberal" Mennonite world.

The question that emerged for me, then, had a personal dimension. To be sure, I was well aware that German Mennonites had accommodated themselves to both the Nazi regime and Nazi ideology to a considerable degree. But given that Nazism was based on an anti-liberal ideology, it seemed likely that these liberal freedom-embracing principles may have – at least to some degree – insulated German Mennonites from that ideology.

This supposition proved false. Rather than insulating German Mennonites, liberal free-church principles did more to facilitate the German Mennonite accommodation to the Nazi world view. True, they did not *cause* that accommodation; there were many different dynamics at play guiding German Mennonites – indeed, most Germans – toward identification with the Nazi *Volksgemeinschaft* (national or racial community).[7] But the unsettling role of liberal free-church concepts and principles in facilitating the German Mennonite identification with the goals of the Nazi state is the central point of this chapter.

A secondary point addresses the complex relationship between Nazi church-state policy and the liberal principles embraced by free churches. Without question, Nazi ideology was fundamentally antiliberal. Nonetheless, Nazi leaders did not shy away from liberal ideas if they served their own ends – such as using them to buttress their own racial conception of "German religious freedom," or implementing them as part of a wider strategy of eroding the societal authority and influence of the provincial churches.

Alongside these two points, a question hovers over the chapter as a whole. These three forms of Christian community – the provincial church, the free church, and the sect – were more than abstract ideal types. They were categories used both by the regime and by the population as a whole, and how a Christian community was categorized had very specific consequences. Given that, did one of these three forms remain truer to the heart of the Christian message? And if so, are there any enduring conclusions that Christian communities today might draw from this?

The Defining Characteristics of the Provincial Church, the Free Church, and the Sect

Figure 1 lists the key characteristics that have been associated with the provincial church, the free church, and the sect. I borrow the overarching distinction between them – the locus of charismatic authority – from the conceptual vocabulary of Max Weber.[8] In Weber's analysis, both (state/provincial) church and sect make exclusive claims to Christian truth, thus asserting their respective monopolies over charismatic authority. Despite this commonality, the location of charismatic authority is not the same: in the church, its base is *bureaucratic* (*Amtscharisma*), residing within the clerical hierarchy; in the sect, its base is *collective*, residing within a spiritual virtuosity that is shared relatively evenly by the sect's members.

By contrast, the free church and the denomination place the seat of charismatic authority within the individual conscience of each individual member. This conclusion relies on the work of church scholars on denominationalism.[9] The free church is best understood as a variant of the denomination that exists in contexts where a state or provincial

Figure 2.1. Sect, Free Church, Provincial Church Properties

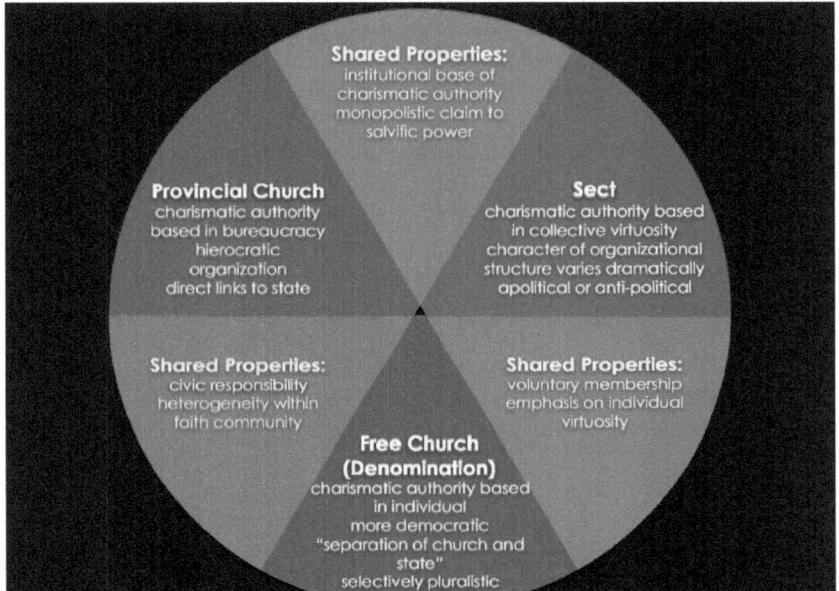

church predominates. Neither the free church nor the denomination makes exclusive claims to charismatic authority. As a general rule, both also reject the provincial church's hierarchical location of charismatic authority and the sect's collective location of charismatic authority.[10] In a sense, they declare the charismatic independence of each believer before God.

It must be noted at this point that the term denomination is seldom used in Germany. The closest German equivalent to "denomination" is *Konfession*. But "confession" is conceptually problematic for describing free churches since not all of them – including Mennonites – define themselves on the basis of a confession.

In fact, the historical context for the emergence of denominationalism was an anti-confessional campaign. During the seventeenth-century English Civil War, Puritan Independents raised objections to the Westminster Confession. Their aim was not to fix it; the problem – as they perceived it – lay in the process itself, which remained vulnerable to error: "in many councils, Jesus Christ hath been outvoted by antiChrist." Instead, the Independents sought a "church" that could – at least for a time – tolerate confessional ambiguity: "[i]n the dark, all colors be alike; but in the light, they appear diverse." Citing Daniel 12:4, they asserted that the time had come for many to "run to and fro, and by this means knowledge shall be increased." While "the truth and true measure be one, the persons measuring it are very various and much different."[11]

Thus, the Independents' denominational discourse identified *any* confession as a human document and *any* church as a human institution.[12] Diversity and dialogue were requisite components of discernment. Indeed, multiplicity is embedded in the term denomination itself, since one can only denominate where there is more than one. Admittedly, the pluralism the Independents were promoting was selective, but it marked a bold departure from the monopolistic claim to Christian truth that had thus far characterized "the church."

Alongside pluralism, church scholars have associated the denomination with a trend toward adopting freedoms that most German Mennonites would call their own. These include freedom from hierarchy as established by Anabaptist anticlericalism and freedom of choice as realized by adult baptism. Furthermore, German Mennonite congregations had embraced the notion of the freedom of the individual conscience even *within* the congregation. Finally, the principle of congregational autonomy endured among German Mennonites; while confessions were not foreign to their tradition, the identity of nineteenth- and twentieth-century German Mennonites is best characterized "in nonconfessional and non-dogmatic" terms.[13]

Admittedly, historical developments had somewhat modified the characteristics distinguishing the provincial church from the free church. For example, the experience of the provincial churches during the Weimar Republic instilled in them a greater appreciation for autonomy from the state.[14] Furthermore, not every German free church possesses the characteristics of denominationalism in equal measure.[15] Nonetheless, through their publications, German Mennonites demonstrated repeatedly their affinity for denominational characteristics during both the Weimar Republic and the Third Reich. They did this to justify an institutional existence beyond the provincial churches as well as to distance themselves from a sectarian status.

Freedom of Conscience, Non-Resistance, and German Freedom

The denominational characteristic that had the most decisive impact on the German Mennonite response to Nazi ideology was freedom of the individual conscience. Most German Mennonite congregations had integrated this principle into their congregational statutes by the end of the nineteenth century. This shifted the status of German Mennonites away from sectarianism and toward denominationalism. It also conformed to contemporary liberalizing trends in industrializing countries, which tended to promote individual rights.

But for most of these German Mennonite congregations, the integration of "freedom of conscience" was not about becoming more liberal; it was a means to a very specific end. The issue at hand was the rise of the modern nation-state, which indeed granted individual rights, such as "freedom of conscience." But alongside those rights came duties. And one of those duties was military service.

Certainly until the second half of the eighteenth century, German Mennonites held to a sectarian course on the refusal to bear arms. It remained a defining component of Mennonite collective virtuosity. This was possible because the scattered Central European principalities that tolerated a Mennonite presence had granted those Mennonites an exemption from bearing arms. But as corporative legal structures gave way to the principle of equality before the law, Mennonites lost their status of subjects bound to a separate set of legal parameters. Their new status, as citizens of a nation, threatened their "freedom" from military service. This liberalizing process prompted the onset of emigration by rural Prussian Mennonites to Russia during the second half of the eighteenth century.

That migration illustrates how seriously rural German Mennonites still took non-resistance at that time. But at the very same time, urban German Mennonites had begun questioning the same principle. Exposure to Enlightenment trends had inspired them to reflect on their roles in society. As a consequence, the bourgeois Mennonite elite of Krefeld concluded that their exemption from bearing arms had degenerated from a religious principle into a self-serving "symbolic demarcation."[16] A parallel self-questioning had plagued my own generation as we weighed our response to the draft during the Vietnam War. Indeed, since the advent of the modern nation-state, multiple generations of Mennonites with access to some form of exemption from bearing arms have asked themselves whether that exemption amounted to anything beyond hollow entitlement.[17]

This provides *one* reason why a growing proportion of German Mennonite young men – even though they had been granted the right to serve as non-combatants in 1868 – came to believe they could truly fulfil their obligation to the German nation only through the form of military service expected of *any* German man. It was to accommodate such "qualms of conscience" that the parameters of congregational membership were changed. But this change was about membership retention, not about turning German Mennonite congregations into bastions of liberalism. The matter of whether to refuse to bear arms was thus transformed from a question answered by the community to one answered by the individual. And this change took place one congregation at a time. It started during the second half of the eighteenth century and was largely complete by the end of the nineteenth.[18]

Thus, the integration of freedom of conscience into German Mennonite congregational statutes fundamentally shaped the German Mennonite response to Nazi Germany. This freedom did not cause the decline of non-resistance as a defining dimension of German Mennonite identity, but it did facilitate it. Had a sectarian approach to non-resistance been maintained, then an ideological accommodation to the profoundly militarist Nazi ideology would have been impossible. During the first four years of Nazi rule, multiple statements emanating from the *Vereinigung* (Alliance) – that is, from the largest association of German Mennonite congregations – asserted that German Mennonites had "fully abandoned" the principle of non-resistance.[19] The intent of such declarations was to publicly signal the demise of non-resistance among German Mennonites.

However, the Alliance's public assertions fell short of the full truth. The principle of non-resistance did not vanish entirely among German Mennonites; it did, however, retreat into the shadows, where it persisted among an intimidated remnant.[20] No congregational statutes were changed; they retained freedom of conscience in regard to bearing arms. And a good number of German Mennonite leaders remained committed to helping members with qualms about bearing arms to inconspicuously find their way.[21] In an isolated but more public move, one lone German Mennonite signed the Mennonite Peace Manifesto at the 1936 Mennonite World Conference in Amsterdam.[22] With the start of war, some German Mennonites sought and secured non-combatant status, but Lichdi speculates that this may have been in about the same proportion as the German population as a whole. Still, Lichdi asserts that a non-resistant conscience lived on through the "numerous cases" of German Mennonite soldiers who carried their convictions into the field by surreptitiously sidestepping direct involvement in killing.[23]

Arguably, the German Mennonite integration of the principle of freedom of conscience facilitated this secluded persistence of non-resistance. Congregational statutes mandated respect for those with qualms about killing. This non-resistant remnant exercised this freedom behind the closed doors of the "private" sphere – and it is indeed the private sphere that liberalism remains most intent on protecting, whether it is a matter of principle or of property. And in defence of this remnant, the pre-modern principle they were preserving was *not* designed to have any impact on any public sphere in any way. Oddly, it was precisely those German Mennonites who secretly shot their weapons into the air who may have had an – admittedly infinitesimal – impact on the German war effort if their qualms of conscience prevented the deaths of some small number of Allied soldiers.

There is some evidence that the Nazi regime did not fear religious opposition to bearing arms as long as those who sought non-combatant military status remained numerically small, qualified as "racially" German, and kept their "pacifist" principles to themselves, ensuring that any such ideas remained impotent in terms of their impact on society or state policy.[24] Indeed, some of the highest-ranking Nazi leaders explicitly defended freedom of conscience within the *religious* sphere. These men included Hitler's immensely powerful private secretary, Martin Bormann; a key architect of the Nazi ideological creed, Alfred Rosenberg; and the mastermind of the Holocaust, Heinrich Himmler.[25] Each defended religious freedom as an inalienable component of *German* freedom, as an exclusively *German* right for the *German* race.

To be sure, each of these Nazis had abandoned Christianity. But their ideology still bound them to theism, since it viewed atheism as the creation of "Jewish materialism." So they guarded their Nazi fortress of theism. And in the discourse of that fortress – which at that point still housed quarters for German paganists, Catholic and Protestant provincial churches, and German free churches – freedom for the religious conscience still played a role, albeit as a prerogative exclusive to the master race.[26]

This regard for freedom of conscience in terms of religious convictions served several aims of the regime's church-state strategy. It legitimized Nazi anticlericalism and curbed the authority of established confessions, which undermined the authority of the provincial churches over their members.[27] Freedom of conscience also shielded church members with Nazi racial views from conflicts with their clergy, their confession, or their congregation. It secured a point of entry into any congregation for views that reconciled Christianity with Nazi racial ideology, such as those promoted by the German Christians.

At its best, freedom of the individual conscience guards the communal process of discernment; at its worst, it privatizes, atomizes, and relativizes religious piety. Dietrich Bonhoeffer, for one, questioned the authority of the conscience, arguing that it was guided in part by the interests and concerns of the ego.[28] This returns us to the question of the role played by freedom of conscience in facilitating the dramatic decline of non-resistance among German Mennonites once the Nazis came to power. Was an anti-egoist sense of liberal responsibility the defining dynamic in the qualms of young German Mennonites at the end of the nineteenth century? Or were they driven by nationalist egoism – which the Nazis later transformed into racial chauvinism?[29]

Nazi Church-State Policy and "Separation of Church and State"

Initially, Nazi church-state policy attempted to restructure the provincial churches and fully align their functions with the aims of the state. One aspect of that restructuring would have involved integrating the free churches – including German Mennonites – into the provincial churches. But within two years, this approach was abandoned. While a significant proportion of provincial church leaders were prepared to fall in line behind the goals of the new regime, a nearly equal proportion insisted on maintaining the degree of institutional autonomy they had achieved during the Weimar Republic.[30]

The regime then shifted its church-state strategy, seeking instead to limit church influence over German society by confining its influence to the private sphere as much as possible. Nazi leaders also realized rather quickly that there was little point in eliminating free churches. First of all, free churches had little if any influence on German society. Furthermore, free churches proved to be as compliant as the provincial churches, if not more so. Finally, free churches generally viewed the Nazi regime as a return to a "Christian state" and as their best guardian against the threat of Bolshevist atheism. Indeed, it was possible to interpret some interactions between the free churches and the regime as suggesting a trend in Nazi church-state policy toward favouring the free church over the provincial church, such as the fact that while Hitler forbade any representation by clergy from the Protestant provincial churches at the Ecumenical Conference on Life and Work in Oxford in 1937, two free church representatives were able to attend.[31] Arguably, the free church model fell in line with a broader trends in Nazi church-state policy that suggested privatizing "charismatic authority" as a means of atomizing Christian life and circumscribing churchly influence on both German society and Nazi state policy.

This may help explain why, by 1935, German Mennonite leaders had fallen for Nazi church-state policy hook, line, and sinker. In their commentaries, they characterized that policy as the realization of a cherished denominational principle: separation of church and state. Moreover, they praised the Nazi approach to this principle as distinctively "clean," "clear," and "modern." While the Danzig pastor Erich Göttner preferred the adjective "clear,"[32] the youthful pastor Horst Quiring congratulated the fascist state – "the modern form of the state" – for finally implementing this Anabaptist principle.[33] And the long-time liberal pastor of Krefeld, Gustav Kraemer, anointed the Nazi regime as the *first* to achieve a "clean" separation of church and state.[34]

In a sense, clean, clear, and modern were apt adjectives for Nazi church-state policy. On its face, the regime's approach lacked ambiguity: it granted full authority over the "hereafter" to the church while retaining full authority over the "here" for the state. This take on the respective roles of church and state conformed tidily with the fascist tendency toward binary compartmentalization. It also held firm to Nazi aims of totalitarian control over society while permitting a temporary flexibility with one sphere of society that most Germans still identified as intrinsically German.

But the true significance of Mennonite praise for the regime's "liberal-denominational" church-state policy – regardless of how accurate their assessment was – lay in the fact that it enabled German Mennonites to advance themselves as "the model church." Prior to that point, it was the provincial church that provided the German norm. With the shifts in Nazi church-state policy that had taken place by the mid-1930s, German Mennonites now presented themselves as exemplifying the *new* norm. It was they – and, by implication, other free churches – who were distinctively compatible with this new *clean, clear, and modern* church-state policy.

German Mennonite periodicals brought this point home to their readers by pointing out how it was the free churches that remained free of the conflicts plaguing both sects and provincial churches. To be sure, the "church struggle" (*Kirchenkampf*[35]) aroused sympathy, and some German Mennonite leaders maintained direct contacts with the Confessing Church.[36] More publicly, German Mennonite periodicals contrasted the *Kirchenkampf* with the *absence* of a struggle between German Mennonites and the Nazi state. As an observer asserted in a Mennonite youth periodical, the "correctness" of separation of church and state "has been demonstrated by the current church struggle. The proper separation of religion and politics, the so hotly contested separation of state and church (but please not between *Volk* and church!) was realized four hundred years ago in our founding principles."[37]

This diagnosis surfaced repeatedly between 1935 and 1938. And each time, German Mennonite periodicals stated or implied that in instances of conflict between a church and the Nazi state, the fault lay with the church, not the state.[38] After all, Jesus died because the "Jewish church" had interfered in the affairs of the Roman state. Thus the Nazi state's "legal limitation" on the sphere of the church served as a positive and modern contribution that even possessed a biblical basis.[39] One could thank the regime for guiding "our sister [provincial] churches step by step out of an unholy fusion" with the state, as well as leading Mennonites "into a much warranted service to our *Volk* [people or nation]."[40]

A deficient understanding of a clean, clear, and modern separation of church and state also explained the plight of Protestant sects. It is interesting that in *Gemeinde-Blatt*, critical commentary on sects remained limited to articles by non-Mennonite authors. Still, these articles were selected for publication for their Mennonite audience, presumably by *Gemeinde-Blatt*'s Mennonite editor, Christian Schnebele. And when the Nazi regime outlawed a sect with the disturbingly familiar name – "the Anabaptists" (*die Wiedertäufer*) – Schnebele inserted his own commentary. He declared that German Mennonites had "absolutely nothing" to do with this sect; therefore, its dissolution "leaves our congregations completely untouched. We enjoy complete freedom of faith and practice as much as ever."[41]

A revealing article in *Gemeinde-Blatt* delineated how – in the contemporary context of Nazi Germany – a sect might transform itself into free church. The details of such a transformation align with the ideal-type analysis in Figure 1 to a remarkable degree. In the fall of 1937, *Gemeinde-Blatt* praised the transformation of *Christliche Versammlung* into the *Bund freikirchlicher Christen* (Association of Free-Church Christians). The regime had dissolved the sect on 28 April 1937; to legitimate itself, the new *Bund* provided its free church credentials. It began by praising the Nazi regime as "the instrument" that had torn down *Christliche Versammlung*'s "dividing wall" of sectarianism. Along with integrating "free church" into its new name, the *Bund* had done away with *Christliche Versammlung*'s "coercion of conscience and thought, intolerance, and judgmental spirit." It further committed itself to greater internal heterogeneity, greater openness to believers outside its community, and greater openness to the affairs of the world.[42] In seeking legitimacy in Nazi Germany, the *Bund* had adopted the defining characteristics of denominationalism as closely as if it had been following a recipe.

The German Mennonite embrace of Nazi church-state policy sealed their relationship of compliance with that state. The provincial churches, by contrast, had never embraced separation of church and state. They would have to define their relationship to the Nazi state differently.

This was easy for those sectors of the Protestant provincial churches that embraced the state's agenda and ideology: they simply conformed to the role of subservient "state churches." But sectors within the Protestant provincial churches intent on greater independence – specifically, those that had emerged during the *Kirchenkampf* and came to be known as the Confessing Church – strove to preserve some semblance of what they viewed as the rightful role of the church in society. They put this in writing in May 1934 with the Barmen Declaration. Representatives from almost every Protestant provincial church gathered in the city of Barmen with the aim of preserving the integrity of their various confessions in the totalitarian context. The declaration that emerged provided a bottom line to which members of the Confessing Church could hold themselves accountable – which is, indeed, one virtue of a confession.[43] The declaration also secured for the church a role in holding the state accountable to Christian doctrine.

To do this, the representatives at Barmen had to break with the characterization of the state as a created "order of God" (*Ordnung Gottes*). This assertion of the state's God-given nature became dominant particularly among Lutherans by the end of the nineteenth century; the broad extent of its influence is illustrated by its presence in German Mennonite periodicals. Pastor Erich Göttner, for example, repeatedly referred to the state as an "order of God" when buttressing his definition of a "clear" understanding of separation of church and state. In the Barmen Declaration, the state is not an "order of God" but an *Anordung Gottes* ("command of God"). This seemingly subtle change enabled the declaration's authors to shift the state's authority from an immutable "order" to a "mandated arrangement." On that basis, then, the authors empowered the church to claim the role of "admonisher" and hold the state accountable to "God's commandment and justice."[44]

Admittedly, the Barmen Declaration represented what was a minority position from within the provincial churches. Nonetheless, it possessed a sense of societal authority lacking in the German Mennonite response to Nazi church-state policy. Max Weber maintained that the *Amtscharisma* of the church legitimates the state; the Barmen Declaration preserved *Amtscharisma* to the extent that it retained a role for the "church" by monitoring the boundaries of that legitimation.

Yet "churches" in the setting of Anglo-American denominationalism have also assumed the mantle of admonisher of the state. This mantle is then not – by definition – denied a free church. As laid out in Figure 1, "civic responsibility" is one of the shared properties linking the free church to the state church. But up until this point, the German free churches had more or less cowered in the shadow of the German provincial churches. They lacked the societal stature that would have conferred on them an authoritative posture. The term "free church" appeared to concede that they had something like churchly status; it would be more accurate, though, to say that the ecclesiastical setting of Germany in the 1930s was such as to insist that free churches prove themselves worthy of the status of "church."

This raises the question of the extent to which the German Mennonite response to Nazi church-state policy typified German free churches in general. Two other German free churches – Seventh-day Adventists and Quakers – allow for an interesting comparison since, in both cases, their responses to church-state relations were shaped in part by their own teachings against bearing arms.

The German Seventh-day Adventist (SDA) position on church-state relations paralleled the German Mennonite position closely. SDAs follow a "dual citizenship" model that tends to presume an absence of conflict between "earthly" and "heavenly" citizenships.[45] As Kurt Sinz, editor of *Adventbote*, put it, "history vividly teaches that neither church nor state may encroach on regions foreign to each other."[46] German SDA commentary further asserted that freedom of worship was both a fascist and a Nazi principle.[47]

At the same time, more nuanced positions on separation of church and state *did* surface in both German Mennonite and German SDA periodicals. In 1933 and 1934, there were some strikingly bold commentaries, especially in *Mennonitische Jugendwarte*.[48] And Pastor Christian Neff of Weierhof – who had the clarity to reject the concept of a "Christian state" – reminded readers of the limits of worldly authority as late as 1939: "there is an abuse of office that is contrary to God when evil is protected and good is suppressed. A Christian cannot and must not participate in such abuse."[49] In SDA periodicals, it was one of German SDA's most adamant defenders of the Nazi state, Hulda Jost, who cautioned her readers in 1935 that worldly authorities "do not constitute the highest authority. ... The Christian must from time to time scrutinize whether or not the demands of earthly authority stand in contradiction to the will of the highest authority, Jesus Christ."[50]

But such statements remained isolated in both Mennonite and SDA periodicals. Far more typical were affirmations of the Nazi notion of "positive Christianity": "The positive Christian submits to 'all worldly authority.' He submits even when his faith and his behaviour are wrongly expounded upon, as happened to Christians of yore. The life that he leads before God demonstrates that he is *an irreproachable citizen* [emphasis in original]."[51] This preoccupation with *irreproachability* was pervasive among free churches. It was up to free churches to prove – on an ongoing basis – that they were "churches" and not "sects."[52]

Unlike German Mennonite periodicals, German SDA periodicals avoided commentary on the "church struggle."[53] But like German

Mennonites, German SDAs anxiously distanced themselves from more radical Adventists, whom the Nazi regime had classified as sects and banned. In the same breath, they expressed gratitude for the regime's "religious tolerance."[54] Indeed, German SDA periodicals harped repeatedly on the "freedom" they enjoyed in Nazi Germany.[55]

By contrast, the German Quaker periodical *Der Quäker* challenged the tidy delineation between the spheres of church and state.[56] Also unlike Mennonite and SDA periodicals, *Der Quäker* made no attempt to distance the German Yearly Meeting from outlawed sectarians with whom it could be associated. The dissolution of the *Rhönbruderhof* by the Gestapo in 1937 presents a striking example. Both German Mennonites and German Quakers had close ties to the Hutterite community. And since both Mennonites and Hutterites trace their origins to Anabaptism, it was arguably not so far from the mark when some press reports on the *Rhönbruderhof*'s dissolution identified the commune as "Mennonite." In response, German Mennonite periodicals scrambled to distinguish themselves from the pacifist and "communist" community.[57] By contrast, *Der Quäker* publicly noted that *exiled* members of the *Rhönbruderhof* were sitting in on the Dutch Yearly Meeting. True, the *Rhönbruderhof* had not been mistakenly labelled as Quaker. Nonetheless, *Der Quäker*'s content indicates solidarity, not distancing.[58]

Der Quäker's commentary on the "church struggle" was also distinctive. While German Mennonite and German SDA commentary faulted the Confessing Church for political engagement, *Der Quäker* faulted the Confessing Church for political *dis*engagement. The author of most of this criticism, Emil Fuchs,[59] accused the Confessing Church of limiting "Christian responsibility to the sphere of the church," excusing itself "from the burden of full responsibility for conduct of state," and expressing its recognition of Nazi state leaders as Christians "exuberantly." Fuchs also had few kind words for the positions on church-state relations voiced by Confessing Church luminaries such as Martin Niemöller and Karl Barth.[60]

Fuchs's boldness in *Der Quäker* was unrelenting. In 1937, he cited Martin Buber's assertion that religious institutions "lose their power" whenever they "retreat to the hereafter to avoid responsibility for the present."[61] That same year, Fuchs condemned the Nuremberg Racial Laws' prohibition of marriage between a Jew and a German.[62] Such commentary in *Der Quäker* calls forth the question: could German Mennonite or German SDA periodicals have gotten away with equally bold content? At a minimum, the repeatedly forthright content of *Der Quäker* suggests that the narrowness of commentary in other free-church periodicals simply cannot be written off as a consequence of Nazi press restrictions.

Selective Pluralism as an Antisemitic Strategy

A third denominational principle, selective pluralism, was not merely a free church characteristic: it was specifically promoted by the 1920 Nazi Party platform.[63] The platform's reliance on this liberal principle illustrates the genius of Nazi nationalism. Germany was a divided nation beset with deeply entrenched regional, religious, and class barriers. Nazi nationalism took on the challenge of bridging such barriers.[64] With this aim in mind, the 1920 platform challenged centuries of confessional conflict in Germany by replacing confessional divides with its own concept: "positive Christianity." This suggested that Nazism and Christianity were compatible, a point that Hitler drove home by incorporating a theistic vocabulary into his speeches more thoroughly than any previous German chancellor.[65]

Here, Nazi ideology was implementing a liberal denominational principle in pursuit of its antisemitic agenda. But one can ask how liberal this denominational principle was to begin with. To be sure, the dynamics binding the international ecumenical movement were diverse, but a shared fear of Marxism was certainly one of them. And this was the virtue of the Nazi platform's concept of "positive Christianity": it provided a vague umbrella concept to unite diverse Christian orientations behind the Nazi campaign against "Jewish materialism." A common materialist (here the Christian would read "Bolshevik") foe thus aligned the ecumenical agenda with the Nazi agenda on at least one point.

German Mennonites were probably not particularly enthusiastic about the open hand the Nazi Party platform extended to Roman Catholicism. But they did embrace the idea of "positive Christianity." The expression served as the Party's welcome mat for anti-secular Christians – which pretty much included all church-attending Christians in Germany. Such anti-secularism extended even to liberal Mennonite pastors like Alfred Fast of Emden, who in a 1930 commentary labelled the secular state a "bastard" of the French Revolution, destined to degenerate into Bolshevism.[66] Here, Fast was targeting the Weimar Republic, whose secular policies had ironically benefited free churches.[67] Nonetheless, German Mennonites – like most churchgoing Protestants – remained wary of that secular democracy. For them, secularism was an assault on Germany's "intrinsically" Christian character, particularly as the birthplace of Protestantism. Furthermore, they remained deeply suspicious of the parties that most reliably stood by the Weimar Republic, such as the Center Party with its Vatican ties and the Social Democrats with their Marxist origins. Additionally, the continued growth in voter support for the German Communist Party during the Great Depression only increased German Protestant anxieties about the Weimar Republic's ability to resist revolution.[68] Into that context stepped Hitler as Christianity's bulwark against Bolshevism. The Nazi promotion of "positive Christianity" then provided a platform that could unite denominations against the common foe of "Jewish materialism."

A profound fear of communism was arguably as important as any other factor in shaping German Mennonite support for Nazism. As Jonas J. Driedger convincingly demonstrated, Bolshevism ranked as the dominant bogeyman in *Mennonitische Blätter* from the end of the First World War through the ascent of Nazism.[69] Without question, it was more than reasonable for any denomination to be concerned about the fate of its members in the Soviet Union, and there were substantial numbers of both Mennonites and SDAs there.

Even so, German SDAs and German Mennonites approached this particular crisis in very different ways. While German Mennonites shared the hostility to socialism that was pervasive in German Protestantism, German SDA periodicals tended to express sympathy with socialist internationalism during the Weimar Republic. This may have reflected SDA experience: in 1925, one SDA author noted that "human freedom, especially religious freedom, has been incomparably greater under the Bolshevist government than under the Czarist regime."[70] Also, SDA periodicals articulated arguments favouring socialism by linking capitalism to militarism.[71] And even when SDAs did critique socialism, their principal bogeyman remained the papal menace, not the Red menace: for SDAs, the real problem with Germany's Social Democrats was *not* their Marxist origins but their readiness to form coalitions with the Catholic Center Party.[72]

Nonetheless, as Stalin's persecution of religious communities grew more brutal and bloody, both German Mennonite and German SDA periodicals raised protests. During the Nazi years, both communities repeatedly condemned the "Godless" materialism of international socialism as a "satanic" or "demonic" force.[73] Still, the character of their critiques of Soviet anti-religious policies differed dramatically: German SDA periodicals objected to *all* forms of Soviet religious persecution whether it targeted Christian, Jew, or Muslim.[74] By contrast, German Mennonites remained preoccupied with the specific fate of their fellow Mennonites there.

But even if German SDAs had focused their concern more narrowly on SDAs in the Soviet Union, their commentaries would still have been drastically different. German SDA periodicals were proud that the SDA population in the Soviet Union spanned *twenty-nine* different nationalities.[75] By contrast, German Mennonites identified Mennonites in the Soviet Union as members of precisely one nationality: their own.[76]

Thus the German Mennonite concern for the religious freedom of Soviet Mennonites was fully in alignment with the Nazi pursuit of German freedom. And this aim had assumed mythic proportions in the historic imagination of German nationalists. The basic outline of this millennia-long saga surfaced in an address delivered during the second year of the First World War by the Mennonite pastor of Danzig, Hermann G. Mannhardt. His overview of the "long road" of "our German *Volk* for its freedom" started with the Teutonic struggle against invading Romans and concluded with the Franco-Prussian War, leading "through ascent and decline, finally to the most magnificent of destinations."[77] The First World War did not lead to Mannhardt's happy ending. Still, the German nationalist imagination clung to this notion of a sacred quest for German freedom by casting the German signatories to the Treaty of Versailles and the leading parties of the Weimar Republic as traitors who had deprived Germany of this grail.

Nazi ideology took this narrative of German freedom one step further, encasing it in the ideological framework of a social Darwinist racial struggle. The seemingly innocuous habits of genealogy and "the Mennonite game"[78] dovetailed all too tidily with these racial notions: a susceptibility to Nazi racial ideology ran through German Mennonite congregations and surfaced even in periodical content.[79] Nazi propagandists used this racialized version of Mennonite history to their own ends, promoting the "racial purity" of Mennonite communities throughout the world in racial periodicals, popular novels, and a feature-length studio movie.[80]

This meant that German Mennonites were much more than a model free church: they were the model *German* free church. As evidence, their credentials were historic (with their Central European Anabaptist origins), cultural (with their diaspora committed to the preservation of German language), behavioural (with their reputation for integrity and hard work), and racial (as reflected in their preoccupation with genealogy). By contrast, most other German free churches were of Anglo-American origin, which made them increasingly suspect with the onset of the Second World War.

This contrast surfaced in the differing treatment of Mennonites and Baptists in the Warthegau, which Nazi Germany annexed after its invasion of Poland in September 1939. According to Reich Governor Arthur Greiser, the Warthegau was to be a "drill field for the National Socialist *Weltanschauung* [world view]"; it would circumvent established channels of church-state policy in Nazi Germany, operating under the direct authority of Hitler.[81] Greiser's stated vision could be read as seeking to undermine provincial churches while promoting free churches. Steigmann-Gall summarized Greiser's policy as "no longer" having "state churches, but voluntary, independent church societies." The specific details of Greiser's model church aligned so closely with Mennonite and Baptist congregational models that one might ask whether they *provided* the model.

But Andrea Strübind makes clear that the Nazi administration of the Warthegau severely undermined the basic operation of Baptist congregations there. True, some of Greiser's policies – such as his insistence that only adults could be members of congregations – aimed more squarely at the provincial churches. Even Greiser's insistence that "the National Socialist idea of separation of church and state" demanded that "the church take on the form of an association (federation)" would have been no hindrance.[82] But Warthegau's Baptists were never allowed the legal status of a public body. And the list of restrictions that targeted the provincial churches – such as severing contact with co-religionists in the rest of Germany and prohibiting collections – hit Warthegau's Baptists hard.[83]

By contrast, Benjamin Goossen's account of Mennonites in the Warthegau portrays a positive relationship with Greiser, who, for example, permitted active coordination between those Mennonites and the Alliance and other Mennonites in Germany. This was doubtless because these Mennonites served Greiser's most important goal: Germanizing his *Gau* (district). The region was overwhelmingly Polish, and the regime aimed to expel both Poles and Jews from the region and repopulate it with Germans. Here, Mennonites – first of all from portions of Poland initially conquered by the Soviet Union and later from portions of the Soviet Union conquered by the Nazi regime – played their part in this scheme of territorial, racial, and ultimately genocidal expansion.[84]

While the free church status of the Baptists proved meaningless in the Warthegau, this was not altogether true of Mennonites. True, the apparent favouritism enjoyed by Mennonites there had more to do with racial credentials than with free church credentials. But Greiser was intent on eliminating all vestiges of provincial church influence. Mennonites provided the model free church for his "model *Gau*."

Was Denominationalism an Asset or a Liability?

Key principles of denominationalism – freedom of conscience, pluralism, even separation of church and state – fell in line with the Nazi approach to German religious freedom. As a free church of Anabaptist origin, German Mennonites embraced those denominational principles and portrayed the Nazi state as a defender of those principles. But they were able to do this only because they themselves were racially qualified for the entitlements of German freedom. This is what enabled them to blindly defend a genocidal regime as "free."

Clearly, denominationalism as an approach to Christian community had serious vulnerabilities in Nazi Germany. To be sure, even in countries associated with denominationalism, the track record of "the denomination" has been far from even.[85] The weak points of denominationalism may, in part, explain the criticisms that surface regarding the German free church response to National Socialism. But the history of free churches in Germany differs substantially from, say, the history of denominations in the United States. Karl Heinz Voigt asks whether the sudden recognition that free churches enjoyed in Nazi Germany thrust a "new dignity" and a "craving for societal recognition" upon these politically inexperienced communities, which were burdened with the "collective memory" of centuries of past struggles.[86]

It is interesting, then, that it was a denomination that formed only in 1925 – one lacking in that history of repression – that maintained such a steady distance from Nazi ideology: the German Yearly Meeting. Especially certain aspects of the Quaker response – such as their outreach to Jews – were without parallel. And the denominational characteristics of the Yearly Meeting clearly played a role in its response to Nazism.[87]

But if boldness is to be the measure, nothing compares with the response of Jehovah's Witnesses to National Socialism. The scholarly assessment of this sect in Nazi Germany began with the branding of Jehovah's Witnesses as "totalitarian"; the point here was to draw an ironic parallel between the persecuted and the persecutors.[88] True, Jehovah's Witnesses did not profess democracy at that time, and they still do not today.

Still, labels such as totalitarian suggest a robotic-like subservience that does not do justice to the activities of Jehovah's Witnesses. They faced the Nazi state as a largely autonomous entity operating in isolated units; as a consequence, they responded on their own initiative. And the circumstances that confronted them demanded dynamic responses. In the camps, they held their own in arguments with Communist inmates, creatively circumvented regulations, and thoughtfully drew lines as to when to conform and when to defy.[89] The response by Jehovah's Witnesses to Nazi Germany demonstrated the power of sectarian faithfulness, reliant as it is on collective virtuosity as the basis for its charismatic authority.

By comparison, the Confessing Church – as the preserve of those Protestants within the provincial churches who clung more faithfully to their confessional origins – fell short. The Barmen Declaration was certainly a partial victory, but it remained subject to varied interpretations. And even among its bolder interpreters within the Confessing Church, "only a very few ... demonstrated resistance worthy of mention."[90] Yet there was still a sense of *churchly* authority in the critical voices there that one finds only rarely in free churches, such as in the published statements by Emil Fuchs. Perhaps the point here is that Fuchs presents a rare hybrid: he was a Lutheran pastor who also maintained membership in the German Yearly Meeting. As such, Fuchs synthesized clerical authority with denominational independence of thought.

These considerations show that some of the weaknesses of denominationalism – such as its decentralizing, relativizing, and atomizing potential – are not evident in either the state church or the sect to the same extent. Thus, instead of an answer to the question posed at the beginning of this chapter – whether the provincial church, the free church, or the sect remained truer to the heart of the Christian message – I can only add more questions. Does the truest and most faithful form of Christian community lie perhaps somewhere between these three ideal types? And does that "optimal spot" on Figure 1 also vary depending on historical context?

Nonetheless, I shall end with a quote from a confirmed denominationalist. Josef Gingerich – like Emil Fuchs – maintained membership in two "denominations": the German Mennonite congregation of Königsberg and the German Yearly Meeting. His commentary on the plight of German Mennonite congregations in 1934 demonstrates the endurance of a self-reflective and self-critical spirit in German Mennonite periodicals into the early years of Nazi rule, even if such commentaries were few and far between: "The danger is particularly great because we have become faint-hearted and unaccustomed to struggle after a long period of religious peace and freedom, and because we quite naturally bristle at recognizing a danger that will shoo us out of our compliant contentedness, since it may well shatter our religious as well as our economic well-being."[91] While Gingerich was addressing the situation of German Mennonites at the start of the Nazi regime, the resonance of his words echoes into the present day.

NOTES

1 On German Mennonites and the oath, see Heinold Fast, "Die Eidesverweigerung bei den Mennoniten," in *Eid – Gewissen – Treuepflicht*,

ed. Hildburg Bethke (Frankfurt: Stimme-Verlag, 1965). I will return to the question of the relationship between German Mennonites and nonresistance later in this chapter.
2 At the time, this question did not confront only Mennonites; Baptists in Germany faced it as well. Andrea Strübind, *Die unfreie Freikirche. Der Bund der Baptistengemeinden im "Dritten Reich"* (Neukirchen-Vluyn: Neukirchener, 1991), 52.
3 The degree to which surveillance of churches and religious communities was a priority of the Nazi Security Service (*Sicherheitsdienst*) during the 1930s is striking: Wolfgang Dieker, "'Niemals Jesuiten, niemals Sektierer'. Die Religionspolitik des SD gegenüber 'Sekten' und völkisch-religiösen Gruppen," in *Die völkisch-religiöse Bewegung im Nationalsozialismus. Eine Beziehungs- und Konfliktgeschichte*, ed. Uwe Puschner and Clemens Vollnhals (Göttingen: Vandenhoeck & Ruprecht, 2012), 356–63.
4 James Irvin Lichti, *Houses on the Sand? Pacifist Denominations in Nazi Germany* (New York: Peter Lang, 2008), 10–12; Erich Geldbach, *Freikirchen – Erbe, Gestalt, und Wirkung* (Göttingen: Vandenhoeck & Ruprecht, 1989), 29. In Germany, the provincial churches included the Lutheran, Reformed, and Union confessions.
5 Gustav Kraemer, "Wir und unsere Volksgemeinschaft 1938" (Krefeld: Krefeld Mennonite congregation, 1938), 20.
6 "It is part of the gist and essence of Anabaptism that it embraces the most diverse elements and currents within itself, not only tolerating them respectfully or skeptically, but welcoming them as the requisite range of manifestations of the one life of God that belong together by virtue of necessity and organically complement each other." Ethelbert Stauffer, "Das Testament unsre Väter," *Mennonitische Blätter*, September 1925, 34–40. Reprinted in August 1927. It is noteworthy that *Mennonitische Blätter*, the most widely read German Mennonite journal, chose to publish Stauffer's article promoting these assertions twice.
7 This process is boldly sketched out by Peter Fritzsche in works such as *Germans into Nazis* (Cambridge, MA: Harvard University Press, 1998) and *Life and Death in the Third Reich* (Cambridge, MA: Belknap Press of Harvard University Press, 2008).
8 The key insight of Weber that I rely on here his assertion of the role of the *location* of charisma ("access to saving grace"). Weber borrowed the term charisma from Rudolf Sohm; both Weber and Sohm looked to the term's New Testament meaning, which understood charisma as "gift of grace" in the epistles of Paul. While Weber also applied charisma to non-religious settings, his use of this concept always signifies *a power or quality that has its source beyond the normative order* that breaks into – and thereby interrupts – the normative order. In the religious context, this "seat of charisma" is the location of access to the sacred, to transcendence; it is the place where the

gift of grace may be received or is in some manner fundamentally present. H.H. Gerth and C. Wright Mills, *From Max Weber: Essays in Sociology* (New York: Oxford University Press, 1958), 52, 245ff; Hans Mol, *Identity and the Sacred: A Sketch for a New Social Scientific Theory of Religion* (Oxford: Basil Blackwell, 1976), 44; Talcott Parsons, "Introduction," in *Max Weber, The Sociology of Religion*, xxxiii.

9 For scholarly definitions of denominationalism, see Russell Richey, *Denominationalism* (Nashville: Abingdon, 1977); Russell Richey and Robert Bruce Millin, *Reimagining Denominationalism: Interpretive Essays* (New York and Oxford: Oxford University Press, 1994); D.A. Martin, "Denomination," *British Journal of Sociology* 13, no. 1 (March 1962); or Winthrop S. Hudson, "Denominationalism," in *The Encyclopedia of Religion*, ed. Mircea Eliade (New York: Macmillan, 1987).

10 To be sure, the denomination seeks to foster the relationship between the individual believer and God, but it rejects "the claims of any institution or creature to possess men in the name of God." H. Richard Niebuhr, *The Kingdom of God in America* (New York: Harper & Row, 1937), 25.

11 Quotes are from Independents such as John Cook, Joseph Burroughs, and Praise-god Barebones: Winthrop Hudson, "Denominationalism as a Basis for Ecumenicity," *Church History* 24, no. 1 (March 1955): 32–50.

12 Among the biblical passages referenced by these Independents was 1 Corinthians 13:9 – "For we know in part and we prophesy in part, but when completeness comes, what is in part disappears" (NIV). In heeding Paul, Independents insisted that "the church" must acknowledge the limitations imposed by the human condition.

13 Karl Koop, "Bekenntnisse," *Mennonitisches Lexikon*, vol. 5: *Revision und Ergänzung*, ed. Hans-Jürgen Goertz (Mennonitischer Geschichtsverein, 2010), http://mennonitisches-lexikon.de/doku.php?id=top:bekenntnisse. To be sure, there was an expectation in Germany that a societally acceptable ecclesiastical institution should have a confession. Benjamin Goossen notes this tension between urban German Mennonites desiring a more mainstream and unifying confession and more conservative rural German Mennonites resisting it during the late nineteenth century: *Chosen Nation: Mennonites and Germany in a Global Era* (Princeton: Princeton University Press, 2017), 73–4.

14 The Weimar Constitution had formally declared "separation of church and state," which facilitated the greater autonomy mentioned above. At the same time, provincial churches continued to enjoy significant forms of state support not extended to free churches. Martin H. Jung, *Der Protestantismus in Deutschland von 1870 bis 1945* (Leipzig: Evangelische Verlagsanstalt, 2002), 113–47. Furthermore, the term "provincial churches" indicates a multiplicity of provincial churches in Germany, which raises the question of how authoritative the "monopolistic claim to charismatic

authority" of each was. As a rule, each province had no more than two provincial churches: a Catholic one and a Protestant one (either Lutheran, Reform, or Union). Nonetheless, each provincial church – regardless of whether it was Catholic or Protestant – proceeded from the basis of a *territorial* claim to "charismatic authority."

15 Karl Heinz Voigt, "Freikirchen im Nationalsozialismus – Anmerkungen zur Freikichenforschung," in *Christen im Dritten Reich*, ed. Philipp Thul (Darmstadt: WBG, 2014), 96.

16 This response by Krefeld Mennonites paralleled a self-questioning process already taking place in Dutch Mennonite congregations. One issue for Krefeld Mennonites was that the exemption did not distinguish them from the remainder of the Krefeld bourgeoisie: this social class enjoyed this exemption as a whole. Christoph Wiebe, "Die Krefelder Mennoniten und die Wehrlosigkeit. Eine symbolische Abgrenzung im Wandel der Zeit," *Mennonitische Geschichtsblätter* 65 (2008): 114–46.

17 During my adolescence, it was Rudy Wiebe's *Peace Shall Destroy Many* – published in 1962 – that asked these difficult questions. Wiebe's novel developed this problematic from the perspective of a young Canadian Mennonite man during the Second World War. The novel was discussed openly within my home congregation, which was emblematic of that congregation's liberal character. But Wiebe did lose his position as founding editor of the *Mennonite Brethren Herald* over the response to the novel. For a complex and recent assessment of the novel's reception, see Paul Tiessen, "Re-framing the Reaction to *Peace Shall Destroy Many*: Rudy Wiebe, Delbert Wiens, and the Mennonite Brethren," *Mennonite Quarterly Review* 90, no. 1 (January 2016): 73–102.

18 The many dimensions of that process – such as, for example, the conflicting roles played by nineteenth-century German liberalism in that process – are presented by Mark Jantzen, *Mennonite German Soldiers: Nation, Religion, and Family in the Prussian East, 1772–1880* (Notre Dame: University of Notre Dame Press, 2010).

19 That particular phrase is from a 1937 statement: Diether Götz Lichdi, *Mennoniten im Dritten Reich: Dokumentation und Deutung* (Weierhof/ Palatinate: Mennonitischer Geschichtsverein, 1977): 134.

20 One phrase used by Lichdi is that the principle was discussed "behind closed doors." Lichdi was characterizing how some German Mennonites "privately" responded to public statements from sources such as the *Vereinigung*'s declarations that non-resistance had become a principle of the past. Ibid., 123.

21 Ibid., 124–6.

22 His name was Richard Nickel. Lichti, *Houses on the Sand*, 18.

Enjoying the Entitlements of German Freedom   95

23 From his interviews, Lichdi offers a number of strategies for this, such as purposefully missing targets when firing weapons. *Mennoniten im Dritten Reich*, 135–8.
24 For example, the Nazi regime appears to have tolerated qualms about bearing arms for certain small but "racially" German Protestant communities. While I was welcomed by German Evangelical Baptists in Baden during a visit in 1992, they were not comfortable with formal interviews. However, they assured me repeatedly during informal conversations that during the Nazi years, Evangelical Baptists served only in non-combatant military positions. In the state files of Baden at the Karlsruhe General State Archives, government authorities consistently referred to Evangelical Baptists as *Altmennoniten*, which permitted their inclusion in the 1868 cabinet order permitting German Mennonites to serve in non-combatant positions. Lichti, *Houses on the Sand*, 13, 36–7. Also see Hermann Rüegger, *Aufzeichnungen über Entstehung und Bekenntnis der Gemeinschaft evangelisch Taufgesinnter (Nazaraner)* (Zürich: Bücherverlag der Gemeinschaft Evangelisch Taufgesinnter, 1961).
25 In 1942, Alfred Rosenberg fought to preserve religious freedom for Christians in the newly annexed Wartheland. Martin Bormann's positive reference to religious freedom was his defence of paganists who did not believe in a hereafter. However, his specific point was the reminder that Germany was "a land of 'religious freedom.'" Richard Steigmann-Gall, *Holy Reich: Nazi Conceptions of Christianity, 1919–1945* (Cambridge: Cambridge University Press, 2003): 132, 229, 250. A personal concern expressed by Heinrich Himmler was that the racially untainted members of his SS must enjoy a "National Socialist version of the age-old German right of freedom of conscience." Also interesting is that both Himmler and the head of the Reich Security Service Reinhard Heydrich took a more "liberal" – that is, less suspicious – approach to leaders of the Confessing Church. Ibid., 176, 183. In addition, Himmler and Bormann were both involved in the release of Bishop Berggrav of Norway from prison, here acting in defence of a "Germanic" Norwegian Lutheran who had objected to excessive intervention in Norwegian church affairs by the Nazi occupying forces: Sabine Dramm, *Dietrich Bonhoeffer and the Resistance* (Minneapolis: Fortress Press, 2009), 147–9.
26 The defence of freedom of conscience was voiced particularly by Germanic pagan movements and by defenders of those movements. Uwe Puschner and Clemens Vollnhals, "Forschungs- und problemgeschichtliche Perspektiven," in *Die völkisch-religiöse Bewegung im Nationalsozialismus. Eine Beziehungs- und Konfliktgeschichte*, ed. Puschner and Vollnhals (Göttingen: Vandenhoeck & Ruprecht, 2012), 20.

27 Martin Bormann, for one, argued for limiting the religious authority of the clergy because they "could not possibly know more about the hereafter than anyone else." And Joseph Goebbels "argued that an *Überkonfessionalismus* is innate to the character of German greatness." Steigmann-Gall, *Holy Reich*, 54, 220.

28 Bonhoeffer's earlier works expressed his belief that an individual's ego drove the dictates of the conscience at least in part. His final works concluded that the conscience stood among humanity's noble weapons but had failed to prove sufficient "in the present struggle." Clifford J. Green, *Bonhoeffer: A Theology of Sociality*, rev. ed. (Grand Rapids: W.B. Eerdmans, 1999), 202, 305–6. Similarly, Erich Geldbach, a key German scholar of German free churches, commented on the danger of free-church subjectivity "because of course feelings shift with mood": "Religiöse Polemiken gegen 'neue Religionen in Deutschland des 19. Jahrhunderts," in *Toleranz und Repression. Zur Lage religiöser Minderheiten in modernen Gesellschaften*, ed. Johannes Neumann and Michael W. Fischer (Frankfurt am Main: Campus Verlag, 1987), 181.

29 One example of nationalist shaming would be when German Mennonites distanced themselves from non-resistance through public portrayals of the principle, such as when a popular play mocked Mennonites about this principle (Ernst von Wildenbruch's *Der Menonit*). See Jantzen, *Mennonite German Soldiers*, 228–34. More broadly, the 1871 founding of the German empire was based on a striking string of military victories that linked German national identity to a victor mentality. When the First World War and the ensuing Treaty of Versailles challenged that mentality, some Germans responded with acceptance, but others felt betrayed. During the Weimar Republic, the German right – Nazis included – fed off that sense of betrayal. And as members of the German right, Nazi ideologues transformed that German nationalist egoism into a sense of German racial superiority. Benjamin Goossen charts this course in detail in *Chosen Nation*.

30 Jung, *Protestantismus in Deutschland*, 159–161; Karl Heinz Voigt, *Kirchliche Minderheiten im Schatten der lutherischen Reformation vor 1517 bis nach 2017* (Göttingen: V&R unipress, 2018), 278–80.

31 The German Methodist Bishop Friedrich Heinrich Otto Melle and the German Baptist leader Paul Schmidt were both permitted to attend on behalf of the Union of German Free Churches. See Strübind, *Die unfreie Freikirche*, 231–44.

32 Erich Göttner, "Ein Wort zum Ausgang des Menno-Jahres," *Mennonitische Blätter*, December 1936, 87; and *Gemeinde-Blatt*, 1 December 1936, 112.

33 Horst Quiring, "Kirche, Volk und Staat in mennonitischer Sicht," *Mennonitische Jugendwarte*, 5 October 1937, 106–7.

34 Kraemer, "Wir und unsere Volksgemeinschaft 1938," 15.
35 *Kirchenkampf* (church struggle) was the expression used for the early conflict arising from the Nazi regime's attempts to exert control over German churches and efforts within certain sectors of those churches to maintain autonomy. Those sectors asserted the authority of their respective confessions and came to be known as the Confessing Church.
36 On relations between German Mennonite leaders and the Confessing Church, see Lichdi, *Mennoniten im Dritten Reich*, 84–7.
37 Ernst Fellmann, "Warum und wozu Jugendarbeit?" *Mennonitische Jugendwarte* 3 (1936): 72.
38 "The way Anabaptists separated political and religious questions has proven to be the right course; the Lutheran state church and the Reformed theocracy have been judged by history." Quiring, "Kirche, Volk und Staat." "Our forefathers fought for this clear separation of state and religious community with tremendous sacrifice of property and person [*Gut und Blut*]. In principle, we owe to their struggle the fact that our Mennonite congregations have been spared the church struggles of our day." Göttner, "Ein Wort zum Ausgang des Menno-Jahres," 87; and *Gemeinde-Blatt*, 1 December 1936, 112. "If our congregations have up until now remained spared the direct intervention of the church struggles of today, we have the sacrifices of our forefathers in their plentiful struggles for a clear separation of church and state. ... We wish to render state and nation – as orders put in place by God – our due service as citizens and as members of the Volk, and deploy our strength for them as German Mennonites." Göttner, "50 Jahre 'Vereingung der Deutschen Mennonitengemeinden," *Mennonitische Blätter*, January 1938, 2. As Christian Neff put it, "Protestant pastors trespass beyond their competence when they make themselves accountable for political assaults." "Wir Mennoniten und die heutige Zeit," *Mennonitische Jugendwarte*, October 1935, 114.
39 Stadtpfarrer Weismann, Stuttgart, "Was soll ich denn machen mit Jesus, von dem gesagt wird, er sei Christus?." *Gemeinde-Blatt*, 15 April 1939, 30; J. Dohmann, "Geschichte und Gegenwart," *Gemeinde-Blatt*, 1 January 1940, 23. Any Mennonite reader will note that these authors were not Mennonites; the decision to include them in a Mennonite periodical was presumably made by *Gemeinde-Blatt*'s editor, Christian Schnebele.
40 Pastor Walter Fellmann, "Warum sind wir Mennoniten noch Mennoniten?" *Mennonitische Blätter*, May 1935, 44. Interestingly, Fellmann also expressed sympathy with the trials of the Confessing Church in Hesse. And Christian Neff, often a more astute commentator, voiced a parallel sentiment that cast contemporary conflicts between church and state as a function of a failure of separation of church and

state: "Menno Simons in seiner Bedeutung für die Gegenwart," ibid., September 1935, 68.
41 "Andere religiöse Vereinigungen," *Gemeinde-Blatt*, 15 December 1935, 119.
42 "Bund freikirchlicher Christen," *Gemeinde-Blatt*, 1 October 1937, 91–2. Schnebele appears to have been unaware that a small, covert remnant of *Christliche Versammlung* endured and persisted in its sectarian refusal to swear oaths and perform military service. File 58:7651, Central State Archive of Rhineland/Westfalen. For some basic details, see also Lichti, *Houses on the Sand*, 63–4n72.
43 The representatives at Barmen came from Union, Reformed, and Lutheran confessions. Their point of view was largely conservative. The contingencies of totalitarian rule led them to cooperate in a manner they would not otherwise have done. Admittedly, they did not consider the Barmen Declaration a confession, but it has acquired something like that status over time. Thomas Martin Schneider, *Wem gehört Barmen? Das Gründungsdokument der Bekennenden Kirche und seine Wirkungen* (Leipzig: Evangelische Verlagsanstalt, 2017), 40–5.
44 Klaus Scholder, *Die Kirchen und das Dritte Reich*, vol. 2: *Das Jahr der Ernüchterung 1934: Barmen und Rom* (Berlin: Ullstein, 1988), 196, 197, 406. This is the twentieth-century version of the two-kingdom teaching (*Zweireichelehre*): God had vested the state with authority over the "kingdom of the world" and the church with authority over the "kingdom of God." While ascribed to Luther, the two-kingdom teaching did not become part of the established discourse of German Protestantism until the Confessing Church sought to delineate its sphere of influence from that of the Nazi state. References to a two-kingdom teaching appeared as early as 1922, but Harald Diem provided its first coherent formulation in 1938, inspired by Karl Barth. Kurt Nowak, "Zweireichelehre: Anmerkungen zum Entstehungsprozeß einer umstrittenen Begriffsprägung und kontroversen Lehre," *Zeitschrift für Theologie und Kirche* 78, no. 1 (February 1981), 105–27. Were the state to invade the sphere of conscience, Luther called for passive resistance and a preparedness to die for one's convictions. At the same time, Luther's writings evidence a preoccupation with defending and securing the power of the state. His twentieth-century interpreters picked up on the latter trend; thus, the resulting Lutheran two-kingdom teaching one-sidedly emphasized Luther's respect for the divinely instituted authority of the state. See Erich W. Gritsch, "Luther and the State: Post-Reformation Ramifications"; and Thomas A. Brady, Jr, "Luther and the State: The Reformer's Teaching in its Social Setting," in *Luther and the Modern State in Germany*, ed. James D. Tracy (Kirksville: Sixteenth Century Journal Publishers, 1986), 40, 49–52.

45 "[Believers] must be subject to worldly authorities as citizens of the state on earth and pray for the rulers of their country. But as children of God they must also continually keep in mind that spiritually they are citizens of a heavenly country and members of the family of God." "Botenmeldungen von nah und fern," *Adventbote*, 15 August 1936, 256.
46 Kurt Sinz, "Zions Wächter," *Adventbote*, 1 March 1935, 80; and "Christliche Dienstpflicht," ibid., 15 May 1935, 145.
47 "Botenmeldungen von nah und fern," *Adventbote*, 15 January 1936, 32; 1 April 1936, 112; 1 September 1938, 272.
48 In the summer of 1933, Pastor Walter Fellmann expressed concern regarding the "requisitioning of the entire human being and the relegation of all of life to the goals of the state. Won't our youth become totally absorbed by the concept of the nation?" "Staat und Evanglium," *Mennonitische Blätter*, July–August 1933, 72. Otto Lichti of Branchweilerhof asked the same question a few months later, insisting that the lines delineating separation of church and state were not as neat and tidy as those drawn by the state: "Friedensgesinnung und Wehrhaftigkeit. Antwort und Gegenwort auf den gleichnamigen Vortrag von Gerhard Hein, erschienen in der Oktobernummer 1933 auf Jugendwarte," *Mennonitische Jugendwarte* 1 (1934), 9. Finally, a Mennonite youth gathering during Easter 1934 voiced the fear that the *Führerprinzip* would "absolutize" the state: "No Weltanschauung but National Socialism is to possess validity. It is in this sense that youth are to be educated. This trespasses on God's terrain. ... The church has become guilty of handing God's law over to the state." "Bericht über das Rundbrieflertreffen Ostern 1934 auf dem Weierhof in der Pfalz," *Mennonitische Jugendwarte* 3 (1934), 68.
49 Christian Neff, "Der erste Petrusbrief. 1. Petri 2, 13–17. Untertan aller menschlichen Ordnung!," *Gemeinde-Blatt*, 1 February 1939, 11. Neff's views on the relationship between Christianity and the state surface in "Wir Mennoniten und die heutige Zeit," *Mennonitische Jugendwarte*, October 1935, 111–15.
50 Hulda Jost, "Gemeinde Gott und Obrigkeit," *Adventbote*, 15 January 1935, 22.
51 Kurt Sinz, "Seid untertan aller menschlichen Ordnung," *Adventbote*, 15 February 1934, 49.
52 And each free church often had additional burdens to bear in supplying this proof. In the case of SDAs, their distinctive teachings left them susceptible to association with both pacifists and Jews. German Seventh-day Adventism maintained a low profile on the denomination's affirmation of non-combatancy; this had for a long time been a matter of "individual conscience," but the denomination was committed to supporting those

members who chose non-combatant military service over bearing arms. German SDA scholars estimate that one third of German SDAs served as non-combatants in Nazi Germany. SDA Sabbath observance left the denomination open to accusations of being "judaized."
53 One exception to this was a letter addressed to all German SDA congregations in the fall of 1933. In that letter, Wilhelm Mueller, chair of the East German Association of SDA Congregations, expressed regret regarding "what was going on in the Protestant Church," but asserted: "Some representatives of religious communities do not always show the necessary reserve in political questions, whereby extraordinary measures are incurred. This is different with us." Copy of letter in Johannes Hartlapp, "Die Lage der Gemeinschaft der Siebenten-Tags-Adventisten in der Zeit des Nationalsozialismus" (Friedensau, 1979), 100.
54 "Von nah und fern," *Adventbote*, 15 January 1938, 32.
55 Lichti, *Houses on the Sand*, 51.
56 For example, Hans Albrecht, the clerk of the German Yearly Meeting, approached the desire for such delineation as a temptation; while acknowledging that Quakers were "citizens of two worlds, the divine and the worldly," he observed that we are "too readily inclined to separate these two worlds." "Die Grundlagen der Gemeinschaft," *Der Quäker*, February 1939, 39.
57 When the Gestapo initially dissolved the *Rhönbruderhof* on the basis of its "sectarian" beliefs, not all German Mennonite leaders – especially Emil Händiges – were comfortable with distancing themselves. When the regime then shifted its justification for dissolving the *Rhönbruderhof* to economic dysfunction, this better accommodated German Mennonite sensibilities, and German Mennonites switched to this justification. For a detailed overview, see James Irvin Lichti, "Rhönbruderhof," *Mennonitisches Lexikon*, vol. 5: *Revision und Ergänzung*, ed. Goertz, http://www.mennlex.de/doku.php?id=top:rhoenbruderhof.
58 Lura van Honk, Haarlam, "Die Niederländische Jahresversammlung," *Der Quäker*, July 1937, 171. For a full overview of *Der Quäker*'s coverage of the *Rhönbruderhof* from 1927 to 1937, see Lichti, *Houses on the Sand*, 150n146.
59 Fuchs – a Quaker, a Lutheran pastor, and a religious socialist – was one of the better-known members of the German Yearly Meeting. After the Second World War, he went on to have an influential and moderating impact on church-state relations in the German Democratic Republic. His even better-known son, the theoretical physicist Klaus Fuchs, was convicted for supplying information from the Manhattan Project to the Soviet Union in 1950.

60 Fuchs blasted Martin Niemöller's *Das Bekenntnis der Väter und die bekennende Gemeinde* as a "shocking limitation of the teaching on justification in which faith becomes a passive, innerchurchly, individual matter." This was in the context of Fuchs's critique of a series published by the Confessing Church and edited by Th. Ellwein and Chr. Stoll. *Der Quäker*, January 1935, 27–8. See also Emil Fuchs, "Karl Barth," *Der Quäker*, August 1934, 199–201.
61 Martin Buber was still in Germany at this point. He immigrated to the British Mandate of Palestine in the following year. Emil Fuchs, "Die Frage an die Zeit – an die Frommen und die andern – !" *Der Quäker*, January 1937, 9.
62 Specifically, he asserted that that racial theory may *not* serve as the framework for the "choice of a life companion, the elevating experience of love." Emil Fuchs, "Geist und Körper im Erleben der Liebe," *Der Quäker*, April–May 1937, 122.
63 This selective pluralism was expressed in Point 24 of the 1920 NSDAP Platform: "We demand liberty for all religious confessions in the State, so far as they are not a danger to it and do not militate against the moral feelings of the German race."
64 Peter Fritzsche charted the course that led both to a national identity that spanned these boundaries and to the means by which the Nazi Party successfully portrayed itself as the party that truly embodied that national spirit, *Germans Into Nazis*.
65 On Nazism's confessional pluralism, see also Steigmann-Gall, *Holy Reich*, 51–85; and Manfred Gailus, " 'Ein Volk – ein Reich – ein Glaube'? Religiöse Pluralisierung in der NS-Weltanschauungsdiktatur," in *Religion und Gesellschaft. Europa im 20. Jahrhundert*, ed. Friedrich Wilhelm Graf and Klaus Große Kracht (Köln, 2007), 247–68. On Hitler's speeches, see Thomas Schirrmacher, "Hitlers religiöse Sprache – Propaganda oder Glaube?" in *Christen im Dritten Reich*, ed. Philipp Thull (Darmstadt: wbg Academic, 2014): 11–20.
66 Alfred Fast, "Die Stellung der Taufgesinnten oder Mennoniten zu den Fragen der Kultur," *Mennonitische Blätter*, July–August 1930, 70–2, 82–5. Walter Fellmann reaffirmed this distrust of a secular state in "Staat und Evangelium," *Mennonitische Blätter*, July–August 1933, 73.
67 The secular Weimar Republic had granted German Mennonites an unprecedented level of parity with provincial churches. The Weimar Constitution (1919) provided a strong legal basis for eliminating any remaining fees and taxes still levied by the provincial churches on members of Mennonite congregations. By the 1930s, German Mennonites faced such fees only outside of Germany proper, such as in the Free State of Danzig. "Eingabe des Ausschusses der Westpr. Mennonitengemeinden

für kirchenrechtliche Fragen an den Senat der Freien Stadt Danzig," *Mennonitische Blätter*, May 1935, 43–4.
68 This is one of Fritzsche's key arguments regarding the role of the Great Depression in increasing the vote for the Nazi Party between 1929 and 1932 so dramatically. *Germans into Nazis*.
69 Jonas J. Driedger, "'Wohin wir blicken, sehen wir Feinde.' Wie sich preußische Mennoniten von 1913 bis 1933 als Teil einer christlich-antibolschewistischen Volksgemeinschaft neu erfanden," *Mennonitische Geschichtsblätter* 71 (2014), 71–102.
70 Phylax, "Ein Wendepunkt," *Kirche und Staat* 1925, 41. Obviously, this indicates that czarist Russia treated Mennonites and Seventh-day Adventists differently.
71 "Die Lösung des Weltstaatproblems," *Kirche und Staat* 1 (1932): 6–7.
72 F. Albert, "Zehn Jahre deutsche Republik," *Kirche und Staat* 1 (1929): 26. See also Phylax, "Ein Wendepunkt," 41. The SDA attitude toward Roman Catholicism was shaped by SDA eschatology.
73 For examples of Mennonite references to this effect, see Hermann Funck, "Was der Verstand des Verständigen nicht sieht," *Mennonitische Jugendwarte* 4 (1931), 78; Bernhard Peters, "Die Kirche Christi in der Völkerwelt," *Gemeinde-Blatt*, 15 March 1936, 25–6. For parallel SDA references, see Gauger, "Ein Schauspiel der Welt," *Adventbote*, 15 July 1937, or Hulda Jost, "Wohlfahrtspflege," *Adventbote*, 1 April 1937, 104. For further examples, see Lichti, *Houses on the Sand*, 129.
74 See Lichti, *Houses on the Sand*, 146n105.
75 "Vom nahen und fernen Erntefeld," *Adventbote*, 1 November 1929, 329–30.
76 Ethnic identification is a mutable affair; the Mennonite colonies of tsarist Russia had been settled largely by Mennonites of Frisian and Flemish origin, although there was likely some intermarriage during the sojourn in West Prussia, and some Swiss Mennonites made their way to the colonies as well.
77 Helmut Foth, "Mennonitischer Patriotismus im Ersten Weltkrieg und die Kriegsrede des Danziger Predigers Hermann G. Mannhardt," *Mennonitische Geschichtsblätter* 72 (2015): 62–63.
78 One scholarly definition of "the Mennonite game" runs as follows: "The goal of this game is to see how quickly two Mennonites, often meeting for the first time, can get to know each other's familial ancestry and establish how many of each other's relatives they know." Bruno Dyck, "Exploring Congregational Clans: Playing the 'Mennonite Game' in Winnipeg," *Journal of Mennonite Studies* 21 (2003): 137. The Mennonite game is largely limited to Mennonites who trace their ancestry to Late Modern European Mennonite communities. Privileges granted by the isolated principalities that tolerated Mennonites did not permit intermarriage or proselytizing.

Even after Mennonites migrated away from those communities or were released from those privileges, endogamy tended to persist. While in itself innocuous, the Mennonite game inevitably acquired a sinister character in the Nazi context.

79 See Lichti, *Houses on the Sand*, 120–7. This topic was developed considerably further by Helmut Foth in "Wie die Mennoniten in die deutsche Volksgemeinschaft hineinwuchsen," *Mennonitische Gechichtsblätter* (2011). It is addressed comprehensively in terms of the current historical literature in Goossen's chapter "The Racial Church" in *Chosen Nation*.

80 Benjamin W. Goossen, "Mennoniten als Volksdeutsche: Die Rolle des Mennonitentums in der nationalsozialistischen Propaganda," *Mennonitische Geschichtsblätter* 71 (2014): 55–70.

81 Kurt Meier, *Der Evangelische Kirchenkampf*, vol. 3: *Im Zeichen des zweiten Weltkrieges* (Göttingen: Vandenhoeck & Ruprecht, 1986), 116. Strübind drew my attention to Meier's characterization of Greiser's policy: *Die unfreie Freikirche*, 299.

82 Meier, *Der Evangelische Kirchenkampf*, 124.

83 Strübind, *Die unfreie Freikirche*, 299–300.

84 Goossen, *Chosen Nation*, 165–72.

85 For an overview, see James Irvin Lichti, "Denomination," *Mennonitisches Lexikon*, vol. 5, ed. Goertz, http://www.mennlex.de/doku.php?id=top:denomination.

86 Voigt, *Kirchliche Minderheiten*, 291.

87 There was a Quaker presence in Germany by the seventeenth century, but all organized forms of that presence had disappeared by the end of the nineteenth century. Also, the German Yearly Meeting was very young and followed the lead of British Quakers closely. For a thorough account, see Hans A. Schmitt, *Quakers and Nazis: Inner Light in Outer Darkness* (Columbia: University of Missouri Press, 1997). Michael Seadle arrived at a more nuanced assessment, isolating "quietist" and "activist" sectors: "Quakerism in Germany: The Pacifist Response to Hitler," PhD diss., University of Chicago, June 1977. For an analysis of periodical content in *Der Quäker* and a tight summation of German Quaker activity on behalf of Jews, see Lichti, *Houses on the Sand*, 185–96.

88 Michael H. Kater, "Die Ernsten Bibelforscher im Dritten Reich," *Vierteljahrshefte für Geschichte* 17, no. 2 (April 1969): 181–218.

89 See Lichti, "Model Denomination or Totalitarian Sect?" in *The Routledge History of the Holocaust*, ed. Jonathan C. Friedman (New York and London: Routledge, 2011): 358–74.

90 Schneider, *Wem gehört Barmen?* 150.

91 Josef Gingerich, "Wachet!" *Mennonitische Jugendwarte* 2 (1934), 30.

Chapter Three

Antisemitism and the Concept of *Volk*: The Mennonite Youth Circular Community at the Beginning of the Nazi Dictatorship

IMANUEL BAUMANN

In 1928, four young Mennonite men and one young Mennonite woman decided to exchange views on the matters that interested them by way of circular letters.[1] The group grew from one year to the next until by around 1940 it comprised more than 250 young men and women from all over the German Reich.[2] Subgroups or "circles" of about ten young men and women each communicated on various topics by entering a paragraph in a notebook and then sending the notebook on to the next person in round-robin style. One member of the circle then summed up the discussion for all the others in a booklet that was then reproduced. Unique testimonies to the times were thus created, and have survived – at least in part – to the present. The circular community was special in that, for one thing, it was not a structural subdivision of a larger organization, but succeeded in bringing together young members from various German Mennonite associations – as much from Baden, Bavaria, and the Palatinate as from northern Germany, eastern and western Prussia, and even abroad, for example from as far away as South America. What is more, these young adults followed widely different professional paths. They included theology students as well as farmers and metal workers. Young women played an active role.

The Mennonite Youth Circular Community brought people together in a specific way, through regular exchanges and group meetings. Phenomenologically, with Max Weber we can see this as the creation of a community (*Vergemeinschaftung*), which he defines as "a social relationship" in which "the initiation of social interaction ... depends on the subjectively felt (affective or traditional) cohesion of the participants."[3] In observing the social interactions within the Circular Community, we can see these group identity creation processes at work. The members experienced community as they sent on notebooks in which they had written their contributions, when they sent occasional private letters to others in their "circle," prayed for one another, and met once a year at Circular Community meetings, which included additional elements designed to foster community.

In asking here what these participants thought about the term *Volk* (people or nation) and what their attitudes were toward Jews, we are joining a long tradition of confronting the Nazi past. For German Mennonites this process began in the 1970s with two texts from Hans-Jürgen Goertz and Diether Götz Lichdi. Goertz examined the actions of official Mennonite representatives and institutions, which saw themselves as the direct descendants of the Reformation Anabaptists, especially Menno Simons. He wrote about a "religious downfall" in the form of a "decline in understanding freedom," which he saw "as the result of a centuries-long process of acculturation and self-preservation."[4] This is not the place to unpack the subsequent debate over the history of Mennonites under the Nazis, which has been renewed recently with important additional contributions.[5] Nor can we pause to consider the literature about the non-state churches in the Third Reich. Today we have good information about the Methodists,[6] Baptists,[7] the Brethren,[8] and the Seventh-day Adventists.[9] Additional research – for example, on Pentecostals – is under way.[10]

The literature on the subject already paints a clear picture of the free churches' loyalty to the Nazi regime. In this regard, the circular notebooks are an excellent source for advancing our efforts to determine the *reasons and motives* for a positive attitude toward, or involvement in, the Nazi state. The voices of individuals can be found in the sources of the Circular Community, which has yet to be adequately researched.[11]

In recent years the Mennonite community's views on *Volk*,[12] antisemitism,[13] and "race"[14] have been closely examined. This chapter follows up on the excellent work done by James Irvin Lichti, an American historian who argued that Mennonites, in contrast to other non-state churches, were seen as being prototypically German and that they themselves embraced this view: "German Mennonites not only basked in this praise: they also embraced a sense of *völkisch* [racial nationalistic] duty."[15] *Volk* was thus expanded to encompass not just people or nation but also "race," and this was justified with the theological doctrine of "orders of creation."[16]

This doctrine was not of Mennonite origin, but rather came from creation ethics, most notably as expounded by the Erlangen theology professor Paul Althaus. Martin Honecker describes this paradigm as a typical conceptual construct of national Protestantism as it reconstituted itself after the First World War. "The context and cause of the fervid discovery of peoplehood or nation [*Volkstum*] as a direct creation of God can only be explained by seeing it as a reaction to the Treaty of Versailles which was seen as a great humiliation."[17] This understanding of nation as an order established by God was conveyed by applying "the institutional and historical philosophical metaphors of the state as developed by German idealism and romanticism."[18]

Lichti has shown how this conception was processed by Mennonite theology, especially in the work of the Danzig pastor Erich Göttner. Lichti has posited that the "racial" understanding of peoplehood in Mennonite thinking was relativized by the Kingdom of God, where all "racial" boundaries would be removed. This, however, only related to the church. The state was an "order of creation" that was to be organized "racially." This move served to legitimize the racist outlook of the National Socialists. "The church may possess a transnational and transracial character, but nation and race remained components of a divine 'order of creation.'" Mennonites "provided a churchly discourse that legitimated racial policy without interfering with that policy."[19] It is at this point that my analysis begins. This "racial" understanding dominated the thinking of younger Mennonites and was virulent even among those who were at first somewhat critical of National Socialism. Such thinking legitimized individual participation in the Nazi state; it also created a blind spot for Nazi crimes. This process is illustrated by the attitude of the community members toward the anti-Jewish politics of the first half of the 1930s. Contributors to the Circular Community not only used the older anti-Jewish stereotypes but also viewed events through the lens of "racial" thinking.

My analysis will focus on the concepts of *Volk* and antisemitism as they stood at the time the National Socialists assumed power. This will help us better understand why members of the Circular Community upheld the Nazi brand of racism, and how they did so. But I will also take into account other issues – for example, the Mennonites' stance on the new church order and the topics of military conscription and violence. I will begin with these last-mentioned points.

I will take a targeted look at written testimonies by those Mennonites who, in the early 1930s, claimed to be the *voice of youth*.[20] This claim reflected their self-perception, given that they had been born during the first decade of the twentieth century and thus were between twenty and thirty-five years of age at the beginning of Nazi rule. They were firmly anchored in congregational life, and some already had or soon would have official roles in that life. Their influence on Mennonite institutions must, however, be seen as indirect, for they had no formal mandate to speak for the youth or the congregations. Temporally, I will focus on the phase marked by the Nazi "seizure of power," during which, on a fundamental level, the course was set in the sphere of the free churches as in German society as a whole. I will, however, explicitly *not* be arguing that the patterns formed regarding perceptions and interpretations of *Volk* and "race" remained in place or that the protagonists' Nazi world views were in any way automatically upheld until the end of the regime.

The Conception of the Church

At the start of the Nazi dictatorship, there was basic agreement within the Mennonite community in Germany that their various organizations should join forces so as to be able to speak and act in concert vis-à-vis the state. During this phase, many Mennonite leaders could even imagine entering into an alliance, if only a loose one, with the Protestant Reich church. Many considered this option preferable to becoming part of a "third pillar" in Germany (i.e., a free church pillar, the other two being the Protestant Reich churches and Catholicism), because the Mennonites conceived of themselves as a reform church and had issues with the evangelical missionary approach of the classical free churches such as the Baptists. In 1933–34, however, the Mennonite unification process made only very slow progress; ultimately it would fail altogether. One reason for this was that questions pertaining to the theological profession of faith were bound up with the regulation of organizational matters. The young generation of Mennonites were dissatisfied that their seniors could not agree. What is more, young Mennonites – more precisely, the leading figures in the Circular Community around Theo Glück – made a specific contribution to the debate over Mennonite unity.

Within the Mennonite community, the group around Glück promoted a conception of church and community linked with the idea of the "congregational church." They contended that the term "church" could be used to designate the community of believers who, at least outwardly, confessed to the lordship of Christ. The congregation, then, was the part of the church that dedicated itself entirely to following Christ. Moreover, they considered this distinction between church and congregation characteristic of Mennonitism, and they viewed the concept of the "Mennonite congregational church" as a way of strengthening the flock of *ecclesia* (literally, "those summoned forth"). Glück and his circle believed that Mennonites had been called upon by God to make a specific testimonial, but at the same time they saw justification in the existence of the other churches in Germany.

This point of view concurred with another key concept held by the young circular generation: that of community. This grew out of the Circular Community's generational circumstances. Here two generations were especially important: those born around 1900, who were already working in their professions in the early 1930s; and those born around 1910, many of whom were still taking vocational training. The latter were part of the war youth generation who had been teenagers in the postwar years and had been strongly influenced by that war without themselves having participated in it. Particularly among this group, born around 1910, the idea of being part of a specific community was highly developed. Many of them, including Theo Glück, had their roots in the sector of the German youth movement known as the *Bündische Jugend* and brought this influence with them to the Circular Community. Their concept of community found expression when, for example, the members of this generation referred to the term "people's community" (*Volksgemeinschaft*). At the time, I should add, this term was not yet being used exclusively in the National Socialist sense. Another manifestation was the particular importance they attached to the category *Volk*, which, in keeping with nationalist-racialist-tinged Protestant ethics, they conceived of as a divine "order of creation." This important connection will be examined again later. Even this rough outline gives a sense of how deeply the Mennonite religious community was embedded in the contemporary context and influenced by its culture.

The Stance on Military Conscription and Violence

As is well known, in 1933 the largest Mennonite conference (*Vereinigung*) came out in favour of military service. There would be no claiming of special privileges when the draft was reinstated. This was a topic of lively discussion among young Mennonites, some of whom were outspoken advocates of military service. Ultimately, the German Mennonites did not come out as conscientious objectors.

That members of a traditional peace church pledged themselves to the *Sturmabteilung* (Storm Detachment, SA) – an organization notorious for its extreme violence – requires an explanation. Particularly in the first months after the Nazis seized power, this subdivision of the Nazi Party was a driving force in the crimes and abuses committed by the new regime. Among other activities, it established "wild" concentration camps, it persecuted, tortured, and murdered political opponents, and it played a large role in the campaign to boycott Jewish businesses. Violence was at the *core* of Nazi politics and the SA. By the time some Mennonites joined the SA, it boasted more than 400,000 members, and it would continue to grow, reaching 4 to 5 million by 1934. Naturally, only a part of the troop would have taken active part in the SA's bloody rampages, and presumably they would have had little or nothing to do with the Mennonite community. Unfortunately, the sources provide too little information on this to allow a reliable assessment. That said, the SA's violent orientation and image could not have gone unnoticed by the Mennonites. Nevertheless, the participants in the Mennonite youth circulars of 1933 made no mention of this.

How, then, did they discuss their involvement in the SA? Their motives for joining that organization varied. On 27 January 1934, a theology student, writing to the others in his "circle," explained his decision as follows: "Incidentally, I have now been a member of the SA since Nov. [1933]. I very much enjoy the service, even if it's often time-consuming. The SA can also become a school for charity and brotherly love."[21] The act of joining might have been based quite simply on the desire for "camaraderie," though in part linked to a motivation to perform "service to the *Volk*" in the Christian sense. A further motivation would have been a deeply rooted, Christian-based anti-Bolshevist sentiment. Elements of Nazi ideology that contradicted a person's own Christian convictions were in some cases dealt with by making a distinction between politics on the one hand and world view, or (*völkisch*) religion, on the other. In general, membership in the SA was a young Mennonite's way of underscoring his participation in the building of the Nazi "people's community."[22]

The Perspective on *Volk* and Antisemitism

This brings me to my third point: *Volk*, "race," and antisemitism. As far back as June 1932, one of the group's important representatives, Hilde Funk, reported on the discussion in "Circle 2" of the Circular Community. In a piece she titled "Can a Christian Be a National Socialist?" she levelled her criticism at a core element of the Nazi world view and politics: racism. Significantly, however, she focused entirely on "idolization" – that is, on the overvaluation of the category "race" – without fundamentally condemning it. At the same time, she and most of the Circular Community expressed acceptance of a biological conception of *Volk* based on the categories of "blood" and "race." Here *Volk* was conceived of as a "biological" category and theologically legitimized as a divine "order of creation." In September 1933, Hilde Funk wrote to the Circular Community:

> You are used to hearing about politics from Circle 2 and so you will not be surprised to hear that we talked about the Nazis at the Thomashof

discussions [a gathering of the Circular Community at a Mennonite centre – I.B.]. At that point we said yes to politics, but hung a question mark on the worldview. The two are, however, always connected. So do we have to agree to the worldview on account of the politics or doubt the politics on behalf of the worldview? That was our question in Circle 2. Our answer was to find out where the two agree. If that is good, we can say yes to both. That approach also raised a lot of pros and cons, but I think we found that sweet spot in the middle. It is the German people. We say a loud yes to that. Nonetheless we also know that this good that we love cannot be made an absolute above all else, as the Nazis are unfortunately sometimes wont to do. We know there is an even higher loyalty for us, the will of God. It is only in obedience to this higher authority that we serve our people, since they are His creation. To reiterate: His will is above all, His demand, 'You shall have no other gods besides me.'[23]

As mentioned above, this stance was not a specific Mennonite doctrine, but an approach that had been elaborated on in detail above all within Protestant theology. At the same time, however, it was also widespread within the Mennonite community, including among the Circular Community, with no critical examination of its theological justification ever having taken place.

Erich Göttner (1899–1945?), a shrewd theologian and member of the Circular Community, had referred to this way of thinking on the eve of the Third Reich as if it was obvious.[24] He had emphatically rejected the idea of a "master race" (*Herrenvolk*), stressing that there were no "value differences" between the races, and in early 1933 he had even criticized Hitler personally for regarding "the blood value as a basic human value."[25] But at the same time, there was something problematic about Göttner's openness to theological doctrines of the orders of creation. He cited those doctrines to legitimize the "racial" category of *Volk* as a factor in the spiritual evaluation of the social. Yet if the "racial" category *Volk* was not rejected but accepted as a criterion to consider in the interpretation of the social – and Göttner did in fact accept it as such – it was a viewpoint that differed only in nuances, not fundamentally, from the "overvaluation" of the "race" factor, from the "idolization" of the state.

Göttner conceded in May 1933 in a lecture that "the reality of *Volk* as a community of blood and fate, as a determining characteristic of the soul and a spiritual nature is something we experience anew today."[26] Horst Quiring, a Mennonite theologian and Circular Community editor, would note something similar in his 1938 monograph *Grundworte des Glaubens*, which he structured like a dictionary. Under the entry for

Volk he wrote: "What it means to be a people [*Volk*] has only recently become clear to us Germans. A people is not formed by a commonality in land, language, or history, but has its deepest foundation in the community of blood or race."[27] Arnold Neufeldt-Fast analyses Quiring's theology in more depth in chapter 4 of this volume.[28]

Ernst Fellmann, an important organizer of and participant in the Circular Community, took an approach quite different from those of Hilde Funk and Erich Göttner. In 1935 he was made youth pastor for two Mennonite conferences, those of the south Germans and the West Prussians.[29] He favoured a dialectical approach. Funk and Göttner warned about an "overemphasis," whereas Fellmann argued that both the Nazi state and the Gospel made claims on the *whole* person. In both cases he found these demands to be justified. He did not ignore possible tensions between the two areas. In a December 1933 meeting of the circle leaders he went so far as to talk about the "anti-Christian aspects" of the National Socialists.[30]

Therefore in his view the necessary commitment of the individual to the German people consisted of more than the sense of civic duty that had arisen among Mennonites in the nineteenth century. It has been well documented how Mennonites left the position of being merely tolerated and gained civic freedoms. In an era of rising nationalism they had gradually given up non-resistance out of a sense of patriotic duty.[31] The commitment to one's people, for which Fellmann made an exemplary argument, was of a different quality, for it was based on a biological model that by its own logic ruled out emigration, an option exercised in the nineteenth century by part of the West Prussian Mennonite community.[32] Thus Herbert Schmutz summarized in this way the address Fellmann gave at the Easter 1934 address Circular Community gathering, which he titled "The Community of the Gospel and the New German People's Community":

> The new German People's Community [*Volksgemeinschaft*] consciously does not discuss "I" but embeds it in "we." This development places us in the midst of a new people's community which says, One People, One State, One Leader! This innovation has been given to us as a gift that we are part of. … It demands our whole person for community is more than mere participation, it is dedication with one's whole being. One cannot try to escape this community, for that would be to denounce one's own blood and land.[33]

Going perhaps even a step further was the young theology student, Circular Community activist, and later pastor in Krefeld, Dirk Cattepoel

(1912–1976). He revealed his *völkisch* thinking with astonishing clarity in a series of articles he was allowed to publish in 1934 in *Mennonitische Blätter*, the main German Mennonite newspaper. His views were not shared by the editor, who appended this caveat: "The views in this article are the responsibility of the author alone and we are publishing it without expressing our differing views on some points." Cattepoel placed his hand right on the hot potato – his three-part article "Mennonites and the Desire for Military Service" sought to explain theologically why Mennonites were duty-bound to serve in the military.[34] His line of argument is revealing, but here we will only examine how the acceptance of the concept of people as a "racial" category served to bind one to the Nazi state.

To be a Christian, according to Cattepoel, one must live facing the world and striving to fulfil the command to love. Since, however, it is not possible for a person to love all of humanity, one must concentrate on one's "neighbours," for whom love can be expressed concretely. To illustrate his point, he highlights geographical distance: "One's love cannot be abstract, loving a Mister X in Chicago and a Miss Y in Tierra del Fuego." Following this attempt at humour, he offers a definition of neighbour that makes a decisive racial turn. For a Christian, one's *neighbour* is one "with whom one shares one's being, in whom your blood also flows, a soul of one's soul. One's people is the area in which a Christian extends love. ... We are part of the German people. ... The German is our neighbour, to whom we declare our love and give our strength."[35] Here is a clear break with the basic teaching of the biblical parable of the Good Samaritan through which Jesus illustrated the nature of loving one's neighbour and to which Cattepoel alluded with his reference to "neighbour." Jesus told this parable to demonstrate concretely what love of neighbour looks like (Luke 10:25–37). The only one who helped the man who was attacked by robbers was a Samaritan, a member of a group that at the time was despised for its religion and mixed ethnic heritage.

In this parable, love of neighbour overcomes human barriers and crosses ethnic boundaries. Cattepoel, however, placed back those barriers with his discussion of race and blood in an attempt to redirect love of neighbour into the "correct" channel.[36] He continued emphatically that "our neighbour cannot be any old Negro or Japanese or Jew."[37] This short sentence combines both arenas, the spatial and the racial. Spatially the reference is to distant Africa and Asia. The conception of the Jew as a member of a foreign "race" or "people" demonstrates that the line can be drawn even in the immediate surroundings, so as to exclude Jews in Nazi Germany. Perhaps it is not too much to say that Cattapoel's line of reasoning served to justify discrimination against Jews. He continued, "certainly divine justice and grace will allow them access to love and preserve their lives. But our more limited strength demanded by our neighbours cannot be extended to them, although we know we will accrue guilt if we limit our love as well."³⁸

Cattepoel's views were apparently widely shared. Circle 17 embraced them wholeheartedly, although according to the distributed summary of October 1936, Cattepoel was not a member. Daniel Schneider reported in 1935 for this group that

> before God there is no difference among believers of all nations. They are all brothers in Christ. Nonetheless even there the order of creation is still valid, for it allowed us to be born as Germans. It is this people's community that has a just claim on our service and we gain by helping to bear its burdens. In practical terms that means in all outward matters we must join in it without any reservations whatsoever.³⁹

It seems that by accepting a "racial" definition of people or nation (and extending it to form a theological category), many young Mennonites simultaneously accepted the National Socialist understanding of people and people's community. This clouded their judgment regarding illegal acts of exclusion that began with the Nazi seizure of power.

Circle 12 discussed the "race issue" in the winter of 1933–34. Among other things, the writers cited the "Aryan Paragraph," in which context they referred directly to events taking place in a number of Germany's regional churches at the time. The "Law for the Restoration of Professional Civil Service," which went into effect on 7 April 1933, was the Nazi state's first anti-Jewish law. It reintroduced legal discrimination against Jews and paved the way for the "elimination of Jews" from all key public institutions (such as universities).⁴⁰

On 9 December 1933, a thirty-one-year-old farmer complained in a circular entry of Circle 12,

> Erich, you picked a touchy subject, the race question. Looking at it as a livestock breeder one would have to agree with the demand to exclude foreign racial material from our people. Every breeder values breed purity. If one can preserve a pure-blooded people, the result will be a healthier, more resistant, home-grown breed [illegible inserted word] preserving people better than a people that is a mixed-up mess.⁴¹

The author of these lines understood that in the church, or at least in some congregations, other standards applied, but this did not prevent him from applying them to the state as well,

> How we as Christians need to act in this regard will depend on different perspectives than this one. One of these points will be the question of what

to do with the Jews, who are in the midst of our people. The Jews would not be admitted to Palestine even if they all wanted to go there. If the worst of them would be punished now as an example for the others, that would only be as it should be. Often, however, when you ask what this or that one did, the only answer is, "Well, he's a Jew."[42]

Clearer still are the reflections of a farmer studying to be a missionary who had maintained a critical distance from the Nazi state. His commentary is noteworthy for showing how far even a more critical observer was willing to go toward accepting the early Nazi state's Jewish policy. He wrote on 9 January 1934:

> Still what is our attitude to the current race question? There is no doubt that each nation has its own "people's feeling." So I would not simply [want] to condemn the idea that every civil servant has to be Aryan. But it will always be an injustice to expand this principle to all areas of life. The special branding of non-Aryans in private life is unjust and from the church's perspective completely unjustified. The "Aryan paragraph" is and will remain a scandal for the state churches, a fact that is much more important than the question of whether the man in question has a Jewish background or not. As Friedchen already said, the Jewish people are the carriers of God's promise. That they are now under God's curse is certainly not because Aryan blood has achieved a special "high breeding." We have absolutely no right to disrespect the Jews. No, Friedchen, your expression is not strong enough when you say "there is a regular cult being created about Germandom." Germandom has been deified and Aryan blood is the highest God.[43]

This entry is remarkable for the clarity with which the author opposes racially based enmity against Jews. Yet he is unable to formulate an equally clear opposition to anti-Jewish laws.[44]

When assessing the Nazi state's anti-Jewish policies, the circular letter writers made a significant distinction: for the realm of the church and congregation, they established in a clear and theologically well-founded manner (though evidently rather reluctantly in some cases) that Jews were to be treated without discrimination and were to be placed on an equal footing with all Christians. When it came to the state, however, a racial approach and eugenic measures were acceptable.

The "Jewish question" was discussed again by the Circular Community in 1936–38. Antisemitic actions and the Nazi state's juridical anti-Jewish measures had by then intensified, a development that culminated in the Nuremberg Laws of 1935. From that time on, Jews were mere "citizens of the state," distinct from "'Aryan' citizens of the Reich," who enjoyed full rights. What is more, by prohibiting relationships between Jews and "Aryans," the Nazi laws had brutally invaded the private sphere.

Given the backdrop of Nazi policies to deny Jews in Germany all rights, ban them from public life, and compel them to emigrate, the newly elected leader of Circle 1 assigned a new discussion topic: dealings with Jews. In notebook 23, he wrote on 17 December 1936: "How would it be if we reflected on the Jewish question in light of the Holy Scripture? I know that is a delicate question that would require all of us to remain measured and objective. ... I think it would be good if we would take up the Scripture and not the hot button questions of the day related to Jews, although we would certainly need to discuss them later."[45]

What was meant here by "measured?" One hint is given by the text of a postcard the circle leader wrote on the same day to Theo Glück: "I decided to address the Jewish question, although I know it will not be easy and that's why I asked people to be disciplined and objective. I think we have to be careful in judging this question of our people that we don't act out against what are after all racial necessities."[46]

Apparently the circle leader worried that in this discussion, Nazi politics – which at this point he found to be correct – would come under attack. He had joined the SA in 1933. In his contribution of 13 May 1937, in notebook 24, he argued theologically, which is what he now wanted the other participants to do. He saw Jews as members of the people of God who stood under a curse. This was tinged with a political judgment that had been shaped by strong anti-Jewish stereotypes. Thus, at one point he mentioned the "Jews' desire to rule the world." And he continued: "We know what a world power and world danger deformed Judaism is, we know that the real leaders of Soviet Russia are Jews. But are those the same kind of Jews as Moses, the prophets, or the first disciples were?" In this one hears sympathy for "racial actions" that the author wrote about in a card to Theo Glück, and thus apparent support for the Nazi state's anti-Jewish laws.

And, finally, we also encounter antisemitic tirades – for example, this one, launched by a female contributor to this discussion on 26 July 1937 in notebook 24:

> The goals of Jewdom are apparent today. Disintegration, disintegration at any cost. Therefore I agree that they need to be removed from any positions where they can contribute to disintegration. There is so much talk of decent Jews and I could be persuaded by it if I knew of any. ... We know that a true

Christian must suffer and be scorned since it is written in the Bible. If a Jew, however, is persecuted we are all dismayed. All of them ... hold the blazing torch of all Jews, following Judah's cry to fight against all who put them on the cross, and what does Rome say and the rest of the world? They are dismayed at our government and get up to their dirty tricks.[47]

That this writer took up slogans from the worst of the Nazis' antisemitic vocabulary can perhaps be accounted for by her biography. She showed her affinity for the Nazi state and world view through her work with the League of German Girls (*Bund deutscher Mädel*), and topped that by announcing on 27 December 1935 that she had joined the Nazi Women's League.[48] Michaela Kipp has described this group as the "core of devout female supporters of the Nazi regime." The group held weekly educational evenings, which members had to attend at least once a month, in order to prepare women "for their leadership roles and the ideological control function associated with leading women's organizations."[49] Thus occupation and Nazi world view were one and the same for this Circular Community activist; she was, as the title of Birgit Breidig's book put it, a "brown sister."[50] On 14 January 1937, so about half a year after she penned the antisemitic tirade quoted above, she reported to her circle with evident satisfaction: "So today I send you greetings as a Nazi sister. I have been working for almost a year at the Rudolf Hess hospital in Dresden."[51] For Nazi sisters the "belief in the National Socialist world view was assumed," given that joining this Party organization including swearing an oath "to the Führer."[52] If, in addition to schooling in the world view, ritualistic elements were included in the political formation of NS sisters, we can assume that our writer was also exposed to such. It remains an open question whether her antisemitic expressions as quoted above were based on attitudes she had picked up before 1933 (from family, friends, etc.) or whether they were a more direct result of her ties to the League of German Girls, the Nazi Women's League, and the Nazi Sisters. There is no doubt, however, that beginning in 1933 this activist was incrementally exposed to such influences and that she made a public confession to National Socialist leanings following her engagement with these groups.

In this context, we find an important testimony of goodwill toward ostracized Jews. In July 1937, a female contributor to the same circular discussion expressed her sympathy for the Jews, regarding discrimination against them as unjust. Here I quote the rather long passage:

> Signs saying: "Jews unwelcome" are posted at the entrances to public establishments or on the doors of post offices. This week I went to a municipal

bathing facility, and there it said: "Jews not admitted." I must confess, I can only shake my head at this, and I have unending sympathy for those it concerns. If one of them enters a shop, you're hardly allowed to talk to him, and if you do, then in such a way as to ensure that he doesn't return. How can these people help the fact that they are born as Jews? If someone breaks a law, he should be punished, and there are a number of ordinances to enforce that. But that they should be despised for nothing, and that they are barred from every means of enjoying life with others … that is something I cannot condone.[53]

However – and this brings me to the problematic aspect of this writer's striking statement – even she, who so courageously voiced her opinion within her circle of friends, elsewhere considered it opportune to justify the antisemitic measures practised by the Nazi state. Again I quote:

The fact that the Jews were the ones who damaged our *Volk*, and sucked it dry, is something we can presumably agree on. And that they are no longer permitted to hold leading or high-level positions is also entirely correct, as "opportunity makes a thief," and they would unerringly soon practise their clean craft again. But the fact that they are repressed to the extent that they are, I sometimes find outrageous.[54]

Conclusion

I conclude with three points. First, comparing these discussions from different times and circles demonstrates that antisemitism grew sharper over the course of the 1930s as well as more radical in tone. One should be cautious, however, about applying this finding about two specific topics of conversation to the Circular Community as a whole. It is a fact that in both 1933–34 and 1936–38 there were critical voices that opposed anti-Jewish discrimination even while – a key point for me – not fundamentally denying that anti-Jewish politics were justified. In a recent essay, Diether Götz Lichdi argued that "in the written sources … there are only a few mentions of Jews or the Jewish religion" and that "none of the Mennonite publications discussed the 'Aryan paragraph' or the *Kristallnacht* (Night of Broken Glass) pogrom and its consequences. From the available texts there is no way to know how well these events were known or discussed."[55] He explicitly mentions the Circular Community, in which "'the Jewish question' was raised in only a few places" between 1935 and 1937 and without elaboration. Thus the findings in this chapter expand our knowledge of the relationship between Jews and Mennonites under National Socialism. As Lichdi attempted to speculate plausibly, "even if the sources do not explicitly document it, the impression nonetheless remains that most [Mennonites] did not oppose German officials' behavior and some even justified it."[56] The passages from the circular notebooks quoted and analysed here document that hunch.

Second, I have argued that many members of the Mennonite youth Circular Community – even those who took a critical stance on National Socialism – proved to be very open to racial thought. The spread of the racial mentality and the related conception of the *Volk* as a divine order of creation, I hold, served to bridge the gap to the Nazi concepts of *Volk* and the "people's community." It was also a way of legitimizing active political involvement. And it helped soften criticism of illegal measures aimed at ostracizing both Jews and political opponents of Nazism. Antisemitic outlooks not only were fed by setpieces of traditional Christian anti-Judaism but also bore a relation to a racist understanding of *Volk*.

Third, not all of the contributors to the circular letters adhered to conservative *völkisch* Protestantism such as that championed by the theology professor Paul Althaus of Erlangen. The position of Karl Barth was also discussed within the Circular Community – specifically by Cornelius Krahn, a student of Barth's. Eric Jantzen proved this in a History Seminar paper.[57] Yet the fact that Krahn emigrated to the United States in the 1930s speaks for itself – his theological orientation did not predominate within the Circular Community.

There was a powerful stance, based on religious convictions, that forbade antisemitic and racist attitudes toward Jews at least within the realm of the congregation and the church. Yet at the same time, the members of the Circular Community voiced no fundamental criticism of the National Socialist policies towards Jews of the years 1933 to 1936. The reason for this, I argue, is that those policies were essentially perceived as warranted.

NOTES

This chapter was translated by Mark Jantzen and Judith Rosenthal.

1 A portion of this chapter was previously published as "Volksbegriff und Antisemitismus bei der mennonitschen Jugend-Rundbrief-Gemeinschaft in der Etablierungsphase des NS-Regimes," *Kirchliche Zeitgeschichte* 29, no. 1 (2016): 123–48, https://www.jstor.org/

stable/24894366. We thank the editor, Andrea Strübind, for granting permission to reprint it here.
2 See the assessment of Theo Glück, "RB-Teilnehmer 1928–1940," box 2, Theo Glück Papers, Mennonitische Forschungsstelle (MFSt), Weierhof, Germany. The basis for my analysis in this chapter was the circular notebooks deposited with the Theo Glück papers at MFSt. I am deeply grateful to Jochen Schowalter for making these sources, which are at the MFSt, available to me. I also want to thank my father, Helmut Baumann, who along with my brother, Dr Thomas Baumann, transcribed the handwritten documents, which in part are otherwise difficult to read.
3 Max Weber, *Wirtschaft und Gesellschaft. Grundriss der verstehenden Soziologie*, rev. ed., ed. Johannes Winckelmann (Tübingen: Mohr, 1972), 21.
4 Hans-Jürgen Goertz, "Nationale Erhebung und religiöser Niedergang. Mißglückte Aneignung des täuferischen Leitbildes im Dritten Reich," *Mennonitische Geschichtsblätter* 31 (1974): 61–90; reprinted in *Das schwierige Erbe der Mennoniten. Aufsätze und Reden* (Leipzig: Evangelische Verlagsanstalt, 2002), 121–50 at 142. Diether Götz Lichdi responded to that with *Mennoniten im Dritten Reich. Dokumentation und Deutung* (Heilbronn: Mennonitischer Geschichtsverein Weierhof, 1977).
5 Goertz and Lichdi agreed finally to use the term identity crisis. See Diether Götz Lichdi and Hans-Jürgen Goertz, "Gemeinsame Erklärung – Zur Kontroverse um die Mennoniten im Dritten Reich," *Mennonitische Blätter* 12 (1978): 189. For recent contributions see, for example, James Irvin Lichti, *Houses on the Sand?: Pacifist Denominations in Nazi Germany* (New York: Peter Lang, 2008); or Benjamin W. Goossen, *Chosen Nation: Mennonites and Germany in a Global Era* (Princeton: Princeton University Press, 2017).
6 Herbert Strahm, *Die Bischöfliche Methodistenkirche im Dritten Reich* (Stuttgart: Kohlhammer, 1989).
7 Günther Kösling, *Die deutschen Baptisten 1933/1934. Ihr Denken und Handeln zu Beginn des Dritten Reiches* (PhD diss., Theologische Fakultät Marburg, 1980); Andrea Strübind, *Die unfreie Freikirche. Der Bund der Baptistengemeinden im "Dritten Reich"* (Neukirchen-Vluyn: Neukirchener, 1991); Uwe A. Gieske, *Die unheilige Trias. Nation, Staat, Militär. Baptisten und andere Christen im Hitlerismus* (Berlin: WDL-Verlag, 1999); Franz Graf-Stuhlhofer, *Öffentliche Kritik am Nationalsozialismus im Großdeutschen Reich. Leben und Weltanschauung des Wiener Baptistenpastors Arnold Köster (1896–1960)* (Neukirchen-Vluyn: Neukirchener, 2001.)
8 Andreas Liese, *verboten – geduldet – verfolgt. Die nationalsozialistische Religionspolitik gegenüber der Brüderbewegung*, 2nd ed. (Hammerbrücke: Jota Publikationen, 2003).

9 For the Seventh-day Adventists, see Johannes Hartlapp, *Sieben-Tags-Adventisten im Nationalsozialismus unter Berücksichtigung der geschichtlichen und theologischen Entwicklung in Deutschland von 1875 bis 1950* (Göttingen: V&R unipress, 2008).

10 Sven Brenner is working on a dissertation about Pentecostals under the Nazis at the University of Heidelberg; see Brenner, "Pfingstler in der Zeit des Nationalsozialismus. Ein Forschungsbericht," *Freikirchen-Forschung* 21 (2012): 274–86; see also Paul Schmidtgall, "Die Pfingstbewegung im NS-Staat," in *Christen im Dritten Reich*, ed. Philipp Thull (Darmstadt: WBG Academic, 2014), 85–94. See the reflections of Karl Heinz Voigt, "Freikirchen im Nationalsozialismus. Anmerkungen zur Freikirchenforschung," in *Christen im Dritten Reich*, ed. Thull, 95–104, as well as the earlier monograph Karl Zehrer, *Evangelische Freikirchen und das "Dritte Reich"* (Berlin Ost: Evangelische Verlagsanstalt, 1986).

11 See, for example, Eric J. Jantzen, "A Call to Questioning: The German Mennonite Youth and Their Response to Questions of the Day as Found in the Rundbrief Gemeinschaft, 1930–38" (History Seminar paper, Bethel College, North Newton, Kansas, 1996). Theo Glück at the end of the 1970s put together the earliest extremely useful documentation about the Circular Community, which unfortunately is not entirely free of apologetic tendencies. Glück, "Die Auseinandersetzung der mennonitischen Rundbrief-Freundeskreise mit dem Nationalsozialismus," in Lichdi, *Mennoniten im Dritten Reich*, 199–236.

12 See Lichti, ch. 3, "One in Faith but Not in Flesh: Sanctifying Racial Hygiene," in *Houses on the Sand?* (New York: Peter Lang, 2008), 73–114; Benjamin W. Goossen, "Mennoniten als Volksdeutsche. Die Rolle des Mennonitentums in der nationalsozialistischen Propaganda," *Mennonitische Geschichtsblätter* 71 (2014): 55–70; Helmut Foth, "Wie die Mennoniten in die deutsche Volksgemeinschaft hineinwuchsen: Die Mennonitischen Geschichtsblätter im Dritten Reich," *Mennonitische Geschichtsblätter* 68 (2011): 59–88.

13 See Lichti, ch. 5 "'Your father the devil': The Christian Biblicist Discourse on Jews," Lichti, *Houses on the Sand?*, 151–249; Gerhard Rempel, "Mennoniten und der Holocaust. Von der Kollaboration zur Beteiligung an Verbrechen," *Mennonitische Geschichtsblätter* 67 (2010): 87–133; Diether Götz Lichdi, "Mennoniten und Juden in der Zeit des Nationalsozialismus," in *Freikirchen und Juden im "Dritten Reich." Instrumentalisierte Heilsgeschichte, antisemitische Vorurteile und verdrängte Schuld*, ed. Daniel Heinz (Göttingen: V&R unipress, 2011), 65–76. See as well the other chapters concerning additional free churches in this important volume.

14 In addition to the chapters by James Lichti and Arnold Neufeld-Fast in this volume, see also Lichti, "One in Faith but Not in Flesh," 73–114; Goossen, "Mennoniten als Volksdeutsche," 55–70; Foth, "Wie die Mennoniten in die deutsche Volksgemeinschaft hineinwuchsen," 59–88; Lichti, "'Your father the devil'"; Rempel, "Mennoniten und der Holocaust"; Lichdi, "Mennoniten und Juden in der Zeit des Nationalsozialismus." See as well the other chapters concerning additional free churches in this important volume, and on "race," Goossen, *Chosen Nation*.
15 Lichti, *Houses on the Sand?*, 75.
16 The chapters by Pieter Post and Arnold Neufeldt-Fast in this volume also highlight the importance of the "Orders of Creation" for Mennonites' acceptance of racism and Nazi ideology.
17 Martin Honecker, "Nationale Identität und kollektive Verantwortung," *Evangelische Christenheit in Politik, Gesellschaft und Staat. Orientierungsversuche*, ed. Martin Honecker, (Berlin: De Gruyter, 1998), 149–71 at 161.
18 Martin Honecker, "Evangelische Theologie vor dem Staatsproblem," in *Evangelische Christenheit*, 59–97 at 69. On the topic as a whole see also Martin Honecker, *Profile – Krisen – Perspektiven. Zur Lage des Protestantismus* (Göttingen: Vandenhoeck und Ruprech, 1997), 128.
19 Lichti, *Houses on the Sand?*, 81.
20 Theo Glück, Ernst Fellmann, Hermann Funck and Hilde Funk, "Mennonitische Gemeindekirche! Ein Beitrag der Jugend zum Neubau des deutschen Mennonitentums," reprinted in *Mennonitische Blätter* 81, no. 1 (January 1934): 3–4; meeting participants from Baden, Württemberg, Bavaria, the Palatinate, Rhine Hesse, the Free State of Danzig, western Prussia, Berlin, the Province of Saxony, and the Rhineland, "Offener Brief an die Vertreter in den Verhandlungen zur Einigung des deutschen Mennonitentums," *Mennonitische Blätter* 81, no. 5 (May 1934): 41.
21 [Anon., b. 17 July 1912], circle 1, notebook 16, box 1, Theo Glück Papers, MFSt. From private correspondence it follows that the student later quit the SA. We are unfortunately uninformed as to the timing of and motives for his leaving; nothing on this person is found in the SA records of the German federal archive. (Incidentally, this same person later, in 1937, strove to become a member of the Nazi Party.) Series PK, Bundesarchiv (BArch) (formerly Berlin Document Center [BDC]).
22 Regarding the aspects of camaraderie and the possibility of using membership in the SA to prove one's loyalty to the Nazis' *Volksgemeinschaft*, see Daniel Siemans, *Stormtroopers: A New History of Hitler's Brownshirts* (New Haven: Yale University Press, 2017), 332–6.
23 Hilde Funk, Mitteilungen der Freunde des mennonitischen Jugend-Rund-Briefes Nr. 5, September 1933, 6: Bericht aus Kreis 2, "Der

Absolutheitsanspruch Gottes!," folder "Rundbrief-Mitteilungen 1932–1936," box 2, Theo Glück Papers, MFSt.

24 Erich Göttner had studied theology in Marburg, Munich, and Berlin in the years 1919 to 1923 and subsequently served as a Mennonite parish pastor in the Palatinate and Hesse before becoming the pastor of the Danzig congregation in 1927. He was thus among the professionally established circular protagonists and, as a member of the board of the "Vereinigung der Mennonitengemeinden im Deutschen Reich," carried out an important supra-regional function.

25 Erich Göttner, "Die völkische Religiosität der Gegenwart. Auf Grund eines Vortrages in der Danziger Mennonitenkirche, gehalten im Februar 1932 ...," pt 3, *Mennonitische Blätter* 80, no. 2 (1933): 14.

26 Erich Göttner, "Welche Aufgabe hat die Gemeinde in der Gegenwart?," lecture, second West Prussian Youth Convention, Steegen (near Danzig), 21 May 1933, *Mennonitische Jugendwarte* 13, no. 4 (1933): 87–94 at 87.

27 Horst Quiring, "Volk," *Grundworte des Glaubens. Achtzig wichtige biblische Begriffe für den Menschen der Gegenwart dargestellt von Dr. Horst Quiring*, (Berlin, 1938), 221–5 at 221–2.

28 See my own reflections in Imanuel Baumann, "Volksbegriff und Antisemitismus bei der mennonitischen Jugend-Rundbrief-Gemeinschaft in der Etablierungsphase des NS-Regimes," *Kirchliche Zeitgeschichte* 29, no. 1 (2016): 123–48.

29 See Lichdi, *Mennoniten im Dritten Reich*, 74–9; Hans-Jürgen Goertz, "Mennoniten und der Nationalsozialismus," in *Christen im Dritten Reich*, ed. Thull (Darmstadt, 2014), 68–84 at 75–7. See also the letter from Johs. Foth, 8 October 1935, Konferenz der Süddeutschen Mennoniten, box 24 "Jugendarbeit/Sitzungen," MFSt.

30 Typewritten essay by Ernst Fellmann, "Stellung und Aufgabe des Rundbriefes in der politischen und kirchlichen Umwälzung unserer Zeit. Einleitung beim Kreisleitertreffen in Durlach vom 30.–31.12.33," folder "Jugendarbeit, Rundbriefe, 1937–1938," box 2, Theo Glück Papers, MFSt.

31 Christoph Wiebe provides a different interpretation, "Die Krefelder Mennoniten und die Wehrlosigkeit. Eine symbolische Abgrenzung im Wandel der Zeit," *Mennonitische Geschichtsblätter* 65 (2008): 114–46.

32 See also the argument in Lichti, *Houses on the Sand?*, 75, 77.

33 "Unser R-B-Treffen Ostern 1934 auf dem Weierhof Pfalz," folder "Rundbrief-Mitteilungen 1932–1936," box 2, Theo Glück Papers, MFSt.

34 Dirk Cattepoel, "Mennonit und Wehrwille," *Mennonitische Blätter* 81, no. 2 (February 1934): 9–11; (Fortsetzung 1), no. 3 (March 1934): 23–5;

(Fortsetzung 2), no. 4 (April 1934): 33–35; (Fortsetzung 3 und Schluss), no. 5 (May 1934): 42–44.
35 Cattepoel, "Mennonit und Wehrwille" (Fortsetzung 3 und Schluß): 43.
36 The commandment in Lev. 19:34 – To love the stranger as a member of one's own community – was ignored here.
37 Cattepoel, "Mennonit und Wehrwille" (Fortsetzung 3 und Schluß): 43.
38 Ibid.
39 "Mitteilungen des mennonitischen Jugend-Rund-Briefes Nr. 8, Januar 1935: Bericht aus Kreis Nr. 17 von Daniel Schneider unter der Überschrift 'Führung Gottes – Sendung der Gläubigen heute,'" folder "Rundbrief-Mitteilungen 1932–1936," box 2, Theo Glück Papers, MFSt.
40 See Saul Friedländer, *Nazi Germany and the Jews: The Years of Persecution, 1933–1939* (London: Weidenfeld and Nicolson, 1997), 27f.
41 Notebook Circle 12 (Copies), box 1, Theo Glück Papers, MFSt.
42 Ibid.
43 RB-Circle 12 (Copies), First round, notebooks 1 and 2, box 1, Theo Glück Papers, MFSt.
44 Cf. "Mitteilungen des mennonitischen Jugendrundbriefes Nr. 7, Sommer 1934: Bericht aus Kreis 12 von Rudolf Funk unter der Überschrift "Einigung – Rasse," folder "Rundbrief-Mitteilungen 1932–1936," box 2, Theo Glück Papers, MFSt.
45 Folder "Circulars dating from 1921 and later, possibly from the estate of Paul Schowalter," box 3, Theo Glück Papers, MFSt.
46 "Karte des Kreisverantwortlichen an Theo Glück vom 17.12.1936," folder "Korrespondenz Rundbriefe Treffen u.a. 1932–1938," box 2, Theo Glück Papers, MFSt.
47 Ibid.
48 [Anon., b. 8 May 1912], Series FS, BArch (formerly BDC).
49 Michaela Kipp, "Die NS-Frauenschaft (NSF)," Lemo (*Lebendiges Museum Online*), http://www.dhm.de/lemo/kapitel/ns-regime/ns-organisationen/frauenschaft.html, 16 September 2015 (accessed 14 May 2018).
50 Birgit Breiding, *Die Braunen Schwestern. Ideologie, Struktur, Funktion einer nationalsozialistischen Elite* (Stuttgart: Steiner, 1998).
51 Rundbrief: circle 1, notebook 23, box 1, Theo Glück Papers, MFSt.
52 Breiding, *Die Braunen Schwestern*, 49, 53f. Breidig demonstrates how the focus on National Socialism was intended to shape the thoughts and emotions of the NS Sisters. "In order to embed the National Socialist worldview in the consciousness of the NS Sisters and to link it to their emotions, in addition to ideological education 'times of celebration' were held in the sister homes, during trainings or other gatherings, for example, at the summer solstice or on November 9. The main point of these 'times

of celebration' was the ritual of dedicating oneself to Hitler following different pre-determined formulas." Ibid., 76.
53 Folder, "Circulars dating from 1921 and later, possibly from the estate of Paul Schowalter," box 3, Theo Glück Papers, MFSt.
54 Ibid.
55 Lichdi, *Mennoniten und Juden*, 70, 71, 69.
55 Ibid., 69.
57 See Jantzen, "A Call to Questioning."

Chapter Four

German Mennonite Theology in the Era of National Socialism

ARNOLD NEUFELDT-FAST

What logic or force was at play that could check every Mennonite ethic and coordinate the action of German Mennonites to pursue immoral ends during the Nazi era? And could this happen again? In his book titled *Modernity and the Holocaust*, Polish philosopher Zygmunt Bauman has argued that grand visions of a "better and different kind of society," which might include the defamation, relocation, and eradication of populations, are deeply linked to the order-making, instrumental rationality of modernity. He offers a simple yet compelling picture of modern social engineering as landscaping the human garden. Gardeners identify certain cultured plants for care, and others for segregation, containment, removal, and even destruction, as part of the creative construction of the "gardening" state.[1] If in an earlier era the state was like a leisurely "gamekeeper" who merely watched over his realm, the modern state is like a diligent gardener, who with his zealous apprentices creates a thoroughly designed and fully controlled world. Building on the unfinished agenda of Hannah Arendt and Theodor Adorno, Bauman argues that the Holocaust was not so much an aberration in modern history; rather, it displayed the very logic of modern bureaucracy. German Mennonite leaders accepted the purposive, calculated, ordered, efficient violence required for this evolving "garden" project of a Jew-free *Reich* – and eventually Europe – at every stage without sustained interference from the ethical norms of their tradition. Was this an aberration? As one elderly German Mennonite recalled years later, Nazism "came over us like a revival."[2]

I begin with some early responses by Mennonite leaders to National Socialism and then survey four different Mennonite groups in the Nazi era: first, the liberally disposed (*freisinnige*) north German congregation of Krefeld, whose Pastor Emeritus was Gustav Kraemer; second, the Pietist-influenced Federation (*Verband*) of German Mennonite

Congregations in Baden, Württemberg, and Bavaria; third, the Conference of East and West Prussian Mennonite Congregations, of which Horst Quiring, a young systematic theologian from Heubuden, was a member; and fourth, the Soviet Mennonites evacuated to the new German state "Wartheland" in annexed Poland, where they were naturalized as German citizens. I will close with a recommendation for confession and the development of a post-Holocaust Mennonite theology.

When Hitler was appointed chancellor in January 1933, Russian Mennonites in Canada closely followed the events as they unfolded, including the 1 April nationwide economic boycott against Jews and the rapid implementation of racial laws that removed Jews from public administration, education, and the judiciary.[3] After this first harsh cleansing of Jewish influence, Ontario elder Jacob H. Janzen wrote in May 1933 to his one-time Molotschna Mennonite colleague Peter J. Braun in Germany:

> And now to National Socialism and your strong sense of national consciousness. The newspaper clippings from there appear to have found the Jews guilty for Germany's troubles. All of the evil lies upon their conscience, and [apparently] Germans – especially those with blue eyes and blond hair – have absolutely nothing for which they should do penance. ... This German self-glorification concerns me; why must one always brag so much over there? Why demean the other in order to assert oneself?[4]

While glad for the new German self-confidence, Janzen chided his friend with the German idiom that "there are people living on the other side of the mountain as well" (*hinter dem Berg wohnen auch Menschen*). He then shared his personal story: "You are probably not aware of this, but I was once saved from death in Russia by my Jewish tailor, and I had also done the same earlier."[5] Janzen told Braun he awaited with "eager anticipation" what would unfold: "Will Hitler be the awakened Barbarossa," who famously stirs from the cave to meet the country's greatest need, "or the Antichrist, who will rise above everything that is divine?"[6]

Warnings from co-religionists in North America and the Netherlands fell on deaf ears. The early enthusiasm for National Socialism is captured well in reports of the September 1933 special meeting of the Alliance (*Vereinigung*) of Mennonite Congregations in the German Reich and its member conference of Prussian Mennonite congregations. The following is a composite of the reports by Pastors Emil Händiges of Elbing and Erich Göttner of Danzig.[7] Germans as a whole had been humiliated, demoralized, and impoverished by the conditions of the

Treaty of Versailles at the conclusion of the First World War and were threatened by anti-Christian Bolshevism. The national "arising" (*Erhebung*) was a new birth or "becoming" (*Werden*) of the *Volk* (people or nation) after a long period of testing. Hitler as Führer was "a divine gift of salvation to our people," wrote Göttner. "God has called men to the head of the government who have placed themselves with a clear confession on the foundation of Christian faith."[8] Yet this would require a transformation of the heart – and not just of individuals but of the *Volk*, wrote Händiges.[9] Göttner argued that for this to happen, Christianity and Germanness would need to find each other, and the church, including the Mennonite church, would have to emerge out of ossified Christendom and traditionalism.[10] The promise by the Führer and the Nazi Party of religious freedom and legal protection, as long as it did not "conflict with the manners and moral sentiments of the Germanic race," was unprecedented good news and opportunity for Mennonites.[11] In these 1933 reports, there was a shared perception that Germany would benefit from a single and totalitarian ordering of life, including coordination of state and church for the building up of the German *Volk* and to address perceived morality gone wild. "The challenge today is to become aware, in a new way, of what these goals mean for our congregations, and to wrestle for a 'new becoming' amongst ourselves as well," wrote Göttner.[12] If German Mennonites had struggled to clarify the shape of Mennonite non-conformity in the shift from a pre-modern world to a modern world, Diether Götz Lichdi argued, the path vis-à-vis the totalitarian society of National Socialism was even less clear.[13]

The well-known Nazi hymn "Deutschland erwache!" called on Germany to "awaken" from its "bad dream," and this was coupled with the call to "deny space to foreign Jews" and to "struggle for [Germany's] resurrection" and against the "complete destruction of Aryan blood."[14] Mennonite leaders did not address early warnings about basing this renewal on racial biology, nor did they scrutinize the Party's vaguely defined "positive Christianity" platform. Indeed, the new national arising and its opportunities for a fresh German-appropriate articulation of faith reminded a few – including the official representative of Russian Mennonites in Germany, Benjamin Unruh – of the populist beginnings of the sixteenth-century Anabaptist–Mennonite movement.[15] The Führer's rise to power was embraced and lauded theologically as a turning point in history, as a rescue from humiliation and moral disintegration, and as a shield against communism – a real Barbarossa! There were no expressions of abhorrence toward the early policies or violence already being used to contain Jewish life so central to this "rescue." Even at this early point, redemptive words or efforts to support Jewish neighbours were absent, as was any repudiation of the new racial doctrine as heresy.

Fast-forward five years. Bauman's thesis linking the Holocaust to the logic of modernity – that is, its capacity to justify purposive, calculated, efficient violence – was on full display in the 1938 lecture by Krefeld's Pastor Emeritus Gustav Kramer titled "We and Our *Volk*-Community" (*Wir und unsere Volksgemeinschaft*).[16] The address was commissioned for the five-year anniversary of the National Socialist regime and written for a broader Mennonite community. It was structured along the Nazi Party (NSDAP) platform and praised what had been accomplished in five short years.[17] Kraemer argued that there were "decent and base elements" in every community; "personal hatred against individual Jews" was not relevant, and he did not follow those who claimed that "each Jew is a devil."[18] However, the "fate of individuals" had to be seen within the larger developments, intentions, and goals of National Socialism. Its party platform was not antisemitic, according to Kraemer; however, the state was compelled to "break the bondage of usury" that had crippled farms and businesses.[19] This financial regime "in principle and in fact is embodied most fully by Jewry [*Judentum*]" – according to Kraemer's government sources. Like parasites, Jews had economically choked German farmers to death and then simply moved on when there was nothing left to take, according to Kraemer.[20] When reviewing the cultural achievements of the past five years, Kraemer celebrated the exclusion of "Jewish media bandits," whose writings were full of political lies and "mockery of all that is German and Christian."[21] Kraemer praised new marriage regulations designed to "eliminate the hopeless contaminants of the race" and "to promote healthy breeding."[22] He acknowledged that Jews had been excluded but noted that every revolutionary movement involved risks.[23] While Kraemer knew and respected many Jews and people in mixed marriages, and while he felt very sorry for their individual suffering, he also understood the need for "the hard exclusionary battle against Jewry [*Judentum*]." The tone did not suit him, he admitted, but it was necessary – "the sound of slaughtering has never made beautiful, harmonic music."[24] At first, the new anti-Jewish laws "appeared very brutal and unjust to me, but later I could appreciate that ... in the ordering of this world, which of course is God's order ... we live as members of a community, in both good times and in bad." And now the old Jewish law – that children are to be punished for the sins of the parents "to the third and fourth generation" (Exodus 34:7) – was falling upon the decent and innocent Jews as well, according to Kraemer.[25]

According to Kraemer, Jews as a people had sinned against the *Volk* that had offered them hospitality, and they always refused to take any responsibility. Again, he declared that he was "very saddened for individuals ... but state necessities and private happiness are [two] very different things. The whole is more than its parts and pieces," he reminded his Mennonite co-religionists. "Great floods engulf the guilty and the innocent alike in the life of a people."[26] To underscore his point, he referred to the German diaspora and to the innocent "millions in Russia who are being tortured and martyred by Jewish-led Bolsheviks." However, in the case of Jews in Germany, it was mostly "evil seed sown that is now being reaped."[27] He argued that Mennonites would do well to look upon the intent and work of National Socialists as they cast out demons and created space and form for the good, just as Jesus had.[28]

The Kraemer document's reception by the Alliance's executive was equally disturbing. Chair Emil Händiges judged the pamphlet to be "of such great significance, that it is recommended for distribution to all our congregations and families for study and discussion. It is eminently suitable for establishing with complete clarity the positive disposition of German Mennonitism toward the Third Reich."[29] This was hardly controversial: an "overwhelming majority of [Mennonite] elders and ministers in West Prussia and Danzig" were "members of the [Nazi] party," according to Benjamin Unruh; and "as party members they wear the swastika on their chest with pride and joy," according to Händiges.[30] Only months after this endorsement, the renowned Classical-style Krefeld synagogue – spiritual home to more than 1,800 Jewish families – was gutted by fire during the *Kristallnacht* (Night of Broken Glass) pogrom. Kraemer visited the Chief Rabbi of the synagogue to offer his condolences; this act was consistent with his 1938 address – "sadness for the individual" within the frame of "state necessities."[31] For years, Händiges would remain deeply convinced that concerns raised by co-religionists in the Netherlands and abroad were based on misunderstandings and that it would "take some time before a better understanding prevails of the new Europe for which our FÜHRER [*sic*] is striving."[32] Before and after *Kristallnacht*, the Alliance executive was silent about basic human rights and pursued official recognition as the "oldest Reformation free church"– not sect – in good standing with state, party, and its organizations,[33] especially the SS (*Schutzstaffel*).[34] The window for renouncing the sin of antisemitism with boldness and determination had closed.[35]

Importantly, the theologically conservative Federation did not differ substantially in its response to Jewish defamation, exclusion, and persecution from liberally disposed Mennonite congregations like Krefeld. The reflections in its newspaper, the *Gemeindeblatt*, are pious and congregationally minded, comprehensive in choice of biblical and dogmatic themes, and largely attentive to Anabaptist history and its perspectives and emphases. Attacks on the Old Testament by the German Christian Movement, and on Good Friday as a "remnant of the Jewish spirit," are rejected frequently with clarity of conviction. Yet mixed in with all of these informed, well-intentioned biblical reflections are asides that are context-blind and tone-deaf, emphasizing that Jews were the first to reject Christ, had failed in their divine calling, and had lost any status as the elect people of God[36] – a hard supersessionist replacement theory consistent with conservative German scholarship of the day.[37] By 1933, biblical columnists were declaring at length how "everything sinister [*unheil*] comes from the Jews."[38] This editorial perspective continued even after *Kristallnacht*.[39] One 1939 article, for example, claimed that the German church had become diseased because of the Jewish synagogue, which was "a corpse, surrendered to decay." Not only had the "blood of the murdered Lord been a curse upon Israel for two thousand years," but the "honor of our *Volk* too is impacted," the author argued, echoing the 1935 Nuremberg Law "On the Protection of German Blood and German Honor."[40] Editor Christian Schnebele allowed the German Christian claim to stand that a "Judaized [*verjudete*] Christendom is alien to our kind [*artfremd*] with its repentance and dream of heaven" and that "its fear and humility before God, is not appropriate for such a great nation."[41] In some columns, the defamation, isolation, and exclusion of Jews from cultural and economic spheres was plainly recommended "in light of revelation" as wholly consistent with the Nuremberg Laws of 1935.[42] The *Gemeindeblatt*'s editor was aware of regime-critical movements – the "Young Church Movement," the 1934 Barmen Declaration, Eberhard Arnold's *Bruderhof* movement – but withheld all signs of solidarity.[43] Critical theological insights on the church and the state by Menno Simons and other early Anabaptists were offered, but without connection to other discussions about the call of the church to be "cruciform."[44]

A broader interest in anthropology would dominate German Mennonite theology in the 1930s, evident especially in Horst Quiring's 1938 *Grundworte des Glaubens* – a rich and accessible compendium of the basic terminology of Christian faith published by a promising Mennonite theologian.[45] Quiring had recently completed his doctoral work in Heidelberg under Walter Köhler, together with two later prominent American Mennonite historians, Harold S. Bender and Cornelius Krahn, and had been elected co-minister in Berlin. In his methodology, Quiring valued conversation with contemporary science and embraced the "newly awakened preoccupation with the origins of human races," that is, the recognition that we "are formed in large part by racial origin."[46]

He had published on the anthropology of the sixteenth-century Anabaptist leader Pilgram Marpeck[47] and was glad for those contemporary anthropological works that "once again take seriously" the individual's responsibilities to the *Volk* "as a whole."[48] He viewed "racial-biological differences" between peoples as "significant for the history and future of a *Volk*." He argued that the "call to keep blood pure" and "the cultivation of a healthy race ... finds a clear echo in the Christian worldview."[49]

For this reason, he suggested, kinship research (*Sippenkunde*) too had "always found fertile soil in Christian circles." Missionaries and most governments recognized that the "mixing of blood hides danger" and is simply "not good"; even the Apostle Paul and the early church worked against a "mush of humanity," Quiring told his readers.[50] He accepted the claims of Nazi science that blood testing cannot show a "genealogical unity of the human race"[51] and that some "residual ethnological stock" of lower human races – though very difficult to identify – is still in the gradual process of extinction, as had happened with the Neanderthals of prehistoric Europe.[52] As a theologian he recommended that the unity of humankind be thought with the Apostle Paul, namely, in terms of the common *search* for God.[53] "Every human being, whether he is of pure blood or of a combination of various races," knows the inner struggles of good and evil.[54] Even so, it was not the "image of God" or the Sermon on the Mount that provided the basic rubric for his Christian account of moral obligation, but the categories of blood, *Volk*, and race: "With the extensive treatment of racial questions and with the *völkische* renewal movement, a significant transition has taken place in the German person. The German person experiences impressively the mightiness of blood, the importance of the biological background of existence. Taking seriously this natural foundation of life leads to the recognition that even morality and all cultural creations arise from the depths of this *Volk* identity."[55]

Quiring's approach – which precluded the possibility of the Jew as neighbour – was hardly unique within the Mennonite community.[56] Yet according to him, humility as service to one's neighbour in one's *personal* life remained an appropriate Christian virtue for Germanic peoples and had early Germanic Christian precedents.[57] He praised the cultural contribution and vigour of "Frisian" Mennonites who had established attractive villages on the "barren and inhospitable" Russian steppe, "always creating space for the next generation" thanks to their "hereditary industriousness and competence for colonization."[58] In an article on German Volhynians – who counted among their number a Mennonite group on the Polish border with Ukraine – Quiring claimed that they were the "biologically healthiest *Volk*-German group with the largest families in the *Reich*" – healthiest, that is, in the sense of being least tainted with Polish or Ukrainian blood.[59]

A highly influential Manitoba Mennonite elder, Johann Enns, reviewed *Grundworte* and was satisfied that Quiring took appropriate pride in the newly awakened German Reich without displaying racial haughtiness, and recommended the volume.[60] In Germany, Benjamin Unruh praised Quiring for including racial-biological theory in his theological handbook and strongly recommended it to all Mennonite ministers, youth workers, and the younger generation.[61]

These same theories were presented with less nuance and theological commitment in the popular Mennonite genealogical articles and publications of Heinrich Schröder, a Russian Mennonite émigré who had studied with Unruh in Russia. Schröder, who was not a theologian, proposed a pseudo-religious, trinitarian "synthesis of Blood, Soil and Holy Spirit."[62] Specifically, he contended that deep religiosity – characteristic of Frisians, according to the author – awakened concern for "blood purity," which alone could ensure the health, vitality, and survival of clan and race. He promoted a non-dogmatic third option between modernity, on the one hand, and an increasingly archaic understanding of faith, on the other: "Body and blood are never 'incidental,' but rather bring about healthy moral existence and life. Unfortunately, this fundamental fact has not been recognized by either the church or the Enlightenment."[63] In a judgment typical of Schröder's writings, the beloved Mennonite missionary and elder Heinrich Dirks – "one of the most striking Russian Frisians in the field of church" – had a son who no longer "honoured the body" and who by marrying a Javanese woman had "desecrated the race."[64] But his most hateful comments were reserved for "Jewish Bolshevism," which he alleged had been behind the murder of the "Mennonite heroes of the *Volks*-body" during the Russian Revolution.[65] In the racial state, race supplanted class or the classless society as the primary binding power.

Let us return to Bauman's model of social engineering as landscaping the human garden. German Mennonite leaders across the theological spectrum "got their hands dirty" and participated with conviction as certain cultured plants were identified for care and others weeded out or destroyed.[66] This model is helpful for interrogating the place assigned to and quickly embraced by Mennonites in German-occupied Ukraine. They were recent victims of Bolshevik social gardening, and in that regard, Nazi Germany offered them a new quasi-theological, racial interpretive framework for their suffering under Stalin; this in turn fuelled older, latent forms Christian antisemitism.[67] The *Ukraine Post* – distributed in Chortitza and Molotschna and part of the sophisticated Nazi propaganda apparatus – displayed this well. The *Post* carefully laid out all key National Socialist concepts and Nazi Party policies in order to initiate the newly liberated into the new world view.[68] Laws such as the one prohibiting marriage between Germans and other peoples – and if undertaken, such marriages were legally void – were explained to the youth.[69] The *Post* defined the *Volk* as a "lived community bound by blood and destiny; the racial forces living within it create and shape its own language, custom, etc."[70] Using this definition, the *Post* reported that Mennonites of Chortitza and Molotschna were among the "most successful" German settlers in the east, with an exceptionally high birth rate, and were of extraordinarily high "German racial purity." Consequently, the work of the Hitler Youth and the League of German Girls "finds fertile soil" among them.[71] Elbing pastor Emil Händiges received a similar impression in a letter from a nephew serving near the Mennonite populations: "The boys aged sixteen to eighteen-years-old in German military uniform are strapping and very proud. Many girls look like our Reich League of German Girls: blue skirts, white blouses and black neckerchief … slim and blond, most obviously German."[72] He sent greetings from an eighty-four-year-old Molochans'k (Halbstadt) midwife Helene Berg, who was "curious about everything" and had "studied the Führer's [*Mein*] *Kampf* with the appropriate interest."[73] He reported that these Mennonites were happy and friendly despite enduring "endless suffering" and being "pushed aside and robbed by Jews." In language consistent with news reports, he speculated that this resilience was due to their "German essence and nature [*Art*]."[74]

Antisemitic columns in the *Ukraine Post* fuelled paranoia about an apocalyptic struggle between Jews and the rest of humankind. Readers were told that "Bolshevism equals Judaism," that the Soviet Union was a "state of Jews," and that wherever Bolshevism arose, it was only as the shock troops in a worldwide Jewish conspiracy to enslave and exploit.[75] Columns by Professor Johann von Leers, whom Goebbels had appointed to the Ministry of Propaganda, explained why the eradication of all Jews – regardless of individual acts – was not only rational but morally imperative:

> The Jew is the primordial evil in the world, completely satanic and devilish— we are now fighting this fight against him until his ultimate end. That is why this fight has become so hard and so ruthless. The Jew wants our blood and the blood of our children, and we want his destruction [*Vernichtung*] in Europe. In between, there is no compromise.[76]
>
> If the Jew wins, then all who are of German blood will be destroyed, sterilized, tortured to death, slaughtered. If we win, then Judaism will – according to the words of the Führer – be eradicated [*ausgerottet*] from the world.[77]

In support of such theses, the *Post* published testimonials and photographs of Soviet-era torture chambers with the claim that "such methods" of torture "can only be devised by a Jewish-Oriental mind."[78] Interviews in the *Post* soon reflected the language of the regime: "the Jews tortured us the most," soldiers were told by an ethnic German woman in the Caucasus, a region where some Mennonite communities were located.[79] What Mennonites thought of the *Post* and two other Nazi papers in Ukraine is unclear, but they provided new constructs for antisemitism to flourish.[80] Bolsheviks were bent on the death of European culture and civilization, the ethnic Germans were told, and the "common root" nourishing all of their enemies was Jewry.[81] In 1943, the powerful Chortitza district mayor Johann Epp told Benjamin Unruh – who had been absent from Russia for two decades – how "Jews and Jewish comrades [*Judengenossen*] sat in our villages and played their wicked games on us."[82] A climate of opinion had been created by the German occupiers that provided new guidelines for behaviour and action as communities surrendered their last Jews. Anecdotally, my grandmother often bartered dried fruit and geese for dry goods from a Jewish woman whose family lived on the edge of Marienthal/Panfilivka, Molotschna. The village cobbler – a Mennonite – identified this Jewish family for the authorities; they were taken to a cemetery behind the school and shot.[83] Another relative in Paulsheim/Pavlivka remembered how two Jews in the village were similarly led out by soldiers, made to dig their own grave, forced to their knees, and shot.[84]

The administrative and logistical roles played by appointed community leaders are, in part, recorded in surviving 1942 village reports, which include an accounting of Jews in the villages before and after occupation. Because so-called racial hygiene and genetic improvement were a top priority, "mixed" marriages and individuals determined to be biologically inferior with heritable diseases were designated for remedial action – typically sterilization.[85] Mayor Kröger of Nova Khortytsya, for example, singled out one family as inbred, noting that "all three children are intellectually disabled."[86] The *Ukraine Post* assured ethnic Germans that the singular, rational goal of these racial policies was "to give back and maintain the health, resilience, and performance capacity of the German *Volk*."[87]

District mayor Johann Epp of Chortitza showed little mercy to Mennonites who had chosen to adapt culturally or politically during the Soviet period:

> There are many of our families, especially in the cities, who were the type of German who no longer wished to be German and had declared

that they were Russian or Ukrainian. They are swine and should choose their colour. ... In this regard I am hard and brutal [*grausam*]. ... They have disowned Germandom [*Deutschtum*], they have disowned their forefathers, they have disowned their own self and trampled it under foot into the dirt, and now they should be equal to the brave, the honourable, who suffered for their Germanness? That would be false. Imaginable perhaps if their confession of sin was sincere, but I can't trust them! In my view, they are useless to us ... dangerous. [Solely] with the children something might still be possible.[88]

This was not an isolated perspective or tone, especially toward children of mixed marriages.[89] Data having been amassed for each village, German ethnographer Walter Kuhn was tasked "to provide a genealogical and *Volks*-biological accounting of the ethnic Germans in Ukraine."[90] Supported by Mennonite migration records from Prussia to Russia collected and submitted to the German Foreign Institute (Deutsches Ausland-Institut) by Benjamin Unruh and his team of Mennonite kinship researchers over a period of years, Kuhn concluded that the "unconscious powers" of Germanness had not been extinguished and that they *"will become a valuable element with the new construction of the German order in eastern Europe"* (italics in original).[91] In particular, Mennonites had not "allowed themselves to be confused and did not believe the Jewish-communist lies. Their hope was set on Germany."[92] There was an immediate concern about the youth, however, whom they deemed to have been significantly exposed to "Jewish-Marxist influence" by educational materials "written largely by Jewish emigres."[93] These materials were destroyed, and ethnic German teachers were put through a three-week re-education program to introduce them to "the National Socialist body of thought [*Gedankengut*],"[94] which at its core was antisemitic.

Kuhn's research, supported by the work of Special Unit (*Sonderkommando*) Dr Karl Stumpp, complemented efforts to achieve the National Socialist goal of "an ethnically separable and racially homogenous state."[95] Hitler spoke of creating a "Garden of Eden" in his newly acquired eastern territories; it was to be a German-blooded aristocratic garden linked by an *Autobahn* from Berlin to "Germany's own Riviera" on the Black Sea, with fortified "pearls" of German communities and bases along the way.[96] In 1941 he calculated that 3 million prisoners – Jews and Slavs – would be required to construct highways and bridges over the next twenty years.[97] This would require forced population transfers, enslavement, and mass murder. Adjacent to the Mennonite villages of Gnadental/Vodiana and Novokhortytsya in the

Baratov Settlement, for example, the entire Jewish village of Rotfeld was euphemistically "evacuated" and resettled with 188 neighbouring Mennonite ethnic Germans in June 1942, according to the village report by Mayor Peters.[98] These reports spearheaded by Stumpp identified all non-Germans as threats to the health, resilience, and vitality of the mythical German racial corpus, as hindrances to their settlement requirements, and ultimately as subhuman material most suited for servitude – or in the case of Jews, extermination. The quasi-scientific ethnic research accentuated difference, incompatibilities, hierarchy – not similarities, and not the rich history of cultural exchange and mutual interdependence in this ethnically mixed context.[99] By spring 1942 the racial identification of peoples in southern Ukraine was complete, and Mennonites were issued identity cards attesting that the holder was an ethnic German and "under the protection of the Greater German Reich," that is, by force of the death penalty for crimes committed against them.[100]

Mennonites benefited from this extreme racial policy even after they had fled Ukraine with the retreating German armies, for Wartheland in annexed Poland beginning in the fall of 1943. In March 1944 in Łódź/Litzmannstadt, Benjamin Unruh met with one of the architects of the Holocaust in Poland, *Gauleiter SS* Arthur Greiser.[101] On 14 March, Greiser welcomed the "millionth resettler" to the Reich and addressed a large gathering of newly arrived ethnic Germans. In a telegram to Hitler earlier that week, Greiser had reported to the great satisfaction of the Führer that the Wartheland milestone had been reached and that "save for a tiny remnant, Jewry has completely disappeared, and Polishdom has been reduced from formerly 4.2 million to 3.5 million persons."[102] Unruh reported to the *Vereinigung* executive that despite complications, Greiser "has firm intentions of giving land to farmers from the eastern zone, and he especially values Mennonite farmers."[103] While the elimination of Jews may not have been a direct result of the resettlement, at the very least the "two occurred simultaneously and served a common purpose," as Valdis Lumans argues, and "the Holocaust would have occurred with or without the resettlement program."[104] In his visits to resettlement camps, Unruh repeatedly admonished his brethren "to give evidence of your thanks in convictions, attitudes, and deeds to our Führer, the *Reichsführer SS* [Heinrich Himmler, whom Unruh had met], the director and officials of the Ethnic German Liaison Office, and above all to the district and local camp officials for the marvelous rescue [*Rettung*] from the hellish violence of Bolshevism."[105]

Regarding Wartheland from this time until the end of the war, we have one important church document related to the resettler Mennonite leadership. In March 1944, under the legal guidance of Gustav Reimer of Heubuden and Benjamin Unruh, Mennonites submitted to the state their articles of incorporation (*Satzung*) for the new "Conference of Mennonite Congregations of German Nationality in the Province of Wartheland" (Mennonitische Gemeindekirche Deutscher Nationalität im Reichsgau Wartheland). Its statutes limited membership to those of "German nationality," strictly defined in Nazi Germany by blood and *Volk*, thus excluding on principle Christians of Jewish or Slavic background. The same proposal recognized that the Reich Governor (*Reichsstatthalter*) was allowed to remove a person from denominational leadership for political reasons, which restricted the church's authority to serve as the conscience of the state or offer a culturally critical embodiment of the Gospel.[106] While in the resettlement camps, Unruh and Johann Epp divided the resettlers into wards, each with a designated lay pastor (no new elder/bishop had yet been ordained), who would organize two worship services per month. Unruh confirmed that "our people, together with their spiritual leaders," would participate in the Nazi Party "Morning Celebration" (*Morgenfeier*) on one Sunday per month.[107] Its purpose was "to awaken and kindle forever anew the forces of instinct, of emotion and of the soul which are vital for the struggle for existence and the bearing of our people and our race for all times."[108]

Unruh's prewar associate from the German Foreign Institute, SS Storm Unit Leader Karl Götz – principal of the teachers' training school in Prischib/Pryshyb (since 1938 part of Molochans'k) during the occupation, relocated to Lutbrandau, Warthegau – advised in a confidential SS report that Mennonite leaders in Germany would be able to guide co-religionists from Ukraine, over time, toward an appropriate and "thoroughly German religiosity":

> For the Russian Mennonites ... the Lord God [*Herrgott*] or the divine as such remained as most essential to their religious feeling. For the most part, all Christian-dogmatic aspects have faded. ... They are groping for religious models again. Understandably, they also come upon dogmatic-confessional matters on occasion. But with astute guidance regarding world view, the Mennonites in particular – but also the rest of the German Russians – will be led away from dogmatic-confessional matters to a clear and thoroughly German religiosity [*Gottgläubigkeit*]. Their desire is for the divine, for awe before the Almighty, the inconceivable, the sublime. Mennonite leaders are now working to lead the world of Mennonitism [*Mennonitentum*] toward this German God-believing, religious attitude.[109]

Götz did not free Mennonite teacher candidates for worship, though he required their participation in Nazi Sunday "Morning Celebrations," where they sang and "learned about the beginnings of the SS and the SA and were encouraged to fight faithfully for this movement," as one student recalled.[110] His report, with reference to Unruh, Horst Quiring, and Gustav Reimer, was consistent with the larger outcomes of the Ethnic German Liaison Office, which assumed that adherence to religious doctrine was a "temporary phase" that over time would be replaced by *völkisch* values. The longer-term goal was to attract Mennonites' co-religionists from North and South America – with their "German blood," "valuable genetic biological material," and financial resources – to serve as "advance troops" of National Socialism in the new settlement territory. With that, the Nazi human landscaping project in Wartheland would be complete – and Jew-free. With this goal in view, the resettlers were not to be "ambushed" with the new values in the camps. "We cannot afford to multiply the legion of dissatisfied resettlers," wrote SS Senior Squad Leader Dr R. Foerster in Łódź.[111]

In hindsight there is little question whether Hitler was the "awakened Barbarossa" – the secret code name for the war on the Soviet Union – arising to meet the country's greatest need or, as Jacob H. Janzen feared a decade earlier, "the Antichrist, who will rise above everything that is divine."[112] Following Zygmunt Bauman, perhaps the Holocaust – and Mennonite involvement – was not simply a horrible aberration, but rooted in the very rationality of modernity – so much so that each strand of German Mennonite theology, ethics, and piety proved impotent before National Socialism and its call to separate and eliminate the Jews.[113] Could something similar happen to Mennonites again? If Bauman is correct – and I think he is – the powers of that calculative logic continue to linger.

What, if anything, can the facts of Mennonite complicity in the Holocaust tell us about the hidden capacities of present-day life, and about the hidden capacities of present Mennonite theology? Consistent with Bauman's thesis, German Mennonites in the Nazi era continued to calculate a time in which love and justice would reign, but only after *order* had been achieved by the Führer. Toward that end, Mennonites like Kraemer and his Krefeld colleague Dirk Cattepoel, Händiges, Schnebele, and Quiring could delimit neighbourly love to make space for the most horrific crimes against humanity. Benjamin Unruh reckoned that the best solution to the "Jewish problem" would have been the Hitler-endorsed plan for an SS police state or "super ghetto" (*Großgetto*) on the former French-controlled African island of Madagascar, to hold some 4 million European Jews – a perfect example of Bauman's "gardening state."[114] And to secure an honourable place in that garden – Unruh's overriding concern – Mennonite kinship researchers organized a massive bureaucratic, genealogical undertaking that would strengthen a Mennonite "feeling of solidarity" as a "family and community of destiny [*Schicksalsgemeinschaft*]" rooted in the larger German *Volk*, the goal being to bind Mennonites "more firmly and completely to our Lord and Savior Jesus."[115] *Schicksalsgemeinschaft* was a Nazi slogan employed to understand the individual as part of a quasi-divine order of blood, ancestry, and destiny.

In the years after the devastation of the Second World War, German Mennonite leaders publicly declared their support for Mennonite non-resistance.[116] In a sermon given to his Krefeld congregation at the conclusion of the Nuremberg Trials in 1946, Krefeld pastor Dirk Cattepoel acknowledged that that which had overcome them over the past twelve years was the particular stance of a very particular *Weltanschauung*: "What is surprising and terrifying is how very much of this *Weltanschauung* – theoretically and practically – is found in each of us. ... God can be confused with the devil, truth with lie, love for hate, good for evil – and it is even considered ingenious and wise to do so." Cattepoel spoke of a "spirit" that allowed them to believe "in the power of hate, violence, deceit and irrationality" and called for repentance. On behalf of German Mennonites at the 1948 Mennonite World Conference in United States, Cattepoel offered an official apology – particularly to "Dutch and French brothers and sisters" – for what they had endured at the hands of the German nation. Surprisingly, however, he spoke of a "general ignorance" of Jewish persecution before 1938 and did not speak to his own antisemitic texts and those of his colleague, Gustav Kraemer.[117] A major examination of Mennonites in the Third Reich was first published in 1977, and with the fiftieth anniversary of the war's end in 1995, German Mennonites confessed that "nearly all Mennonites remained silent in the face of Nazi crimes against Jews and others," and asked for forgiveness.[118] Descendants in Canada and South America of ethnic German Mennonites from Ukraine, however, did not participate in that European process. Though traumatized by and burdened with their own story of suffering under Stalin and of displacement during and after the war, their relations with Jewish and Slav neighbours did change dramatically under German occupation. Many survivor memoirs have been written, but their story as favoured and willing objects of German liberation, occupation, re-education, and resettlement is still largely underdocumented and unanalysed.[119]

In conclusion, the impact of this research opens a door for Mennonites to acknowledge and apologize for past transgressions, and to (re)establish relationships with the Jews for the integrity of a Mennonite witness that calls "the nations (and all persons and institutions) to move toward justice, peace, and compassion for all people."[120] More recent Mennonite biblical-exegetical studies have sought to explore God's commitment to those who are oppressed and suffering, together with the specifics of the Exodus message of God's election and covenant with Israel.[121] A reassessment of the legacy of sixteenth-century Anabaptism too must be ongoing. At the Mennonite World Conference in the Netherlands in 1967, German Mennonite historian Hans-Jürgen Goertz posited that the real trajectory and central theological rediscovery of that movement is not anthropological, but "eschatological," namely "faith in the coming of God's Kingdom to this world," which is "aroused and strengthened by the Word and the Spirit of God."[122] This helped open the door to reconciliation and peace ministries with a cosmic account of the redeemed creation that includes Jews and Christians together. Theologically, there has been a growing consensus – best articulated by Jürgen Moltmann in *The Crucified God* – that all *Christian* talk of God requires reference to God's own Trinitarian self-definition in weakness and death for the sake of life. Moltmann takes Elie Wiesel's book *Night* as his theological starting point to dismantle an indifferent God: "Where is he? He is here. He is hanging there on the gallows."[123] I have been deeply critical of Horst Quiring's work, yet Quiring was also the strongest Mennonite theologian of the Nazi era, and the only one who – like Moltmann in the postwar era – adopted Luther's significant teaching of the "hidden God" – a God who displays his goodness and power most clearly in its opposite, namely, through suffering, catastrophes, and pain. "*The revealed God always remains at the same time the hidden God. In the weakness of the cross he hides his victory*" (italics in original).[124] Sadly, Quiring did not develop this theme for Mennonites as Jews became "'strangers' *par excellence* in Europe."[125] The accommodations made by Mennonites during the Hitler years, and their complicity, have been too significant for Mennonites not to be explicit in the development of a post-Holocaust theology – so that it might never happen again. The above proposals are, in my assessment, a few steps and strategies to keep Mennonites faithful to the longer Christian tradition, and largely disentangled from modernity's powerful spirit of order-making, instrumental rationality embodied so terribly in the antisemitism of National Socialism.

NOTES

1 See Zygmunt Bauman, *Modernity and the Holocaust* (Ithaca: Cornell University Press, 1989), 28, 13. For a more recent discussion of this construct, cf. Amir Weiner, ed., *Landscaping the Human Garden: Twentieth-Century Population Management in a Comparative Framework* (Stanford:

Stanford University Press, 2003). Except where otherwise noted, all translations are my own. I wish to thank John Thiesen, Benjamin Goossen, Peter Letkemann, and Willi Vogt for providing primary sources.

2 Dean Taylor, "Mennonite Nazis: A Lesson from History," *Ephrata Ministries* (blog), Ephrata Christian Fellowship, http://www.ephrataministries.org/remnant-2012-11-mennonite-nazis.a5w. For a good local example of such enthusiasm, see the 1934 annual report of the Heubuden-Marienburg congregation in *Mennonitische Blätter* 81, no. 5 (May 1934): 46f. https://mla.bethelks.edu/gmsources/newspapers/Mennonitische%20 Blaetter/1933-1941/DSCF0920.JPG.

3 Cf. the *"Reich* Law for the Restoration of the Professional Civil Service," 7 April 1933, and the Nazi call for a nationwide economic boycott against Jews on 1 April 1933.

4 Jacob H. Janzen to Peter J. Braun, 17 May 1933, 2, MS 91 (Peter Jacob Braun Papers), folder 4, Mennonite Library and Archives (hereafter MLA), Bethel College, North Newton, Kansas, https://mla.bethelks.edu/archives/ms_91/folder_4/SKMBT_C35107121311010_0014.jpg.

5 Jacob H. Janzen to Peter J. Braun, 17 May 1933, 2, MLA.

6 Ibid., 3.

7 Erich Göttner and Emil Händiges, "Zur Kirchenfrage der Mennoniten. Bericht über die außerordentliche Zusammenkunft der Vorstände der Ost- und Westpreußischen und Freistaat-Danziger Mennonitengemeinden zu Kalthof am 25. August 1933," *Mennonitische Blätter* 80, no. 9 (September 1933): 85–91 at 89, https://mla.bethelks.edu/gmsources/newspapers/Mennonitische%20Blaetter/1933-1941/DSCF0873.JPG.

8 Ibid., 89.

9 Ibid., 85.

10 Ibid., 89.

11 Cf. "National Socialist German Workers' Party Program," §24 (The Avalon Project, Yale Law School: Lillian Goldman Law Library), http://avalon.law.yale.edu/imt/nsdappro.asp.

12 Göttner and Händiges, "Zur Kirchenfrage der Mennoniten," 90.

13 "Zum Staatsverständnis der deutschen Mennoniten im 19. Jahrhundert," *Mennonitische Geschichtsblätter* 68 (2011): 56.

14 On the hymn "Deutschland erwache!" cf. Brian Murdoch, *Fighting Songs and Warring Wars: Popular Lyrics of Two World Wars* (New York: Routledge, 1990), 120.

15 Benjamin Unruh, *Mennonitische Blätter* 80, no. 12 (December 1933): 114; Göttner and Händiges, "Zur Kirchenfrage der Mennoniten," 90.

16 Gustav Kraemer, *Wir und unsere Volksgemeinschaft* (Mennonitengemeinde Krefeld, 1938). Kraemer was highly respected in the *Vereinigung;* cf. Emil Händiges in honour of Kraemer's seventieth birthday, in *Mennonitische Blätter* 80, no. 12 (December 1933): 113.

17 Kraemer, *Wir und unsere Volksgemeinschaft*, 10. On the planning and messaging of the national celebration from the Ministry of Propaganda, cf. Karen Peter, ed., *N-S Presseanweisungen der Vorkriegszeit* 6/I, 1938 (Munich: Saur, 1999), 84. Notably, the twenty-five-point program of the Nazi Party had also been printed in the Canadian publication *Mennonitische Rundschau* on 13 September 1933. In contrast to 1932, Kraemer argued that the economy was now (1938) strong, with high employment; Germany was no longer exploited by its enemies and had been spared the "hellish chaos of Bolshevism"; Germany's capacity to wage war and keep order had been re-established; its voice was now heard on the world stage, and its institutions and innovations were respected – all because of Hitler's faith in a higher justice, in destiny, and in the German people, according to Kraemer.
18 Kraemer, *Wir und unsere Volksgemeinschaft*, 12.
19 Cf. "National Socialist German Workers' Party Program," § 11–18.
20 Kraemer, *Wir und unsere Volksgemeinschaft*, 12.
21 Ibid., 8, 13. Cf. "National Socialist German Workers' Party Program," § 23, § 13.
22 Kraemer, *Wir und unsere Volksgemeinschaft*, 8. Cf. "National Socialist German Workers' Party Program," § 21.
23 Kraemer, *Wir und unsere Volksgemeinschaft*, 5f. There was broad awareness of the German Jewish refugee crisis in 1938. Cf. "Nichtarische und andere Flüchtlinge" – a paper received by the *Vereinigung* for the meeting of the World Alliance for Promoting International Friendship through the Churches, August 1938. Vereinigung Collection, file folder 1938, Mennonitische Forschungsstelle, Weierhof, Germany (hereafter MFSt).
24 Kraemer, *Wir und unsere Volksgemeinschaft*, 13.
25 Ibid., 14.
26 "National Socialist German Workers' Party Program," § 24.
27 Kraemer, *Wir und unsere Volksgemeinschaft*, 15.
28 Ibid., 29.
29 The booklet was distributed to executive members in May 1938. See Händiges's review in *Mennonitische Blätter* 85, no. 6 (June 1938): 44–45, https://mla.bethelks.edu/gmsources/newspapers/Mennonitische%20Blaetter/1933-1941/DSCF1248.JPG. Similarly, Daniel Dettweiler (Munich) to Vereinigung Executive, 6 June 1938, 1, Vereinigung Collection, file folder 1938, MFSt.
30 "Bericht über die Verhandlung im Braunen Haus in München betreffend die Regelung der Eidesfrage," recorded by Gustav Reimer, 4 July 1938, 3; see also Emil Händiges to Vereinigung Executive, 23 June 1938, in Vereinigung Collection, file folder 1938, MFSt.
31 Frank Deisel, "Kraemer, Gustav," *MennLex* 5 (2013), http://www.mennlex.de/doku.php?id=art:kraemer_gustav.

32 Emil Händiges, "Anlage zu dem Schreiben von Ds. Postma v. 20. 5. 1942," Vereinigung Collection, file folder 1942, MFSt.
33 See "Auszug aus einer Entscheidung des Gaugerichts der NSDAP in Stuttgart," copied by Abraham Braun to Vereinigung Executive, 8 March 1938; in Vereinigung Collection, file folder 1938, MFSt.
34 See the flurry of concerned Alliance Executive correspondence in June and July 1938 concerning the SS refusal for its member, Heinrich Krüger, to marry the Mennonite Erika Driedger: Vereinigung Collection, file folder 1938, MFSt.
35 The language and encouragement were available, but not leveraged; cf. the 1937 report from German Free Church representatives to the gathering of World Council of Churches in England, in *Gemeindeblatt der Mennoniten* 68, no. 18 (15 September 1937): 87.
36 *Gemeindeblatt* 68, no. 15 (1 August 1937): 71; cf. also *Gemeindeblatt* 68, no. 5 (1 March 1937): 23; 68, no. 5 (1 March 1937): 23; 69, no. 3 (February 1938): 13. The argument is stated most succinctly in Horst Quiring, *Grundworte des Glaubens. Achtzig wichtige biblische Begriffe für den Menschen der Gegenwart dargestellt* (Berlin: Furche, 1938), 225. After the war Quiring published a highly edited second edition (Stuttgart: Evangelischer Missionsverlag, 1949); in this paper I refer exclusively to the first edition.
37 Cf. Anders Gerdmar, *Roots of Theological Anti-Semitism: German Biblical Interpretation and the Jews, from Herder and Semler to Kittel and Bultmann* (Leiden: Brill NV, 2009).
38 Karl Engler, "Das heutige Judentum und das biblische Israel," *Gemeindeblatt* 64, no. 15 (1 August 1933), 71–73 at 72, https://mla.bethelks.edu/gmsources/newspapers/Gemeindeblatt%20der%20Mennoniten/1933-1941/DSCF7450.JPG.
39 E.g., *Gemeindeblatt* 70, no. 1 (1 January 1939): 1.
40 *Gemeindeblatt* 70, no. 8 (15 April 1939): 31.
41 On Schnebele as editor, see James I. Lichti, *Houses on the Sand? Pacifist Denominations in Nazi Germany* (New York: Peter Lang, 2008), 18f.; Diether Götz Lichdi, *Mennoniten im Dritten Reich. Dokumentation und Deutung* (Weierhof/Pfalz: Mennonitischer Geschichtsverein, 1977), 147–9. *Gemeindeblatt*, 70, no. 8 (15 April 1939): 31.
42 In response to the 1936 murder of philosopher Friedrich Schlick on the steps of the University of Vienna, the author noted that Schlick – a Protestant German – was an "idol of the Jewish intelligentsia" who had "one male and two female Jewish assistants" and whose "satanic doubt" and "devilish wisdom" was the "despair of morally sensitive and Christian youth." After a brief critique of the murdered philosopher's thought, the writer asks, "Is it any wonder, that in Vienna there are more

and more calls to cleanse the university of this faithless Jewishness?" Cf. *Gemeindeblatt* 67, no. 19 (1 October 1936): 92.
43 *Gemeindeblatt* 67, no. 17 (1 September 1936): 85. Cf. *Gemeindeblatt* 68, nos. 12–13 (15 June–1 July 1937): 62. The context of this joint statement by ministers representing each Mennonite region was the expulsion from Germany of the Anabaptist-inspired, non-resistant *Bruderhof* movement led by Eberhard Arnold. The incident was wrongly reported in the Swiss and Dutch press in 1937 as "Mennonites expelled from Germany." Mennonites were quick to respond officially and to distance themselves from the convictions of the *Bruderhof*.
44 Cf. Christian Neff, "Die heilsgeschichtliche Entwicklung der Gemeinde Gottes im Laufe der Zeit," *Gemeindeblatt* 68, no. 10 (15 May 1937): 48f: "The burning centre of the religious battle presently that arouses emotions especially in my German home [*Heimat*] is the question of church in its relation to the state. It could have been solved for all times 400 years ago if one could have agreed to follow the fundamental principle of the Anabaptists. ... The church of God on earth has always been cruciform [*Kreuzgemeinde*]. ... Menno Simons always pointed to this, that the church of God is and remains a church of the cross, with which its true and actual essence is recognized. We begin to see and feel something of this truth in recent times. The events taking place in Russia and Spain [regularly highlighted in Hitler's speeches] display this in the harshest and most frightening light." *Gemeindeblatt* 68, no. 10 (15 May 1937): 49. The lack of application to his own context is stunning.
45 Dirk Cattepoel – a younger colleague of Kraemer in Krefeld – also argued that the early church's focus on the kingdom of heaven as the goal of our action or desire was no longer appropriate, and instead endorsed the Reformation focus on anthropology. In this regard Mennonites had a unique understanding of humanity, according to Cattepoel, "because of our perspective on scripture." Specifically, "we are able to do good, because God accomplishes the good through us." "Mennonit und Wehrwille (Fortsetzung 3)," *Mennonitische Blätter* 81, no. 5 (May 1934): 42–4, https://mla.bethelks.edu/gmsources/newspapers/Mennonitische%20 Blaetter/1933-1941/DSCF0916.JPG.
46 H. Quiring, *Grundworte des Glaubens*, 160.
47 Cf. Horst Quiring, "The Anthropology of Pilgram Marbeck," *Mennonite Quarterly Review* 9, no. 4 (October 1935): 155–64; and the modified German version: "Die Anthropologie Pilgram Marbecks," *Mennonitische Geschichtsblätter* 2 (1937): 10–17.
48 H. Quiring, *Grundworte des Glaubens*, 159. Similarly in 1937, Quiring was pleasantly "surprised" with the strength of "*völkische* responsibility to Germany" expressed in the Canadian Mennonite paper *Der Bote*, and also

by Mennonites in Paraguay. "Kirche, Volk und Staat in mennonitischer Sicht," *Mennonitische Jugendwarte* 17, no. 5 (1937): 103–10 at 108, https://mla.bethelks.edu/gmsources/newspapers/Mennonitische%20Jugendwarte/DSCF9370.JPG.

49 Quiring, *Grundworte des Glaubens*, 36. Quiring's method gave theological weight to what the Protestant tradition has called the orders of creation – including work, family, marriage, and the state. With many contemporaries, Quiring included *Volk* and race among those orders entrusted to us by God in which God's law could be perceived. Thankfulness to God for "*Volk* and *Volkstum*" as creation orders should include "the love and unconditional allegiance to the *Volk*," according to Quiring, as well as responsibility for the physical and cultural heritage of the *Volk*, including its language (*Grundworte des Glaubens*, 222, 221). Quiring was convinced that "a *Volk* as a whole is called to Christ" and that the church was responsible for communicating the Gospel appropriately "into the *Volk*." Here Quiring was echoing the language of the German Christian Movement (*Grundworte des Glaubens*, 32), though he cautioned against their extremism: "race and *Volkstum* are divine orders," but they "are not the ultimate values in which we believe": *Grundworte des Glaubens*, 104. In this connection, see ch. 3 by Imanuel Baumann and ch. 5 by Pieter Post in this volume.

50 Quiring, *Grundworte des Glaubens*, 223; 96. The implementation of the 1935 Nuremberg racial laws spawned small armies of kinship researchers, who scoured church registers and created elaborate card catalogues and genealogies to document the Aryan bloodlines of Germans in the Reich and abroad. Cf. Manfred Geilus, ed., *Kirchliche Amtshilfe. Die Kirche und die Judenverfolgung im "Dritten Reich"* (Göttingen: Vandenhoeck & Ruprecht, 2008). Mennonites eagerly participated, organizing their most influential denominational leaders and historians for the Working Group for Mennonite Kinship Research, with the leading Mennonite figure Benjamin Unruh as its expert consultant on Frisian racial heritage, and as a splinter German group. B. Unruh, "Die Herkunft der Rußlanddeutschen mennonitischen Glaubens als Beitrag für die sippenkundliche Erfassung des Rußlanddeutschtums," *Jahrbuch für auslandsdeutsche Sippenkunde* 2 (1937), 124–33.

51 Quiring, *Grundworte des Glaubens*, 160.
52 Ibid., 161.
53 Ibid., 160.
54 Ibid.
55 Ibid., 161. An article by Dirk Cattepoel, referenced often by denominational leaders, argued that the neighbour "is the one who shares his being, whose blood flows through him, whose soul is his soul. ... Because he must love

and help his neighbor, he will have to destroy the one who threatens the development of that life. ... The German is our neighbor, to whom we are committed with our love and strength. Our neighbor cannot be a Negro, Japanese, or Jew. ... Our limited strengths are claimed by the neighbor and cannot take the others into consideration." Cattepoel, "Mennonit und Wehrwille [Fortsetzung 3]," 43, https://mla.bethelks.edu/gmsources /newspapers/Mennonitische%20Blaetter/1933-1941/DSCF0916.JPG. As a reference point, cf. Emil Händiges to Vereinigung Executive, 27 May 1941, Vereinigung Collection, file folder 1943, MFSt.
56 Quiring, *Grundworte des Glaubens*, 52.
57 Ibid.
58 Horst Quiring, "Kolonisten," *Mennonitisches Lexikon* 2 (Frankfurt am Main/ Weierhof, 1937), 524f.
59 Walter Quiring, "Die Deutschen in Galizien und Wolhynien. Ein abgeschloßenes Kapitel aussendeutscher Volksgeschichte," *Deutschtum im Ausland* 23 (1940): 6–10 at 10; on the importance of the blood purity, see also Quiring, "Kirche, Volk und Staat in mennonitischer Sicht," *Mennonitische Jugendwarte* 17, no. 5 (1937): 103–10 at 108.
60 Johann H. Enns, elder of the Schönwiese Mennonite Church group in Manitoba, in *Mennonitische Warte* 4, no. 42 (1938): 238–9 at 239, https:// mla.bethelks.edu/gmsources/newspapers/Mennonitische%20Warte /DSCF3709.JPG. In explicit contrast to the Germanic-Nordic rhetoric of the day, see the German original of H. Quiring's "Die Anthropologie Pilgrim Marpecks," 10; and Quiring, *Die Begegnung zwischen Deutschtum und Christentum* (Berlin, 1939). While Quiring challenges the extremes of Nordic-Germanic faith, his proposal fits the pattern of those religious-nationalist synthetic conceptions of Germandom and Christendom promoted nationally for a decade, that is, for a fuller permeation of the life of the *Volk* with the spirit of the Gospel. Cf. Kurt Maier, *Die theologischen Fakultäten im Dritten Reich* (Berlin: DeGruyter, 1996), ch. 3.
61 Benjamin Unruh, in *Gemeindeblatt* 69, no. 9 (1 May 1938), 45. Erich Göttner also affirmed the importance of racial research: "Vom Glauben an Gott, III: Gottes Walten und die Rätsel des Daseins," *Mennonitische Blätter* 85, no. 5 (May 1938): 34–35, https://mla.bethelks.edu/gmsources/newspapers /Mennonitische%20Blaetter/1933-1941/DSCF1238.JPG.
62 Heinrich Schröder, *Rußlanddeutsche Friesen* (Döllstädt-Langensalza, 1936), 31. For background, see Gerhard Rempel, "Heinrich Hajo Schroeder: The Allure of Race and Space in Hitler's Empire," *Journal of Mennonite Studies* 29 (2011): 227–54.
63 Schröder, *Rußlanddeutsche Friesen*, 31.
64 Ibid., 85, 30.
65 Ibid., 54. Schröder's work was endorsed without concerns by a range of Mennonite reviewers, including Christian Hege (*Mennonitische*

Geschichtsblätter 1, nos. 1 and 2 (1936), 57f.; Walter (Jacob) Quiring, *Deutsche erschließen den Chaco* (Karlsruhe: Schneider, 1936), 184n41; and Benjamin Unruh, "Die Herkunft der Rußlanddeutschen mennonitischen Glaubens," 132.

66 Cf. Bauman, *Modernity and the Holocaust*, 28, 13.
67 Peter Holquist, "State Violence as Technique: The Logic of Violence in Soviet Totalitarianism," in *Landscaping the Human Garden*, ed. Amir Weiner, 20–2. See also ch. 7 by Dmytro Myeshkov and ch. 8 by Aileen Friesen in this volume.
68 Cf. "Hunger nach dem Deutschen Wort," *Ukraine Post*, no. 12 (3 October 1942): 3f., https://libraria.ua/en/numbers/877/32385. The twenty-five planks of the party platform were unfolded weekly. Platform no. 24 on "positive Christianity" appeared in *Ukraine Post*, no. 10 (13 March 1943): 6, https://libraria.ua/en/numbers/878/32428: "All religions must be tolerated" except "Marxist Judaism," which "tries subversively to immerse itself in the Aryan peoples for its revolutionary ends." Cf. the *Ukraine Post*'s regular column, "Notizbuch der Gegenwart," for example, issues no. 12 (3 October 1942): 4, https://libraria.ua/en/numbers/878/32403; no. 17 (7 November 1942): 6.
69 "Deutsches Eherecht für Volksdeutsche," *Ukraine Post*, no. 30 (10 August 1943): 8, https://libraria.ua/en/numbers/878/32427.
70 "Gemeinschaft des Blutes," *Ukraine Post*, no. 5 (6 February 1943): 4, https://libraria.ua/en/numbers/878/32425.
71 "Deutsche Leistung in der Ukraine," *Ukraine Post*, no. 11 (26 September 1942): 3f., https://libraria.ua/en/numbers/878/32407; "Das Bluterbe der Väter," *Ukraine Post*, no. 9 (6 March 1943): 3, https://libraria.ua/en/numbers/878/32418. Mennonite settlements are also mentioned in "Der Deutsche Zug nach der Ukraine," *Ukraine Post*, no. 15 (24 October 1942): 3, https://libraria.ua/en/numbers/878/32402. "Jugend im Gleichschritt: Lehrgang für Jungen und Mädel im Generalbezirk Dnjepropetrowsk," *Ukraine Post*: no. 22 (5 June 1943): 7, https://libraria.ua/en/numbers/878/32443. Cf. also "Deutschland lebt in seiner Jugend," *Ukraine Post*, no. 12 (3 October 1942): 5, https://libraria.ua/en/numbers/878/32403.
72 Hans Spittler to Emil Händiges, 7 May 1942, copied by Händiges to Benjamin Unruh and Abraham Fast, 18 May 1942, Vereinigung Collection, file folder 1942, MFSt.
73 Ibid. See Helene Berg's memoir of the flight from Russia: *Unsere Flucht. Erinnerungen von Frau Helene Berg, frueher Halbstadt, Sued Russland* (Thomashof bei Karlsruhe/Winkler, MB, 1947).
74 Hans Spittler to Emil Händiges, 7 May 1942, MFSt; Spittler's father was a Ludwigshafen city missionary. Cf. "Deutsche Art dringt durch. Es geht vorwärts in Chortitza," *Ukraine Post*, no. 15 (17 April 1943): 3, https://libraria.ua/en/numbers/878/32431.

148   Arnold Neufeldt-Fast

75 "Bolschewismus = Judentum," *Ukraine Post*, no. 14 (17 October 1942): 4, https://libraria.ua/en/numbers/878/32396; similarly, "Vom Ziel dieses Krieges," *Ukraine Post*, no. 21 (5 December 1943): 1f., https://libraria.ua/en/numbers/878/32397.
76 "Die dunkle Spur des Judentums. Warum ist unser Kampf so hart und schonungslos?," *Ukraine Post*, no. 22 (12 December 1942): 4, https://libraria.ua/en/numbers/878/32406; similarly, "Vor dem Angesicht Jahwes," *Ukraine Post*, no. 19 (15 May 1943): 3, https://libraria.ua/en/numbers/878/32419. On von Leers, see Emil Fackenheim, *The Jewish Thought of Emil Fackenheim: A Reader*, ed. M.L. Morgan (Detroit: Wayne State University Press, 1987), 141.
77 Johann von Leers, "Judas Kriegsziel," *Ukraine Post*, no. 15 (24 October 1942): 1, https://libraria.ua/en/numbers/878/32402; cf. also von Leers, "Vor dem Angesicht Jahwes," *Ukraine Post*, no. 19 (15 May 1943): 3, https://libraria.ua/en/numbers/878/32419.
78 "Folterkammer 7, 8, 9. Inquisitionen in den Gefängnissen," *Ukraine Post*, no. 24 (19 June 1943): 3, https://libraria.ua/en/numbers/878/32439. Similarly – with a twisted use of the biblical text – cf. "'Du wirst alle Völker zehren.' Jüdische Massenmorde in der Geschichte," *Ukraine Post*, no. 26 (3 July 1943): 4, https://libraria.ua/en/numbers/878/32447. "Trotz schwerer Prüfungen. Volksdeutsche Bauern packen wieder an," *Ukraine Post*, no. 26 (3 July 1943): 7, https://libraria.ua/en/numbers/878/32447.
79 "'... daß ihr endlich da seid:' Volksdeutsche umjubeln unsere Soldaten," *Ukraine Post*, no. 24 (24 December 1942): 8, https://libraria.ua/en/numbers/878/32416.
80 Cf. also the *Deutsche Ukraine-Zeitung*, which reported regularly on villages in Molotschna, https://libraria.ua/en/numbers/875. In June 1942, the village of Chorititza received twenty-three copies of each issue of the *Deutsche Ukraine-Zeitung*; cf. "Chorititza [Dorf], Chortitza Kolonie Dorfbericht," 1 June 1942, "Fragebogen Nr. XII b," 7. Reichsminister für die besetzten Ostgebiete, R6, Mappe 622, 81. *Bundesarchiv Koblenz*, https://tsdea.archives.gov.ua/deutsch/table.php?rnum=R_6_622.
81 *Deutsche Ukraine-Zeitung* 1, no. 242 (31 October 1942): 3, https://libraria.ua/en/numbers/875/32007.
82 Former Chortitza district mayor Johann Epp, cited by Unruh for the *Vereinigung* leadership, in Benjamin Unruh to Johann Epp, 5 December 1943, 3a, Vereinigung Collection, file folder 1943, MFSt.
83 Albert Dahl and Katharine Bräul Fast, interview with author, 26 July 2017. Both were children at the time and told the story independently of the other.
84 Nelly Bräul Epp, interview with author, 2016. For similar accounts, cf. Pamela E. Klassen, *Going by the Moon and the Stars: Stories of Two Russian*

Mennonite Women (Waterloo: Wilfrid Laurier University Press, 1994), 85. Similarly, see Susanna Toews, *Trek to Freedom: The Escape of Two Sisters from South Russia during World War II*, translated by Helen Megli (Winkler: Heritage Valley, 1976), 20; "Anna," in Gerhard Lohrenz, ed., *The Lost Generation and Other Stories* (Steinbach: self-published, 1982), 136; Jacob Braun, *Long Road to Freedom* (Winnipeg: Word Alive, 2011), 66f.

85 Cf. Dmytro Myeshkov's work on Dr. Ivan Klassen in chapter 7 of this volume.

86 "Neu-Chortitza, Baratow Kolonie, Dorfbericht," May 1942, "Fragebogen Nr 4," 4. Reichsminister für die besetzten Ostgebiete, R6, Mappe 623, 244–87. *Bundesarchiv Koblenz*, http://chort.square7.ch/Stumpp/stumpp.html. For background, cf. Maria Fiebrandt, *Auslese für die Siedlergesellschaft. Die Einbeziehung Volksdeutscher in die NS-Erbgesundheitspolitik im Kontext der Umsiedlungen 1939–1945* (Göttingen: Vandenhoeck & Ruprecht, 2014), 51.

87 "Schutz gegen Volkszerfall," *Ukraine Post*, no. 8 (27 February 1943): 4, https://libraria.ua/en/numbers/878/32422.

88 Benjamin Unruh to *Vereinigung* Executive, "Vollbericht über die Lagerbesuche," 7 January 1944, 4, Benjamin Unruh Collection, file folder: Correspondence with Abraham Braun, 1930, 1940, 1944–45, MFSt.

89 Cf. Heinrich Hamm, formerly of Dnjepropetrovsk, to kinship researcher in Danzig, Franz Harder, 6 October 1943, *Bundesarchiv Koblenz*. "Auswanderung aus Preussen nach Russland 1787–1854 (Auszüge aus Hypotheken)," 18–20, http://chort.square7.ch/AuswPr.htm.

90 "Das Bluterbe der Väter: Die biologische Kraft der Volksdeutschen in der Ukraine," *Ukraine Post*, no. 9 (6 March 1943): 3, https://libraria.ua/en/numbers/878/32418.

91 Cf. *Mennonitische Blätter* 85, no. 9 (1938): 61, https://mla.bethelks.edu/gmsources/newspapers/Mennonitische%20Blaetter/1933-1941/DSCF1265.JPG; Emil Händiges to Gustav Reimer, 13 May 1942, 2, in Vereinigung Collection, file folder 1942, MFSt; Walter Kuhn, "Die mennonitische Altkolonie Chortitza in der Ukraine," Sonderabdruck aus den *Deutschen Monatsheften. Zeitschrift für Geschichte und Gegenwart des Ostdeutschtums* 9, no. 19 (September–October–November 1942): 1–40 at 40 (Kuhn's italics).

92 Kuhn, "Die mennonitische Altkolonie Chortitza in der Ukraine," 38.

93 Ibid. Cf. "Neue ukrainische Schulbücher," *Deutsche Ukraine-Zeitung* 1, no. 92 (8 May 1942): 3, https://libraria.ua/en/numbers/875/32088 (11).

94 "Umschulungslager für volksdeutsche Lehrer," *Deutsche Bug-Zeitung* 1, no. 8 (8 April 1942): 4, https://libraria.ua/en/numbers/1/32541.

95 Cf. Alexander Pinwinkler, "Walter Kuhn (1903–1983) und der Bielitzer 'Wandervogel e.V.,'" *Zeitschrift für Volkskunde* 105, no. 1 (2009): 29–51 at 44, 45. Benjamin Unruh and Karl Stumpp had worked together in the Stuttgart-based Deutschland Ausland-Institut in the late 1930s; its goal

was to do "family-oriented and racial-biological research on all Russian Germans across the world": Eric J. Schmaltz and Samuel D. Sinner, "Nazi Ethnographic Research of Georg Leibbrandt and Karl Stumpp in Ukraine, and Its North American Legacy," *Holocaust and Genocide Studies* 14, no. 1 (2000): 28–64 at 56. Cf. also *Mennonitische Geschichtsblätter* 3, no. 1 & 2 (December 1938): 97, 99.

96 Meeting notes, 16 July 1941, in Czeslaw Madajcyzk, ed., *Vom Generalplan Ost zum General-Siedlungsplan* (Munich: Sauer, 1994), no. 3, 15–19. Adolf Hitler, "17 September 1941," in *Hitler's Table Talk, 1941–1944: His Private Conversations*, 3rd ed., trans. N. Cameron and R. H. Stevens (New York: Enigma, 2008) 29, 436.

97 Adolf Hitler, "October 17, 1941," in Madajcyzk, *Vom Generalplan Ost zum Generalsiedlungsplan*, no. 6, 22.

98 "Rotfeld, Baratow Kolonie, Dorfbericht," July 1942, "Fragebogen Nr 4," 2. Reichsminister für die besetzten Ostgebiete, R6, Mappe 623, 288–312. *Bundesarchiv Koblenz*. http://chort.square7.ch/Stumpp/stumpp.html.

99 Cf. Pinwinkler, "Walter Kuhn (1903–1983)," 46f. Notably, Kuhn's divisive racial perspectives were welcomed in North America well after the war. Cf. Walter Kuhn, "Cultural Achievements of the Chortitza Mennonites," *Mennonite Life* 3, no. 3 (July 1948): 35–48, esp. 38.

100 See sample in Justina D. Neufeld, *A Family Torn Apart* (Kitchener: Pandora, 2003), 102. For context, cf. J. Otto Pohl, *Ethnic Cleansing in the USSR, 1937–1949* (Westport: Greenwood, 1999), 44f.

101 In Litzmannstadt from March 14 to 16, 1944, Greiser hosted the first conference of the Regional and District Leaders of the Nazi Party (NSDAP) Wartheland. In the addresses, the resettlement challenges were addressed; cf. "Die Parole. Alles für den Sieg," *Litzmannstädter Zeitung* 27, no. 79 (19 March 1944): 1, http://bc.wimbp.lodz.pl/publication/31097.

102 In Catherine Epstein, *Model Nazi: Arthur Greiser and the Occupation of Western Poland* (Oxford: Oxford University Press, 2010), 191. At this point, about 23 per cent of Warthegau's population was German: Epstein, *Model Nazi*, 192. Cf. "Der millionste Deutsche im Wartheland angesiedelt," *Litzmannstädter Zeitung* 27, no. 75 (15 March 1944): 1, http://bc.wimbp.lodz.pl/publication/31097.

103 Bericht über Verhandlungen in Warthegau im März 1944 (30 March 1944), 6b, Benjamin Unruh Collection, file folder: Correspondence with Abraham Braun, MFSt.

104 Valdis Lumans, "Reassessment of *Volksdeutsche* and Jews in the Volhynia-Galicia Narew Resettlement," in *The Impact of Nazism: New Perspectives on the Third Reich and Its Legacy*, ed. Alan E. Steinweis and Daniel E. Rogers, 81–100 (Lincoln: University of Nebraska Press, 2003), 97.
Lumans challenges the causal claim found in Götz Aly, *"Final Solution"*:

Nazi Population Policy and the Murder of European Jews (London: Arnold, 1999).

105 Bericht an Herrn SS-Obersturmführer Dr. Wolfrum über meine Lagerbesuche in Oberschlesien, January 1944, in Benjamin Unruh Collection, file folder: Correspondence with Abraham Braun, MFSt.

106 "Satzung der Mennonitischen Gemeindekirche im Wartheland" (March 1944 Submission), Vereinigung Collection, file folder 1944, MFSt.

107 Benjamin Unruh to Vereinigung Executive, 27 December 1943, 2, Vereinigung Collection, file folder 1943, MFSt.

108 Cited in Aryeh L. Unger, *The Totalitarian Party: Party and People in Nazi Germany and Soviet Russia* (Cambridge: Cambridge University Press, 1974), 174.

109 Karl Götz, *Das Schwarzmeerdeutschtum. Die Mennoniten* (Posen: NS-Druck Wartheland, 1944), 11f.; cf. "Karl Götz über den Leidensweg der Schwarzmeerdeutschen," *Litzmannstädter Zeitung* 27, no. 88 (28 March 1944): 4, http://bc.wimbp.lodz.pl/publication/31097.

110 Helene Dueck, *Durch Trübsal und Not* (Winnipeg: Centre for Mennonite Brethren Studies, 1995), 49.

111 Ingeborg Fleischhauer, *Das Dritte Reich und die Deutschen in der Sowjetunion* (Stuttgart: Deutsches Verlags-Anstalt, 1983), 228, citing a report by SS-Oberscharführer Dr R. Foerster, Litzmannstadt, March 1942.

112 Jacob H. Janzen to Peter J. Braun, 17 May 1933, 3, MS 91, folder 4, MLA. https://mla.bethelks.edu/archives/ms_91/folder_4/SKMBT_C35107 121311010_0015.jpg.

113 In 1941, Benjamin Unruh attempted to organize a theological working group comprised of Mennonite ministers with graduate theological degrees, but many had already been conscripted. Cf. 3 January 1941 and 12 February 1941, Vereinigung Collection, file folder 1941, MFSt.

114 Cf. Hans A. Schmitt, *Quakers and Nazis: Inner Light in Outer Darkness* (Columbia: University of Missouri Press, 1997), 175, based on conversations with Unruh's son Heinrich. On the Madagascar Plan, cf. Christopher R. Browning, *Origins of the Final Solution: The Evolution of Nazi Jewish Policy, September 1939–March 1942* (Lincoln: University of Nebraska Press, 2004), 85f.

115 Cf. the 1938 annual report by Elder Ernst Regehr of Rosenort, West Prussia, chair, "Arbeitsgemeinschaft für mennonitische Sippenkunde," *Mennonitische Warte* 4, no. 38 (June 1938): 214–20 at 220.

116 Cf. the June 1949 Thomashof Declaration: "Erklärung," *Gemeindeblatt der Mennoniten* 80, no. 24 (15 December 1949): 101. The twenty-five signatories from all parts of Germany included Dirk Cattepoel and Benjamin Unruh. https://mla.bethelks.edu/gmsources/newspapers/Gemeindeblatt%20 der%20Mennoniten/1948-1953/DSCF7989.JPG.

117 Dirk Cattepoel, "The Mennonites of Germany, 1936–1948, and the Present Outlook," *Proceedings of the Fourth Mennonite World Conference, Goshen, Indiana and North Newton, Kansas, August 3–10, 1948* (Akron: Mennonite Central Committee, 1950), 14f. More fully, however, see Cattepoel's 1946 sermon cited in Götz Lichdi, *Mennoniten im Dritten Reich*, 162f.
118 "50 Jahre nach Kriegsende. Erklärung der Mitgliederversammlung der Arbeitsgemeinschaft Mennonitischer Gemeinden in Deutschland am 10. Juni 1995 in Karlsruhe-Thomashof," http://www.mennoniten.de /ressourcen/stellungnahmen/archiv.
119 See also ch. 7 by Dmytro Meshkov, ch. 11 by Hans Werner, and ch. 12 by Steven Schroeder in this volume.
120 "Article 23: The Church's Relation to Government and Society," *Confession of Faith in a Mennonite Perspective* (Scottdale: Herald Press, 1995), 86.
121 Cf. Waldemar Janzen, *Exodus*, Believers Church Bible Commentary Series (Scottdale: Herald Press, 2000), 43; also John E. Toews, *Romans*, Believers Church Bible Commentary Series (Scottdale: Herald Press, 2004), 277–85.
122 Hans-Jürgen Goertz, "Future of the Mennonite Brotherhood," *Mennonite Life* 22, no. 4 (October 1967), 156–8 at 156.
123 Jürgen Moltmann, *The Crucified God: The Cross of Christ as the Foundation and Criticism of Christian Theology* (Minneapolis: Fortress, 1994), 274; citing E. Wiesel, *Night* (New York: Avon, 1969), 75f.
124 H. Quiring, *Grundworte des Glaubens*, 113.
125 Z. Bauman, *Modernity and the Holocaust*, 53.

Chapter Five

Dutch Mennonite Theologians and Nazism

PIETER POST

It is not yet known how many Dutch Mennonite ministers were National Socialists. Based on the portraits he wrote of five National Socialist ministers, Gabe G. Hoekema concludes there were no war criminals among them.¹ Yet, though demonstrating little inclination toward discrimination and murder, they did not distance themselves from such actions in public.

Before entering into the subject of my study on Dutch Mennonite theologians and Nazism, it is necessary to establish that Hoekema reaches this conclusion through his treatment of the question as to why these ministers were attracted to the National Socialist thought involving Hitler's ideal state. There were various reasons for this. As Christians they resisted a socialism that denied religion. They resisted the economically liberal political line followed by the prevailing Christian government in the 1930s. They were influenced by German family ties. Sometimes the choice to take a pro-German attitude was also stimulated by a historical interest.

Hoekema's study is part of a series of articles about Dutch Mennonites in the Second World War. At the same time, it fits in with overviews about the Dutch Mennonite attitude toward National Socialism published earlier, with events in congregations, and with individual experiences of Dutch Mennonites.² For purposes of historiography, a study of the aid Dutch Mennonites provided to Protestant German refugees with Jewish backgrounds in the Netherlands should be mentioned.³ Taken together, these studies provide an overview of Mennonite activities in the period before the war and the time of the German occupation.

What is still missing, however, is the thinking on theology during this dark period. Choosing from the broad range of historical themes, I will focus on the theological thought of two Dutch Mennonite contemporaries who were political opponents. The Mennonite minister Cornelis Bonne Hylkema (1870–1948) was the party ideologist of the violent National Socialist Movement (NSB, Nationaal Socialistische Beweging). Frits Kuiper (1898–1974), by contrast, was a pacifist and a social democrat. In publications on the topic of Mennonites and Nazis, both ministers, but especially Frits Kuiper, among others, are mentioned frequently. A view of their behaviour can be formed from this as background to my own research, which is about their thought. This article, therefore, has two parts: I first provide a sketch of the most important conclusions of the studies about Dutch Mennonite involvement in the years before the war, then discuss the thought of Hylkema and Kuiper.

Elisabeth I.T. Brussee-van der Zee centres her study on this question: what influence did the character of the Dutch Mennonite community have on its attitude toward National Socialism between 1933 and 1940?[4] Her conclusion is that the Mennonites generally tolerated expressions of National Socialism.

In her view, the most important reasons for that tolerance were the non-political character of the Mennonite community and its free-thinking and liberalism. She further observes that there was little reflection in Anabaptist theology about life views that threatened the freedom of the Gospel. She found nothing at all in this period about how the Mennonites thought about the place of the congregation in the world.

Nevertheless, among the anti-militaristic Task Force against Military Service (Arbeidsgroep tegen de Krijgsdienst), led by Frits Kuiper, some attention was given to the dangers of National Socialism. This task force was part of the Church Renewal Movement (Gemeentedagbeweging), a revitalizing movement in the Netherlands, established in 1917 after inspiring visits to the Woodbrooke Quaker Centre in England. The main purpose of this movement was to offer a counterweight to the modernistic, bourgeois trend in nineteenth-century Dutch Anabaptism. That trend had nourished individualism and freedom of belief. Yet strictly speaking, this movement cannot be considered a separate confessional one. The Gathered Church Movement wanted to give new impulse to a life of faith and what it meant to be a congregation. After the horrors of the First World War and over the following century, this movement was of tremendous importance for the revitalization of the principle of non-resistance and anti-militarism. An important result of this movement was the founding of conference centres (*Broederschapshuizen*), Dutch Mennonite fellowship centres, in Elspeet, in the Province of Gelderland, in "Fredeshiem" near Steenwijk, in Overijssel, and in Schoorl, North Holland. These centres were established as meeting places to encourage fellowship. Besides the extensive practical work that preceded the war years, achieved through encounters, spiritual exercises, games, and relaxation, there were also theological lectures and political and religious discussions; but above all, there was much singing. In response to the international tensions of the 1930s and the war years, the Dutch Mennonite community centres took in refugees. This will be discussed further below.

At the same time, the governing body of the General Mennonite Conference (Algemene Doopsgezinde Sociëteit; ADS) feared a break with the international Mennonite community. This was evident in the preparations for the General Congress of Mennonites (Algemeen Congres van Doopsgezinden), the forerunner of the Mennonite World Conference, held in the Netherlands in 1936. The ADS governing body rejected a lecture by Frits Kuiper titled "The Mennonites and Violence," fearing that the German brothers and sisters would not like it. The Americans would have appreciated it very much, but the organizers were loath to invite a confrontation during the conference. Nevertheless, Frits Kuiper and the American C. Henry Smith of Bluffton University, Ohio, held a dual lecture about "Mennonites and Culture," in which an antimilitaristic position was presented, albeit cautiously.

Brussee-van der Zee concluded that all in all, the ADS governing body appeared unable to represent the Dutch Mennonite voice against life views that threatened the church's freeedom. The Church Renewal Movement, however, expressed a position against National Socialism in terms of Anabaptist theology and history. At the same time, the people of the revitalizing movement were not silent with respect to the Mennonites in Germany. Individual Dutch Mennonites committed themselves to helping people who had fled to the Netherlands for reasons of race, faith, or politics.

Frits Kuiper's name appears repeatedly in connection with the Church Renewal Movement and the preparations for the General Congress of Mennonites. Cornelis B. Hylkema is mentioned twice in a footnote in connection with a debate about National Socialism, but that is all.

Gerlof D. Homan conducted empirical historical research on war-related events in the various congregations and on the experiences of members.[5] A number of Mennonite churches and parsonages were destroyed or heavily damaged by enemy as well as Allied bombing. The Germans confiscated other church buildings, and congregations fell apart as a result of evacuations. A particular challenge for congregations was to protect Mennonites with a Jewish background. The German authorities decided that Jews would not be deported if they belonged to a church where their parents were also members before

1 January 1941. Unbaptized Jews were not, however, saved by this measure. "Falsification" in order to indicate that parents were members was one option for keeping not only Jewish Mennonites, but also Jewish Christians of other churches, out of German hands.

The fact that there were NSB members in the church pews made congregations very insecure. In one congregation, a Mennonite NSBer brought two Germans into the church so that they could ascertain whether the sermons were anti-German. In another congregation, a Mennonite NSBer was condemned to death for betraying a member of the underground. A very unusual situation developed in a congregation where an underground leader was arrested. After the liberation, it was discovered that another Mennonite had betrayed him. The judge, the lawyer, and the witnesses all appeared to be Mennonite, with the result that the accused was acquitted.

Some ministers tried to convert NSBers in their congregations, usually to no effect. It is reported that one minister tried to convert the son of a member who belonged to both the NSB and the SS and who assisted in rounding up Jews, but without result. Yet this minister received valuable information from other Mennonite NSBers. The uncertainty the congregations experienced around this time had a great deal to do with how much they could trust the brothers and sisters who were members of the NSB.[6]

According to Homan, Frits Kuiper was one of the most outspoken of the ministers who rejected National Socialism. Quite loudly, he called the governing body of the General Mennonite Conference to account, declaring that they should resist the NSB's interference in the church's work. Homan also views Cornelis B. Hylkema as the most prominent of the NSB ministers. Hylkema accepted the racism of National Socialism in his book *Ras en Toekomst* (Race and the Future), which he wrote with his son.[7] In his view, Jews were not like the Aryans, for they were neither honest, nor proud, nor courageous. Jews were plutocrats and Bolsheviks. He approved of the Nazis' Nuremberg laws against the Jews and was in favour of transferring European Jews to Dutch, French, and British Guyana. Homan ignores the question of whether Hylkema was antisemitic.

Alle G. Hoekema reports on the practical aid given to refugees by Mennonites in the 1930s and later on during the war.[8] In the course of this work, they had close contact with other Protestant aid organizations, representatives of German Protestants, and the Ministry of the Interior. He describes this aid as a high point in Dutch Mennonite history.

With respect to the twentieth century, the Dutch Mennonite Emigration Office (HDEB, Hollandsch Doopsgezinde Emigratie Bureau) in

Rotterdam, established specifically for the purpose, arranged transportation to Mexico, Paraguay, and Brazil for hundreds of fleeing Russian and Ukrainian Mennonites, until at least 1934. Then, two years later, Dutch Mennonites offered the shelter of their fellowship centres to Hutterites from the *Rhonbrüderhof* who had been ordered by the Gestapo to leave Germany within forty-eight hours.[9] With the support of the Mennonite conference, they could continue their journey to their fellow believers in England after a few months. In addition, the Mennonite Aid Office (DHB, Doopsgezinde Hulp Bureau) was established for relief work during the period of mobilization and war. Among other things, this organization sheltered dozens of families from Rotterdam who had lost their homes in the German bombardment of May 1940.

After Germany annexed Austria in 1938, the Mennonite fellowship centres in Elspeet, Fredeshiem, and Schoorl opened their doors to 106 refugees. In Fredeshiem, a few dozen Jewish children from Vienna who had been baptized as Protestants were taken in. These had come without their parents.

When Germany invaded Poland in September 1939, refugees began streaming from Germany. For their relief, the Dutch Mennonites set up the Task Force of Mennonites and Kindred Spirits (WDG, Werkgemeenschap Doopsgezinden en Geestverwanten), with offices in Amsterdam, Rotterdam, and Groningen. Earlier, organized cooperation with the Quakers had failed, although they later appeared to be prepared to assist incidentally. Religion, political convictions, and race did not play a role, however, because of the urgency of relief.

An important project was sending food parcels to the transit camp of Westerbork, where the Nazis corralled Jews before deporting them to extermination camps. Within a year, this endeavour had grown from 10 or 20 parcels a week to 600 or 700 parcels a week. Besides offering aid to German Jewish Christian refugees and poor families from Rotterdam, the organization cared for the relatives of deceased resistance fighters by providing food coupons. In the Zaan area in particular, there was a strong social network among Mennonite industrialists and members of the Task Force against Military Service. They operated an illegal network and hid Jews in their homes. After the war, the WDG declared itself in favour, on principle, of reinstating collaborators in society after they had served their time. The WDG also made a case for finding loving foster homes for the children of parents who had been in league with the Germans. It is not clear whether the WDG actually undertook this. It did, though, constitute the motivation for establishing the Mennonite Peace Group (DVG, Doopsgezind Vredesgroep) in 1946, the successor to the Task Force against Military Service.

Hylkema is not mentioned in Hoekema's report, whereas Kuiper comes up several times. This is not so surprising, given the latter's role in the resistance, his inter-church contacts, and his involvement in *Vrij Nederland* (The Free Netherlands), an underground newspaper of the resistance. Kuiper was a central figure in a large network. He has been described as principled, sharp, keen, clear, and community-minded. For example, he favoured relief work based on the principle of peace work. He also suggested opening community houses for refugees. In the field of theology, he was the only Mennonite who published anything on Israel as a state after the war, viewing it as the benchmark of Christian theology.[10]

Kuiper and Hylkema: Posing the Problem

Cornelis Bonne Hylkema and Frits Kuiper were opponents with respect to the relationship between politics and Anabaptist theology. Hylkema has been referred to as the NSB's fascist ideologist.[11] During the occupation from 1940 to 1945, the NSB collaborated with the Germans. Kuiper was chairman of the Task Force against Military Service, which assisted conscientious objectors, as well as a member of Church and Peace and of the Social Democratic Labor Party (SDAP, Sociaal-Democratische Arbeiderspartij).[12]

These two men took opposing sides at meetings of ministers and at other gatherings, where they expounded their differing views of Christianity and Anabaptism.[13] What position did they, as Mennonites, who are known for their theology of community, take on the state, parliamentary democracy, and the monopoly on violence at a time when Hitler was preparing his politics of annexation? Were their arguments motivated by Anabaptism? Where did they draw the boundary between the faith community and the world? The period of concern here is the first stage of the NSB, beginning in 1933. At that time, Italian fascism, which did not have an antisemitic bias, was still a strong inspiration.[14]

We should position both ministers in a Mennonite context in which non-violence was no longer being propounded as an absolute and the general religious climate was liberal. That is to say, the ADS did not have a generally adopted church order such that sanctions could be imposed on members who were out of harmony with the principle of non-resistance, for instance. The position taken by the ADS was that it should be possible for all political convictions to exist side by side in a congregation. Neutrality and freedom were important characteristics of Dutch Mennonite liberalism. In practice, this meant that people with National Socialist sympathies could continue to perform their ministry, or their service in a governing body.¹⁵ Yet journals and ministerial associations spoke of their uneasiness about what was happening in Germany. There, the ADS governing body was being urged to take a position on the dangers of National Socialism.¹⁶ Clearly, Dutch Mennonites were divided over the ADS's political position. The ADS secretary, Reverend A.A. Sepp, a National Socialist, was not trusted, and he resigned.¹⁷

I will analyse four aspects of the views of Hylkema and Kuiper: (1) the relationship between church and state, (2) Anabaptists and their arguments, (3) non-resistance, and (4) the faith community. But I will begin by asking who they were.

Who Were Hylkema and Kuiper?

Cornelis Bonne Hylkema, PhD, and retired minister of Haarlem, saw himself as a historian and an idealist. He had studied theology at the Mennonite Seminary and served three congregations. Hylkema and his wife Goverta de Clercq were both deeply involved in the Mennonite fellowship centre in Elspeet. Of their three sons and one daughter, all but the second son joined the NSB in 1933. Hylkema was originally a supporter of democracy. Later he adhered to the principle of leadership, being of the opinion that the Dutch parliamentary system should be replaced by a strong leader.¹⁸ Such a leadership system would be characterized by personal responsibility: the responsibility from the bottom up, and the decision-making from above to below.

In 1932, he wrote up a rational, empirical religious ideology in a book titled *Werkelijkheidstheologie* (The Theology of Reality). In it, he declared that we can know God only through reality. And humans have a religious instinct by nature. This instinct had evolved in such a way that humans ultimately attained fulfilment and truth in self-sacrifice.¹⁹ Self-sacrifice was the noblest characteristic of the new era and the new human being, the *homo fascistus*.²⁰

His *Werkelijkheidstheologie* may be viewed as providing the theological foundation for his second book, *Het Nederlandsch Fascisme* (Dutch Fascism), published in 1934. In that book, he tries to give a Dutch twist to a fascism by tracing it back to the humanist tradition of the Brethren of the Common Life and Erasmus of Rotterdam.²¹ *Het Nederlandsch Fascisme* was a bestseller until 1937, when it was banned.²²

After an electoral defeat in 1937, bowing to pressure from within, the NSB leader A.A. Mussert adopted German Nazism, including its racist antisemitism.²³ Hylkema would later claim that he was never a propagandist, even though he was listed as one.²⁴ After the liberation in 1945,

5.1. Cornelis B. Hylkema

he and his wife Goverta were arrested, interrogated, and imprisoned for fifteen months. Hylkema died in 1948.

Reverend Frits Kuiper was a minister in Alkmaar during the war. His family included intellectual Mennonite ministers on both sides. As a theology student, he attended the lectures of the socialist theologian Karl Barth. He helped alleviate the famine among fellow students in the Russian city of Kazan. There he learned to appreciate Bolshevik values, though he later sharply criticized its approach to human rights and the return of capitalism.[25] Back in the Netherlands, he joined the SDAP in 1925. He regarded the party as giving form to the political aspect of the biblical call to justice. Although opponents lumped the SDAP together with the Bolsheviks, the party strongly rejected dictatorship and terror.[26] This explains why the pacifistic Kuiper could join this political party.

During the occupation, in 1941, he published the book *Gemeente in de wereld* (The Faith Community in the World) to give people heart in the event that the church was forbidden.[27] Kuiper was involved in the resistance. He helped to hide Jews and worked on the newspaper of the underground resistance, *The Free Netherlands*, as noted earlier.

5.2. Frits Kuiper

Because of the help he gave to Jews, and also because of his bond with the State of Israel in 1948, he was honoured with a park in the Ben Shemen Forest in Modi'in in Israel after his death in 1974.[28]

Church and State

What positions did Hylkema and Kuiper take regarding the state?

Hylkema emphasized Jesus's devotion to the love of God. This was to serve as an example for National Socialists,[29] who were expected to be prepared to submit themselves to the creation order that the Almighty God had provided, and of which the nation was a part.[30] The National Socialist asked "What can I give?" instead of "What do I get?" The church could function freely in this creation order so long as it presented no danger to the fascist state. Many people in the NSB were perturbed about this.[31] According to Hylkema, it was therefore necessary to pay close attention to what ministers were preaching. The *Weerafdeling*, the NSB's paramilitary wing, would take harsh action against spiritual leaders who raised themselves above others and who took it upon themselves to pass moral judgment on the fascist ideal state.[32] Hylkema opposed the testimony of Church and Peace that the Gospel and war were irreconcilable opposites, and he rejected the organization's call for total disarmament.[33] The church should stay with its calling to proclaim eternity, and it should form politicians into humble personalities.[34] Naturally, God, who is above all governments, should be obeyed above others when the impossible is demanded in a dictatorship. But that pertained to extreme cases, for fascism did not propagate an absolute state.[35] The standard rule for the fascist was always: stay within the law, even when you are treated unjustly, no matter what form the state takes.[36]

Kuiper's objection to National Socialism was based on a strict separation of church and state.[37] The faith community was part of the state, but it needed to keep the interference of other ideologies at bay. By being conscious of Christ, the church maintained its independence and its ability to proclaim God's message to all the powers of the world.[38] That meant the church's task was to remind the individual and society of God and his commandments. This involved pointing out to society that it should not slide into idolatry, as was happening in Germany, where the Aryan race, the nation, and the doctrine of leadership were being glorified. In short, the faith community was *in* the world and simultaneously *in confrontation* with it.

Dialectically, Kuiper transferred this to the position of Christ against Pilate.[39] The faith community and the world were always in conflict because they both wanted to control human beings. But the ultimate victory of Christ meant that the church should turn away from militarism and National Socialism.

Anabaptism

How did Hylkema and Kuiper employ Anabaptism in their arguments?

Hylkema spoke negatively about liberals in general, who were in favour of democracy. He criticized the multi-party system, which upheld the popular sovereignty of the people but undermined corporate popular strength. He referred to democracy as an illusion. Since the liberal Mennonites were on the side of democracy, they were a bad odour for him.[40]

He did not mention Anabaptism explicitly as a source of inspiration for his ideas in either of his books, but he was recognizably theologically Anabaptist when he posited that faith and works are one.[41] For him, faith was belief in self-sacrifice. This clearly revealed the fascist's inner motivation of love and perseverance for the ideal state and for the authority of the general leader.

Kuiper was in favour of social democracy.[42] Such a system allowed Christians to choose freely which party would best fulfil biblical justice. For him, socialism was the expression of justice. And for this reason, he was convinced that Dutch Mennonites should acknowledge Karl Marx and the socialist movement.[43] Mennonites, as Christian socialists, should always take a stand against injustice toward fellow citizens and the working class and against a ban on worship and a Christian upbringing. Kuiper linked the unity of faith and works with resistance to injustice. This could well go hand in hand with making sacrifices, including of one's own life. The faith community had to be prepared to suffer, for that was how it would preserve its independence.[44]

In other sources, Mennonite NSBers drew a parallel between the Anabaptist congregational model and the national community of the NSB. Mennonites came out for the furtherance of community, and not primarily for the minister. In the same way, the individual in National Socialism existed for the national community.[45] Where the importance of the community above the individual was concerned, there was no difference between the NSB and the Anabaptist faith community.[46]

Non-Resistance

What role did non-resistance play in their considerations?

Hylkema agreed that violence and war were not in the spirit of Christ, but he himself was not a pacifist.[47] He did not reject anti-militarism, but neither did he approve of conscientious objectors. For him, the latter betrayed a faulty understanding of Christianity: a Christian people was armed and able-bodied. The fascist had to fight in the name of God. In this light, it is remarkable that, while being interrogated after the war, he wrote off German violence off as "psychotic unpleasantness."[48] He illustrated his view by pointing to Anabaptist ancestors who were against the Inquisition, the death penalty, and bearing arms. The NSB displayed the opposite. Actually, Hylkema was trapped between his fascist ideology, which had failed, and the reality of Anabaptist non-violent history.

Kuiper realized that non-resistance had not penetrated deeply enough in the congregations. He connected non-resistance to a total concentration on Christ's victory. In this light, every nation was transient and there was no reason to worship the nation or authorities. It was the Christian's calling to witness to God and his kingdom. Christians had the freedom to say no to military service.[49] But he experienced a turning point when the Germans executed two of his nephews by firing squad. Shortly after the liberation, he let his good friend Cornelius Krahn know that he no longer had the courage to continue with peace work.[50] He realized that he did not truly hold to non-resistance any longer. But later he would attend Mennonite peace conferences again.

Faith Community

What was their vision of the faith community of which they were members?

According to Hylkema, the church derived its meaning from the proclamation of grace.[51] Grace restored our self-confidence and our trust in God. This made the church "a place of refuge for the spirit" in a "turbulent reality." This applied to people inside and outside the faith community. All would find forgiveness and justification there. Hylkema proceeded from a common grace, granted to all people with no regard for their religion. This idea was in keeping with classical Dutch Anabaptism, which teaches a common grace, but it was also in keeping with the universalism and humanism of the fascist ideal.[52] He put this into practice by appearing at the Sunday service the day after his release, but a colleague asked him not to show up again. He felt pierced to the heart, as he wrote to the church council. He withdrew into solitude. The question is whether he was able to enter into the feelings of the faith community enough. But there is also the question: how abundant is common grace?

During the war, there were members of the NSB in Kuiper's congregation, but this did not lead to betrayal. He continued to preach openheartedly, and he held firmly to the principle of the faith community as a service of reconciliation.[53] As in many other congregations, the burning question after the war was how to deal with the brothers and sisters who had been released from detention camps.[54] In Kuiper's congregation, members considered it a Christian duty to take those who had been condemned back into the congregation immediately. Sometimes it took years before reconciliation occurred.[55]

> It was 1967. As the June wind blew softly across the Redstar, they sighed: If we were to organize a teach-in. ... A month later it happened.[56] The little Mennonite Church in Oudebildtzijl filled up nicely that evening with

older Mennonites *and* young people of all sorts. Homework and handball suddenly seemed unimportant. The church council was delighted, though a bit nervous. … Then there were the obligatory little introductions. From a dark church pew, a polite question was put. But it did not catch on at all.

Outside, the rushing around of a late potato farmer could be heard. Then it happened. The sea wind tugged a wagonload of *ruach* along, setting two people in motion. Suddenly Bouwe de Boer stood up, a man of age 60 at the time. Determined, unstoppable, he said in Bildts, the language of the village:

> You all know that I was on the wrong side during the war. And if you didn't know it yet, you know it now. I was an NSB-er. I regret that choice. I did not see it in the right way, and I did wrong. But I had to get on with things after the war. And it was this here, this congregation here, this was the place where I could start over.

He began perspiring. He looked around and concluded, "I feel that you should know this." Bouwe de Boer had spoken, in utter vulnerability. It was deathly quiet in the Mennonite Church in Oudebildtzijl.

Then the late wind from the Wadden was pleased to set Inne de Groot on his feet.[57] He was a big man, and strong, and very emotional. He began in this way:

> I have something to tell you, too. I was on the other side in '40–'45. I was in the resistance. And I do not regret it. If it becomes necessary anew, I will do it again. But when the war was over, in our village, too, I thought, "Where can I make a new start?" And then I got baptized. For this little church here was that place at that time. And we succeeded pretty well, starting over, eh Bouwe?"

And then the carpenter Inne de Groot went over to the farmer Bouwe de Boer, and they shook hands with great emotion. And the Holy Spirit drifted off to the Frisian shallows and was satisfied. Two highly respected men had witnessed of their Resurrection. Both rose from the dead, a fascinating messianic event.

Conclusion

In summary, we have situated the Mennonites Kuiper and Hylkema in an Anabaptist-historical and social-political context. What theological positions did they take as supporter and opponent of National Socialism?

In systematic terms, Hylkema maintained the idea of a creation order, and he applied the principle of leadership to this. Decisions were made from above to below, which required responsibility from below to above. In this watertight hierarchy, there could be no contribution from outside the line.

Kuiper condemned this as enslavement and fatalism.[58] According to Kuiper, social democracy gave direction to society, for which everyone was personally responsible. He thought and acted with the kingdom of Christ as starting point, against the powers of the world, whereby Christ was presumed the victor even though his struggle was not yet over.

What made their positions even more complicated were their hermeneutics. Here and there they applied the same biblical texts to their personal vision of faith. A Bible text such as "Do not rule, but serve," was used by Hylkema as support for subjection to fascism, while Kuiper saw it as support for the faith community in the world.[59]

The result of the positions taken by these two was that Dutch Mennonites kept quiet about Hylkema soon after the war, while Kuiper was honoured for a long time after.[60]

NOTES

This article was translated from Dutch into English by Lydia Penner. An earlier, Dutch version of this article appeared in *Doopsgezinde Bijdragen* 45 (Hilversum: Verloren, 2019): 271–94.

1 Gabe G. Hoekema, "Idealisten en baasjes met oogkleppen voor. Voorgangers van doopsgezinde gemeenten die van 1933 tot 1945 aangesproken werden door het gedachtegoed van de NSB of tijdens de oorlog meewerkten met de Duitse bezetter," *Doopsgezinde Bijdragen* 41 (2015): 183–246.
2 E.I.T. Brussee-van der Zee, "De Doopsgezinde Broederschap en het nationaal-socialisme, 1933–1940," *Doopsgezinde Bijdragen* 11 (1985): 118–29; Gerlof D. Homan, "Nederlandse doopsgezinden in de Tweede Wereldoorlog," *Doopsgezinde Bijdragen* 21 (1995): 165–97. Other works by Homan include: "'We hebben ze lief gekregen.' Het verblijf van Russische mennonieten in Nederland van 1945–1947," *Doopsgezinde Bijdragen* 32 (2006): 225–53. See the English version of this article, "'We Have Come to Love Them': Russian Mennonite Refugees in the Netherlands, 1945–1947," *Journal of Mennonite Studies* 25 (2011): 39–59. See also Gerlof D. Homan, "Een doopsgezinde gemeente in oorlogstijd. Zuid-Limburg, Heerlen," *Doopsgezinde Bijdragen* 31 (2005): 263–76. Further, see *Doopsgezinde Bijdragen* 41 (2015), with the theme "Mennonites during the Second World War."

3 Alle G. Hoekema, *'Bloembollen' voor Westerbork. Hulp aan Zaanse en andere doopsgezinden aan (protestants) Joodse Duitse vluchtelingen in Nederland* (Hilversum, 2011). Hoekema (b. 1941) is Gabe G. Hoekema's brother; he was a lecturer for the Doopsgezinde Zendingsraad (Mennonite Mission Board) in Indonesia, minister in two Dutch congregations, lecturer at the Mennonite Seminary in Amsterdam, and senior lecturer of missiology at the VU University. He has published various books and many articles about Christian theology in Asia, among other things. In English there's also Alle G. Hoekema, "Dutch Mennonites and German Jewish Refugee Children, 1938–1945," *The Mennonite Quarterly Review* (April 2013): 133–54. See also ch. 9 on Mennonites and Yad Vashem recognition in this volume.
4 Brussee-van der Zee, "De Doopsgezinde Broederschap." E.I.T. Brussee-van der Zee (1948–2019) was minister in seven Mennonite congregations and lecturer in Practical Theology at the Mennonite Seminary. See also L. van der Zee and A. Klinefelter-Koopmans, *Mediation in het Pastoraat* (Utrecht 2012). In English: "Mediation in Pastoral Care," Elkhart, IN, Institute of Mennonite Studies (2012).
5 Gerlof D. Homan (1929–2017) was born in the Netherlands and immigrated to the United States in 1952. He earned his PhD in history at the University of Kansas in 1958. After teaching in Edmond and Norman, Oklahoma, and in Pittsburg, Kansas, he went to Illinois State University in Normal. Professor Homan retired in 1994. He has published three books and many articles on French, Dutch, and American history and on peace history, see note 2 for some examples.
6 Gerlof D. Homan, "Nederlandse doopsgezinden in de Tweede Wereldoorlog," in *Doopsgezinde Bijdragen* 21 (1995): 195. Homan mentions the congregations of Grijpskerk, Workum, Oudebildtzijl, and Zaandam East.
7 G.W. Hylkema, *Ras en Toekomst* (Amsterdam: De Amsterdamsche Keurkamer, 1941); See also Gabe G. Hoekema, "Idealisten en baasjes mit oogkleppen voor. Voorgangers van doopsgezinde gemeenten die van 1933 tot 1945 aangesproken werden door het gedachtegoed van de NSB of tijdens de oorlog meewerkten met de Duitse bezetter," *Doopsgezinde Bijdragen* 41 (2015): 188–210. Gabe G. Hoekema deals with this more extensively than Homan does.
8 See note 3.
9 Described in more detail in Lichti, ch. 2 in this volume.
10 See note 3.
11 Robin te Slaa and Edwin Klijn, *De NSB. Ontstaan en opkomst van de Nationaal-Socialistische Beweging, 1931–1935* (Boom: Igitur, 2009), 664.
12 Church and Peace, founded 1924, is the oldest Christian peace organization in the Netherlands. It focuses on disarmament and non-violence.

13 "De Strijd der kerken in Duitschland. Dr [sic] F. Kuiper spreekt voor de Vereeniging van Noord-Hollandsche Predikanten," *Algemeen Handelsblad*, 18 June 1935; "De Nationale Gedachte," *Algemeen Handelsblad*, 1 March 1938 evening ed., 19; notice of a meeting of the Task Force against Military Service, led by F. Kuiper, and C.B. Hylkema among others in the Vredeshuis in The Hague. See further Alle G. Hoekema and Pieter Post, *Frits Kuiper (1898–1974) Doopsgezind theoloog. Voordrachten en getuigenissen over Kuiper en een selectie van zijn brieven* (Hilversum: Verloren, 2014), 192.

14 C.B. Hylkema, *Het Nederlandsch Fascisme, wat het is, wat het leert, hoe het geworden is*, 1st ed. (Utrecht: Nenasu, 1934), 129; 9th ed., 1937. Subsequent citations are from the 1st edition.

15 Gabe G. Hoekema, "Idealisten en baasjes met oogkleppen voor," *Doopsgezinde Bijdragen* 41 (2015): 183–246.

16 Ger van Roon, *Protestants Nederland en Duitsland 1933–1941* (Utrecht: Het Spectrum, 1973), 292–3.

17 Gabe G. Hoekema, "Idealisten en baasjes met oogkleppen voor," *Doopsgezinde Bijdragen* 41 (2015): 218–24.

18 Hylkema, *Het Nederlandsch Fascisme*, 14–15; 52–5, 120, 156; and see review by F. v. d. W, "Een verzwegen boek," *De Zondagsbode* 48, no. 14 (3 February 1935).

19 C.B. Hylkema, *Werkelijkheidstheologie. Hoofdlijnen eener empirische godsdienstideologie* (Haarlem: Tjeenk Willink, 1932), 22–3; this approach harmonized with the ideology of the Italian fascist leader Benito Mussolini; Te Slaa and Klijn, *De NSB*, 27; Hylkema, *Het Nederlandsch Fascisme*, 120: "Fascism puts great power into the hands of one person. But then, it places responsibility on this one person for all its decisions. A leader can never hide behind a nameless majority of votes."

20 Hylkema, *Het Nederlandsch Fascisme*, 72–3, "What could be fulfilled of his demand to serve and to sacrifice if it is not rooted in a religious, a Christian world view?" *Homo fascistus*, see Te Slaa and Klijn, *De NSB*, 27–8.

21 Hylkema, *Het Nederlandsch Fascisme*, 127–9. He also mentions Geert Grote, Johannes Ruysbroeck, and Thomas à Kempis.

22 Hylkema's other books with regard to National Socialism are *De vrouw in de nieuwe maatschappij* (Utrecht: Nenasu, 1935) and *De N.S.B. en ons christelijk volkskarakter* (n.d.). For further references, see Homan, "Nederlandse doopsgezinden in de Tweede Wereldoorlog," *Doopsgezinde Bijdragen* 21 (1995), 171.

23 A.A. Mussert wrote a brochure titled *De bronnen van het Nederlandsche nationaalsocialisme* (1937). This defines the transition from Italian fascism to German National Socialism, https://www.bibliotheek.nl/catalogus/titel.851199194.html/de-bronnen-van-het-nederlandsche-nationaal-socialisme.

24 Hylkema, *Het Nederlandsch Fascisme*, 5; folder T990, inventory number 105015, Dossiers inzake het verzamelen van gegevens voor de opsporing en eventuele berechting van politieke delinquenten, reference no. 2.09.09, Ministerie van Justitie: Centraal Archief van de Bijzondere Rechtspleging (CABR), The National Archive of the Netherlands, The Hague.
25 Frits Kuiper, *Sovjet-Rusland en het Christendom* (Amsterdam, 1937), 100ff.
26 Rob Hartmans, *Vijandige broeders? De Nederlandse sociaal-democratie en het nationaal-socialisme, 1922–1940* (Amsterdam: Ambos/Anthos, 2012), 28.
27 Hoekema and Post, *Frits Kuiper* (2016), 231. A year later the book was banned by the German authorities.
28 Pieter Post, *Naar Messiaans Communisme. Frits Kuiper (1898–1974) dopers theoloog* (Gorinchem: Narratio, 2014), 12.
29 C. B. Hylkema, *Werkelijkheidstheologie*, 111.
30 Hylkema, *Nederlandsch Fascisme*, 144.
31 Te Slaa and Klijn, *De NSB*, 131.
32 C.B. Hylkema, *Werkelijkheidstheologie*, 117–18; Hylkema, *Nederlandsch Fascisme*, 97–8; Hylkema, "De N.S.B. en 'Kerk en Vrede,'" *Kerk en Vrede. Orgaan van de groep van godsdienstige voorgangers en gemeenteleden tegen oorlog en oorlogstoerusting* 9, no. 16 (15 January 1934): 131.
33 "Beginselverklaring" (statement of principles) of the Task Force of Mennonites against Military Service 1929, *Evangelie en Krijgsdienst* (Arnhem, 1929), overleaf. Hylkema polemicizes implicitly with the Task Force against Military Service. The description "irreconcilable contradiction" appears here too. Rob Hartmans, *Vijandige broeders?* (Amsterdam Ambo, Anthos, 2012), 212. The SDAP declared itself in favour of disarmament. During the First World War, workers from all countries appeared to be prepared to kill their proletarian brothers. The fact that one nation placed itself above other nations led to the principle of disarmament. Hylkema, *Nederlandsch Fascisme*, 110. Also see Hylkema, "N.S.B. en Kerk en Vrede," *Kerk en Vrede* 10, no. 20 (15 March 1935): 187.
34 Hylkema, *Nederlandsch Fascisme*, 104–6.
35 Ibid., 62–3.
36 "Remain within the law, even beyond the boundary of injustice done you, 'legal'!" Hylkema, *Nederlandsch Fascisme*, 105.
37 He mentioned this topic in the magazine *Kerk en Vrede*, and later he developed it in his book *Gemeente in de wereld*. Frits Kuiper, "Oorlog en Christendom," *Kerk en Vrede* 9, no. 17 (1 February 1934): 137–8; Frits Kuiper, "Christus voor Pilatus," *Gemeente in de wereld* (Haarlem, 1941), 113–47.
38 "Does it have to show itself off in the field of education and upbringing … social and political order? … It can do no other." Kuiper, *Gemeente in de wereld*, 135.

39 Kuiper, *Gemeente in de wereld*, 120ff. On these pages Kuiper treats a lie over against truth, suppression over against freedom, sin over against grace, and death over against life.
40 Hylkema, *Nederlandsch Fascisme*, 118–19, 121. Here he accuses liberal churches and societies of having a "democracy" that he refers to as narrow-minded, hardly noble, and tyrannical, and to "democratic freedom" as humbug. Liberalism and democracy are false gods.
41 Hylkema, *Werkelijkheidstheologie*, 111; Hylkema, *Nederlandsch Fascisme*, 28, 30, 95.
42 Frits Kuiper, *Christen en Socialist 1933* (Zeist: NCSV/ds. Frits Kuiper Stichting, 1979), 64–6; 69–71; 123–5.
43 Frits Kuiper, *Met de gemeente de wereld in (1914–1969). Herinneringen van een theoloog* (Amsterdam: Algemene Doopsgezinde Sociëteit, 1969), 24.
44 Kuiper, *Gemeente in de wereld*, 170; Frits Kuiper, "De grenzen van onze Doopsgezinde Vrijheid," *Doopsgezind Jaarboekje 1939*, vol. 38 (Assen: L. Hansma, 1938), 51.
45 Tj.S. Visser, "'Het Nationaal-Socialisme," *Brieven*, published by the Vereeniging voor Gemeentedagen voor Doopsgezinden, 17, no. 1 (1934), 8–9.
46 Hylkema, *Nederlandsch Fascisme*, 2.
47 Hylkema, *Nederlandsch Fascisme*, 108, 110; Hylkema, *Kerk en Vrede* 9, no. 16 (15 January 1934): 131; interview with his daughter-in-law by R.M.M. Hoogewoud-Verschoor.
48 Folder T990, inventory number 105015, reference number 2.09.09, National Archive of the Netherlands, The Hague.
49 Kuiper, *Doopsgezind Jaarboekje 1939*, 50–51.
50 Hoekema and Post, *Frits Kuiper*, 229.
51 Hylkema, *Werkelijkheidstheologie*, 90–93; 118–119.
52 Hylkema, *Nederlandsch Fascisme*, 127–129. And also other streams of thought, such as De Gemeenschap des Gemeenen Levens of Geert Grote in the fourteenth century; Alfred R. van Wijk, *Plicht tot leren & plichten leren. Een onderzoek naar de ontwikkeling van de doperse geloofsopvoeding in de Lage Landen (ca. 1540/1811), aan de hand van de in druk verschenen geloofspedagogische geschriften*, 2 vols. (Kampen: Kok, 2007), 391; J. A. Oosterbaan, "De reformatie der Reformatie. Grondslagen van de doperse theologie," *Doopsgezinde Bijdragen* 2 (1976), 44–45.
53 Kuiper, *Gemeente in de wereld*, 126. Paraphrased: We are living in a broken world, and we must set ourselves to the task of reconciliation.
54 Hoekema and Post, *Frits Kuiper*, 96.
55 Jaap Gulmans, "Fryslân oerein. Een Paasverhaal," *Schots en Scheef. Van vermaning tot verwondering* (Amsterdam: Algemene Doopsgezinde Sociëteit, 2001). Jaap Gulmans (1939–2017) was minister of the Mennonite Church of Oudebildtzijl (1964–68).

56 The Redstar is a variety of potato.
57 Geographically the "Wadden" is the sea between the northern coast of the Province of Friesland and the island of Ameland.
58 "There is a different relationship between believers and their Lord than between the followers of some worldly movement and its leaders." Frits Kuiper, "Solidariteit," in *Christen en Socialist* (Zeist: NCSV, 1933), 50. Kuiper criticizes the idea that faith in God as Almighty and in world government can easily lead to fatalism: "everything that happens, has to happen in any case." Kuiper, "Solidariteit," in *Christen en Socialist*, 142. See Kuiper, *Gemeente in de wereld*, 127, 140, concerning God's leading in his covenant.
59 Hylkema, *Nederlandsch Fascisme*, 95; Kuiper, *Gemeente in de wereld*, 135. Mark 10:45.
60 G.W. Hylkema, "C.B. Hylkema (1870–1948): Between Two Worlds," *Mennonite Life* 10 (January 1955): 43–4. His son Govert W. wrote a short article about his father seven years after he died. It could probably not be published in the Netherlands because of the sensitivity for the past. It is remarkable that he remained silent about his father's political ambition.

Chapter Six

Mennonite Collaboration with Nazism: A Case Study of the Responses of Mennonites in Deutsch Wymyschle, Poland, to the Plight of Local Jews during the Early Nazi Occupation Period (1939–1942)

COLIN P. NEUFELDT

Introduction

In 1940 my Mennonite grandparents, Peter and Frieda Ratzlaff, moved 7 kilometres from the Mennonite settlement of Deutsch Wymyschle (now "Nowe Wymyśle") to a vacated building on the town square of Gąbin, in occupied Poland, where they hoped to open a hardware store. They were prompted by the German occupation authorities' promise that prime commercial property would soon be available in Gąbin at favourable rents. One of the authorities who influenced their decision was Peter's cousin Erich L. Ratzlaff, a former teacher from Deutsch Wymyschle who had risen to the position of senior civil administrator and local group leader of the Nazi Party (*Ortsgruppenleiter der NSDAP*) of the Gąbin area shortly after the German occupation in 1939. Over the course of the Second World War, at least twenty Mennonites took up this offer and left Deutsch Wymyschle for Gąbin, where they moved into residences and started businesses in properties that had been violently seized from Jewish families.[1]

Shortly after the Ratzlaffs moved to Gąbin, the German Wehrmacht began drafting young ethnic German men in occupied Poland. Peter Ratzlaff received his notice in early 1940, and before the end of the year he was serving in the Wehrmacht. One day, while managing the hardware store in Peter's absence, Frieda was approached by a Jewish man whose home and business had been Aryanized. He was living in

6.1. Frieda and Peter Ratzlaff with daughter Ella, circa 1940, mother of Colin P. Neufeldt and author of *Ella's Story: The Journey of a Mennonite Girl from Poland to Canada*.

Gąbin's recently established Jewish ghetto and was desperately trying to liquidate what little personal property he still possessed; Frieda purchased several bedspreads from him, as well as two gold rings, which thereafter would serve as Frieda and Peter's belated wedding rings. This was not the only time Frieda crossed paths with the Jews of Gąbin. Frieda witnessed the persecution and ghettoization of Gąbin's Jews, not just by nameless Nazi occupation forces but by fellow Mennonites as well, including Erich L. Ratzlaff, who walked down the streets of Gąbin with a whip on his belt and forced Jewish inhabitants to doff their hats and bow in deference to him. Between 1940 and 1942, Frieda and other residents watched Jews being rounded up in the Gąbin town square, where they were beaten, loaded into trucks, and removed from the town. Most of them were eventually transported to the extermination camp at Chełmno.[2]

Deutsch Wymyschle Mennonites and Their Relationship with the Surrounding Community

The origins of Deutsch Wymyschle date back to the 1760s, when West Prussian Mennonites began migrating to the Mazovian region of Poland and settled on the flood plains of Gąbin, on the edge of the Kutno Plain. By 1762, some of these Mennonites had settled in Olędry Czermińskie (later referred to as "Deutsch Wymyschle" or "Wymyśle Niemieckie" by the local Polish population). Most of the Mennonites

6.2. The wedding of Agnes Pauls to Gustav Ratzlaff, Peter's brother, 6 March 1942. Under the words for Mennonite Church, the sign reads "No Jews allowed," a reading confirmed by several former residents.

who settled in Deutsch Wymyschle were subsistence farmers, but their descendants diversified their businesses to include an oilseed mill, a lumber mill, a flour mill, a dairy, a wagon-building shop, and several merchant operations.[3]

After the partition of Poland in the 1790s and the Napoleonic Wars, the village of Deutsch Wymyschle came under the control of the Russian

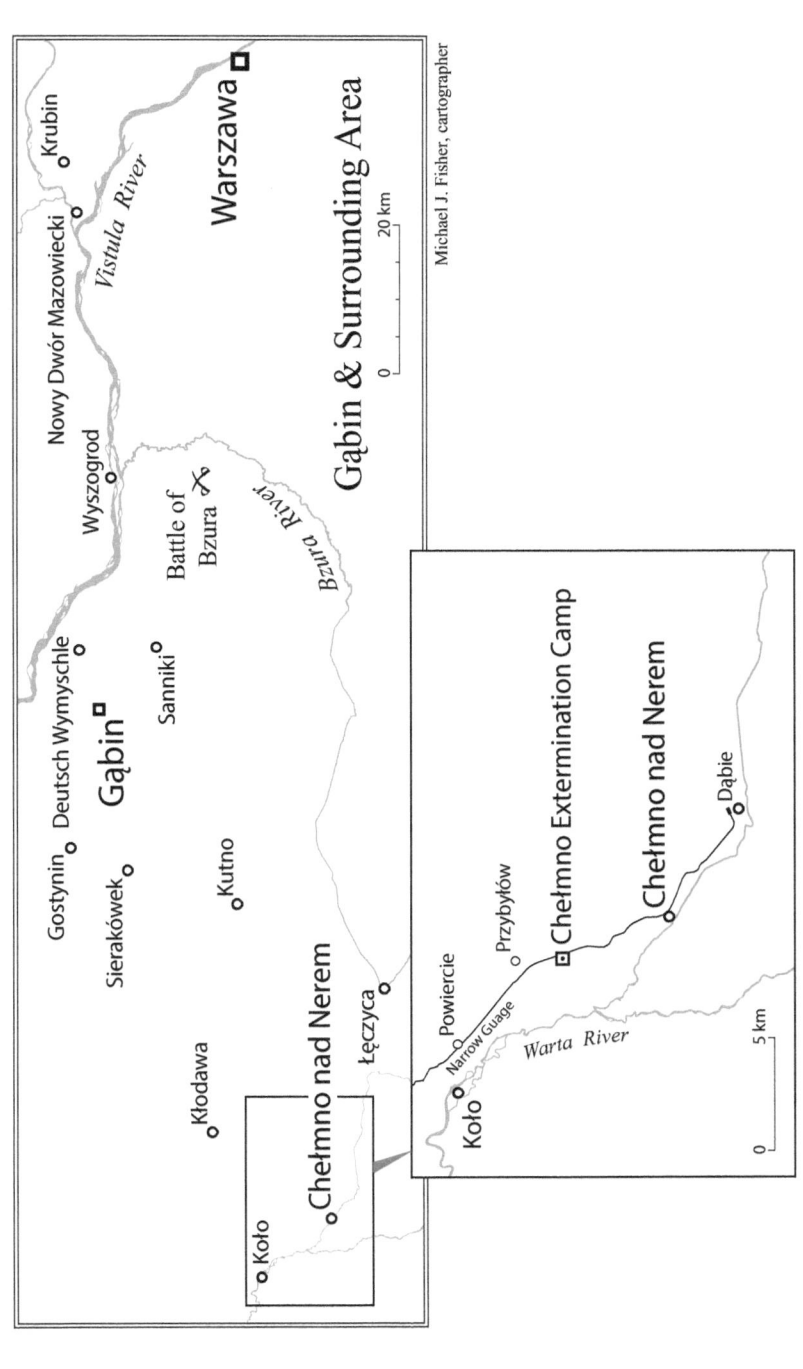

empire until 1918, when Poland regained its sovereignty and independence from the Russian, German, and Austro-Hungarian empires.

Two Mennonite denominations coexisted in Deutsch Wymyschle: the Mennonite Church (*Mennonitengemeinde*), which constructed its first sanctuary between 1764 and 1770, and the Mennonite Brethren Church (*Mennoniten-Brüdergemeinde*), which did not establish roots in the village until the 1880s. In 1940 the Mennonite Brethren Church had 176 members, and the Mennonite Church around 50.[4]

Deutsch Wymyschle residents had frequent business interactions with the residents of the nearby town of Gąbin. That town had Polish and ethnic German residents, but Jews constituted the largest ethnic group and dominated the town's businesses and social welfare system.[5] In 1921 the population of Gąbin was 5,777, more than 2,560 of whom were Jews.

Life in Deutsch Wymyschle in the Interwar Years

Mennonite life in Deutsch Wymyschle was not easy in the 1920s and '30s. Shortly after the Second Republic of Poland was founded in 1918, the Polish government introduced policies that made life increasingly difficult for ethnic minorities.[6] With the onset of the Great Depression in the 1930s, a series of government measures – including a reduction in the number of German minority schools, limitations on German-held businesses, the government expropriation of large tracts of ethnic German property, and new restrictions on the right of ethnic Germans to inherit real property – exacerbated the situation for ethnic Germans.[7]

The German government funnelled money to governmental and non-governmental organizations to provide economic, cultural, educational, and welfare support to the ethnic German minority in Poland.[8] Hitler's rise to power in 1933 brought little change to this situation other than to cause bitter public feuds among pro-German organizations in Poland competing for the favour of Nazi authorities.

In Deutsch Wymyschle, the deteriorating economic, political, and social conditions of the 1920s and '30s made life challenging. The Great Depression had a direct impact on the livelihoods of Deutsch Wymyschle residents. That impact is evident in the number of Mennonite families who emigrated: between 1926 and 1938, for example, seventy-three residents left – a significant portion of the village's overall population of less than five hundred.[9]

After 1933, pro-Nazi organizations tried to gain the support of the Mennonite communities in Poland; initially, they were unable to persuade Deutsch Wymyschle Mennonites to consider Nazism as a viable political option, but over time this began to change. Mennonite newspapers from Canada, which circulated among Deutsch Wymyschle residents in the 1930s, often provided favourable coverage of the Nazi regime.[10]

Mennonite support for the Nazi cause manifested itself in various ways prior to the war. According to some accounts, the first Nazi propaganda meetings in Deutsch Wymyschle were held in 1938 and 1939 when the village mayor (*Schulze*), Ferdinand Rennert, began hosting them.[11] The Mennonite men in attendance included Wilhelm Schroeder, Erich L. Ratzlaff, Gustav Kliewer, and Daniel Prochnau.[12] The extent to which Deutsch Wymyschle Mennonites participated in such meetings is unclear, but the fact that the village mayor publicly supported them must have had a strong impact on Mennonites and non-Mennonites in the community.

The Early Years of the Second World War: 1939–1942

Tensions in Deutsch Wymyschle and Gąbin rose significantly in 1939. In August, the Polish army launched a massive military draft. At least six Mennonite men from Deutsch Wymyschle and the surrounding area were drafted into the Polish army. Some of these men were later accused of being enemies of the Polish state and were incarcerated by Polish authorities; all were eventually released and permitted to return to Deutsch Wymyschle by late 1939 or early 1940.[13]

When the Nazis invaded Poland on 1 September 1939, Deutsch Wymyschle Mennonites, like other ethnic Germans in Poland, became targets of Polish hostility. The Polish government began widespread arrests of ethnic Germans in Poland; in the chaos that ensued, local Polish authorities often applied arrest orders in an arbitrary manner. During the brief September campaign, around 5,000 ethnic German civilians were murdered in Poland.[14] During that time the Mennonite male population in Deutsch Wymyschle was subjected to arrests, forced marches, kidnappings, internment in concentration camps, and various acts of terror. Local Polish police arrested at least three Deutsch Wymyschle Mennonite men; the families of some of those who were arrested were evicted from their homes.[15] Local Polish civilians kidnapped at least twelve men and male teenagers from Deutsch Wymyschle and ferried them to secret locations, where some were severely beaten.[16]

The arrests and kidnappings caused panic in Deutsch Wymyschle, prompting many Mennonite men and adolescents to hide in barns or the local forest. Meanwhile, local Polish mobs terrorized Mennonite women and children in Deutsch Wymyschle, stealing or destroying property and produce, and searching for German spies and enemy agents.[17]

178   Colin P. Neufeldt

The German invasion in early September heightened the anxiety and panic in Deutsch Wymyschle. While no German bombs or shells struck the village itself, the sound of German fighters overhead, an exploding bomb in a nearby field, and the roar of advancing German artillery during the Battle of Bzura (9–19 September 1939) left many villagers scrambling for shelter and wondering if their community would survive the German onslaught. As of 17 September 1939, German troops occupied and controlled Deutsch Wymyschle, Gąbin, and the surrounding area. For the residents of Deutsch Wymyschle, German occupation seemed like an answer to prayer: the villagers were now safe from Polish vigilantism, their menfolk could return home, and they could resume a more normal life.[18]

The new German military administration in Gąbin immediately acted against Jewish residents, burning the synagogue, levying fines, imposing forced labour, and expropriating businesses and homes.[19] Over the next two and a half years, violence against the Jews of Gąbin intensified, culminating in the clearing of the Gąbin ghetto and the transport of its surviving residents to the Chełmno death camp.[20] The German officials responsible for administering the Jewish ghetto at various times during the war included Rode, Ferdinand Schneider, Erich L. Ratzlaff, and Richard Hacke.[21] Of the approximately 2,310 Jews who lived in Gąbin in 1939, only 212 survived the war.[22]

Deutsch Wymyschle Mennonites as Nazi Collaborators and Perpetrators

Deutsch Wymyschle residents directly and indirectly participated in a wide spectrum of collaborative activities while the Nazis occupied the Gąbin area.

Acknowledgment of and Engagement with the Nazi Regime

The overwhelming majority of Deutsch Wymyschle residents welcomed the Nazi occupation of their territory. The German Wehrmacht put an end to the depredations of the Polish police and local Polish mobs, who had terrorized Deutsch Wymyschle residents during the early weeks of the war. Deutsch Wymyschle residents who moved to Gąbin to participate in the Aryanization of Jewish businesses and homes benefited directly from this preferential access to prime property at reduced rates; moreover, their departure from the village freed up land for the remaining residents. It also injected money into the local economy, since families who relocated to Gąbin purchased food and other supplies from family members still living in Deutsch Wymyschle. The German Wehrmacht and Nazi occupation forces purchased agricultural produce, lumber, and other products from Deutsch Wymyschle residents, which further boosted the local economy and significantly increased many Mennonite household incomes. All told, the Nazi occupation resulted in the greatest economic boom in the history of Deutsch Wymyschle.[23]

In return for these security and economic benefits, Deutsch Wymyschle residents complied with the rules the German authorities instituted: they permitted German officials to direct the administration of the community, and they allowed a schoolteacher from Germany to run the village school. Deutsch Wymyschle residents turned a blind eye to the Nazis' mistreatment of local Jews, Poles, Roma, Sinti, and other non-German groups in the area. For the residents of Deutsch Wymyschle, the benefits of collaborating with and publicly demonstrating support for the Nazi authorities outweighed the disadvantages, even if it meant that their Jewish, Polish, and non-German neighbours suffered as a result.

Organizing and Participating in a Selbstschutz *(Self-Defence Militia)*

In the fall of 1939, German officials encouraged the residents of Deutsch Wymyschle to organize their own self-defence unit (made up of local ethnic Germans and Mennonites) to provide ongoing protection for the village and to demonstrate to the surrounding non-German populations that the residents of Deutsch Wymyschle supported the Nazi occupiers.[24]

What did participation in the Deutsch Wymyschle self-defence unit entail? According to some eyewitness accounts, the participants were often young Deutsch Wymyschle Mennonite men who wore white armbands, practised military exercises (marching and shooting a weapon), and guarded the village, sometimes with unloaded guns. The unit was reportedly a short-lived affair, operating for no more than a few months and certainly less than a year. The Gąbin self-defence unit was actively involved in actions that targeted local Jewish populations; however, it is not clear whether and to what extent the Deutsch Wymyschle unit participated in these attacks.[25] Whatever the case, joining the village self-defence unit amounted to an intentional collaborative act on the part of participants, and the fact that the Deutsch Wymyschle community permitted that unit to operate and made no effort to stop it demonstrated to the neighbouring communities the village's willingness to align itself with the Nazi regime.

Adopting an "Ethnic German" (Volksdeutsche) *Identity*

Many Deutsch Wymyschle residents readily identified themselves as *Volksdeutsche* (ethnic Germans). Nazi officials, however, were not prepared to grant *all* Deutsch Wymyschle Mennonites ethnic German status automatically. Nazism was antagonistic toward Christianity, and for that reason, Mennonite piety and religious observance initially disqualified many Deutsch Wymyschle residents. Nazi officials also criticized Mennonite ministers for encouraging young people to participate in church activities. As the war ground on, however, the Nazi authorities broadened the definition of ethnic German as a means to grow the ranks of the German armed forces and increase the number of possible inhabitants and officials available to occupy and administer the newly acquired territories.[26]

Mennonites from Deutsch Wymyschle did not object to being registered on the Ethnic Germans List (*Deutsch Volksliste*), and many willingly completed the requested paperwork in 1940. In fact, many Deutsch Wymyschle residents qualified as ethnic Germans without having to provide much evidence; in some cases, the names of those who vouched for the individuals were Mennonites who were self-proclaimed Nazi sympathizers or activists in the NSDAP. Deutsch Wymyschle ethnic Germans were now eligible for higher positions in the local civil administration, the NSDAP, and German civilian organizations. They also received higher wages, more food ration cards, and better access to schools for their children than non-Germans. They also enjoyed preferential access to Aryanized property and possessions taken from dispossessed Jews and Poles at discounted prices or rents. At the same time, most male ethnic Germans were automatically eligible for German military service.[27] Thus, passing the ethnic German test meant that an individual was ineluctably tied to the Nazi regime.

Co-opting Deutsch Wymyschle Children to Support the Nazi Regime

Shortly after the German occupation began, Nazi authorities helped Deutsch Wymyschle residents organize Hitler Youth *(Hitler Jugend; HJ)* and League of German Girls *(Bund Deutscher Mädel; BDM)* organizations in the village. The purpose of both *HJ* and *BDM* was to educate children and youth in the spirit of National Socialism. In the annexed territories of Poland, the *HJ* and *BDM* had an additional purpose: to educate ethnic German children – and indirectly their parents – in the language, customs, and practices of the German Reich. In Deutsch Wymyschle, Mennonite children who enrolled in *HJ* and *BDM* sang

Volkslieder (German folk songs), practised marching, read from *Mein Kampf*, and learned how to salute with "Heil Hitler." Female members received domestic training in cooking, sewing, and childcare. Some Deutsch Wymyschle youth spent several weeks at a time at *HJ* or *BDM* summer camps.

Not all villagers permitted their children to participate in *HJ* or *BDM*, but most of them did. Their reasons for doing so varied, from demonstrating their ethnic German identity, to teaching their children respect for authority, to getting their children out of the house for a few days a month. At the same time, Deutsch Wymyschle children acknowledged that they enjoyed participating in the Nazi youth groups, both the domestic and more militaristic elements.[28] By permitting their children to join, Deutsch Wymyschle parents were showing their non-ethnic German neighbours they supported the Nazi regime.

Benefiting from the Aryanization of Jewish Property

The Nazi occupation of Gąbin created new economic opportunities for the residents of Deutsch Wymyschle, and some took advantage of them. They demonstrated their support for the Nazi regime when, at the invitation of the Nazi-controlled Gąbin town administration (*Stadtverwaltung*) in late 1939 and early 1940, they moved to Gąbin to start new businesses in buildings that had once belonged to Jews. Mennonite families and individuals from Deutsch Wymyschle took possession of former Jewish properties and opened businesses in them. These included a hardware store (operated by Peter and Frieda Ratzlaff and Leonard and Minna Schmidt), the Wohlgemuth coffee house and confectionary (operated by Heinrich, Kornelius, and Lina Wohlgemuth), the Kliewer shoe store (operated by Reinhold Kliewer and his wife), the Wilhelm Heier clothing and textile store, the Witzke business (operated by Rudolf Witzke), and a dry goods store (operated by David Ratzlaff and his sister Alma).[29]

Most of the Deutsch Wymyschle Mennonites who moved to Gąbin as part of the Nazis' Aryanization program lived in the town until the Red Army retook it in early 1945, and they had witnessed or at least known about the deadly violence perpetrated against Gąbin's Jews between 1939 and 1942. In light of such atrocities, how did these Mennonites justify their actions? David Ratzlaff, who operated a variety store with his sister Alma, writes: "We leased [the store] from the new German government on a trustee basis; it was one of the expropriated stores. We did not think it wrong, because the profit we made selling the merchandise would be handed over to the Jewish owners as soon as possible."[30]

182　Colin P. Neufeldt

Frieda Ratzlaff, who operated a hardware store in Gąbin and witnessed the persecution of Jews and Poles first-hand – including the public execution of ten Poles in June 1941 – desperately wanted to abandon her store and move back to Deutsch Wymyschle with her daughter after her husband Peter was drafted into the German armed forces in early 1940. Frieda was overwhelmed by the prospect of running a store by herself while also looking after a small child. But Peter and Frieda would have lost most of their investment in hardware inventory if Frieda had walked away from the store, so instead she asked some of her siblings to move to Gąbin to help her run the business. In January 1945, she and her children were forced to evacuate the town.[31]

Participating in the German Military

In early 1940, the German military began drafting Deutsch Wymyschle Mennonite men, including those who were operating businesses in Gąbin. For a number of reasons, Deutsch Wymyschle Mennonites did not oppose military conscription. First, Deutsch Wymyschle Mennonites viewed the Germans as their liberators, given that they had brought an end to the attacks on their village in the first weeks of the war. Moreover, the German occupation brought financial prosperity to Deutsch Wymyschle as well as economic opportunities in Gąbin. Refusing to participate would have shown ingratitude and jeopardized a family's ethnic German status. Second, the principles of pacifism and non-resistance were not strongly emphasized in the Deutsch Wymyschle Mennonite Brethren Church: the ministers preached very few sermons on the topic, so most young men did not strongly identify with these principles.[32] Third, refusal to participate in the military on the basis of conscientious objection was not seen as a realistic option, since German law deemed conscientious objection or helping someone avoid military service as subversive, indeed a capital crime.[33] Finally, Deutsch Wymyschle ministers made little or no attempt to approach German military officials to advocate on behalf of the young men in the congregation, nor did they provide them with moral guidance on the issue of military service.[34]

In many family photographs taken during the war, Deutsch Wymyschle men on military leave are wearing the German uniform with obvious pride.[35] Participation in the military affected almost every Deutsch Wymyschle family: 46 Mennonite men from the village (of fewer than 500 residents) were conscripted, as well as another 35 from the surrounding area.[36] Such a high participation rate in a small community clearly demonstrated where the allegiances of the Mennonites of Deutsch Wymyschle lay.

Confessional Support for the Third Reich

The Mennonite Brethren Church in Deutsch Wymyschle collaborated with the Third Reich. Throughout the war, church leaders permitted grooms to wear the military uniform during marriage ceremonies in the church, thereby signalling their tacit approval for the Third Reich and its soldiers. At the same time, the Deutsch Wymyschle Mennonite Brethren Church ministers Gustav P. Ratzlaff and Leonhard P. Ratzlaff regularly corresponded with the leaders of the pro-Nazi Association of German Mennonite Churches (*Vereinigung der Deutschen Mennonitengemeinde*) between 1939 and 1941. Most of that correspondence focused on the trauma the Deutsch Wymyschle congregation had experienced at the outbreak of the war, the benefits that same congregation would enjoy if it joined the association, the activities of Mennonite congregations in the territories of western Poland annexed by the Third Reich, and the reasons why non-resistance was no longer relevant to Mennonite faith and practice. The effusive support both sides offered the Nazi regime was reflected in the "Heil Hitler" periodically used to end their letters. In this respect, the association and the Deutsch Wymyschle congregation shared much: they no longer practised non-resistance, and they both supported the Nazi regime's efforts to defend the Fatherland and create a new German state.[37]

This overt congregational support for the Third Reich came at a price. The church ministers Gustav P. Ratzlaff and Erich L. Ratzlaff were required to report once a month to the Nazi authorities in Gostynin about the church's activities. They also had to promise they would not prevent Mennonite youth in the Deutsch Wymyschle church from participating in the *HJ* and *BDM*. Under pressure from Nazi officials, Gustav P. Ratzlaff no longer preached non-resistance from the pulpit.[38]

In the long run, the Deutsch Wymyschle church leaders' efforts to cooperate with Nazi officials did not save the congregation: the number of members and young people who attended declined significantly during the war, in part due to the church's lack of moral leadership. When Red Army troops advanced into the region in January 1945, the Deutsch Wymyschle church closed its doors permanently.[39]

Seeking Employment with the Third Reich

The Nazi occupation provided employment opportunities for residents of Deutsch Wymyschle in financial and government institutions in Gąbin.[40] Minna (Ratzlaff) Pauls, for example, found work as a postal clerk and telephone operator; Maria Ratzlaff worked in the district

6.3. Minna and Peter Pauls

savings bank; and Erhard Ratzlaff was employed by the town comptroller, initially as a clerk and later as a manager, where he was in charge of collecting taxes and handling the payroll for town employees.[41] These Mennonites had witnessed Nazi brutality toward the Jews, yet they chose to continue working for the Nazi authorities – at least until they were drafted into the Wehrmacht (as was the case for Erhard Ratzlaff in 1943) or were forced to flee the advancing Red Army in January 1945.[42] Why did these Mennonites not do anything to help the Jews? As Minna (Ratzlaff) Pauls explains: "If you were seen talking to a Jew, then the Germans would treat you like a Jew. Mennonites did not help Jews or hide Jews. It was too dangerous to be associated with the Jews."[43]

Another Deutsch Wymyschle resident who sought employment in Gąbin was the Mennonite youth minister and choir leader, Gustav P. Ratzlaff.[44] During the first months of the German occupation, Gustav and his family lived and worked in Deutsch Wymyschle, but in 1940 he found employment in Gąbin as an accountant and tax assessor in the treasury of the Nazi-controlled Gąbin town administration. In 1941, he moved his family to Gąbin, where they settled in an expropriated Jewish home on Schusster Street. The summer kitchen (*Sommerküche*) at the back of that property housed a Jewish family until German officials deported them in 1942.[45] Besides working in the tax department, Gustav P. Ratzlaff was chief of the Gąbin fire brigade.[46] According to one eyewitness, he led fire drills on Sunday mornings in an SA uniform.[47] His activities in Gąbin often prevented Gustav from fulfilling his ministerial responsibilities at the Deutsch Wymyschle Mennonite Brethren church. Thus the congregation had to rely on the leadership of Gustav's brother, Leonhard P. Ratzlaff, a much older minister who lacked the energy required to lead a congregation through turbulent times. When reflecting on this difficult time in the history of their congregation, a number of Deutsch Wymyschle Mennonites noted that as Gustav P. Ratzlaff spent more and more time in Gąbin, the spiritual life of the congregation declined rapidly.[48]

While Gustav P. Ratzlaff worked in Gąbin between 1940 and January 1945, he and his family witnessed some of the most brutal actions against the town's Jews. Yet Gustav did not quit his job and leave Gąbin; indeed, he continued his accounting and fire-prevention work for the Nazi-controlled civil administration until January 1945. Moreover, he encouraged his children to obtain employment with these same German authorities in Gąbin: his daughter Wilhelmine worked in the telephone office, and his daughter Erna was initially employed as a telephone operator and librarian, and then as a secretary for Richard Hacke, the mayor of Gąbin between 1943 and January 1945.[49]

A man named Albert Foth was another Mennonite from the Deutsch Wymyschle area who provided services to Nazi authorities in Gąbin during the war. According to Erich L. Ratzlaff, Foth was employed as the assistant to Ferdynand Schneider, the first mayor of Gąbin following the Nazi occupation. When the local district administrator (*Landrat*) removed Schneider from his position, he appointed Foth as interim mayor of Gąbin. Unfortunately, Ratzlaff's account does not clarify which Albert Foth was interim mayor; at least three different individuals with the same name lived in the Gąbin, Deutsch Wymyschle, and Płock areas during the war.[50]

An Albert Foth was linked to the mass murder of Poles in Gąbin in June 1941. After a German policeman was found dead, local police, the SS, and members of Nazi organizations retaliated by arresting eighty-six Poles from the Gąbin area, some of whom were incarcerated and tortured in a Gąbin church. After several detainees escaped, Nazi police and paramilitary forces hunted them down and summarily executed nine of them. According to one account, an Albert Foth played a major role in the round-up and execution of these Polish victims, but once again, it is not clear which of the three Albert Foths participated in this nefarious activity.[51]

One of the most prominent Deutsch Wymyschle residents to have worked for the Nazi authorities was the teacher Erich L. Ratzlaff, who served in the Gąbin town administration from September 1939 until he left to work as a teacher in Sierakówek (near Gostynin) in August 1940. Ratzlaff briefly discusses this one-year period in his life in his autobiography *Vom Don an den Fraser,* in which he states that he was a schoolteacher when the local headquarters (*Ortskommandantur*) of the German military authority asked him to help Mayor Schneider with the administration of Gąbin and to serve as his secretary. In Ratzlaff's words, he served as the mayor's liaison with the local military headquarters, the district administrative office (*Landratsamt*), the local police sergeant (*Polizeimeister*), the Gendarmerie, the Security Service (*Sicherheitsdienst*), the Gestapo, and the NSDAP. In his dealings with these bodies, Ratzlaff describes himself as someone who "protested" against the beatings of Jewish and Polish leaders, who defended the interests of local Poles, and who was held in "high esteem" by the Polish population.[52] Eyewitness accounts of Mennonites who lived in Gąbin in 1939–40 confirm that Erich L. Ratzlaff served as mayor of Gąbin during the first year or so of the Nazi occupation.[53] Non-Mennonite sources – including a letter from Eduard Eichmann (a German auxiliary police officer or *Hilfspolizist*), who lived in Gąbin in 1940 and who knew Ratzlaff before and after the war – identify Ratzlaff as Gąbin's chief civil administrator (*Amtskommissar*) during the first year of the Nazi occupation.[54]

Ratzlaff's autobiography may be true in parts, but it fails to disclose important details about Ratzlaff's activities in the Gąbin city administration. For example, Deutsch Wymyschle Mennonites state that it was he who invited them to move into expropriated Jewish properties in Gąbin and who implemented the harsh rules that governed Jewish life in Gąbin during the occupation; also, that he participated in the dispossession of Jewish property and assisted in the creation of the Gąbin Jewish ghetto. According to some Deutsch Wymyschle eyewitnesses, Gąbin's Jews despised Ratzlaff because of the harsh labour demands he imposed on the community and the demeaning deference to German authority that he demanded (Jews were expected to doff their hats in his presence and walk on the streets instead of the sidewalks).[55] At the same time, Ratzlaff was disliked by some Deutsch Wymyschle Mennonites because of his inflated opinion of himself and his demanding manner when dealing with other Mennonites. One

Mennonite reported that when he saw Ratzlaff walk down a street in Gąbin, he crossed to the other side to avoid him.⁵⁶

Ratzlaff's April 1940 Ethnic Germans List questionnaire reveals that he was a member of the Gąbin self-defence unit and an SS company (*SS Sturm*) – facts that are not mentioned in *Vom Don an den Fraser*. These Nazi paramilitary organizations were directly involved in attacks on local Jewish populations. Ratzlaff's acknowledgment of his participation in these Nazi paramilitary groups demonstrates that the involvement of Deutsch Wymyschle Mennonites in Nazi depredations against Gąbin's Jews was not incidental or indirect, but included Mennonites who had a direct hand in making and implementing decisions that affected the lives of thousands of Gąbin's Jews during the war.⁵⁷

The Role of Deutsch Wymyschle Mennonites in the NSDAP

Eyewitness accounts confirm that some Deutsch Wymyschle Mennonites (including Wilhelm Schroeder, Erich L. Ratzlaff, Erhard Ratzlaff, Albert Foth, Daniel Prochnau, Gustav Kliewer, and Ferdinand Rennert) were heavily involved in local NSDAP affairs during the war. These individuals organized Nazi Party meetings in the village, defended NSDAP ideas and values, helped spread Nazi propaganda in the area, wore Brownshirt uniforms to public events, and encouraged fellow Deutsch Wymyschle residents to participate in local Nazi events.⁵⁸ Some Deutsch Wymyschle Mennonites also participated in auxiliary organizations closely linked to the NSDAP: Albert Foth, for example, served as leader of the *HJ* and NSDAP cells in Gąbin during the war, while Erich L. Ratzlaff served as a member of the Gąbin unit of the SS during the first year of Nazi rule.⁵⁹

NSDAP documents from the Federal Archives in Berlin indicate that two different individuals from the Gąbin area, both named Albert Foth, applied for and received NSDAP membership: Albert W. Foth (member no. 8123403) and Albert J. Foth (member no. 8390784). It is not clear, however, whether it was Albert W. Foth or Albert J. Foth who led the Gabin *HJ* and NSDAP, or whether that distinction belonged to a third Albert Foth (Albert P. Foth) who also lived in the area but did not have NSDAP membership.⁶⁰

Erich L. Ratzlaff makes no mention of his NSDAP affiliations in his memoir *Vom Don an den Fraser*, but wartime German government and NSDAP correspondence, now located in Polish archives, confirms that Ratzlaff was the local group leader (*Ortsgruppenleiter*) of the NSDAP organization in Gąbin from 1939 until the fall of 1940. At this time, Ratzlaff was not a Party member; even so, he was selected as group leader for his dedication to Nazi ideology, his ardent support for the Nazi cause, and his potential leadership abilities. Some of this correspondence was generated by a charge that Gąbin auxiliary policeman (*Hilfspolizist*) Eduard Eichmann made against Ratzlaff. In September 1940, Eichmann complained that Ratzlaff had participated in a Polish political party meeting in 1937–38, that Ratzlaff frequently conversed in Polish, and that he had promoted the appointment of a local Pole as a school manager, notwithstanding the objections of local ethnic Germans.[61] After much back and forth, Ratzlaff was cleared.[62]

If Erich L. Ratzlaff had any qualms about his relationship with the NSDAP after the Eichmann allegations, they did not last long. Only a few months later, on 1 January 1941, he became a member (no. 441225) of the National Socialist Teachers League (*Nationalsozialistische Lehrerbund*). In March 1941, he submitted his application to become a member of the NSDAP, and on 1 August 1941 he became an NSDAP member (no. 8442988).[63]

After the war, Ratzlaff and his family immigrated to Germany and then to Canada. Eventually he became editor of the Mennonite Brethren publication *Die Mennonitische Rundschau* (1967–79) as well as an influential force in the Canadian Mennonite Brethren Conference. It is unclear, however, whether he ever disclosed his past activities to Canadian immigration authorities, members of the *Rundschau* hiring committee, or the leadership of the Canadian Mennonite Brethren Conference.[64]

Resistance to the Reich

There is little evidence that Deutsch Wymyschle Mennonites resisted the Nazi authorities or provided aid and comfort to Gąbin's Jews.[65] There are a number of possible reasons why Deutsch Wymyschle Mennonites were unlikely or unwilling to oppose the regime or help Jews in their hour of need. First, Deutsch Wymyschle Mennonites were very appreciative of the German Wehrmacht when it arrived in mid-September 1939, and they made a tacit collective decision to align themselves with the Nazi regime – a decision that may have been made before many Deutsch Wymyschle community members became aware of the extent of the brutality and oppression the Nazis would unleash against Jews, Poles, and other non-German minorities. Deutsch Wymyschle residents were not inclined to resist a regime that had saved them from Polish depredations, provided them with protection, given them jobs, and improved their lives economically. Helping Jews would have jeopardized the Mennonites' mutually beneficial relationship with the regime.

Second, extending compassion to Jews or opposition to the Nazi regime required enormous courage: either one carried great risk. It was not uncommon for Deutsch Wymyschle families to have one or more members serving in the German Wehrmacht or working in administrative positions or civilian organizations closely associated with the Nazi regime. In this context, resistance against the regime was often tantamount to resistance against one's own family. Few individuals had the fortitude to participate in resistance activities that would imperil large numbers of immediate and extended family members.

Third, the Deutsch Wymyschle population and the Mennonite Brethren Church supported the regime throughout the war; thus, any Deutsch Wymyschle Mennonite who resisted the Nazi regime or helped local Jews would be viewed as opposing the Deutsch Wymyschle community and church. Doing so might result in serious retaliation against the entire church or community (including innocent children, the disabled, and the elderly) as a whole – another excuse for not resisting the regime or assisting Jews.

Fourth, the size and composition of the Deutsch Wymyschle community made it difficult to participate in resistance activities or hide Jews from Nazi authorities without being detected. There were only a few hundred people in the village, which meant that everyone in it knew the business of everyone else. That was especially true of the Mennonite residents, who interacted with one another on a daily basis. In such a confined area it would have been a challenge for anyone to plan or participate in resistance activities or to assist or hide Jews without others in the community knowing about it.

It is difficult to tell how antisemitic the Deutsch Wymyschle community was before and during the war, but it is hard to argue that a community that tacitly permitted its members to participate in Nazi Party meetings, and to take leadership positions in local Nazi Party cells and government offices, and that did nothing to oppose Nazi propaganda and policies during the German occupation, was not antisemitic. When asked if any Deutsch Wymyschle Mennonites hid Jews during the war, one former resident said: "No one considered it. No one did it."[66]

Fifth, support from outside the Deutsch Wymyschle community to assist Jews or participate in resistance activities against the Nazi regime was lacking. Deutsch Wymyschle was an isolated Mennonite community surrounded by non-Mennonite populations – mostly Poles, who had few close relationships with Deutsch Wymyschle Mennonites. Given this reality, a Deutsch Wymyschle resident who wanted to resist the Nazi regime or support local Jews would not have been likely to find support from non-German neighbours. Moreover, political loyalties were not always clear-cut: a significant number of Poles in the Gostynin-Gąbin area collaborated with the Nazi regime or at a minimum supported the Nazis' antisemitic agenda during the early years of the war; consequently, it would have been difficult for a Mennonite who wanted to help local Jews or participate in anti-Nazi activities to know with certainty which Polish neighbours were not collaborators with the Nazi regime.[67]

Finally, there was no confessional or ministerial support within the Deutsch Wymyschle congregation for anyone contemplating hiding a Jew or participating in Nazi resistance. A Deutsch Wymyschle Mennonite who wanted to resist the regime or help a local Jew could not count on the church or its ministers (one of whom was working for Nazi authorities in Gąbin) for support.

So did anyone from Deutsch Wymyschle participate in the resistance during the war? Yes, someone did, but he was not a Mennonite. A Lutheran businessman, Reinhold Wegert, divided his time between Deutsch Wymyschle, Gąbin, and Sanniki, where he ran a mill and had regular contact with the Nazi authorities. This gave him the opportunity to come and go from Deutsch Wymyschle as he pleased, and because he was one of the few Lutherans in the village, he was not under as much scrutiny or pressure to conform to village expectations. During the war, Wegert reportedly supported the activities of the Polish underground and the Home Army by providing them with information about the activities of the Nazi authorities, leading Poles through the territory of the *Generalgouvernement*, organizing escapes, and delivering flour to internees at a prison camp in Krubin.[68] So resisting the Nazis was possible, though not common in Deutsch Wymyschle, and it involved non-Mennonites, not Mennonites.

Some Final Observations

Deutsch Wymyschle Mennonites played significant and varied roles in the destruction of Gąbin's Jewish community, although this was not their original intent at the outbreak of the war. In the early weeks of September 1939, Deutsch Wymyschle Mennonites feared for their lives after suffering violence at the hands of local Polish mobs. Not surprisingly, Deutsch Wymyschle Mennonites were relieved when the German Wehrmacht appeared and brought a quick end to the chaos and brutality that had disrupted their village; consequently, Deutsch Wymyschle Mennonites viewed the Nazi occupiers as their liberators and were eager to show their gratitude. As the war progressed, more and more Deutsch Wymyschle Mennonites became ensnared in the implementation of Nazi policies, including policies that targeted Jews. These Mennonite agents of the Nazi regime carried out government orders that determined the pace of the Holocaust in Gąbin, punished those who resisted or expressed opposition to Nazi plans for the region, and assisted in the ghettoization, arrest, and deportation of Gąbin's Jews. And the reward for their service was lucrative. As Nazi sympathizers and ethnic Germans, Deutsch Wymyschle Mennonites were now near the top of the local political, social, and economic hierarchy in the Gąbin area, and they were given access to valuable Jewish real and personal property through the Aryanization program. Clearly, Mennonites bear some responsibility for the tragic events that befell Gąbin's Jews.

In carrying out their Nazi duties, these Mennonite agents also functioned as a transformative force in Deutsch Wymyschle. They helped undermine the religious authority of their home congregation, an institution that had largely abandoned its historic peace position and now supported the Nazi regime in uncomfortable ways. These Mennonites also lent legitimacy to Nazi-sponsored violence against Jewish, Polish, and other non-German minority groups, besides working to convince fellow Deutsch Wymyschle residents that supporting and serving the Nazi regime was in their best interests. In so doing, these Nazi-aligned Mennonite leaders helped legitimize antisemitic attitudes among Deutsch Wymyschle residents; encouraged them to ignore, denigrate, or abandon many of the values, beliefs, and practices (such as Anabaptist peace theology, helping the needy, religious toleration, and separation of church and state) that historically defined who was a Mennonite; and facilitated the moral and religious deterioration of the community. Over time, a growing number of Deutsch Wymyschle residents became less concerned about following the Anabaptist principles of their forefathers and more preoccupied with reconstructing their Mennonite identity in ways that conformed to what the Nazis required of ethnic Germans. As members of a Mennonite ethnic German community, Deutsch Wymyschle residents still acknowledged their Mennonite heritage, but they also countenanced the Nazis' brutal practices and participated in the destruction of those who were alien to the racial community (*Gemeinschaftsfremde*) in the surrounding area.

Of course, not all residents of Deutsch Wymyschle were fanatical supporters of the Nazi regime. There were undoubtedly some residents who found the Nazi ideology and policies abhorrent, but unfortunately the extant documentation does not indicate that any of them participated in resistance to the Nazi regime. There may well have been Deutsch Wymyschle Mennonites who were philosophically opposed to the Nazi regime but who felt powerless to act.

And what were the consequences for Deutsch Wymyschle's close association with the Nazi regime during the war? They were very harsh for some village residents, and deadly for others. As the Red Army advanced into western Poland in January 1945, chaos erupted as retreating German troops engaged with Red Army forces in the Gąbin area. Elderly Deutsch Wymyschle men were conscripted into the People's Militia (*Volkssturm*) as a last-ditch defence against Soviet troops. Many of the spouses and children of Deutsch Wymyschle soldiers in the German military were permitted to leave for Germany on military trains beginning in mid-January 1945. Extended family members, however, were left to fend for themselves. A large convoy of Deutsch Wymyschle families left for Germany – by horse and wagon and on foot – in the third week of January but were quickly overtaken by Red Army forces and ordered back. Some of the men and adolescent boys in that convoy were arrested and transported to the Soviet Union; almost all of them died in the Soviet Gulag. The Deutsch Wymyschle women, children, and handful of men left behind were often separated from one another and forced to perform labour service for the Poles, who now controlled former Mennonite farms in Deutsch Wymyschle.[69]

NOTES

The author thanks Lynette Toews-Neufeldt, Weronika Böhm, Richard Ratzlaff, Wojciech Marchlewski, Heinz Ratzlaff, Benjamin W. Goossen, Conrad Stoesz, Sven Devantier, Richard D. Thiessen, John D. Thiesen, Mark Jantzen, Alexandra Neufeldt, Olivia Neufeldt, Arnold Neufeldt-Fast, Claire Rosenson, and the anonymous reviewers for their assistance in locating documents, translating sources, or providing editorial comments and suggestions for this chapter. The author also thanks the family of Erich L. Ratzlaff for granting access to the personal papers of Erich L. Ratzlaff. This paper was first presented at the Mennonites and the Holocaust Conference at Bethel College, North Newton, Kansas, in March 2018.

Writing about one's own family's historical experience is rarely an easy undertaking, especially when your family is on the wrong side of history and actively collaborated with the Nazis during the Second World War. For me, however, writing about my family's often beneficial relationship with the Nazi regime in occupied Poland was a positive experience for two reasons. The first relates to my mother's decision to write her autobiography (see *Ella's Story* below), wherein she focuses on her family's relationship with the Nazi occupation troops in Deutsch Wymyschle and Gąbin, in a very candid manner and with no desire to hide uncomfortable historical realities. In this respect, my mother provided me with a role model for writing family history – that is, in as straightforward and honest a manner as possible, regardless of how shameful our family's role was in that history. The second reason is that many of my extended family members wanted me to share "their story" – Nazis, warts and all – and encouraged me to do so, so that they could come to terms with their past. As individuals who had experienced both the good and the bad of the Nazi occupation and who had the good fortune to emigrate to Canada after the war, many of my relatives told me they wanted to document their experiences during the Nazi occupation, but that they lacked the educational background and command of the English language that was necessary to do so. They were happy I was interested in what had happened to them and that I planned to publish something that preserved some of their experiences during the war. For these reasons, I know I have the affirmation and blessing of many of my extended family.

1 Peter and Frieda Ratzlaff, interview by Colin P. Neufeldt, June and August 1991, Coaldale, AB; Ella Neufeldt, *Ella's Story: The Journey of a Mennonite Girl from Poland to Canada* (Coaldale: printed by the author, 2003), 16–18.
2 Peter and Frieda Ratzlaff interview; Neufeldt, *Ella's Story*, 19–26, 31–4.
3 Concerning the founding of the Deutsch Wymyschle community in Poland and the relationship between Mennonites and Poles from the eighteenth century to the twentieth, see Robert Foth, *Die Geschichte der Mennoniten zu Deutsch-Wymyschle, Polen* (printed by the author: 1949), Mennonite Library and Archives, Bethel College, Kansas; Erich Ratzlaff, *Im Weichselbogen: Mennonitensiedlungen in Zentralpolen* (Winnipeg: Christian Press, 1971), 12–15, 22–8; Ratzlaff, *Familien – Stammbaum der Mennonite von Deutsch Wymyschle und Umgebung* (Abbotsford: printed by the author, n.d.); Wojciech Marchlewski, "Religious Contacts among Lutherans, Mennonites, and Catholics in Mazovia in the Nineteenth Century," *Mennonite Quarterly Review* 66, no. 2 (1992): 199–213; Paweł Fijałkowski, "Mennonite Religious Communities in Mazowsze prior to 1945: Material Relics," *Catalogue of Monuments of Dutch Colonization in Poland*, 2001; Marchlewski, "Mennonici w Polsce (O Powstaniu Spolecznosci Mennonitów Wymyśla Nowego)," *Etnografia Polska* 30, no. 2 (1986): 129–45; E. Kizik, "Uwagi o Mennonitach w Związku z Artykułem Wojciecha Marchlewskiego," *Etnografia Polska* 33, no. 1 (June 1989): 261–4; Marchlewski, "Odpowiedź na Uwagi P. Edmunda Kizika w Związku z Moim Artykułem 'o Mennonitach w Polsce," *Etnografia Polska* 33, no. 1 (1989): 264–6; Marchlewski, "Holendrzy w Polsce," *Konteksty. Polska Sztuka Ludowa* 66, no. 3–4 (2012): 343–51; Marchlewski, "The 'Hollander' Settlements in Mazovia," *Mennonite Life* 41 (March 1986): 5–10. For nostalgic works on Deutsch Wymyschle, see Erich L. Ratzlaff, *Keine Bleibende Stadt. Darbietungen und Vortraege auf dem zweiten Wymyschler Treffen in Three Hills, Alberta* (Abbotsford: printed by the author, n.d.); Ratzlaff, *Auf Tabors Höhen. Wymyschle-Treffen 1977 in Three Hills, Alberta* (Abbotsford: printed by the author, n.d.).

194   Colin P. Neufeldt

4   Foth, *Die Geschichte der Mennoniten*, 5–8; 72–4; Peter J. Klassen, *Mennonites in Early Modern Poland and Prussia* (Baltimore: Johns Hopkins University Press, 2009), 96; "Robert Foth Papers," Erich L. Ratzlaff personal documents; Ratzlaff, *Im Weichselbogen*, 33, 38, 56, 89.

5   Janusz Szczepański, *Dzieje Gąbina do roku 1945* (Warsaw: Państwowe wydawn. naukowe, 1984), 14–15; Hanna Krzewińska, "Zagłada Żydów gąbińskich," (cz. 1), *Notatki Płockie* 3, no. 184 (2000): 8–13; Jan Borysiak, *Z Dziejów Ochotniczej Straży Pożarnej w Gąbinie. W Latach 1898–1998* (Gąbin: OHP, 2000); "Gombin" (Gabin, Poland)," *Encyclopedia of Jewish Communities in Poland*, vol. 4, Translation of "Gombin" chapter from *Pinkas Hakehillot Polin* (Jerusalem: Yad Vashem 1989), 154–6, https://www.jewishgen.org/yizkor/pinkas_poland/pol4_00154.html.

6   Klassen, *Mennonites in Early Modern Poland*, 96–7; Richard Blanke, *Orphans of Versailles: The Germans in Western Poland, 1918–1939* (Lexington: University Press of Kentucky, 2015), 54–89; Winson Chu, *The German Minority in Interwar Poland* (Cambridge: Cambridge University Press, 2012); Karl Cordell, "Memory, Identity and Poland's German Minority," *German Politics and Society* 27, no. 4 (93) (2009): 1–23; Richard Blanke," The German Minority in Inter-War Poland and German Foreign Policy – Some Reconsiderations," *Journal of Contemporary History* 25, no. 1 (January 1990): 90.

7   Blanke, *Orphans of Versailles*, 95–162, 208–14.

8   Winson Chu, "*Volksgemeinschaft unter sich*: German Minorities and Regionalism in Poland, 1918–39," in *German History from the Margins*, ed. Neil Gregor, Nils Roemer, and Mark Roseman (Bloomington: Indiana University Press, 2006), 108–9.

9   Foth, *Die Geschichte der Mennoniten*, 84. Between 1926 and 1938, 27 adults and 9 children emigrated to Canada, 10 adults and 2 children to Brazil, 17 adults and 7 children to Paraguay, and 1 adult to the United States. For *Die Mennonitische Rundschau* articles on Deutsch Wymyschle, see *Die Mennonitische Rundschau* (hereafter *MR*): 29 January 1930, 8; 26 March 1930, 8; 21 May 1930, 5; 11 June 1930, 8; 16 July 1930, 3; 23 July 1930, 12; 20 August 1930, 3; 24 September 1930, 4; 7 January 1931, 12; 11 February 1931, 8; 6 May 1931, 4; 22 July 1931, 5; 9 December 1931, 5; 23 March 1932, 9; 27 July 1932, 4; 4 January 1933, 5; 30 August 1933, 8; 13 April 1938, 2; 29 June 1938, 4; 2 November 1938, 4; 8 March 1939, 6.

10 Archiwum Państwowe w Płocku (hereafter "APPł"), Starostwo Powiatowe w Gostyninie 1918–1939, syg, 1 s. 28, as cited in Wojciech Marchlewski, "Hollanders during World War II and Their Post-War Situation – Social, Political and Economic Issues. Mennonites in Mazovia 1939–48," *Catalogue of Monuments of Dutch Colonization in Poland*, http://holland.org.pl/art.php?kat=art&dzial=maz&id=13&lang=en; L. Olejnik, *Zdrajcy narodu? Los Volksdeutschów w Polsce po II wojnie światowej* (Warszawa: 2006). For *Die Mennonitische Rundschau* articles supportive of the Nazi regime,

see *MR*: 28 September 1932, 12; 13 November 1935, 4; 2 March 1933, 12; 18 October 1933, 12; 10 May 1939, 12; 14 March 1934, 2; 5 June 1935, 4; 12 January 1938, 12.

11 Peter and Minna Pauls interview by Colin P. Neufeldt, June and July 1992, Calgary; Erna Ratzlaff interview by Colin P. Neufeldt, January and February 1996, Calgary; Peter and Frieda Ratzlaff interview.

12 Peter and Minna Pauls interview; Erna Ratzlaff interview.

13 Foth, *Die Geschichte der Mennoniten*, 170; Daniel Prochnau, "Autobiography of Daniel Prochnau" (Calgary: printed by the author, January 1978); Bruno Rennert, *Meine Lebensgeschichte* (Printed by the author, n.d.).

14 Blanke, "The German Minority in Inter-War Poland," 98–9; Borysiak, *Z Dziejów Ochotniczej Straży*, 23–4. See also Karol Marian Pospieszalski, "W Sprawie strat niemieckiej mniejszości w Polsce przed wybuchem wojny i we wrzesniu 1939," *Przegląd Zachodni* 36, no. 2 (April 1980): 206–9.

15 Erhard Ratzlaff, *Entstehung des Dorfes Deutsch Wymyschle* (printed by the author, n.d.). Erich L. Ratzlaff, *Vom Don an den Fraser. Forschung und Erinnerung* (Abbotsford: printed by the author), 36.

16 Bernard E. Ratzlaff, "Eine Persönliche Erlebnisgeschichte von Bernhard E. Ratzlaff," (Linden: printed by the author, n.d.), 1–7; Ratzlaff, *Entstehung des Dorfes Deutsch Wymyschle*; Foth, *Die Geschichte der Mennoniten*, 86–91; Ratzlaff, *Im Weichselbogen*, 119–21; "Robert Foth Papers," Erich L. Ratzlaff Documents; Edith Hooge, ed., *A Celebration of Family: The Legacy of Kornelius Kliewer* (Abbotsford: printed by the author, 2004); Karol Marian Pospieszalski, *The Case of 58,000 "Volksdeutsche": An Investigation into Nazi Claims Concerning Losses of the German Minority in Poland before and during September 1939* (Poznań: Western Institute, 1981); Peter Ratzlaff interview; Neufeldt, *Ella's Story*, 14–16; Ratzlaff, *Vom Don an den Fraser*, 36; David and Martha Pauls, interview by Colin P. Neufeldt, December 1991, Coaldale, AB; Rennert, *Meine Lebensgeschichte*.

17 Ratzlaff, *Entstehung des Dorfes Deutsch Wymyschle*; Peter and Frieda Ratzlaff interview; Foth, *Die Geschichte der Mennoniten*, 86–91.

18 Foth, *Die Geschichte der Mennoniten*, 86–91; Peter and Minna Pauls interview; Peter and Frieda Ratzlaff interview; Erna Ratzlaff interview. During the Nazi occupation, Gąbin and Deutsch Wymyschle were located in Reichsgau Posen (later Reichsgau Wartheland). For information on the Nazi administration of Wartheland, see Joseph Robert White and Martin Dean, "Warthegau Region (Reichsgau Wartheland)," in *The United States Holocaust Memorial Museum Encyclopedia of Camps and Ghettos, 1933–1945*, vol. 2: *Ghettos in German-Occupied Eastern Europe*, gen. ed. Geoffrey P. Megargee, vol. ed. Martin Dean, pt A (Bloomington: Indiana University Press in association with the United States Holocaust Memorial Museum, 2012), 34–9; Michael Alberti, *Die Verfolgung und Vernichtung der Juden im Reichsgau Wartheland 1939–1945* (Wiesbaden: Harrassowitz Verlag,

196 Colin P. Neufeldt

2006); Benjamin W. Goossen, *Chosen Nation: Mennonites and Germany in a Global Era* (Princeton: Princeton University Press, 2017), 166–73.
19 Melvyn Wrobel, ed., *Gombin Ghetto and the Joint, 1940: Correspondence between the Gombin Jüdisches Hilfskomitee and the Warsaw Office of the American Joint Distribution Committee* (San Diego: Gombin Jewish Historical and Genealogical Society, 1997), 8–12; Ben Guyer, "In the Gombin Ghetto and in the Nazi Camps" in *Gombin: The Life and Destruction of a Jewish Town*, ed. Jack Zicklin (New York: Gombiner Landsmanshaft in Amerike, 1969), 45–55; Jack Frankel, "Gombin Children in Nazi Camps" in *Gombin: The Life and Destruction of a Jewish Town*, 79–82; Abraham Zeideman, "Survived in Soviet Russia," in ibid., 83–95; Szczepański, *Dzieje Gąbina*, 52, 269–74; "Gabin (Gombin)," Museum of the Jewish People – Beit Hatfutsot, Tel Aviv, Israel, accessed 30 March 2018, https://dbs.bh.org.il/place/gabin-gombin; Rabbi Shimon Huberband, *Jewish Religious and Cultural Life in Poland during the Holocaust* (New York: Yeshiva University Press, 1987), 305–7; Anna Ziółkowska, "Gąbin," trans. Katrin Reichelt, in *The United States Holocaust Memorial Museum Encyclopedia of Camps and Ghettos, 1933–1945*, vol. 2, 52–3; Borysiak, *Z Dziejów Ochotniczej*, 13–4; Ratzlaff, *Vom Don an den Fraser*, 39–40; Izabella Bates, Yad Vashem Archives, RG 0.33, file number: 5854; Norm Lupu, "Gabin, Mazovia" International Jewish Cemetery Project, International Association of Jewish Genealogical Societies, http://www.iajgsjewishcemeteryproject.org/poland/gambin.html (accessed 30 March 2018).
20 Wrobel, *Gombin Ghetto*, 10, 20–7, 78–9; Izabella Bates, Yad Vashem Archives, Record Group: 0.33, file number 5854; Rose Greenbaum – Dinerman, "Survived as an "Aryan," in *Gombin: The Life and Destruction*, 67–70; Ratzlaff, *Vom Don an den Fraser*, 40–1; David and Martha Pauls interview; Peter and Frieda Ratzlaff interview; Zeideman, "Survived in Soviet Russia," 83–5; Albert Greenbaum, "Saved by a Peasant Family," in *Gombin: The Life and Destruction*, 56–7; Ziółkowska, "Gąbin," 52; Frankel, "Gombin Children in Nazi Camps," 79–81; "Konin" in *Encyclopedia of Jewish Communities in Poland*, vol. 1 (Poland), *52°13′ / 18°16′*. Translation of "Konin" chapter from *Pinkas Hakehillot Polin* (Jerusalem: Yad Vashem), https://www.jewishgen.org/yizkor/pinkas_poland/pol1_00235.html.
21 Wrobel, *Gombin Ghetto*, 10; Borysiak, *Z Dziejów Ochotniczej Straży*,13–14; "Gombin," in *Encyclopedia of Jewish Communities in Poland*; "Hanna Blawat," http://pages.ucsd.edu/~lzamosc/gblawat.html; Ziółkowska, "Gąbin," 52; Greenbaum-Dinerman, "Survived as an 'Aryan,'" 69–70; Szczepański, *Dzieje*, 274–5, 281; Ratzlaff, *Vom Don an den Fraser*, 39–40; Peter and Minna Pauls interview; David Ratzlaff, *So sah ich die Welt* (Calgary: printed by the author, n.d.).
22 Ziółkowska, "Gąbin," 52; "Gombin" (Gabin, Poland)," *Encyclopedia of Jewish Communities in Poland*; Shmuel Krakowski, *Das Todeslager Chełmno/*

Kulmhof: Der Beginn der "Endlösung," trans. Rachel Grunberg Elbaz (Jerusalem: Yad Vashem, 2007); Łucja Pawlicka-Nowak, ed., *Chełmno Witnesses Speak* (Konin: Council for the Protection of Memory of Combat and Martyrdom in Warsaw and District Museum in Konin, 2004), 205; Szczepański, *Dzieje*, 281–2.

23 Foth, *Die Geschichte der Mennoniten*, 91–2; Ratzlaff, *Entstehung des Dorfes Deutsch Wymyschle*.

24 Peter and Frieda Ratzlaff interview; Peter and Minna Pauls interview; Erna Ratzlaff interview; Christian Jansen and Arno Weckbecker, *Der "Volksdeutscher Selbstschutz" in Polen 1939/49* (Munich: Oldenbourg, 1992), 68–71; Eva Seeber, "Der Anteil der Minderheitsorganisation 'Selbstschutz' an den faschistischen Vernichtungsaktionen im Herbst under Winter 1939 in Polen," *Jahrbuch für Geschichte der sozialistischen Länder Europas* 13, no. 2 (1969): 3–34; Tomasz Sylwiusz Ceran and Centralny Projekt Badawczy IPN, *Im Namen Des Führers ... Selbstschutz Westpreussen i zbrodnia w Łopatkach w 1939 Roku*, Publikacje Gdańskiego Oddziału IPN, vol. 43 (Bydgoszcz: Instytut Pamięci Narodowej. Komisja Ścigania Zbrodni przeciwko Narodowi Polskiemu. Oddział w Gdańsku, 2014); Izabela Mazanowska and Tomasz Sylwiusz Ceran, *Zapomniani Kaci Hitlera. Volksdeutsche Selbstschutz w Okupowanej Polsce 1939–1945 Wybrane Zagadnienia*, vol. 54 (Gdańsk: Instytut Pamięci Narodowej, 2016).

25 Peter and Frieda Ratzlaff interview; David and Martha Pauls interview.

26 Doris L. Bergen, "The Nazi Concept of 'Volksdeutsche' and the Exacerbation of Anti-Semitism in Eastern Europe, 1939–45," *Journal of Contemporary History* 29, no. 4 (October 1994): 575–8; Bergen, "Tenuousness and Tenacity: The *Volksdeutschen* of Eastern Europe, World War II and the Holocaust," in *The Heimat Abroad: The Boundaries of Germanness*, ed. Krista O'Donnell, Renate Bridenthal, and Nancy Ruth Reagin (Ann Arbor: University of Michigan Press, 2005), 269.

27 *Deutsche Volksliste Frieda Ratzlaff*, APPŁ; *Deutsche Volksliste Peter Ratzlaff*, APPŁ; *Deutsche Volksliste Albert Foth*, APPŁ; *Deutsche Volksliste Erich L. Ratzlaff*, APPŁ; Markus Krzoska, " Die Volksdeutsche im Warthegau," in *Umgesiedelt–Vertrieben: Deutschbalten und Polen 1939–1945 im Warthegau*, ed. Eckhart Neander, Andrzej Sakson, Deutsch-Baltische Gesellschaft, and Instytut Zachodni (Marburg: Verlag Herder-Institut, 2010), 66–82; Alexa Stiller, "On the Margins of *Volksgemeinschaft*: Criteria for Belonging to the *Volk* within the Nazi Germanization Policy in the Annexed Territories, 1939–1945," in *Heimat, Region, and Empire: The Holocaust and Its Contexts*, ed. C.-C.W. Szejnmann and M. Umbach (London: Palgrave Macmillan, 2012), 242–7; John J. Kulczycki, *Belonging to the Nation: Inclusion and Exclusion in the Polish–German Borderlands, 1939–1951* (Cambridge, MA: Harvard University Press, 2016), 33–8;

Karol Marian Pospieszalski, *Niemiecka Lista Narodowa w "kraju Warty."* *Wybór dokumentów z objaśnieniami w Języku polskim i francuskim* (la Liste Nationale Allemande Au "pays De La Warta") (Poznań: Inst. Zachodni, 1949); Johannes Frackowiak, "Die 'Deutsche Volksliste' als Instrument der nationalsozialistischen Germanisierungs Politik in den annektierten Gebieten Polens 1939–1945," in *Nationalistische Politik und Ressentiments. Deutsche und Polen von 1871 bis zur Gegenwart* (Göttingen: Hannah-Arendt-Institut für Totalitarismusforschung, 2013), 183–90, 209–13; Roland Borchers, "Deutsche Volksliste," in *Online-Lexikon zur Kultur und Geschichte der Deutschen im östlichen Europa*, 2014, ome-lexikon.uni-oldenburg.de/p32838 (Stand 19.11.2014); Gerhard Wolf, "Exporting Volksgemeinschaft: The *Deutsche Volksliste* in Annexed Upper Silesia," in *Visions of Community: Nazi Germany, Social Engineering, and Private Lives*, ed. Martina Steber and Bernhard Gotto (Oxford: Oxford University Press, 2014), 137–8; Leszek Olejnik, *Zdrajcy Narodu? Losy Volksdeutschów w Polsce po II Wojnie Światowej*, 1. ed. (Warsaw: "Trio," 2006), 24–31; Andrzej Pasek, "Die Deutsche Volksliste und das polnische Recht," in *Jahrbuch für Ostrecht* 42 (2001): 406–11; R.J. Overy, *The Dictators: Hitler's Germany and Stalin's Russia* (New York: W.W. Norton, 2006), 543–4; Allfred Wollensak, "Die 'Deutsche Volksliste in den eingegliederten Ostgebieten,'" *Das Standesamt. Zeitschrift für Standesamtswesen Personenstandsrecht, Ehe- und Kindschaftsrecht, Staatsangehörigkeitsrecht das Standesamt* 6 (1998): 170–5; Maximilian Becker, *Mitstreiter im Volkstumskampf. Deutsche Justiz in den eingegliederten Ostgebieten 1939–1945* (Munich: Oldenbourg, 2014), 37–8; Gerhard Wolf, "*Volk* Trumps Race: The *Deutsche Volksliste* in Annexed Poland," in *Beyond the Racial State: Rethinking Nazi Germany*, ed. Devin O. Pendas, Mark Roseman, and Richard F. Wetzell (Cambridge: Cambridge University Press, 2017), 431–54; Ratzlaff, *Entstehung des Dorfes Deutsch Wymyschle*; "Volksdeutsche," Yad Vashem, http://www.yadvashem.org/odot_pdf/Microsoft%20Word%20-%206345.pdf; Klaus-Peter Friedrich, "Collaboration in a 'Land without a Quisling': Patterns of Cooperation with the Nazi German Occupation Regime in Poland during World War II," *Slavic Review* 64, no. 4 (Winter 2005): 725–8; Marchlewski, "Hollanders during World War II"; Peter and Minna Pauls interview.
28 Erna Ratzlaff interview; David and Martha Pauls interview. See also Jost Hermand and Margot Bettauer Dembo, *A Hitler Youth in Poland: The Nazis' Program for Evacuating Children during World War II* (Evanston: Northwestern University Press, 1997).
29 Friedrich, "Collaboration in a 'Land without a Quisling,'" 727, 731–3; Foth, *Die Geschichten der Mennoniten*, 91–2; Ratzlaff, *Entstehung des Dorfes Deutsch Wymyschle*; Neufeldt, *Ella's Story*, 17–19; Ausgleich Amt re: Konditorei Wolgemuth, 28 Januar 1986, Erich L. Ratzlaff papers; Richard Ratzlaff,

Autobiography (Abbotsford: printed by the author, 1998); Erna Ratzlaff interview; Ratzlaff, *So sah ich die Welt*; David and Martha Pauls interview; Frieda Claassen, interview by Colin P. Neufeldt, August and September 2010, Edmonton.
30 Ratzlaff, *So sah ich die Welt*.
31 Peter and Frieda Ratzlaff interview; Neufeldt, *Ella's Story*, 17–19, 20–3, 33–4, 39–41; Ella Neufeldt, interview by Colin Neufeldt, 2002–3, Coaldale; Borysiak, *Z Dziejów ochotniczej straży*, 14.
32 Peter and Frieda Ratzlaff interview; Peter and Minna Pauls interview.
33 Neufeldt, *Ella's Story*, 28; Norbert Haase and Gerhard Paul, eds., *Die anderen Soldaten. Wehrkraftzersetzung, Gehorsamsverweigerung und Fahnenflucht im Zweiten Weltkrieg* (Frankfurt am Main: Fischer Taschenbuch Verlag, 1995); Steven R. Welch, "Securing the German Domestic Front in the Second World War: Prosecution of Subversion before the People's Court," *Australian Journal of Politics and History* 53, no. 1 (2007): 44–56; Holger Grimm and Edmund Lauf, "Die Abgeurteilten Des Volksgerichtshofs. Eine Analyse Der Sozialen Merkmale," *Historical Social Research / Historische Sozialforschung* 19, no. 2 (70) (1994): 33–52.
34 Ratzlaff, *So sah ich die Welt*. See also Ratzlaff, *Entstehung des Dorfes Deutsch Wymyschle*; Ratzlaff, *Eine Persoenliche Erlebnisgeschichte*, 10–26; David Ratzlaff, *Der Grosse Betrug: Die Mennonitische Wehrlosigkeit* (Calgary: Ulrich Ratzlaff and Bruno Ratzlaff, 2010), 646–56; Ratzlaff, *Vom Don an Den Fraser*, 47–56; Peter and Frieda Ratzlaff interview; Peter and Minna Pauls interview; Marchlewski, "Holendrzy w. Polsce," 349.
35 Colin Neufeldt, *Unsere Familie: A Pictorial History of the Ratzlaff, Janzen, Pauls, and Schmidt Families* (Edmonton: printed by the author, 2006) 59, 66–7, 77, 83–4, 119, 125, 137, 165, 171, 180, 182–3, 188, 231, 238–40, 244, 247.
36 Foth, *Die Geschichte der Mennoniten*, 172–4, 192; Rennert, *Meine Lebensgeschichte*; Erna Ratzlaff interview; Neufeldt, *Ella's Story*, 40–2; Foth, *Die Geschichte der Mennoniten*, 92–3.
37 Neufeldt, *Ella's Story*, 28; *Vereinigung*, box 3, folders 1939, January–June 1940, July–December 1940 and 1941, Mennonitische Forschungsstelle, Bolanden-Weierhof; Horst Gerlach, "The Final Years of Mennonites in East and West Prussia, 1943–45," *Mennonite Quarterly Review* 66, no. 2 (April/July 1992): 242; *Vereinigung*, box 3, folders 1939, January–June 1940, July–December 1940 and 1941, Mennonitische Forschungsstelle, Bolanden-Weierhof.
38 Erna Ratzlaff interview.
39 Foth, *Die Geschichte der Mennoniten*, 92–3; Peter and Minna Pauls interview.
40 Peter and Minna Pauls interview.
41 Ibid.; Ratzlaff, *Entstehung des Dorfes Deutsch Wymyschle*. Mennonites who lived in Gąbin during the war included Peter and Frieda Ratzlaff, David Ratzlaff, Alma (Ratzlaff) Schulz, Willi Pauls, Aganetha (Pauls) Schmidt,

Annie Pauls, Heinrich Wohlgemuth, Kornelius and Lina Wohlgemuth, Anna Wohlgemuth, Peter Foth, Gustav P. Ratzlaff and Maria Ratzlaff, Erich L. Ratzlaff and Lydia Ratzlaff, Wilhelm Kliewer, Reinhold Kliewer, Albert W. Foth (born 1901), Anna Foth, Albert P. Foth (born 1910), Rudolf Witzke and Wilhelm Heier. Peter and Minna Pauls interview; Erna Ratzlaff interview; Foth, *Die Geschichte der Mennoniten*; Ratzlaff, *So sah ich die Welt*.

42 Ratzlaff, *Entstehung des Dorfes Deutsch Wymyschle*; Peter and Minna Pauls interview; Peter and Frieda Ratzlaff interview; Erna Ratzlaff interview.
43 Peter and Minna Pauls interview.
44 Erna Ratzlaff interview.
45 Ratzlaff, *Entstehung des Dorfes Deutsch Wymyschle*; Erna Ratzlaff interview.
46 Jan Borysiak, Feliks Jankowski, Zbigniew Łukaszewski, and Ochotnicza Straż Pożarna (Gąbin), *Z Dziejów ochotniczej straży*, 72–3.
47 Ratzlaff, *So sah ich die Welt*; Erna Ratzlaff interview.
48 Peter and Minna Pauls interview.
49 Erna Ratzlaff interview; Helen Rose Pauls, "Ratzlaff, Gustav (1892–1985)," in *Global Anabaptist Mennonite Encyclopedia Online*, January 2002, http://gameo.org/index.php?title=Ratzlaff,_Gustav_(1892-1985)&oldid=148902 (accessed 21 April 2018).
50 Ratzlaff, *Vom Don an den Fraser*, 39–40; Peter and Minna Pauls interview; Peter and Frieda Ratzlaff interview; Erna Ratzlaff interview. The three Albert Foths associated with Deutsch Wymyschle were Albert W. Foth (1901–1983), married to Anna (Ratzlaff) Foth; Albert J. Foth (1909–1981), married to Anna (Foth) Foth; and Albert P. Foth (1910–1987), married to Irma (Bergmann) Foth. Erich L. Ratzlaff, "Familienregister Linie C," *Familienregister* (Winnipeg: By the Author, n.d.).
51 Szczepański, *Dzieje*, 275–7; Jan Borysiak, "Rok 1941 – wzmożenie prześladowań Żydów i Polaków," *Echo Gąbina* 6 (2001): 3; Peter and Frieda Ratzlaff interview; Olgierd Budrewicz, "Ostatni Polski Mennonita," *Perspektywy*, 38 (1976): 23; Ratzlaff, *So sah ich die Welt*.
52 Ratzlaff, *Vom Don an den Fraser*, 39–42; Heinz Ratzlaff, "Ratzlaff, Eric L. (1911–1988)" in *Global Anabaptist Mennonite Encyclopedia Online*, September 2013, http://gameo.org/index.php?title=Ratzlaff,_Eric_L._(1911-1988)&oldid=148901 (accessed 22 April 2018).
53 Peter and Minna Pauls interview; Peter and Frieda Ratzlaff interview; Erna Ratzlaff interview.
54 "Gabin, den 24.9.40… Der Hilfspolizist Eduard Eichmann…" APPŁ; Szczepański, *Dzieje*, 274–5; Ziółkowska, "Gąbin," 52; Marchlewski, "Hollanders during World War II."
55 Peter and Minna Pauls interview; Peter and Frieda Ratzlaff interview; Erna Ratzlaff interview.

56 Peter and Minna Pauls interview.
57 *Deutsche Volksliste Erich L. Ratzlaff*, APPŁ; Ratzlaff, *So sah ich die Welt*.
58 Peter and Minna Pauls interview; Peter and Frieda Ratzlaff interview; Erna Ratzlaff interview; David and Martha Pauls interview; Frieda Claassen interview; Ratzlaff, *So sah ich die Welt*.
59 Szczepański, *Dzieje*, 274–5; *Deutsche Volksliste Erich L. Ratzlaff*, APPŁ; Ratzlaff, *So sah ich die Welt*.
60 Bundesarchiv, Berlin (hereafter "BB"), NSDAP Mitgliederkartei, NSDAP-Gaukartei / BArch R9361 -IX KARTEI / 9280251; BB, NSDAP Mitgliederkartei, NSDAP-Gaukartei / BArch R9361 -IX KARTEI / 9280252.
61 "Gabin, den 24.9.40... Der Hilfspolizist Eduard Eichmann...," APPŁ. See also Marchlewski, "Hollanders during World War II."
62 "Gabin den 3 September 1940...," APPŁ; Erich L. Ratzlaff, *Vom Don an den Fraser*, 34.
63 BB, NSDAP Mitgliederkartei, NSDAP-Gaukartei / BArch R9361 -IX KARTEI / 33810994.
64 Ratzlaff, "Ratzlaff, Eric L. (1911–1988)," *Global Anabaptist Mennonite Encyclopedia Online*.
65 My great-grandfather, Erich P. Ratzlaff, reportedly hid property for a Jewish friend and secretly milled wheat for local Poles during the Second World War. Peter and Frieda Ratzlaff interview; Saturnin Sobol, "W mennonickim skansenie," 26.
66 Erna Ratzlaff interview.
67 "Starostwo Powiatowe w Gostyninie 1945–1950/59," APPŁ, syg. 20–26, 33–227; Friedrich, "Collaboration in a 'Land without a Quisling," 739–43; Martin Dean, "Where did all the Collaborators Go?" *Slavic Review* 64, no. 4 (Winter, 2005): 791–8; Jan Grabowski, *Hunt for the Jews: Betrayal and Murder in German-Occupied Poland* (Bloomington: Indiana University Press, 2013), 69–73, 97–8, 106, 108–9, 118–19, 153–5, 171–3; Antony Polonsky, *'My Brother's Keeper?': Recent Polish Debates on the Holocaust* (London: Routledge, 1990), 17–18.
68 Szczepański, *Dzieje*, 284; Marchlewski, "Mennonici w Polsce," 133; Marchlewski, "Hollanders during World War II."
69 Peter and Frieda Ratzlaff interview; Erna Ratzlaff interview; Peter and Minna Pauls interview; David and Martha Pauls interview; Frieda Claassen interview; Neufeldt, *Ella's Story*, 39–52; Neufeldt, *Unsere Familie*, 301–6; 309–15; Foth, *Die Geschichte der Mennoniten*, 140–54, 175–6; Ratzlaff, *So sah ich die Welt*; Ratzlaff, *Eine Persoenliche Erlebnisgeschichte*, 27–32.

Chapter Seven

Mennonites in Ukraine before, during, and Immediately after the Second World War

DMYTRO MYESHKOV

The two world wars in which first the Russian empire and then the Soviet Union fought Germany were the most decisive events in the lives of Russian Germans during the twentieth century.[1] The so-called Golden Age of German and Mennonite settlements in the Russian empire was ended by the First World War and the 1917 Revolution. Now a new stage in their history began, marked by tragedy and bloodshed, culminating in the destruction of the traditional ways of life of Russian Germans in the 1920s and '30s. The deportations ordered by the Soviets during the first weeks of the German–Soviet war marked the beginning of the end of the German and Mennonite presence in Ukraine, Crimea, and the northern Caucasus. That dislocation called into question their ability to maintain their ethnic and confessional identity anywhere in the Soviet Union.[2]

Research on Germans in the Soviet Union during the Second World War has taken many fruitful approaches. German-language publications tend strongly to treat the various German-speaking confessional groups as a single body.[3] The 1980s saw two books dealing with this topic that remain foundational to the field to this day.[4] About a decade later, two further research approaches gave additional direction to this topic. In the first, the German population in Eastern Europe was set in the broader context of National Socialist population politics.[5] In the second, German historians investigated the connections between knowledge and Nazi politics both before and after the 1998 Frankfurt Historians' Convention (*Historikertag*), which directly addressed historians' complicity with Nazi rule.[6] Finally, there are two important recent publications to mention. Eric Steinhart used the example of the activities of SS Special Unit (*Sonderkommando*) "R" to show how, in the Odessa region, ethnic Germans were involved in Nazi crimes; and Benjamin Goossen placed the Nazi policies toward Mennonites in Ukraine in a broader spatial and temporal context.[7]

Meir Buchsweiler argues that the history of ethnic Germans from 1941 to 1944 can only be understood if we first understand their experiences in the Soviet Union before the war. This perspective is not new: by the 1940s attempts were being made to explain or justify their collaboration with the occupiers by pointing to the persecution they had suffered in the 1930s. In my view, this research approach remains important if taken with a proper critical understanding of how both totalitarian regimes functioned.

The recently opened KGB archives have offered a new perspective for those who research Mennonites and Germans in Ukraine, especially with regard to the strategies of accommodation and survival these groups adopted under both the Communist and the Nazi regimes. This chapter will show how fruitful these archival collections can be, as well as the drawbacks to using them.[8]

In the 1920s, Germans and Mennonites resisted with great tenacity the Soviets' efforts to force their ideas and practices onto the various national cultures on the territory of the Soviet Union. This resistance was one reason why the Soviet leadership came to view the German minority as an "enemy" nationality and treated them accordingly.[9] Hitler's seizure of power in Germany and the resulting stark ideological contrast between Nazi Germany and the Stalinist Soviet Union deepened the impression that Soviet Germans were a "fifth column."[10] Thus the German and Mennonite population of the Soviet Union by the end of the 1920s and throughout the 1930s drew the attention of various security agencies and became the focus of a series of repressive ideological campaigns, including ones that targeted capitalist elements and kulaks in German villages, emigration promoters and activists, organizers and recipients of famine relief in 1932 and 1933, intellectual leaders, and members of sects.[11]

During the "Great Terror," the notion that the German-speaking population was a "fifth column" served as the basis for an unparalleled wave of repression by the NKVD as part of operations against both "kulaks" and "Germans."[12] Some historians have calculated that in the territory of Zaporizhzhia, in percentage terms, Germans or Mennonites were victimized far more than the general population.[13]

The mass arrests and bogus accusations of crimes reached their peak in 1937–38. One illustration of this is the events in November 1938 in Crimea, a traditional area of settlement for Mennonites. L.T. Yakushev, the director of the NKVD administration in Crimea at the time, would later be charged with and convicted of cruelty for the way he treated prisoners.[14] That month, within a short three days, on his orders, 770 prisoners were shot in the prison in Simferopol' even though the investigations into their cases had yet to be completed. Mennonites were among the victims of this violence.[15]

State terror became a daily experience for the vast majority of the Soviet population in the 1930s regardless of their background. That terror entailed constant feelings of being under threat. In particular, population groups whose members were judged by authorities to be unreliable were consumed with an ever-present fear of being caught up in the millstone of repression. In their daily lives, people had to learn to survive any way that they could. This meant having to acculturate to the environment by learning to express obedience at all times and by cooperating with the secret police. This was done partly out of conviction but more often with the goal of personal survival and to protect the lives of immediate and wider family members.

By the 1930s, the youth who had been socialized under Soviet rule were coming of age. This generation had been shaped by the Soviet policies toward nationalities, which were not limited to the repression of the German diaspora – they aimed to infiltrate *all* national and confessional communities for the purpose of establishing total control. By the mid-1920s, in the German colonies, the Soviet secret police (Joint State Political Directorate; OGPU) were attempting to recruit agents and informers among the German citizens living in the Soviet Union as well as among Soviet Germans and Mennonites.[16] The results of these efforts, which heightened dramatically in the 1930s, are evident in the details of the network of agents that had been planted in German and Mennonite colonies before the war.

In Crimea at the beginning of 1941, among the 38,000 Germans settled in 166 towns and villages, there were thirty-five agents and three handlers; forty-three more NKVD informants would soon be recruited.[17] In the Simferopol' district of Crimea, where the Mennonite colonies of Spat, Minlerčik (Menglerčik), and Sarabuz (among others) were located, by June 1941 there were two handlers, two agents, and nine informants watching a German population of about 4,000. Half of them had been recruited by the first half of the 1930s. In addition, employees of Soviet institutions such as the House of Culture in Spat were used to gather additional information.[18]

Many informants had been forced to cooperate under the threat of repression and carried out their assignments only reluctantly. For example, one informant with the code name "Janzen" was suspected by officials of playing a double game. He was willing to maintain a close relationship with the targeted suspects, but he did not report any relevant information about them, and he tried to satisfy his handlers by providing only general information about conditions on the collective farm. Others were more helpful, such as the informant "Miller," who stated that Mennonite women were circulating a rumour about an attempt to immigrate to Germany, and who delivered "actionable information against E.P. Wiens, who was repressed."[19] The agents' reports suggest an atmosphere of mutual distrust and fear among Mennonites. People avoided conversations in closed rooms or about certain themes.[20]

Mennonites did not serve merely as low-level secret informants. NKVD Lieutenant David Korneevič Wiens was a Mennonite who expanded and led a network of agents among his own people. Almost nothing is known about him except that he arrived in Crimea in the fall of 1936, having been assigned to organize a network of agents and informants among the peninsula's German population.[21]

Another important figure in the Soviet and Party structures in Crimea at this time was Maria Harms, who was born to a Mennonite farming family in 1907 in the village of Rosental near Pyatigorsk. She moved often until the mid-1920s and was educated in Mennonite villages along the Volga, in the Orenburg region, and in Siberia. After the death of her father and her marriage at age twenty to the teacher Kornej Korneevič Wiens, she left her family and moved to Crimea, where she became a Soviet activist in the German and Mennonite villages. She was elected chairman of several village soviets, working in the area of propaganda and as the manager of a socialist reading room. In the first part of the 1930s she was sent to numerous continuing education courses for leaders of the Komsomol (the Communist youth organization) and the Party. She put this training she had received in Moscow and Simferopol' to use as the instructor for the Party committee of the German district of Bijuk-Onlar. Her family life, due to long absences, was less successful than her career. She divorced K.K. Wiens in 1934 and lived common law for several years with a Soviet activist who was a Crimean Tartar. Later in life, family difficulties continued to plague this mother of two children.

The biographies of these two representatives of the first Soviet Mennonite generation differed sharply from those of most others. They were highly educated and socially mobile. In Harms's case one could say she emphasized the needs of the collective over those of her family. Although the sparsity of documents prevents any conclusion about how dedicated to the values of the new regime Harms and Wiens were, both were certainly successful in their careers. One reason for this success was their Mennonite background. In its efforts to gain total control over this milieu, the government was utterly dependent on such cadres.

Equally typical were their fates during the time of purges. Here, Harms was the lucky one. She was "only" expelled from the Party for her connections to repressed "enemies of the people"; for unknown reasons, she suffered no other consequences. It seems that just before the war she even managed to get back into a position of leadership.[22]

Harms's fate is particularly interesting for us since after the Germans occupied Crimea she had to live and work under a different totalitarian regime, that of Nazi Germany. Her case will be discussed again below.

The German invasion of the Soviet Union resulted in deportations in 1941 that meant the end of Mennonite settlement in Ukraine. Many German Lutheran and Catholic settlements in southern and southwestern Ukraine were quickly overrun by the German army, and thus their inhabitants were not deported; the inhabitants of the traditional Mennonite settlements along the east bank of the Dnieper, in the Azov area, and in the Don Basin were not so lucky and were deported by the Soviets. In August 1941 almost the entire German-speaking population of Crimea was deported.

Local Germans and the "New Order"

The fighting near the city of Zaporizhzhia, where Mennonite settlements were thickest, lasted almost two months. The western bank of the city (Nove Zaporizhzhia/Kitschkas/Einlage), including the areas of Mennonite settlement, had been overrun by the Germans and their allies by 18 August. The eastern bank, with the rest of the city districts of Zaporizhzhia as well as the Molotschna settlements around Melitopol' and Molochans'k, formerly Halbstadt, were taken two months later, in the first days of October. On 1 September the western bank was annexed to the German Imperial Commissariat Ukraine and given a civilian administration. The city districts on the east bank were under military administration for a whole year before a civilian administration was established, staffed largely by local Germans and Mennonites.[23]

The so-called ethnic Germans in Ukraine – and the Nazis counted the Mennonites among them – were a principal target of the National Socialists' nationality policies and were intended to serve as a means to germanize the occupied territories. The Nazis needed them as translators and as experts on the local conditions. Thus, they were awarded privileges and placed "under the protection" of the Third Reich. Many ethnic Germans worked as translators for the civilian administration, for army units, for the *Sicherheitdienst* (Security Service; SD), and for rural and urban police forces. In many ethnic German settlements, *Selbstschutz* (self-defence) units were formed.[24]

Ethnic Germans and Mennonites in Ukraine fell under the jurisdiction of the SS special units. In Transnistria and the Imperial Commissariat Ukraine, the Special Unit "R" of the Ethnic German Liaison Office

Mennonites in Ukraine 207

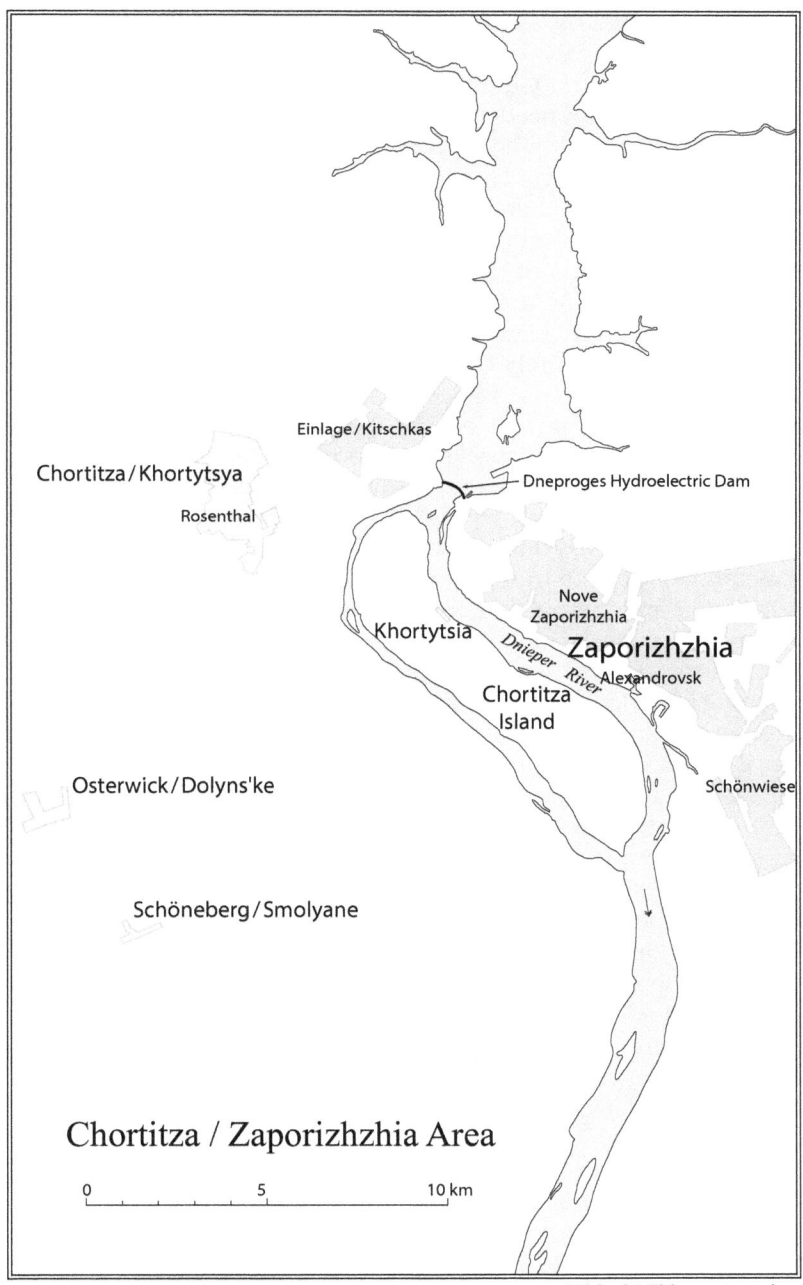

Michael J. Fisher, cartographer

(*Volksdeutsche Mittelstelle*), commanded by Horst Hoffmeyer, had representatives in most of the larger German-populated locales. Their duties were to register "local Germans," run the local administrations, and see to ethnic German needs. Several other institutions and units with responsibilities for fulfilling Nazi policies operated in these areas – for example, the Special Unit Dr K. Stumpp investigated the conditions in the settlements and gathered the information needed to determine the "Aryan ancestry" of local Germans.[25]

The implementation of these policies is better documented for the former Molotschna Mennonite colony. In Molochans'k, the district administrative centre, plans were developed to found an outpost colony (*Stutzkolonie*), a purely German settlement populated by local and resettled ethnic Germans. Molochans'k was visited several times by SS General Hoffmeyer. The local Special Unit "R" representative was Rossman. During the first weeks of the occupation the town became the centre of punitive actions against Soviet activists and Jews. The non-German population was later removed from the colony. In addition to the Germans who had not been deported east by the Soviet army, Germans from around Kharkiv and Donets'k who had lived more isolated lives were resettled here. Some sources suggest that a transit camp was built in Molochans'k for these new settlers. Police and SS personnel recruited translators from the camp for work in Crimea, because after the August 1941 deportations, local ethnic Germans were not available there. As in many other locales, in Molochans'k a self-defence force and a cavalry unit were established. In December 1941 a column of wagons from Molochans'k journeyed to Simferopol', where thousands of Jews had been shot, in order to retrieve the clothing of the murdered for distribution among the ethnic Germans of the Molotschna settlements.

During the occupation, Isaak I. Reimer was installed as the mayor of Nove Zaporizhzhia (Kitschkas), Rudolf Federau as mayor of Molochans'k, and Dietrich Klassen as mayor of Melitopol'. After the changeover to civil administration on the east bank of Zaporizhzhia, Wiebe was made mayor and Toews and Peters department heads of the city administration.[26] At the end of 1941, Reimer was demoted to head of the finance department. During his interrogation after the war he claimed that he had been demoted from mayor because he could not get all the work done. According to other sources, however, the occupiers were quite satisfied with his work: "Reimer is an active, energetic person who is nonetheless lacking in the necessary administrative experience. He does have the necessary perspective and ability, so that his work in part is quite successful."[27] Thus the motives for selecting or removing a candidate from a position remain unclear in many cases.

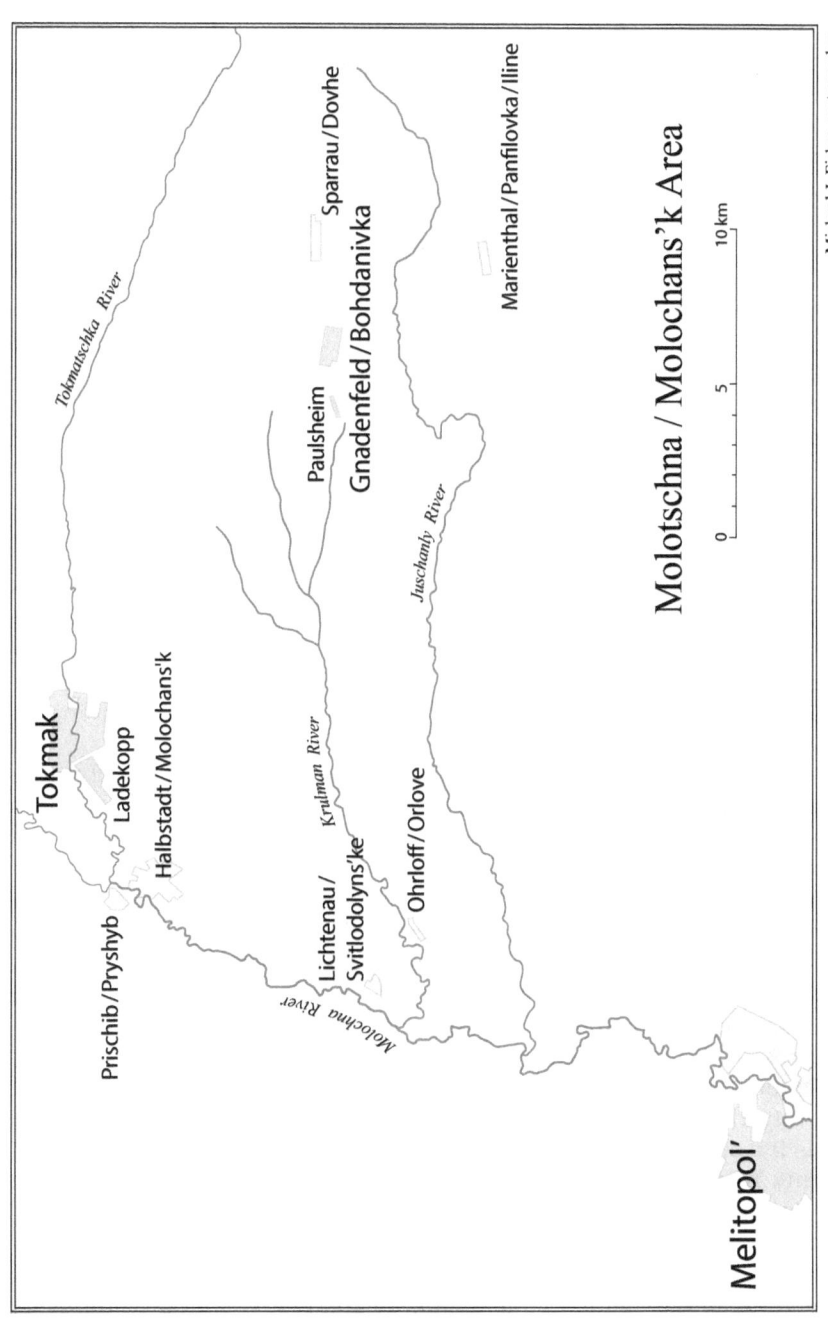

When the city of Zaporizhia was occupied by the Germans in October 1941, the Jewish population numbered 1,841 persons. By spring 1942 at the latest, they had all been murdered. In total, in the Zaporizhia region, more than 14,000 Jews and 10,000 POWs and around 600 Roma were murdered.[28] Individual executions, however, had begun during the very first days of the occupation, in Kitschkas, when Reimer was mayor. His role in the shooting of Jews and Soviet activists is not clear, but given the usual duties of a mayor, it is not likely that he was involved. Based on the investigation of Reimer conducted in 1945–6, it seems he knew about the shootings and offered no resistance to them, given that his duties would have included compiling lists of Jews. Moreover, according to the testimonies of several surviving Jews, Reimer attempted to drive a Jewish family out of their house so that he could move into it himself, punished Zaporizhzhian Jews for appearing on the streets without their Jewish star, and used Jewish labour in his own garden. During the investigation, Reimer denied being actively involved in preparations to shoot Jews or confiscate Jewish property, claiming that these crimes had been committed by the police, to whom he had passed along orders to take Jewish hostages. Reimer's accusation that a number of Mennonite police and SD agents shot Jews has not yet been corroborated by other sources. He admitted to the court that he punished Jews for not wearing the yellow star and that he denied Kitschkaser Jews food ration cards, but he claimed that in so doing he was only following orders that were given to all mayors.[29]

The investigation into the excessive violence of the first days following the arrival of the German military shows that ethnic Germans did not want to practise violence against Jews alone. The common calls for retribution that followed the retreat of the Red Army included diverse targets besides Jews. For example, in Kitschkas a few women whose husbands had been repressed or deported demanded that the new authorities punish those responsible. Following the demands of the Gendarmerie, as part of the cleansing of Nove Zaporizhzhia of anti-German elements, Reimer, with the help of official representatives of the various settlements that were part of the administrative territory, compiled lists of Communist activists for arrest. Of the twenty-three arrested, seventeen were shot immediately. One of these was the activist Antamonov, who shortly before the retreat of the Red Army had himself created a list of Germans and Mennonites to be deported.[30]

Heinrich Wiens led or participated in the execution of activists and Jews around the former Molotschna Colony during the first weeks of the "new order." After being absent for many years, he had returned to his home colony as the commander of Mobile Killing Squad 10-a (*Einsatzkommando*). In these activities he involved local police and collaborators as well as representatives of the civil government such as Piontkovskiy-Federau, the newly appointed mayor of Molochans'k. Molochans'k apparently served as his headquarters until his departure for Crimea at the beginning of November. Wiens and Federau brought those arrested even from distant locales to the edge of the city in order to execute them personally. Among those shot at Wiens's command, for example, was the chair of the Muntau/Yablunivka village soviet, Timošenko. After Wiens left with his group for Crimea, a *Kommando* led by Wenzel took their place in Molochans'k. In November 1941 they shot about one hundred Roma on the edge of town. Federau and other local police allegedly participated in this action.[31] According to a few eyewitnesses after the war, Federau in December 1941 participated in executions that Wiens had organized and implemented on the outskirts of Simferopol' in Crimea, along with a few other ethnic Germans. Later he went to work for the SD in Simferopol'.[32]

Almost all of the officials of the civilian administration denied any involvement in the persecution of Jews in front of Soviet judges; however, the materials accumulated over the course of the investigations suggest something much different. Reimer was finally forced to concede that he was involved in preparations to arrest a group of twenty-three Jews, Communists, and activists. Seventeen of them were shot, including eight Jews who lived in his immediate neighbourhood. This action, it was claimed, was carried out in close cooperation between the police and the newly installed local administration at the request of the Gendarmerie, but it is possible this was a reference to the mobile killing squads that operated directly behind the front lines. Some shootings of Jewish hostages by Hungarian soldiers were carried out on the outskirts of Kitschkas, but this was not in any way a secret: these seventeen were shot in plain light of day in front of the school building in Novyj Kitschkas where the German police were housed. The victims were apparently buried in the nearby vineyard. This event came as a shock to the inhabitants and led to many rumours.[33]

Perpetrators and Active Helpers

This chapter pays the most attention to those Mennonite collaborators who went beyond passive or active assistance in the commission of crimes and became personally involved. Unfortunately, there is little information about people who were not directly the target of inquiry. Even so, it is possible to reconstruct individual events and the roles of those involved by winnowing the files for specific observations, correspondence, and testimonies of suspects and witnesses.

Two Mennonites were able to escape criminal justice although they were suspected of numerous crimes against civilians and Jews: the SS officer Heinrich Wiens, and Rudolf Federau, the mayor of Molochans'k and later head of investigations for the SD in Simferopol'. In both cases, investigations could not be continued because the suspects died. Wiens presumably was killed in the last weeks of the war, and Federau was shot by the SD in May 1943 for misconduct in office.[34]

Some sources suggest that Wiens grew up in Molochans'k and that in 1927 he immigrated to Germany.[35] Other sources make him out to be a German citizen who left Russia in 1928 and remained in Germany until the war began.[36] So far nothing is known about his life in Germany, but there is no doubt he was an enthusiastic Nazi during the 1930s. Historian Michael J. Melnyk, who apparently has seen his SS file, reported that in June 1941 Wiens was assigned to Mobile Killing Squad D as a translator.[37] A few weeks after the Soviet invasion, he was commanding a small group and taking part in executions. In early October, in that function, he returned to occupied Molochans'k, where he reconnected with many acquaintances. Throughout October until he left for Crimea, he arrested and shot many "enemies of the Reich."[38] During this time all the Jewish inhabitants of Molochans'k were arrested and presumably shot.[39]

After the Germans occupied Crimea, Wiens arrived in Simferopol' at the head of a small group known as Special Unit 10-a. Their assignment was to register all the ethnic Germans (from 6 to 11 November, four hundred were recorded there and in the surrounding area),[40] as well as all Jews, and to organize the auxiliary police and city administration. Once Special Units 11-a and 11-b arrived in Simferopol', the peninsula was divided between them, and Wiens transferred to Special Unit 11-b. After the mobile killing squads departed Crimea, the headquarters of the SD for the Taurida region was established in Simferopol'; that region included Crimea as well as the Melitopol' region, with its compact areas of Mennonite and ethnic German settlement.[41]

Matčanbaeva, a translator for the SD in Simferopol', testified concerning Wiens:

> Even before I started working for the SD, I heard rumors about him circulating among people in the city, that he was a beast, that everyone was afraid of him. He was seen as the "Stormtrooper of the Gestapo." He was known for his cruelty, beatings of suspects, which I had to watch myself. He was directly involved in the entire operation to liquidate Jews in 1941 in the city. He also oversaw the registration of all the ethnic Germans as well as the recruitment of Tatars and people from the Caucasus for voluntary

units. He was merciless against Jews and Communists, was vocal about his complete hatred of them, and was full of retribution for them.[42]

Along with the Secret Field Police and under the leadership of the head of the SD Braune and his second-in-command Schulz, Wiens carried out the operation to annihilate the Jews of Simferopol' in two days.[43] In the northern Caucasus, where Wiens arrived with Special Unit 11-b in June, he participated in the execution of civilians.

After returning to Crimea at the end of 1943, he worked at evacuating ethnic Germans, Tatar volunteers, and SD employees along with their families. In the beginning of 1944 he participated in the mass shooting of prisoners in Crimea. At the end of 1944, SS Captain (*Hauptsturmführer*) Heinrich Wiens was reassigned to the reconnaissance unit of the Ukrainian volunteer Waffen-SS division "Galizien." One reason for that reassignment was his fluency in Russian, Polish, and Ukrainian, as well as his experience in fighting partisans on the Eastern Front. His older brother Jakob served in the same unit, having worked earlier in the economic department of the SD in Kiev. In his new position in the Ukrainian division, Wiens again stood out as a sadist who despised Ukrainians.[44] By pure happenstance, the witness Matčanbaeva ran into him in 1945 in Graz. At that time, he was serving in a volunteer division on the Austro-Hungarian border (later the Austrian–Yugoslavian border) with the rank of SS captain.[45]

Rudolf Federau was another notorious figure. According to the records compiled on the activities of Simferopol' SD employees, this SS sergeant (*Scharführer*) was originally from Molochans'k.[46] According to the testimony of an SD agent, before the war he had worked under the name of Piontkovskiy as a school director in the city of Kryvyi Rih.[47] When the occupation began he moved with his family to Molochans'k. His wife's maiden name was Letkemann.

The reports of his activities before the occupation have been partly corroborated by eyewitnesses. Just before the Germans occupied Molochans'k, he was seen in the city wearing the uniform of a Soviet officer. By the time the occupation began, he admitted to being a German spy and that he had crossed the front line many times to gather information from wounded Red Army soldiers about activists, commissars, and Jews.[48] He served as mayor of Molochans'k until February 1942, when he left under the command of Heinrich Wiens, with whom he had often shot Jews on the city outskirts, to serve as a translator for the SD in Crimea.[49]

According to materials in the relevant SD documents relating to Crimea, Federau was "at the same time a translator, agent, and provocateur." He was assigned to the Sixth Informant Department. He had his own large network of agents, and he worked at exposing underground organizations using the false identity of a Soviet partisan. This led to him arresting a large number of people in the district of Melitopol' and in Crimea.[50]

He was highly trusted by Paul Zapp, the head of the SD from September 1942 to September 1943, so he did not need to keep protocols of his investigations against partisans – instead, he could simply recommend several dozen of those arrested for execution. In May 1943, Federau was arrested for bribery, and it was revealed that he exaggerated cases and arrested innocent people in order to polish his image with his superiors. He was accused by the SD department head Berger of robbing and raping victims. Berger led the investigation himself. A search of Federau's apartment in Molochans'k turned up a lot of gold in various forms – coins, watches, and wristwatches, among other items – which he had extorted from the relatives of people he arrested. Federau promised to release people on being paid these bribes; then he typically shot them anyway. His behaviour had fostered many grievances among the inhabitants of the district of Melitopol' and Crimea, which threatened to undermine the SD's authority. Therefore, the head of the SD devoted a great deal of attention to investigating him and then publicized its findings. There are reports that young women whom he had raped were brought from the camp at Konstantinovka to Simferopol' to confront him. Some of them were later freed, others sent to Germany to work.[51] Federau was shot one and a half to two months after his arrest,[52] along with his accomplice Viktor Del', a local ethnic German from Heniches'k. Having uncovered the facts of Federau's dereliction of duty, Berger executed him personally.[53]

It remains unclear what Federau's motives were or whether he participated in crimes. It seems most likely that this man, who worked undercover without any restraints for the German occupiers and who had criminal tendencies, gave in to his worst instincts. In that sense he was quite different from Wiens, who apparently became a fanatical follower of Hitler in the 1930s. For the many victims of the National Socialist Wiens and the "merely" criminal Federau, this difference in motivation had led in any case to the same result.

Translators, Teachers, and Doctors

The SD's activities in Crimea can be divided into two different phases that explain their need for specialist and general workers recruited from the local populace. The first phase lasted from the beginning of the occupation at the start of November 1941 until July or August 1942.

The second stretched from August 1942 until the Germans retreated from Crimea in the second half of November 1943. During the first phase, the front-line units of the SS and then the arriving Special Units 11-a and 11-b were the main actors, remaining in Crimea until late summer 1942. After their transfer to the northern Caucasus, the SD established a stationary staff with branches in all the cities of Crimea and in the districts north of the Sea of Azov, including the Mennonite colony of Molotschna.

The front-line SS units that arrived in Crimea in the earliest days of the occupation brought translators with them. Most of these people came from the German colonies around Odessa (Lutheran, Reformed, and Catholic). In the course of registering the Germans remaining on the peninsula, those who spoke adequate German were offered jobs with the SS. Those who could write legibly and without errors were set to work translating documents.

Once the special units left the Crimea and the SD was reorganized, the lack of translators became more noticeable. The new SD head, Weissboland (?), personally drove to Molochans'k at the beginning of August 1942 to the Germans who had been resettled there from Kharkiv and recruited several people.[54] Over time the percentage of Mennonites from Crimea and Taurida grew among the translators. Many of these Mennonite translators – Maria Harms, A. Wiens, Elizaveta Janzen, and others – were employed by the Fourth Investigation Department, which dealt with the prosecution of Soviet activists, Jews, and partisans.[55] In the roughly eighteen months they served in that job, each translator must have worked at least 500 interrogations. Over the course of that work, more or less stable teams of an SD investigator and a translator evolved. Given the intimate relationship that developed between the two, the influence of the translator on the fate of individual prisoners was immense. Often the translator conducted questioning and wrote up the protocols without the investigator even present. Another typical activity for these translators was translating lists of Soviet activists or Jews.[56]

Elizaveta Jul'evna Janzen, a resident of Simferopol', avoided deportation, perhaps because the father of one of her daughters was an officer in the Red Army. During the occupation she worked for a time in one of the former buildings of the city soviet of Simferopol', where a camp had been set up to sort the property of the murdered Jews and prepare these items for distribution to local ethnic Germans. By her own testimony, Janzen acquired a number of valuable objects here, although she was unable to get all of them out of the camp since some were stolen from her. Neither these facts, nor her acquisition as an ethnic German of a fully furnished apartment, prevented colleagues from describing her as a modest and quiet woman.⁵⁷

Maria Harms, mentioned above, who shortly before the occupation was still working as a Party secretary and leader of the personnel office of the People's Commissariat for Food Acquisition in Crimea, moved into the apartment of an evicted Jewish family after registering as an ethnic German and stocked it with furniture acquired from the Inventory Office, which oversaw the possessions of expelled or murdered Jews.⁵⁸

Despite her past as a Party secretary, Harms was able to win the trust of the Germans at the SD over time and fostered the career of her former husband's sister, the roughly thirty-year-old Agnessa Korneevna Wiens. The trained teacher and wife of a Red Army soldier moved in December 1942 from the northern Caucasus to Crimea with her two small children and started working for the SD.⁵⁹

The main witness in the case against the SD in Simferopol', Matčanbaeva, was also quite critical of another Mennonite translator, the twenty-five-year-old Maria Epp from the district of Melitopol'. The question of whether Epp was involved in persecuting Jews out of greed or hate bears further investigation. According to Matčanbaeva's testimony, Epp did not simply appropriate Jewish property (as Janzen and Harms did) or buy it (like Harms); she entered Jewish apartments along with the investigating official (*Untersuchungsführer*) Tempel to remove property before any decision about how to dispose of it had been officially made. Epp enjoyed strutting her "Jewish plunder" and showed no shame in storing entire suitcases full of clothing in her office and showing the contents to colleagues. In addition, she provided weak and garbled accounts of her (alleged) imprisonment by the Soviets in Feodosija at the time of the Soviet paratrooper landing at the end of 1941. She also misused her position as translator to compromise several prisoners.⁶⁰

The degree to which translators were enmeshed in National Socialist crimes depended in large part on where they worked. In regions where Jews were few, and in the economic offices, the probability was naturally lower than if one worked as a translator for the security apparatus or at locations where even in 1942 and 1943 mass executions of Jews, Roma, and other "undesirable" populations were still taking place. But even translators working in the security apparatus had some room to manoeuvre in their relationship with the executioners and victims of the National Socialist regime, as the Simferopol' SD files reveal. Certainly not everyone saw or used these possibilities.

One of the most important ethnic German specialists the Nazis used was Ivan Ivanovič Klassen from the village of Šestakovka near Stalino/Donets'k. Following his education at the Kharkiv Medical Institute he began work at the hospital in Molochans'k, where his father had been born. Besides working as a doctor, he gave lectures at the medical school there. He was thirty-four years old when the German–Soviet war began and was already the head doctor, a position he retained throughout the occupation. In December 1945 he was arrested by SMERŠ (Soviet military security) in a small town in Mecklenburg to which he had been evacuated in 1944 with his parents, two brothers, and three sisters.[61] Later he was transferred to Zaporizhzhia and sentenced to death by firing squad. He was executed on 17 January 1947.

In addition to the usual charges levelled at most ethnic Germans (availing oneself of the privileges offered by the occupiers, migration to a foreign country, and acceptance of foreign citizenship, which was high treason according to article 54–1 of the Ukrainian SSR legal code), Klassen was charged with a long list of serious crimes committed in the course of discharging his professional duties: working in the "SS hospital"; failing to treat Red Army members, leading in several cases to their deaths; and, finally, ferreting out handicapped people unfit to work in the handicapped home in the village of Orlove (Ohrloff), which resulted in their being shot by SS special units. Here the focus will be only on this final accusation. At issue is a trip Klassen made to Orlove to examine the patients of the home there.

In November 1941 Klassen drove to Orlove under the orders and in the company of the head of the Molochans'k SD, Second Lieutenant (*Untersturmbannführer*) Wenzel, in order to identify those handicapped who could not work. Although no one officially informed him about the purpose of the examinations, Klassen's overhearing Wenzel's comment that a planned "resettlement" of those handicapped would follow was sufficient for him to understand they would be liquidated. At the time, Molochans'k had been occupied for only one month, but Klassen understood the Nazi jargon perfectly well. One reason for that might well have been his acquaintance with SS officer Heinrich Wiens, with whom in the 1920s he had gone to school in Molochans'k. There were two homes in Orlove with approximately one hundred elderly handicapped and about that many handicapped children aged six to fourteen. An SD special unit shot about one hundred of these inhabitants about a month after Klassen's visit.[62] From the outset of the investigation, Klassen admitted his participation in the examinations as well as the circumstance that he knew at once what the consequences would be for patients he declared unfit for work. The testimony of both the accused and witnesses agreed that not nearly all of the patients were actually examined and that the examination itself was perfunctory. Klassen only denied having personally made any marks in the lists, as was reported by some witnesses. At the end of the court process he declared his regret for his actions, mentioning explicitly the episode at the handicapped home in Orlove: "I feel guilty for the killing of handicapped, since I wrote the report. I find my action to be exceptionally culpable, but I saw no other choice at the time, since I feared being arrested any day."[63]

The case of the home for the handicapped should be seen in a wider context. There is no doubt that it was Nazi policy to liquidate a large percentage of these helpless people and to follow that up with relocating what was left of this institution outside of the village limits of Orlove. At the same time, this action was only a part of the larger plan to remove the non-German population from the Molotschna Colony in order to establish a colony for Germans only. The patients of a similar institution in the area, in Lichtenau/Svitlodolyns'ke, most likely met the same fate. Among the materials gathered by the state commission to determine the extent of the losses caused by the German Fascist attackers were accounts of similar actions in the districts of Zaporizhzhia and Brest.[64]

Conclusion

Two important matters must be kept in mind: the problem of identity (or loyalty), and the special nature of the sources used in this chapter. The problem of the identity (or loyalty) of the Mennonites just before and during the Second World War has often been researched. In the investigation at hand, it was of great practical importance and difficulty, for it entailed striving to establish clearly the membership of each person in the Mennonite community. Under both Stalin and Hitler, Mennonites were not recognized as an independent group but rather as part of a larger minority defined by ethnicity, not religion. The Soviets saw Mennonites as "Germans," with the only exception arising during the campaign against "sects," so a phase of their persecution followed that religious criterion. The Nazis, for their part, saw Mennonites as ethnic Germans similar to Aryan Germans.

Therefore, in each case one must ask which characteristic or bundle of characteristics is decisive or sufficient for identifying this or that person as a Mennonite. The profound changes that took place in the Mennonite community in Ukraine and Crimea as a result of social upheavals during this era only make the task more daunting. Violent modernization accelerated the changes in Mennonite identity and exacerbated the generational conflict that was already developing in the early twentieth century. Can those who broke with their community and who worked actively with the Soviet authorities, often to the detriment of their community, still be identified as Mennonites? How should we refer to those who hid their social or national origins and took on a completely or partly new foreign identity? How should we evaluate the common Mennonite practice of adapting to the Soviet and Nazi dictatorships, especially when such accommodations ran counter to traditional Mennonite values and teachings? And, finally, what was the relationship between identity and loyalty to these very different regimes?

An advantage to tapping the sources used here (the risks and drawbacks will be discussed later) is that they allow us to follow the life paths of the subjects at least in part over several decades. People who lived in Ukraine in the 1930s and '40s were shaped by the experience of dictatorship, and the change in regimes in the summer and fall of 1941 makes it essential to recognize the pattern of accommodation as practised under these new conditions. As different as the statuses of "fifth columnist" and "ethnic German" were, many Soviet Mennonites clearly found it useful to declare loyalty and adopt the strategy of accommodation. This process is particularly well illustrated by the cases of those who were forced to cooperate with the secret police during Soviet rule. By his own admission, supported in part by other sources, I. Reimer cooperated with the OGPU–NKVD under the agent name of Friedrich and later Robert beginning in the second half of the 1920s. I. Klassen began such work in the mid-1930s. Abra(ha)m Wiebe, an instructor at the Industry Institute, who during the occupation worked as a translator for the SD and as a newspaper editor, had certainly been a secret informer for the NKVD, along with many other Mennonites.

Conditions under the Soviet dictatorship were such that once persecution of Germans began, many people attempted to disguise their ethnic and social background. One of the most extreme examples of the adoption of a foreign identity was that of Johann Genrichovič Dierksen from Gnadenfeld or Sparrau in the Molotschna colony. His parents, who died before the First World War, were well-to-do farmers. Johann therefore, since he wanted "to disguise his social background," acquired documents during the Civil War that declared him to be the Ukrainian Nikolaj Abramovič Pikolenko (in one of his interrogations he spoke of having gotten "good documents" as part of his demobilization from the Red Army in the 1920 or 1921). He lived under this name in the Mennonite settlement area. Between 1923 and 1934 he worked for the police and continued to hide "his German background ... since he feared persecution by the Soviet power." After the occupation began he volunteered as a translator for Wehrmacht units and worked for the council of a small city in the northern Caucasus. After the Red Army arrived, he switched sides again, fought against the Germans, and was awarded a Soviet medal for bravery. At the time of the investigation, he declared his willingness to work as an informant for the security services in order to escape any punishment for crimes he had committed during the occupation.[65]

Mennonite declarations of willingness to work for the Soviet police, of which there were many (this is in addition to the example of Dierksen-Pikolenko, who had the cover name of "Janzen"), should be seen as attempts to avoid even worse forms of punishment and not necessarily as declarations of loyalty. That is why the Nazis were not particularly bothered by such outward displays of loyalty to the Soviets such as Party membership or being part of the secret police's agent network.[66] When their applications for ethnic German status were reviewed, such people were granted German names even if they had not used them for a long time because they had wanted to avoid the attention of Soviet authorities (e.g., German wives of non-German husbands). Maria Harms was given an internal passport in September 1941 that read Poljakova-Harms, which was probably an attempt to avoid deportation, perhaps by marrying a non-German. It is not possible to document which names she used in the 1930s, especially after her divorce from K.K. Wiens. It is clear that her colleagues in the SD referred to her by her maiden name of Harms or by her previous name of Wiens or as Harms-Wiens. During her evacuation from Crimea in 1943 she had the following documents with her: a German ID and marching orders under the name of Maria Wiens, maiden name Harms, and the Soviet passport mentioned above, as well as a residence permit from the city administration of Simferopol' listing her name as Bogdanova in case she needed to live undercover.[67]

Given the lack of documents and the high number of mixed marriages, it was not easy to confirm one's status as an "ethnic German" during the occupation. Abuses and corruption on the part of both local Germans and German occupiers muddied the boundaries of this group, with the result that acquisition of this status became more an issue of power and access to resources. Many cases are known of people getting these designations without meeting any of the criteria.[68]

The archives of Soviet secret services that have been the main source for this research are a unique historical source. Doubts about their reliability are justified. For example, the pressure on investigators to meet "quotas" and "work norms" in terms of a certain number of protocols per day invited abuses of normal legal practices. Under such conditions common practices included the invention of criminal organizations in order to make one's own work seem more important, the expansion and falsification of protocols, and forcing suspects to make confessions.[69]

Sometimes the accused retracted their confessions even before the investigation or trial was complete. For example, Isaak Reimer in the spring of 1946 repudiated the statement he had made after his arrest in 1945 about Mennonites who were SD agents: "In the interrogation of 23 February 1945 … I was ordered under the threat of violence to name the secret agents in the German network. I decided instead to name those who helped the Germans and had contacts there since I did not know any of their secret agents."[70]

The scepticism one brings when approaching these investigative materials only increases when one considers the wave of revisionism that began after Stalin's death. The interrogators and employees of the NKVD were not generally held accountable, and they denied accusations that they had violated the law, yet one cannot simply ignore the arguments and complaints of their victims. During the war and in the immediate postwar years, trials were held under simplified regulations, at high speed and under war conditions. The suspected crimes were not adequately investigated, and the military tribunals that examined many Mennonites were often conducted without witnesses. The investigations themselves were barely documented. Yet the materials in the investigation files and other materials collected still provide a great deal of new information concerning the Mennonites' final years in Ukraine. They enable us not so much to determine the exact level of guilt of this or that individual as to understand the process as a whole.

Translation: Mark Jantzen

NOTES

The author would like to thank all the employees of the SBU archives in Kiev (Ukraine) and the regional centres for their generous and competent support, especially Andriy Kohut and Maria Panova.

1 Following the research tradition established in Germany and the successor states of the Soviet Union, "Russian German" here refers to all German-speaking minorities on the relevant territory, including Mennonites, even though the historical and confessional particularities of the Mennonites have been extensively researched.
2 The literature on the history of Russian Germans including the Mennonites is extensive. Overviews of the different areas are covered in various bibliographies and encyclopedias: Detlef Brandes and Victor Dönninghaus,

eds., *Bibliographie zur Geschichte und Kultur der Russlanddeutschen*, vol. 2: *Von 1917 bis 1998* (Munich: R. Oldenbourg Verlag, 1999); T.N. Černova, ed., *Rossijskie nemcy. Otečestvennaja bibliografija, 1991–2000 gg. Ukaz. novejšej lit. no istorii i kul'ture nemcev Rossii* (Moscow: Gotika, 2001); V.M. Karev, ed., *Nemcy Rossii*, 3 vols. *Entsiklopediya* (Moscow: ERN, 1999–2006).

3   The German, English, Ukrainian, and Russian language historiography is not the focus of this chapter. Here only the most important publications, including those that have influenced this chapter and the field in general, will be mentioned.

4   Ingeborg Fleischhauer, *Das Dritte Reich und die Deutschen in der Sowjetunion* (Stuttgart: Deutsche Verlags-Anstalt, 1983); Meir Buchsweiler, *Volksdeutsche in der Ukraine am Vorabend und Beginn des zweiten Weltkriegs – ein Fall doppelter Loyalität?* (Gerlingen: Bleicher, 1984).

5   Götz Aly, *"Endlösung." Völkerverschiebung und der Mord an den europäischen Juden* (Frankfurt am Main S. Fischer, 1995). At the same time, Doris L. Bergen published "The Nazi Concept of 'Volksdeutsche' and the Exacerbation of Anti-Semitism in Eastern Europe, 1939–1945," *Journal of Contemporary History* 29, no. 4 (October 1994), 569–82.

6   The foundational work that emerged here included, for example, Michael Fahlbusch, Ingo Haar, and Alexander Pinwinkler, eds., *Handbuch der völkischen Wissenschaften. Akteure, Netzwerke, Forschungsprogramme*, 2 vols. (Berlin: De Gruyter Oldenbourg, 2017).

7   Eric C. Steinhart, *The Holocaust and the Germanization of Ukraine* (Cambridge: Cambridge University Press, 2015); Benjamin W. Goossen, *Chosen Nation: Mennonites and Germany in a Global Era* (Princeton: Princeton University Press, 2017).

8   The research presented here was done as part of the author's work since 2017 at the Institute for the Culture and History of Germans in Eastern Europe at the University of Hamburg (IKGN e. V., Lüneburg). The overall title of the project is "Ukraine Germans before, during, and in the first years after the Second World War."

9   Terry Martin, *The Affirmative Action Empire: Nations and Nationalism in the Soviet Union, 1923–1939* (Ithaca: Cornell University Press, 2001), esp. ch. 8.

10 Savin argued that this stereotype of the Mennonites had developed by the 1920s. A.I. Savin, "Formirovanie koncepcii nemeckoj 'pjatoj kolonny' v SSSR (seredina 1920-ch godov)," in *Voprosy germanskoj istorii: Sb. nauč. trudov.* ed. S.I. Bobyleva (Dnepropetrovsk: "Porogi," 2007), 215–22; idem, "Vvedenie. Mennonity kak celevaja gruppa repressij konca 1920-ch – 1930-ch godov," in *Ėtnokonfessija v sovetskom gosudarstve. Mennonity Sibiri v 1920–1930-e gody. Ėmigracija i repressii. Dokumenty i materialy*, ed. Savin (Novosibirsk: Posoch, 2009), 7–55. See also Goossen, *Chosen Nation*, 121–46.

11 Viktor V. Čencov, "Die Organe der Staatssicherheit als Mittel zur Umsetzung der repressiven Politik der Sowjetmacht in den 30er Jahren," in *Deutsche in Rußland und in der Sowjetunion 1914–1941*, ed. A. Eisfeld, V. Herdt, and B. Meissner (Berlin: LIT Verlag, 2007), 285. Alfred Eisfeld and O. S. Rubl'ov, ed., *Delo "Nacional'nogo sojuza nemcev na Ukraine" 1935–1937 gg. Dokumenty i materialy* (Kiev: TOV "Vydavnytstvo Klio," 2016).

12 In the course of this massive operation by the NKVD, members of Protestant congregations were targeted, including German Lutherans and Mennonites. For additional details, see Savin, "Vvedenie." The history of the operation against "Germans" in Ukraine 1937–38 is the subject of Alfred Eisfeld et al., eds., *"Velykyi teror" v Ukraïni. Nimec'ka operacija 1937–1938 rokiv. Zbirnyk dokumentiv* (Kiev: K.I.S., 2017).

13 F. Turčenko, ed., *Zaporiz'kyj rachunok velykyj vijni 1939–1945* (Zaporižžja: Prosvita, 2013), 54.

14 Among the known cases are the burning of eleven prisoners, public executions, and the extraction of gold teeth from corpses. For more detail on Yakushev, see A.G. Tepljakov, "Amnistirovannye čekisty 1930-ch gg. v period Velikoj Otečestvennoj vojny," *Klio. Žurnal dlja učënych* 67, no. 7 (2012): 69–76.

15 Folder 2, 15.1.1939, GDA SBU (Galuzevyj derzhavnyj archiv Sluzhby bezpeky Ukrajiny = Branch State Archive of the Security Services of Ukraine) (Crimea, spr. 2601, 155–67.

16 Savin, "Vvedenie," 7–55 at 12.

17 "Über die Zahl der registrierten Elemente, das Agentennetz, durchgeführte Verhaftungen und Anwerbungen auf deutscher Linie für 19 Rayone der ASSR Krim mit deutscher Bevölkerung zum 3.01.1941," GDA SBU, f. 13, op. 1, spr. 1139, 6.

18 According to informants' reports, many of these came from or lived in German or Mennonite villages. Lists of the agents and informants, compiled in the Simferopol' district of the NKVD in ASSR Crimea, in the department for counter-intelligence, as of 1 June 1941, as well as other correspondence, GDA SBU, f. 13, op. 1, spr. 1137, 55, 86–87, 112, 118–23.

Half of the eleven members of the agent network had been recruited as of the first half of the 1930s. For the pattern of reports about the attitudes of Mennonites and Germans, see the reports of agents "Lenskaja," "Rusov," and "Gromov"; ibid, 18–20, 111. At first glance, the network of agents was much denser in the German and Mennonite settlements of Crimea than in Ukrainian districts, including those of southern Ukraine with large Mennonite populations. Nadija Kel'm, Petro Bodnar, and Volodymyr Charčenko, eds., "2,3 stukača na tysjaču naselennja," http://texty.org.ua/pg/article/Oximets/read/86836/23_stukacha_na_tysachu_naselenna_Agent_NKVS.

19 The Crimean NKVD administration expected the informant "Janzen" to provide information that would compromise Ivan Wilms from the village of Spat as well as Isaak Dyck and other Mennonites: GDA SBU, f. 13, op. 1, spr. 1137, 55, 86–87, 112, 118–23. There were also examples of the opposite characteristic (opinion about agent) of 30.4.1941: ibid., 76.
20 GDA SBU, f. 13, op. 1, spr. 1137, 21, 22.
21 Information about the composition of the Crimean population (no date): ibid., spr. 1139, 7–9 at 9. Until his arrest in fall 1938 he was the deputy leader of Department 3 (Counter-Intelligence), in charge of work among Germans and against Germany. In the fall of 1938 he was arrested together with his brother Kornej (Kornelius), a teacher in Feodosija, following a denunciation by a Mennonite from Spat. They were accused of working for Nazi Germany. Report of the People's Commissar for the Interior of the Crimean ASSR, Captain Yakushev, no. 31268 from 14.9.1938, SBU Archive in the Autonomous Republic of Crimea, spr. 2601, 1–18.
22 Interrogation M.Ja. Poljakova-Harms from 6.4.1945. GDA SBU Crimea, f. 13, spr. 1431, vol. 12, 213–14.
23 Turčenko ed., *Zaporiz'kyj rachunok velykij vijni*, 136–9.
24 Fleischhauer, *Das Dritte Reich;* Buchsweiler, *Volksdeutsche in der Ukraine;* Goossen, *Chosen Nation*, 121–173; Steinhart, *The Holocaust and the Germanization of Ukraine*.
25 On Stumpp, see Eric J. Schmaltz and Samuel D. Sinner, "The Nazi Ethnographic Research of Georg Leibbrandt and Karl Stumpp in Ukraine and Its North American Legacy," *Holocaust and Genocide Studies* 14, no. 1 (2000): 28–64; Hans-Christian Petersen, "The Making of Russlanddeutschtum: Karl Stumpp oder die Mobilisierung einer 'Volksgruppe' in der Zwischenkriegszeit," in *Minderheiten im Europa der Zwischenkriegszeit. Wissenschaftliche Konzeptionen, mediale Vermittlung, politische Funktion*, ed. Cornelia Eisler and Silke Götsch-Elten (Münster: Waxmann, 2017), 163–91. Petersen is currently working on a biography of Stumpp. About Mennonites who worked for Stumpp on his projects, see also Goossen, *Chosen Nation*, 160.
26 Turčenko ed., *Zaporiz'kyj rachunok velykij vijni*, 148. On Mennonites who were active in the civilian administration, including Isaak Reimer, see Goossen, *Chosen Nation*, 162.
27 The quoted document is report no. 676 of the *Feldkommendatur* of 21 October 1941. Martin Din, "Radjans'ki etnični nimci i Holokost u Reichskomisariati Ukraïna, 1941–1944," in *Šoa v Ukraïni. Istorija, svidčennja, uvičnennja*, ed. Ray Brandon, Wendy Lower, and Natalâ Komarova (Kyïv: Duch i litera, 2015), 368.
28 Turčenko ed., *Zaporiz'kyj rachunok velykij vijni*, 140, 144, 145.

29 For more details see investigation file I.I. Reimer, GDA SBU Zaporizhzhia Region, file 68045, testimony of the witness Fenja G. Šif from 16 June 1946, ibid., 96–7 verso at 97. At the trial, Reimer explained the refusal to give bread ration cards to Jews with the accusation that they had carried out the instructions of the Communists to burn all the grain before retreating. See court protocol from 30 July 1946, ibid., 140–7 verso at 146. On the accusation against the police, see interrogation I.I. Reimers from 7 May 1946, ibid., 50–2 verso at 52.

30 Wives of the repressed by the names of Schmidt, Dierksen, and Thiessen demanded that the mayor arrest Soviet activists and militia. Interrogation I.I. Reimers from 17 June 1946, ibid., 61–4 verso at 62 verso.

31 Interrogation I.I. Klassen on 21 October 1946, GDA SBU Zaporizhzhia Region, spr. 11343, 51–5 verso at 53 verso 54.

32 More details on Federau and Wiens are supplied below.

33 "A meeting was called in the apartment of the Gendarmerie chief. I took part as mayor, along with my assistant Wiens, a few officers, and the chief of police. The Gendarmerie chief [Mobile Killing Squad? – D.M.] read the names of those arrested and for the most part recommended that they be shot. Neither I nor anyone else objected. After the meeting the Gendarmerie chief went to the commandant for approval and received it." Interrogation of 17 June 1946, investigation file I.I. Reimers, GGA SBU, f. 5, spr. 68045, 61–2 at 63 verso. Weins is also discussed in chapter 1.

34 The eyewitnesses' testimonies about Federau were given by the Soviets in the 1960s to the West German Justice Department officials in Ludwigsburg as part of a request for assistance. Bundesarchiv Ludwigsburg. B 162/8566, 253; B162/8569, 134.

35 Interrogation of T.V. Matčanbaeva on 29 January 1946, GDA SBU Crimea, f. 11, spr. 1431, vol. 1, 76–134 verso at 93 verso. Interrogation of Poljakova-Harms on 21 May 1945, ibid., 139–46 verso at 145. Other sources claim that Wiens was born in Muntau near Molochans'k/Halbstadt. Michael James Melnyk, *The History of the Galician Division of the Waffen-SS*, vol. 1: *On the Eastern Front April 1943 to July 1944* (Stroud: Fonthill, 2016), 200, 202. Andrej Angrick's research included an evaluation of Heinrich Wiens's personnel files, which were the source of his published photo. Angrick, *Besatzungspolitik und Massenmord. Die Einsatzgruppe D in der südlichen Sowjetunion 1941–1943* (Hamburg: Hamburger Edition, 2003), 421, 614.

36 Interrogation of I.I. Klassen on 8 August 1946, GDA SBU Zaporizhzhia Region, spr. 11343, 13–20 verso at 19 verso. Other sources suggest he emigrated only in 1930, to Danzig. Goossen, *Chosen Nation*, 159.

37 Michael James Melnyk, *To Battle: The Formation and History of the 14th Galician Waffen-SS Division* (Solihull: Helion, 2002), esp. n106.

38 Klassen relates in an investigation a case where Wiens cynically refused to spare the wounded Jewish POW, Rol. Interrogation of I.I. Klassen on 30 August 1946, GDA SBU Zaporizhzhia Region, spr. 11343, 31 verso, see endnote 36.
39 Interrogation of I.I. Klassen, 22 Septmeber 1946, ibid., 38.
40 Testimony of M.Ja. Poljakova-Harms, "Über Registrierungsverfahren für 'Volksdeutsche,'" December 1945, GDA SBU Crimea, f. 11, spr. 1431, vol. 1, 145.
41 Branches of the SD were opened in Melitopol' and Oleški, ibid., 98 verso.
42 Interrogation of T.V. Matčanbaeva on 29 January 1946, ibid., 76–134 verso at 93, verso 94. The records of the security forces in the countries of Eastern Europe are a unique kind of historical source. Their use has been the subject of intense scholarly attention. Regarding the German-speaking minorities, the issues involved were the subject of a conference, "Aus den Giftschänken des Kommunismus. Methodische Fragen zum Umgang mit den Überwachungsakten in Südost- und Mitteleuropa," held in April 2015 in Berlin. Matčanbaeva's protocols are especially important because she was well-informed and made most of her comments about Nazi agencies as a protected witness for the state after she had already been sentenced.
43 Interrogation of M.Ja. Poljakova-Harms on 21 May 1945, ibid., 139–44 verso at 145.
44 Melnyk, *The History of the Galician Division*, 200, 202.
45 Interrogation of T.V. Matčanbaeva on 29 January 1946, GDA SBU Crimea, f. 11, spr. 1431, Bd. 1, Bl. 145.
46 Interrogation of T.V. Matčanbaeva, 29 January 1946, ibid., 118.
47 Interrogation of A.P. Lukin on 19 April 1944, ibid., 161.
48 Federau also used the uniform of a Soviet officer in his work as a provocateur. Interrogation of A.P. Lukin on 4 May 1944, ibid., 116 verso.
49 Interrogation of I.I. Klassen on 8 August and 21 October 1946, GDA SBU Zaporizhzhia Region, spr. 11343, 13–20 verso at 14 verso; 51–5 verso at 53f. According to other sources he joined the SD in Simferopol' only at the end of 1942, after H. Wiens had already left. Interrogation of T.V. Matčanbaeva on 29 January 1946, GDA SBU Crimea, f. 11, spr. 1431, vol. 1, 76–134 verso at 118.
50 Interrogation of T.V. Matčanbaeva on 29 January 1946, ibid., 118; interrogation of A.P. Lukin on 19 April 1944, ibid., 165.
51 Interrogation of T.V. Matčanbaeva on 29 January and 21 February 1946, ibid., 106; vol. 12, 298–9.
52 Interrogation of T.V. Matčanbaeva on 29 January 1946, ibid., 118.
53 Interrogation of T.V. Matčanbaeva on 29 January 1946, ibid., 88, 88 verso, 98 verso, 103 verso.
54 Interrogation of T.V. Matčanbaeva on 29 January 1946, ibid., 118 verso.
55 Information from Babenko, the deputy leader of the Crimean NKVD 2, on 30 October 1945, ibid, vol. 1, 5–9.

56 A number of Mennonite translators report this, including Dierksen from Priluki, GDA SBU Černigiv Region, spr. 14483, 25, 30 (pt 2 of the file – investigation material).
57 Interrogation of T.V. Matčanbaeva on 29 January 1946, GDA SBU Crimea, f. 11, spr. 1431, vol. 1, 121, 121 verso.
58 Interrogation M.Ja. Poljakova-Harms on 12 May 1945, ibid, vol. 12, Bl. 252; information about people in which the testimony of A.P. Lukin is mentioned, ibid., vol. 1, 152–4.
59 Interrogation of T.V. Matčanbaeva on 29 January 1946, ibid., 123, 123 verso.
60 It is possible that Matčanbaeva's accusations point to certain patterns of behaviour that had developed among the translators. This assumption has not yet been confirmed in other sources and would need additional research. Interrogation of T.V. Matčanbaeva on 29 January 1946, ibid., 130, 130 verso.
61 The family did not know the fate of Heinrich's brother, Andrej, who served with the Gendarmerie, ODA SBU Zaporizhzhia Region, spr. 11343, 24.
62 Interrogation of I.I. Klassen and the eyewitness testimonies of Aleksej Nevojs and Kruglov, ibid., 26 verso, 29 verso, 41–2 verso, 70–7. According to other sources the total number of patients was 140, of whom 88 to 90 were shot; ibid., 78–82.
63 Protocol of the session of the military tribunal on 15 November 1946, GDA SBU Zaporizhzhia Region, spr. 11343, 11–123 verso at 115.
64 Zaporiz'kyj rachunok..., 146; Martin Din, *Radjyns'ki*, 357.
65 Dierksen-Pikolenko on 23 January 1947 was sentenced to ten years in a labour re-education camp and stripped of his medal "Victory over Germany" for disguising his social and ethnic background by the military tribunal of the troops of the MVD of the Region of Černigiv. After serving his time, he settled in the early 1960s under the name of Pikolenko near Dnipropetrovs'k. GDA SBU Černigiv Region, spr. 14483.
66 When a personnel card file listing the secret agents of the NKVD fell into the hands of the Nazis in November 1941 in occupied Crimea, they could see that the people named there had "suffered under the NKVD and the Soviet power, that they were former members of the White Army and generally useful for the Germans." Heinrich Wiens, who was working in Mobile-Killing Squad 10-a, reached the same conclusion and offered several former members of this Soviet system positions in the new Nazi structures. Comprehensive arrests of former NKVD agents began only in 1943 at the start of the German withdrawal from the Caucasus. Interrogation of M.Ja. Poljakova-Harms on 13 July 1945, GDA SBU, f. 11, spr. 1431, vol. 1, 147–8; vol. 12, 264. Maria Harms, who was amazed at how well Wiens was informed about her earlier work for the Communist Party, describes the close supervision by Wiens and his assistant at the beginning

of her work for the SD. Interrogation of M.Ja. Poljakova-Harms on 6 April 1945, ibid, vol. 12, 215–16.
67 Interrogation of M.Ja. Poljakova-Harms on 10 April 1945, ibid., 220. Interrogation of L.I. Legek on 4 May 1945, ibid., 271–3 verso. Interrogation of N.I. Krentovskijs on 17 May 1945, ibid., 362 verso.
68 In the SD in Crimea, Zapp gave his favourite Ivanova from Pyatigorsk a job, arranged Ethnic German status for her and her family, and sent them to his home area around Kassel. Interrogation of T.V. Matčanbaeva on 29 January 1946, GDA SBU Crimea, f. 11, spr. 1431, vol. 1, 76–134 verso at 99 verso, 100. The SD agent Petr Venda in Simferopol' received his documents certifying his German nationality third class by using fake witnesses. Interrogation of M.Ja. Poljakova-Harms on 20 April 1945, ibid, vol. 1, 229. Reimer helped a young Greek woman he was courting and had met in Poland get fictional documents about her German background with the aid of dishonest witnesses. Akte Reimer (as above), 74.
69 Čencov, for example, documented inconsistencies between the interrogation protocols and their copies or excerpts that served to intentionally increase the guilt of the accused by misrepresenting what had been said. The Soviet counter-intelligence agency SMERŠ often fabricated spy networks in the last years of the war in order to inflate the importance of their investigations. Thus, during the investigation of the chief of the district Pokrovsk (Rayon Schorskij), A.I. Dyck was accused of being a handler for a German security (Gendarmerie) network when in fact he only coordinated a small group of informants who wanted to denounce suspicious persons. Permit to extend an investigation, 31 October 1946, GDA SBU Dnipropetrovs'k Region, spr. 13156, 87–8. Instruction concerning the extension of an investigation, 31 October 1946. The unusually long investigation in the case of Dyck was due both to his illness and to the desire of the local MGB to gather information about the members of the agent network. Interrogation Dyck on 21 December 1946, ibid., 96 verso 97.
70 Interrogation of I.I. Reimers on 7 May 1946. Investigation files for Reimer, GDA SBU, f. 5, spr. 68045, 52 verso.

Chapter Eight

A Portrait of Khortytsya/Zaporizhzhia under Occupation

AILEEN FRIESEN

In the spring of 1942, at the end of March or the beginning of April, the last major massacre of Jews in German-occupied eastern Ukraine was conducted.¹ By the order of the German authorities, the Jewish population gathered under the pretence that they were being relocated to Melitopol' for work. One eyewitness, Anastasia Nelyubova, described a chaotic scene as the entire remaining Jewish population assembled and began the long march to Melitopol' under armed guard. Most walked, while the sick, the elderly, and young children were transported by trucks. Leonid Lerner remembered marching with his family, including his mother, grandmother, brother, and cousins, through Zaporizhzhia carrying suitcases. When they were rounded up his family had been preparing to celebrate Passover, the Jewish religious holiday that commemorates the community's exodus from Egypt.² When they arrived at the southern outskirts of the city, they were led to an anti-tank ditch and told to remove their clothing; they were then mowed down with machine guns.³ The shooting started at eight in the morning and ended at five in the evening.⁴ By the end, more than 3,000 Jews had been murdered. The bodies were carelessly covered, and when the spring rains came, they began to wash away.⁵

Shortly after this event, Mennonites gathered in their church in Khortytsya on Easter Sunday (5 April 1942) to celebrate the risen Christ for the first time in nearly a decade. Under the Soviet regime, this church had been converted into a movie theatre. Soon after the start of the German occupation, Mennonites and German soldiers had cleared out Stalin's portrait and reopened it as a place of worship.⁶ Gerhard Fast, a German citizen with Mennonite roots in Russia, who had been assigned to gather information on the ethnic Germans (*Volksdeutsche*) in the region, attended the service. He described how the celebration began with the full church singing "Christ is risen, tell it to Zion" and included prayer, a scripture reading, and a sermon.[7] Even though the massacre did not happen close to the church, it is not hard to imagine that rumours about this event drifted to the Khortytsya side of the Dnieper River.

These images demonstrate in stark terms how the new regime imposed its racial hierarchy. Mennonites benefited materially, socially, and culturally, albeit briefly, from being categorized as ethnic Germans; in contrast, Jews were subjected to unspeakable violence. By combining Jewish, Mennonite, Soviet, and German sources, this chapter will offer a portrait of German occupation in Khortytsya and Zaporizhzhia, describing how Mennonites reacted to this event, including their recruitment into the new administration. While more research is needed into the background of these men and women, as well as the local social networks that supported and facilitated their involvement with the regime, this case study shows that Mennonite collaborators were connected not only to the Mennonite community, but also to the broader local society.

For nearly 150 years, Jews and Mennonites had lived in the region together. In 1789, Mennonite settlers had founded the village of Khortytsya, the first of many Mennonite agricultural settlements that would be established in the locale. Soon afterwards, Jewish merchants and artisans settled across the Dnieper River in the town of Aleksandrovsk (present-day Zaporizhzhia). Although Khortytsya started as a Mennonite enclave, by the end of the nineteenth century it had been transformed into a multi-ethnic and multi-confessional space. Jews worshiped in a synagogue a few streets away from the Mennonite church, and both groups were treated to the ringing of the bells of the nearby Orthodox church.[8] Each group maintained its cultural separateness, yet they interacted extensively through commerce as Orthodox workers laboured in Mennonite businesses and Mennonites shopped at Jewish stores, buying suits from tailor Blum or bread from Izraelski's bakery. Relations between the groups, on the whole, were cordial. The pogroms in Zaporizhzhia, during which Jews lost their lives and livelihoods to mob violence, were not replicated in Khortytsya. In fact, during the shortages of the Russian Revolution, Jews attending synagogue in Khortytsya relied on young Mennonite boys to extinguish candles during the Sabbath to preserve their supplies.[9]

The destruction of the countryside during the Civil War and the building of the new socialist state led to intensive urbanization, which accelerated the transformation of Zaporizhzhia and Khortytsya. The arrival of workers to help build the Dnieper Hydroelectric Station refashioned Khortytsya into a town dominated by Ukrainians with a significant population of Mennonites (and other ethnic Germans) and a small but visible population of Jews.[10] In the past, people had at least vaguely recognized faces on the street; now they passed one another as strangers.[11]

In many though not all ways, the experiences of Jews and Mennonites under the Soviet regime mirrored each other. Religious Jews and churchgoing Mennonites shared experiences as the Soviet regime waged a war against religious beliefs and institutions. Although these groups did not experience the early violence directed at the Russian Orthodox Church, the Soviet regime created an inhospitable atmosphere for religious believers and their leaders.[12] Soviet officials closed Jewish synagogues and Mennonite churches, persecuting their leaders and banning the teaching of the faith to their children.

Even so, secularized Jews and Mennonites found new opportunities under the Soviet regime. In the case of Mennonites, the founding of the German national districts of Khortytsya and Molochans'k provided them with an advantage over their Ukrainian and Jewish neighbours when it came to securing positions in the government. In the district of Khortytsya, hundreds of Mennonite men and women served in the local and regional administration.[13] Besides allowing administrative autonomy, these districts extended Mennonites and other ethnic Germans the opportunity to support their linguistic culture through newspapers and German-language schools for their children.[14] In southern Ukraine, Jews would have their own national districts established in Kalinindorf, Novo-Zlatopol, and Stalindorf.

By the time the Germans invaded, for many ethnic Germans, Soviet nationality politics had merged with a deep sense of victimhood. Still reeling from collectivization, the famine, and the Great Terror, some of them began to believe that as Germans they had endured more suffering than other Soviet citizens.[15] As a perceived diaspora group with ties to a geopolitical competitor, ethnic Germans in the Soviet Union experienced discrimination and repressive policies as Stalin adopted a more Russian chauvinistic stance, targeting specific ethnic minorities whom he viewed as disloyal.[16] As an explanation for their suffering, some Mennonites embraced the notion of Judeo-Communism. Anna Sudermann, a highly educated Mennonite woman, acknowledged that the Jews of Khortytsya had "never shown any unfriendliness or discrimination towards us during the Soviet regime;" yet she readily blamed "Jews" for the persecution that she and other members of her family experienced during the 1930s under Stalin's state security officials.[17] Her memoir shows how Mennonites could hold both ideas together: recognizing the unjustness of Nazi policies, even while justifying those policies as an understandable part of the war waged by the Germans.[18]

Under German Occupation

With the launch of Operation Barbarossa in June 1941, the German Wehrmacht advanced rapidly into the Soviet Union. By mid-August, German troops had reached the banks of the Dnieper, where they occupied the territory of the former Mennonite colony of Khortytsya. By early October, after several weeks of intense fighting, German forces had established a stronghold in Zaporizhzhia. As the German army approached, Soviet officials evacuated key industries behind the quickly receding front line. They also attempted to evacuate/deport segments of the population, including ethnic Germans, whom they viewed as potential collaborators with the enemy. The rapidity of the takeover allowed many Mennonites in this region to elude that fate; in some cases, their Jewish neighbours helped them escape. Helene Peters described hiding with another Mennonite woman among Jews as the NKVD attempted to round up Germans in Zaporizhzhia. She described them as being "very nice to us and anti-Bolshevik."[19] Those living in the former Mennonite colony of Molotschna were not as fortunate as their counterparts in Khortytsya; the NKVD deported tens of thousands of Mennonites and other ethnic Germans from this region in cramped cattle cars, which carried them to the east, where they faced dire conditions in new settlements.[20]

For many ethnic Germans, evacuation meant death; for Jews, it would have saved their lives. Although it is impossible to provide an accurate number, the Yad Vashem central database of Shoah victims includes names from Zaporizhzhia and Khortytsya as evacuees.[21] Otto Klassen's memoir records the presence of thousands of refugees, many of them Jewish, leaving across the river.[22] However, not everyone left. Although some Jews were aware of the Nazis' antisemitic policies and propaganda, many would have been unable to imagine that their policies included genocide. Soviet officials did not readily share this information with the population and did not attempt to move Jewish citizens out of harm's way. Some believed that their roots in the community would shield them from repression; Sudermann offered this as the reason why the Jewish cobbler stayed in Khortytsya with his wife.[23] In other cases, evacuation proved difficult for the elderly and the very young; instead of leaving family members behind, people chose to remain together.[24] Around 4,000 Jews remained in Old Zaporizhzhia at the start of the occupation, according to numbers submitted by the local mayor.[25]

Mennonites caught behind enemy lines enjoyed an elevated position under the new German regime. Having been designated as ethnic

Germans, Mennonites received better treatment than the local population. This status entitled them to more resources, including clothes, goods, and apartments that had belonged to Jews.[26] In contrast, from the outset, the German authorities isolated the Jewish population. Jews were forced to gather in the synagogue in Zaporizhzhia to register with the occupying authorities, and had to wear a white armband with a yellow star of David. Those who were caught without the armband were "shot on the spot."[27] A Jewish ghetto was not established in Zaporizhzhia; however, every morning registered Jews had to gather for their work assignments.[28] During this period, Mennonites continued to live next to Jews. Helene Latter, a woman from a Mennonite family who had embraced the changes initiated by the Soviet system, recalled the mournful singing of her Jewish neighbours one night; by morning, they were gone.[29]

Early in the occupation of Zaporizhzhia, a group of Jews were executed. Holocaust survivor Revekka Egides remembered the day in early November when her father, brother, uncle, and cousin were taken away "for work" to a local stadium, where they were shot.[30] A tall fence surrounded the complex, preventing Egides from witnessing the murder. According to Aleksandr Shilko, who claimed to have witnessed the event, a vehicle carrying twenty-five to thirty people of all ages stopped at the stadium behind a fence; they were forced to remove their clothes, and individuals in German officer uniforms shot them.[31] After the reoccupation of the region, Soviet troops would discover bodies at this site.[32]

Before the beginning of German rule, the population of Verkhnya Khortytsya (which included Khortytsya and Rosenthal) was composed of 2,178 Germans (mainly but not exclusively Mennonites), 11,507 Ukrainians, and 402 Jews.[33] Sudermann, who lived in Khortytsya during the occupation, recorded that police officers rounded up fifty Jews and half-Jews and shot them outside the village.[34] She implied that these officers were from Germany; however, an auxiliary police force composed of local men had been established at the outset of occupation. Included in this round-up likely would have been residents Khaya Tolchinski and her two sons, Semion and Dmitri, who lived in Verkhnya Khortytsya, as well as Meyir and Sara Tzeyikhman, who had lived in the village for more than five decades. All were murdered under the German occupation.[35] By May 1942, the demographics of this place had fundamentally altered: the number of Germans stayed consistent at just over 2,000, but the number of Ukrainians had fallen by almost half to 6,180 (many had likely been transported to Germany as forced labour), and the Jewish population had vanished.[36]

Help Rendered?

In Mennonite memoirs, it is difficult to find examples of rescue or aid given by Mennonites to persecuted Jews. In the stories of life under German occupation there are some references to Mennonites giving food to Jewish neighbours or to strangers passing through their villages whom they assumed to be Jews. A casual conversation with the daughter of a Mennonite woman who lived under the German occupation in Ukraine revealed that her mother knew of houses in which Jewish families were hidden and kept this information quiet. In her memoir, Anna Sudermann recorded that nurses at the hospital in Khortytsya hid a Jewish laboratory technician who had survived a suicide attempt; presumably, Sudermann did not betray this person. In his memoir, Otto Klassen mentions protecting the identity of a Jewish woman who lived with his family in Schöneberg. She had revealed to him that the SS detachment stationed in the village had killed Jews fleeing from the German army on the island of Khortytsya.[37]

The stories of the Righteous Among the Nations (an honorific used by the State of Israel to describe non-Jews who risked their lives during the Holocaust to save Jews from extermination by the Nazis) offer some insight into the actions carried out by the Ukrainian population in Zaporizhzhia.[38] Only a handful of rescuers from Zaporizhzhia province have been awarded this honorific. Natalya Zborik, who lived in Zaporizhzhia, took in two Jewish children who had been separated from their mother during the evacuation. Zborik and her son took care of the boys, pretending they were her nephews. During document checks, Zborik's son took the boys away from the house.[39] In another case, a young Jewish woman escaped from her forced labour assignment and knocked on the door of the Yelnikov family. They opened the door to a young woman named Sara who was wearing an armband with the Star of David and hid her until a neighbour threatened to betray them. Instead of throwing Sara out, they helped her procure forged papers and find employment on a collective farm.[40]

One story of rescue by Mennonites, which cannot be confirmed, does exist. In the summer of 1943, Hans and Suse Wiens of Khortytsya took in a child, a little blonde-haired girl named Tamara. Suse described the event in this way:

> Some time later they brought two orphan girls to our town. One was about two years-old and many were willing to care for her. The other was six years-old and we were asked if we would adopt her. She had seen and suffered much, she was very withdrawn. We think she may have been Jewish.

We thought about it and the next day accepted her as our daughter. We named her Erika and loved her very much.[41]

According to Hans, a state official asked around Khortytsya whether anyone would take in these two children. Many families wanted the toddler but not the six-year-old. According to family lore, the official offered to take back the child if the Wiens could not handle the situation.[42] Erika remained with the Wiens family, travelling with them during the 1943 evacuation of ethnic Germans from the Soviet Union. Her EWZ papers indicated that she was born in Dnipro (formerly Dnepropetrovsk) to an unknown mother and Friedrich Korff, who was *verschleppt*, that is, had been taken away during the Soviet purges.[43] She was fluent in German. According to these records, her religion was unknown, although the Wiens family would later celebrate her acceptance of Jesus. Despite the little information offered or even the fact that a six-year-old could not remember the name of her mother, she was accepted as a full ethnic German.[44] None of her travelling companions at the time heard the Wiens's suspicion that she was Jewish; a cousin who had played with Erika in Poland expressed shock when she was told many years later about this possible Jewish connection.[45] The Wiens family, however, offered little information that could confirm this heritage except for her name, "Tamara Korff," and that she had "seen and suffered much." Hans and Suse would arrive in Canada after the war; Erika would not make the journey, for she passed away from meningitis in Europe.

The Peters family cared for the second child, a toddler. According to them, she was brought to Khortytsya in 1943 by the National Socialist People's Welfare (*Nationalsozialistische Volkswohlfahrt*; NSV) after a bombing raid on Dnipro, probably while the Red Army was fighting to take back the city. Her EWZ papers provide no indication of her background before she joined the Peters family; her parents could offer little information on her origins.[46] The child left Ukraine with her guardians during the 1943 retreat of the German forces. The family would end up in Argentina for a number of years before moving to Canada.[47]

Mennonites as Collaborators

German officials relied on members of the local population to hold administrative and leadership positions under occupation. Men of Mennonite backgrounds took up these positions, becoming mayors, district administrators, translators (women also served in this role), and police officers for the occupying regime.[48] That they were of German background and could speak both Russian and German made them prime candidates for these positions. Shortly after Zaporizhzhia was occupied, German officials appointed Heinrich Wiebe (b. 1889), as mayor of Old Zaporizhzhia; he served in that capacity until the fall of 1942, when he was replaced.[49] In New Zaporizhzhia, the regime installed Isaak Reimer (b. 1898) as mayor. According to the memoirs of one of his contemporaries, Reimer showed a vicious streak in this position. On one occasion he pointed the finger at two Mennonites as former Soviet informers; they were summarily executed. Rempel added that it was unclear whether it was local Mennonites or the occupying forces that carried out this task.[50] In Khortytsya, a recent returnee from the Gulag, Johann (Hans) Epp (b. 1898), was appointed mayor and would quickly become a district administrator, with Karl Hiersack taking over his former position.[51] The appointment of local men helped secure these positions from outsiders; for instance, soon after German forces established control, representatives of the western Ukrainian nationalist organization OUN arrived in Zaporizhzhia, hoping to gain a foothold in the local administration.[52]

Scholars have struggled with the topic of collaboration by local populations under occupation during the Second World War, searching for patterns in behaviour and debating the roles played by ideology and pragmatism in the motivations of individuals.[53] Often overlooked in these discussions is the issue of age, or membership in a generational cohort. While Mennonite mayors of various ages worked for the occupying regime, the similarity in age of the three men working in and near Zaporizhzhia is striking. As young men they had witnessed the jubilation after the fall of the Romanov dynasty, followed by the chaos of the Civil War and the implosion of the Mennonite commonwealth brought about by the Bolshevik Revolution. These men were old enough to remember tsarist Russia as well as the Mennonite religious and cultural traditions that had sustained the community for more than a century.[54]

The case of Heinrich Wiebe provides an example of how some members of this cohort learned to navigate their environment, employing a flexible ideology that allowed them to exploit opportunities and sidestep peril. Born in the southeastern corner of the Molochna colony in the village of Steinfeld, Wiebe was well-educated, having attended the Ohrloff Secondary School (in present-day Orlove) and the Halbstadt Teachers' College (in present-day Molochans'k) before joining a small contingent of Mennonites studying in the imperial capital of Saint Petersburg. These men and women socialized extensively with one another, sometimes gathering for Bible study in the evenings.[55] Wiebe stayed in Saint Petersburg until shortly after the Bolshevik revolution, when he returned to the Molotschna colony, joining the administration in the district village of Bogdanivka.[56] During this period of social and political upheaval, Wiebe displayed a shrewdness combined with a predilection for leadership, exploiting difficulties between the Bolsheviks and Nestor Makhno's men to the benefit of Mennonites.[57] Under the Soviet regime, he managed, unlike many other highly educated Mennonites, to avoid being arrested, although he did resign from a teaching position in Khortytsya, having been brought to realize he would be dismissed if he stayed. He reinvented himself as a bookkeeper in Zaporizhzhia, a position he maintained until the arrival of the German army.[58]

Wiebe, as he had done in the past, adapted quickly to his new circumstances. An early report from the German military hints at how he presented his past to the new regime. Field Commander Kieling reported that Wiebe had been a long-time administrator in local government during the tsarist years, neglecting to mention his administrative experience under the early Bolshevik regime. Wiebe presented himself as both capable and ideologically reliable. For instance, on his trip to Zaporizhzhia in early 1942, Dr. Karl Stumpp, who was conducting research into the ethnic Germans, described Wiebe as "sitting in dignity on his official leather chair; above him hung a large portrait of the Fuehrer." Stumpp gifted this "intelligent official of the old type" a copy of *Mein Kampf*, which Wiebe happily accepted.[59] In 1943, Wiebe retreated with the German army, eventually arriving in Canada on the SS *Goya* in 1951 with his wife, Olga (Kostenetzky).[60]

Mennonite men not only entered into the administrative hierarchy but also joined the German occupiers' security organs. Two significant local perpetrators of direct violence during the occupation were the auxiliary police and the *Sicherheitsdienst* (Security Service; SD). The latter was involved in tracking down and interrogating suspicious elements in their search for communists, Jews, and partisans.[61] Ethnic Germans were recruited to assist both organizations; however, other ethnicities, including Ukrainians, were also well-represented.[62] In Zaporizhzhia, likely the majority of members were Ukrainians, followed by ethnic Germans (both Mennonites and non-Mennonites), and others.[63] Initially, a Ukrainian led the auxiliary police of Old Zaporizhzhia, consisting of 50 men, and a Russian occupied a similar position in New Zaporizhzhia, leading 120 men.[64] However, ethnic Germans were soon inserted into key positions, with Ivan Fast serving as the head of the auxiliary police and his older brother Jacob becoming an important figure in the SD's political department.[65] As only Soviet citizens who self-identified as Mennonite, or were clearly part of that community, should be included under that label, only Jacob can be confirmed as a

"Mennonite." In records generated by the *Einwandererzentralstelle* (Central Bureau for Immigration; EWZ) when ethnic Germans were being resettled, Jacob listed his religion as "Mennonite"; unfortunately, Ivan's records cannot be located.[66]

Soviet interrogations conducted after the war provide insight into the process by which men became involved in the auxiliary police and SD in Zaporizhzhia. Friends, colleagues, and acquaintances already working for the police often encouraged or facilitated applications to join the ranks. According to his interrogation records, Stephan Fomenko joined the police soon after learning about the job from Ivan Fast. Fomenko confided to Fast that he was looking for work, and Fast, an old acquaintance from the agricultural machinery factory Kommunar, who was already serving as chief of police, invited him to apply for a position.[67] A number of the local men who decided to work for the Germans appeared to have come from this factory, illustrating how employment connections served as a recruitment tool. Fast's welcoming of non-ethnic Germans in the force also demonstrates that Mennonites had acclimatized to at least some aspects of Soviet nationality policy, which promoted a sense of camaraderie among different national groups.

Scholarly work on the formation of police units in Ukraine shows that these initial recruits in October 1941 were volunteers; it was not until after the summer of 1942 that the Germans relied on "compulsion" to fill the ranks of the local police.[68] Fomenko worked for the police for only a few months, until mid-January 1942, when he joined the SD's political department. Vladimir Ersak, of Czech nationality, followed this same career path, moving from the auxiliary police to the SD political department. Ersak had worked at Kommunar from 1934 until the beginning of the Second World War; in 1936, he had joined the Communist Party.[69] During his interrogation by Soviet officials he stated that he had joined the police voluntarily after running into his colleague Boris Kolpanov.[70] Kolpanov emphasized that Ersak's communist past placed him at risk and encouraged him to join the police, giving him advice on how to apply. Ersak submitted his application to Ivan Fast and started working for the police soon afterwards.[71] While these two men were not Mennonite, their circumstances point to non-ideological reasons for joining the police.

The evidence suggests that those who helped the SD were not hot-headed youths but rather mature local men with roots in the community. For instance, Jacob Fast was a husband and father of four in his early thirties when the occupation started.[72] His own upbringing had been on the margins of the Mennonite community, but according to Anna Sudermann, who was an aunt to Fast's wife Natalie, his wife's family were pillars of the community.⁷³ Natalie was the daughter of one of the last ministers of Khortytsya, Aron Toews, and a baptized member of the Khortytsya Mennonite church.⁷⁴ As the Soviet state persecuted religious communities and their leaders, Toews remained steadfast in his commitment to the church, continuing to offer spiritual comfort to those in need. Unlike Fast's own father, who had survived the terror of the 1930s, Toews was arrested in 1934, interrogated, and sentenced to five years. Soviet officials accused him of anti-Soviet agitation, of providing the addresses of fascist organizations to people seeking help, and of writing "provocative letters" to people abroad.⁷⁵ These trumped-up charges were based on Toews's activities during the early 1930s as he tried to help ministers and others get in touch with Mennonite aid organizations abroad for assistance during a time of repression and famine. He would never be reunited with his family, although he would communicate extensively with them, sending biblically inspired reflections. Without Toews's leadership, as the Soviets had anticipated, the Khortytsya Mennonite church closed soon after his arrest.⁷⁶

After their marriage, Fast spent a significant amount of time away from home, working as a truck driver as far away as the Caucasus.⁷⁷ The family lived in Khortytsya until Fast began working for the SD at the outset of the occupation, when they moved to Zaporizhzhia. He volunteered for that role only a week after the German army had established its control over Zaporizhzhia. It is difficult to imagine that Anna Sudermann did not know the reason for her niece's move across the Dnieper, although she neglected to raise this issue in her memoir.

The Fast family lived in Zaporizhzhia until they left with the retreating German army in 1943.⁷⁸ Natalie remembered the moment with melancholy, as the departing families boarded packed trains, singing, "God be with you till we meet again."⁷⁹ The Fasts would make their way to Canada aboard the *General Stewart* in the summer of 1947, having spent time in a displaced persons camp in Hannover.⁸⁰ In 2007 the Canadian government revoked Fast's citizenship, having learned he had concealed his wartime activities.⁸¹ Fast would die in 2007 before he could be deported.

One of the main questions of dispute is whether Mennonites participated in the mistreatment of Jews. Recent scholarship exploring the role of local administrators, such as mayors, has concluded that these men contributed significant labour to the implementation of German racial policies.⁸² In the case of Wiebe, Zaporizhzhia depended on the proceeds of confiscated Jewish property to fund its local budget. Identifying and registering the local Jewish population was also one of his duties.⁸³ As for the massacre, Wiebe claimed that he was in the hospital when the Jewish population was killed and thus did not have to witness the event.[84] Extraordinarily, Cornelius Krahn, a Mennonite historian, interviewed Wiebe in the mid-1950s. During this exchange, Wiebe expressed his disgust with Hitler's Final Solution: "The Jewish question is a terrible topic. This question was so terrible that the entire Russian population recoiled and even the Russian GPU was not as terrible as the German Gestapo. The Jews were brought together on the square and shot in broad daylight. If any child was still alive, a dog was set on it, the dog grabbed the child and tore it apart."[85] Testimony collected after the Soviets reoccupied the territory confirm Wiebe's comment about the dogs: "There were so many victims that the whole ravine was full of corpses. Not quite satisfied with the shooting themselves, the butchers set their sheep-dogs on the victims which tore their flesh."[86]

In this interview, Wiebe readily offered his own location during this event; however, he failed to mention the people responsible for carrying out this atrocity. As mayor of Zaporizhzhia, Wiebe had included this information in his report for March 1942, noting that the local police had taken part in the "Judenaktion," a Nazi euphemism for the massacre of the Jewish population.[87] He provided no additional information, unlike the head of the auxiliary police, one of the Fast brothers, who wrote in his official April report, "the Jewish question has been resolved completely and the masses are not in any doubt about its interpretation."[88]

Alexander Rempel, a Mennonite scholar and Soviet émigré, claimed to have personally witnessed Mennonite members of the local police, whom he had known from childhood, celebrating the end of Zaporizhzhia's Jewish population in the spring of 1942. According to Rempel, after the war Mennonite men hid behind a facade of naivety, reluctant to admit their crimes to their families and community.[89] Rempel's accusation was known for decades but was long dismissed on the basis of other nonsensical claims within this document. Brutalized by the Soviet regime, Rempel struggled with his mental health after the war. Rempel, however, was in the town of Einlage, close to Zaporizhzhia, briefly during the spring of 1942. After serving as a translator with the German army, he applied to leave his position, a request that was approved on 8 March 1942. He travelled home to his family before leaving for Germany sometime in April of that year.[90] According to this timeline, he was present in the region as the remaining Jewish population was executed.

Even without Rempel's account, the report by Wiebe confirms that members of the local police force participated in the massacre. This implicates Mennonite men who served in the local police and SD as performing a role in the process by which Jewish families were rounded up, herded, and executed. According to Soviet interrogation records, in the days leading up to the event, locals working for the SD had been active in identifying Jews; these men knew a mass execution was on the horizon.[91] Admittedly, these records need to be used with caution; however, the men under interrogation consistently identified the Fast brothers, along with other men with Mennonite last names, as intimately involved in the violence perpetrated during the occupation.[92]

As Soviet troops reoccupied the territory of Khortytsya and Zaporizhzhia in late 1943, they found a devastated land and a decimated population. The retreating German army had gathered Mennonites (and other ethnic Germans) and evacuated them to Polish Wartheland. Jewish Red Army soldiers, like Pavel Elikinson, returned to the area, not knowing what they would find. As Elkinson remembered, "I didn't know anything about what happened to my parents. I only knew that they had stayed in Zaporizhzhia. And I knew what the Germans did to the Jews. I assumed the worst. My fears were proved true." Elkinson's mother, father, uncle, aunt, grandmother, and brother lay in the mass grave outside of Zaporizhzhia; only his Russian sister-in-law and the family home remained.[93] While Mennonite wartime experience cannot be defined simply by collaboration, it is clear that collaborators were connected to and embedded in the Mennonite community. They also had been part of the multi-ethnic fabric of the local society. Only by combining Jewish, Mennonite, German, and Soviet sources can a portrait emerge of the formation and disintegration of relations in this multi-ethnic space.

NOTES

1 Dieter Pohl, "The Murder of Ukraine's Jews under German Military Administration and in the Reich Commissariat Ukraine," in *The Shoah in Ukraine: History, Testimony, Memorialization*, ed. Ray Brandon and Wendy Lower (Bloomington: Indiana University Press, 2010), 38. There is debate about the date of this massacre.
2 In 1942, Passover started on sundown on 1 April.
3 "Interview with Leonoid Lerner," Yad Vashem, https://www.youtube.com/watch?v=kgRh_NpKxy0 (accessed 1 July 2018).
4 "Report on German-fascist atrocities," USHMM, RG-22.002M.0001.00001695.
5 For a re-creation of this massacre, see Michael Gesin, *The Destruction of the Ukrainian Jewry during World War II* (Lewiston: Edwin Mellen Press, 2006), 230.

6 Waldemar Janzen, *Growing up in Turbulent Times: Memoirs of Soviet Oppression, Refugee Life in Germany, and Immigrant Adjustment to Canada* (Winnipeg: CMU Press, 2007), 44.
7 Gerhard Fast, *Das Ende von Chortitza* (Winnipeg: Regehrs, 1973), 17.
8 See N.J. Kroeker, *First Mennonite Villages in Russia, 1789–1943: Khortitsa– Rosental* (Vancouver: N.J. Kroeker, 1981), 63.
9 Ibid., 62–3, 107–9.
10 Notably, this was not the case in all Mennonite villages; only Khortytsya and Einlage had sizeable Jewish populations before the start of the war. Einlage's Jewish population was 633 before the war and Khortytsya's was 402. Osterwick/Dolyns'ke was the third largest, with a Jewish population of 22. See "Bevölkerungsübersicht vom Gebiet Chortitza," https://tsdea.archives.gov.ua/deutsch/gallery.php?tt=R_6_626+Rayon%3A+Berislaw%0D%0AKreisgebiet%3A+Cherson%0D%0AGenerelbezirk%3A+Nikolajew+Gebiet%3A+Chortitza%0D%0Arussisch+%E2%80%93+Chortitza+&p=R_6_626%5C%D1%821_96-170%0D%0A&fbclid=IwAR3loG_ObrKhSKY4HogcPOca_0q9G_4aNoaYru4IqnrXBF9IZdL-NFghaa4#lg=1&slide=18.
11 Aron P. Toews and Olga Rempel, *Siberian Diary of Aron P. Toews* (Winnipeg: CMBC, 1984), 66.
12 For more on early attacks on Jewish religious life, see Robert Weinberg, "Demonizing Judaism in the Soviet Union during the 1920s," *Slavic Review* 67, no. 1 (2008): 120–53; Jeffrey Veidlinger, *In the Shadow of the Shtetl: Small-Town Jewish Life in Soviet Ukraine* (Bloomington: Indiana University Press, 2013).
13 Colin P. Neufeldt, "Separating the Sheep from the Goats: The Role of Mennonites and Non-Mennonites in the Dekulakization of Khortitsa, Ukraine (1928–1930)," *Mennonite Quarterly Review* 83, no. 2 (April 2009): 231.
14 J. Otto Pohl, "The Deportation and Destruction of the German Minority in the USSR" (n.p., 2001) (accessed 24 July 2019). https://www.norkarussia.info/uploads/3/7/7/9/37792067/deportation_and_destruction_soviet_germans.pdf.
15 See Anna Sudermann, *Lebenserinnerungen* (Winnipeg: Mennonite Heritage Archives, 1970), MHA vol. 3770. A similar phenomenon took place in Poland as Volksdeutsche "had come to feel themselves a community under siege." See Klaus-Peter Friedrich, "Collaboration in a 'Land without a Quisling': Patterns of Cooperation with the Nazi German Occupation Regime in Poland during World War II," *Slavic Review* 64, no. 4 (2005): 725.
16 This situation only worsened after Hitler assumed power in Germany, improving slightly with the signing of the Non-Aggression Pact between Nazi Germany and the Soviet Union. For more on this issue, see James Urry, "Mennonites in Ukraine during World War II: Thoughts and Questions," *Mennonite Quarterly Review* 93, no. 1 (January 2019): 84–6.

17 Sudermann, *Lebenserinnerungen*. A similar statement can be found in the book by Hans (Johann) Epp, the former district mayor of Khortytsya under occupation. See Johann Epp, *Freuden und Leiden der Familie Olga Wiebe und Johann Epp* (n.a: n.a, n.d.), 14.
18 Sudermann, *Lebenserinnerungen*.
19 Mennonite Library and Archives (MLA), OH 4 (Cornelius Krahn interviews with post–Second World War Mennonite refugees), Helene Peters interview.
20 Leona Wiebe Gislason, *Rückenau: The History of a Village in the Molotschna Mennonite Settlement of South Russia* (Winnipeg: Windflower, 1999), 169–70. Approximately 31,320 ethnic Germans were deported from Zaporizhzhia between September 1941 and 1 January 1942. See J. Otto Pohl, "The Deportation and Destruction of the German Minority."
21 "Yad Vashem Central Database of Victims of the Shoah," https://yvng.yadvashem.org/index.html?language=en&s_lastName=&s_firstName=&s_place=Khortytsya&s_dateOfBirth=&s_inTransport= (accessed 30 December 2018).
22 Otto Klassen, *I Remember: The Story of Otto Klassen*, trans. Jakob Klassen (Winnipeg: Klassen, 2013), 40–1.
23 It is interesting to consider how Sudermann knew this information. By her own account, she had ceased speaking to her Jewish neighbours and acquaintances.
24 Gesin, *The Destruction of the Ukrainian Jewry during World War II*, 222–3. For more on this issue of why some stayed, see Anna Shternshis, "Between Life and Death: Why Some Soviet Jews Decided to Leave and Others to Stay in 1941," *Kritika: Explorations in Russian and Eurasian History* 15, no. 3 (2014): 477–504.
25 "Report about the Inspection of the Administration in Zaporizhzhia," US Holocaust Memorial Museum (USHMM), RG-11.001M.0092.00000342. The estimate for the total population was 85,000 for Old Zaporizhzhia. USHMM RG-11.001M. .0092.00000343.
26 Doris L. Bergen has detailed how the construction of the concept of the Ethnic German by the Nazis served to justify the massacre of the local Jewish population. See Bergen, "The Nazi Concept of 'Volksdeutsche' and the Exacerbation of Anti-Semitism in Eastern Europe, 1939–45," *Journal of Contemporary History* 29, no. 4 (1994): 569–82.
27 USHMM RG-22.002M.0001.1547.
28 Martin Dean and Mel Hecker, eds., *The United States Holocaust Memorial Museum Encyclopedia of Camps and Ghettos, 1933–1945*, vol. 2 pt B (Bloomington: Indiana University Press, 2012), 1615. "Eyewitness statement, Alexander Shilko," USHMM RG-22.002M.0001.1548.
29 Helene Latter and Walter F. Latter, *I Do Remember* (Morden: W.F. Walter, 1988), 63.

30 "Interview with Revekka Egides," https://www.youtube.com/watch?time_continue=30&v=BHrVVdE9G0M (accessed 10 December 2019).
31 "Eyewitness statement, Alexander Shilko," USHMM RG-22.002M.0001.1549.
32 A.F. Vysotsky, *Nazi Crimes in Ukraine, 1941–1944: Documents and Materials* (Kiev: Naukova Dumka, 1987), 144. The number of bodies at the stadium provided by this source is too high for them to be only Jews, although POWs, communists, and others were also killed by the occupying regime, in many of the same places in which the killing of Jews occurred.
33 "Dorfbericht Chortitiza," https://chort.square7.ch/Stumpp/Dorfber.htm (accessed 30 December 2018).
34 Sudermann, *Lebenserinnerungen*. Likely this number was higher, based on the Jewish population numbers.
35 "The Central Database of Shoah Victims' Names," https://yvng.yadvashem.org/index.html?language=en&s_lastName=&s_firstName=&s_place=Khortytsya&s_dateOfBirth=&s_inTransport= (accessed 30 December 2018).
36 For more on the *Ostarbeiter*, see Gelinada Grinchenko, "'And Now Imagine Her or Him as a Slave, a Pitiful Slave with No Rights': Child Forced Labourers in the Culture of Remembrance of the USSR and Post-Soviet Ukraine," *European Review of History* 22, no. 2 (March 2015): 389–410. According to Mordechai Altshuler, the Jewish population in 1939 of Zaporozhe province was 43,321. See Mordechai Altshuler, *Soviet Jewry on the Eve of the Holocaust: A Social and Demographic Profile* (Jerusalem: Centre for Research of East European Jewry, Hebrew University of Jerusalem, 1998). Michael Gesin lists the number of Jewish victims in the province (not city) of Zaporizhzhia at approximately 44,000. Gesin, *The Destruction of the Ukrainian Jewry during World War II*, 230.
37 Klassen, *I Remember*, 40.
38 Scholarship on rescue has shown that the category of "rescuer" is not stable and that people rendered aid for complex reasons, not just altruism. See Nina Paulovicova, "Rescue of Jews in the Slovak State (1939–1945)" PhD diss., (University of Alberta, 2013).
39 "Zborik Family," http://db.yadvashem.org/righteous/family.html?language=en&itemId=4039993 (accessed 15 September 2018).
40 "Yelnikova Family," The Righteous among the Nations, http://db.yadvashem.org/righteous/family.html?language=en&itemId=4413308 (accessed 15 September 2018).
41 Paul Dyck, "Suse and Hans Wiens," *Preservings* 13 (1998): 20.
42 Interview with Lottie Klassen, conducted by author on 19 January 2018.
43 According to the Yad Vashem database of victims, a Jewish family with the last name Korf lived in Dnepropetrovsk; they were evacuated east by the Soviets. Korff, however, was also a German name. I was unable

A Portrait of Khortytsya/Zaporizhzhia under Occupation 245

to find records of the father in the database created from the books of rehabilitation in Ukraine. See http://www.reabit.org.ua.

44 Einwandererzentralstelle or Central Bureau for Immigration Collection, "Erika Korff," A3342EWZ50-J016 2820. For more on the production of these documents, see Eric J. Schmaltz, "The 'Long Trek': The SS Population Transfer of Ukrainian Germans to the Polish Warthegau and Its Consequences, 1943–1944," *Journal of the American Historical Society of Germans from Russia* 31, no. 3 (Fall 2008): 11–13.

45 Interview with Lottie Klassen.

46 Einwandererzentralstelle "Karl Peters," A3342EWZ50-G0300280.

47 Interview conducted by author on 28 June 2018. In her memoirs, Anna Sudermann mentions that Olga Lepp was assigned to a social welfare position in the NSV around June 1942. See, Sudermann, *Lebenserinnerungen*.

48 For more on the role of women, including Mennonite women, as collaborators, see Daria Rudakova, "Soviet Women Collaborators in Occupied Ukraine 1941–1945," *Australian Journal of Politics and History* 62, no. 4 (2016): 529–45.

49 For his appointment, see "Report about the Inspection of the Administration in Zaporizhia," USHMM RG-11.001M.0092.00000346. In his book, Benjamin Goossen claims that Wiebe was given this position as a reward for volunteering with Einsatzgruppe C, although no citation is provided. See Benjamin W. Goossen, *Chosen Nation: Mennonites and Germany in a Global Era* (Princeton: Princeton University Press, 2017), 162. In contrast, other researchers have argued that the Germans often used "rank and file" people from Soviet bureaucracy. See Markus Eikel and Valentina Sivaieva, "City Mayors, Raion Chiefs, and Village Elders in Ukraine, 1941–44: How Local Administrators Co-operated with the German Occupation Authorities," *Contemporary European History* 23, no. 3 (August 2014): 412.

50 Johann David Rempel, *Einlage, Chronik des Dorfes* (Regina: H. Bergen, 2009), 117.

51 Janzen, *Growing Up in Turbulent Times*, 46.

52 Eikel and Sivaieva, "City Mayors," 414.

53 See the forum on collaboration in Poland and the Soviet Union published in *Slavic Review* 64, no. 4 (Winter 2005): 711–98.

54 Julius Kliewer, who was born in 1903, had a strong understanding of Mennonite beliefs and history. See "Julius Kliewer interview conducted by David Boder," http://voices.iit.edu/interview?doc=kluverJ&display=kluverJ_en (accessed 10 July 2019). Kliewer also had a position in the administration of Zaporizhzhia under occupation. See Einwandererzentralstelle "Julius Kliewer," A3342EWZ50E016 0880. He would die in mysterious circumstances after visiting Benjamin H. Unruh in Karlsruhe. See Hans Rempel, *Der Weg Der Familie Rempel* (Virgil: self-published, 1980), 144.

55 Wiebe mentions Anna Sudermann as one of his acquaintances in Saint Petersburg, but she does not acknowledge him in her memoir, either in her extensive section on student life in Saint Petersburg or on the one about life under German occupation. See MLA, OH 4 (Cornelius Krahn interviews with post–Second World War Mennonite refugees), Heinrich Wiebe interview.
56 At the time, this village was known as Gnadenfeld. Some scholars have mistakenly identified Wiebe as a non-Mennonite. See Eric J. Schmaltz and Samuel D. Sinner, "The Nazi Ethnographic Research of Georg Leibbrandt and Karl Stumpp in Ukraine, and Its North American Legacy," *Holocaust and Genocide Studies* 14, no. 1 (March 2000): 46.
57 While within this village administration, Wiebe mentions working with Jacob A. Neufeld. MLA, OH 4. For Neufeld's interpretation of Mennonite experience in the 1930s and during the occupation, see Jacob A. Neufeld, *Path of Thorns: Soviet Mennonite Life under Communist and Nazi Rule*, ed. Harvey L. Dyck, trans. Sarah Dyck (Toronto: University of Toronto Press, 2014).
58 Wiebe described himself as being the director of a Mennonite school in Zaporizhzhia; since there were no Mennonite schools in Zaporizhzhia, I assume he meant Khortytsya.
59 Karl Stumpp, "In the Wake of the German Army on the Eastern Front, August 1941 to May 1942," trans. Adam Giesinger, *Journal of the American Historical Society of Germans from Russia* 7, no. 4 (Winter 1984): 21. Stumpp does not identify Wiebe by name; however, he writes about the mayor of Zaporizhzhia, and Wiebe would have occupied that position at this time.
60 See Mennonite Central Committee IX-12–01, box 17, T-Z. For more on MCC's role in refashioning Mennonites with complex backgrounds in postwar Europe, see Steven Schroeder, "Mennonite–Nazi Collaboration and Coming to Terms with the Past: European Mennonites and the MCC, 1945–1950," *Conrad Grebel Review* 21, no. 2 (2003): 6–16.
61 Alexander V. Prusin, "A Community of Violence: The SiPo/SD and Its Role in the Nazi Terror System in Generalbezirk Kiew," *Holocaust and Genocide Studies* 21, no. 1 (March 2007): 4.
62 Daria Rudakova, "Civilian Collaboration in Occupied Ukraine and Crimea, 1941–1944: A Study of Motivation" PhD diss., University of Western Australia, 2018, 94.
63 This can be gleaned from the partial lists of participants produced by members during their interrogations. USHMM RG-22.002M.0001.1561. Some of the possible Mennonite names included Ivan Dik, Ivan Krahn, David Dik, Kornei Andres. These lists also mention Ivan Fast, Jacob Fast, Vladimir Ersak, Stephan Fomenko, and "Interrogation of Nikolai Shubert." USHMM RG-31–018M.0059.1212–1239.

64 "Report about the Inspection of the Administration in Zaporizhzhia," USHMM RG-11.001M.0092.00000343, USHMM RG-11.001M.0092.00000346–7.
65 "Interrogation of Vladimir Ersak," USHMM RG-31.018M.0061.864; "Eyewitness statement, Alexander Shilko," USHMM RG-22.002M.0001.1547.
66 Einwandererzentralstelle "Jacob Fast," A3342EWZ50-B055 1262. This source also confirms that he worked for the Security Service (SD). According to information provided by Nikolai Shubert during an interrogation, Ivan Fast settled in Berlin after the war, where he studied to become a medical doctor. See USHMM RG-31–018M.0059.1239. Stephan Fomenko confirmed hearing from Jacob that Ivan was in Berlin. "Interrogation of Stephan Fomenko," USHMM RG-31.018M.0062.681. Ivan Fast would also eventually settle in Canada.
67 "Interrogation of Stephan Fomenko," USHMM RG-31.018M.0062.646.
68 Martin Dean, *Collaboration in the Holocaust: Crimes of the Local Police in Belorussia and Ukraine, 1941–44* (New York: St Martin's, 2003), 65–6.
69 "Interrogation of Vladimir Ersak," USHMM RG-31.018M.0061.855.
70 Ibid., USHMM RG-31.018M.0061.899.
71 Ibid., USHMM RG-31.018M.0061.857–8.
72 Fast was born in 1910. A number of other men over the age of twenty-five from various ethnic backgrounds joined one of the security organs. See "Interrogation of Nikolai Shubert," USHMM RG-31–018M.0059.1212–1239.
73 Anna Sudermann and Natalie's mother, Maria, were sisters. She also reported the unhappiness of Aron and Maria Toews with this marriage, although Aron conducted the ceremony. Since this memoir was written after the war, it is not entirely clear whether Sudermann felt this at the time or wanted to express indirectly her unhappiness with Fast's alleged wartime behaviour. Sudermann, *Lebenserinnerungen*.
74 She was baptized with nearly one hundred others from Khortytsya and Rosenthal by Reverend David Epp in 1931. See Natalie Fast, "Minister Rev. Aron Toews," translated in Kroeker, *First Mennonite Villages in Russia*, 58.
75 His interrogation file is available at Derzhavnii Arkhiv Zaporiz'koi Oblasti (DAZO), F.R5747, op.3, d.11012, l. 116.
76 For more on Aron Toews, see Aron P. Toews and Olga Rempel, *Siberian Diary of Aron P. Toews* (Winnipeg: CMBC, 1984).
77 Sudermann, *Lebenserinnerungen*.
78 Einwandererzentralstelle, "Jacob Fast," A3342EWZ50-B055 1262.
79 Natalie Fast, "Good-Bye to Khortitsa and Rosental," translated in Kroeker, *First Mennonite Villages in Russia*, 234.
80 MCC, IX-12–01, box 17 A-E. According to this document, they were headed to Arnaud, Manitoba, to stay with H.P. Toews. The family would eventually settle in St Catharines, Ontario.

248 Aileen Friesen

81 Kirk Makin and Jane Taber, "Ottawa Strips Two Nazi Suspects of Citizenship," *Globe and Mail*, 24 May 2007, https://www.theglobeandmail.com/news/national/ottawa-strips-two-nazi-suspects-of-citizenship/article20397970; Government of Canada, "Canada's Program on Crimes against Humanity and War Crimes: 2007–2008," n.d., 12.

82 For local portraits of administrative collaboration in Ukraine, see Yuri Radchenko, "Accomplices to Extermination: Municipal Government and the Holocaust in Kharkiv, 1941–1942," *Holocaust and Genocide Studies* 27, no. 3 (1 December 2013): 443–63; Markus Eikel and Valentina Sivaieva, "City Mayors, Raion Chiefs, and Village Elders in Ukraine, 1941–44: How Local Administrators Co-operated with the German Occupation Authorities," *Contemporary European History* 23, no. 3 (August 2014): 405–28.

83 MLA, OH 4. Initially, there was confusion among the Germans as to how to treat half-Jews or Jewish women married to Aryans who had children. It was clarified that according to official guidelines, these two categories should be exempt from wearing the armband. See USHMM RG-11.001M.0092.00000342. Eventually, children from mixed marriages would be included on the list of undesirables: a story of the murder of a half-Jewish child in Zaporizhzhia by poison in the arms of her Mennonite mother circulated widely within the community. See "Anna Braun interview conducted by David Boder," http://voices.iit.edu/interview?doc=braunA&display=braunA_en (accessed 15 July 2018).

84 While mayors performed their own role in the treatment of the Jewish population, these men rarely participated directly in mass shootings. Eikel and Sivaieva, "City Mayors, Raion Chiefs, and Village Elders in Ukraine, 1941–44," 416.

85 MLA, OH 4 (Cornelius Krahn interviews with post–Second World War Mennonite refugees), Heinrich Wiebe interview.

86 Vysotsky, *Nazi Crimes in Ukraine*, 143. The number of bodies at the ravine provided by this source is too high for them to be only Jews, although POWs, communists, and others were also killed by the occupying regime, in many of the same places in which the killing of Jews occurred.

87 DAZO, f.1433, op.3, d.7, l.26. "Management report for Zaporizhzhia, March 1942, by Heinrich Wiebe."

88 DAZO, F-R. 1433, op.1 d.269, l.132. "Report on the work of the city police for April." Instead of using the correct Russian adjective for Jewish, "*Evreiskii*," Fast used the derogatory term "*Zhidovskii*" to mark the destruction of this group. The recorded is signed "Fast," but without a given name. Likely the report was written by Ivan Fast.

89 Alexander Rempel, *Ein Protest gegen die Judenvernichtung, Untersuchungem zur Frage nach der Beteiligung von Volksdeutschen aus dem Schwarzmeergebiet*

in der Ukraine an der Judenvernichtung während des II-ten Weltkrieges (Winnipeg: Mennonite Heritage Archives, 1984), MHA, vol. 3440: 3.

90 Alexander Rempel and Amalie Enns, *Hope Is Our Deliverance: Aeltester Jakob Rempel: The Tragic Experience of a Mennonite Leader and His Family in Stalin's Russia* (Kitchener: Pandora Press, 2005), 168–9.

91 "Interrogation of Vladimir Ersak," USHMM RG-31.018M.0061.860.

92 For more on the veracity of these types of records, see Diana Dumitru, "An Analysis of Soviet Postwar Investigation and Trial Documents and Their Relevance for Holocaust Studies," in *The Holocaust in the East: Local Perpetrators and Soviet Responses*, ed. Michael David-Fox et al. (Pittsburgh: University of Pittsburgh Press, 2014). See "Interrogation of Iuvenalii Khil'chenko," RG-31.018M.0062.00000968; "Interrogation of Stephan Fomenko," USHMM RG-31.018M.0062.681; "Interrogation of Vladimir Ersak," USHMM RG-31.018M.0061.860.

93 Blavatnik Archive, interview with Pavel Elkinson, http://n2t.net/ark: /86084/b4xt0n (accessed 23 July 2019).

Chapter Nine

Dutch Mennonites and Yad Vashem Recognition

ALLE G. HOEKEMA

After 1933, when Hitler seized power in neighbouring Germany, on the one hand, we find a few Dutch Mennonites (*Doopsgezinden*) who were pro-Nazi and therefore in general (though not always) anti-Jewish.[1] Many of them supported the pro-Nazi party *Nationaal-Socialistische Beweging* (NSB), which during regional elections in 1935 received almost 7 per cent of the vote, but in the following general elections (1937, 1939) no more than 4 per cent. On the other hand, we find a rather large group of Mennonites who by the Second World War certainly were anti-German but who wanted to keep religion and politics separate within their communities; they were represented by the Dutch Mennonite weekly *De Zondagsbode* (The Sunday Messenger), which, until the Germans closed it down in 1942, tried – sometimes in vain – to keep "politics" out of its pages. Many congregations took the same attitude. After the war broke out on 10 May 1940 and the cruel measures of the Nazi regime became more and more visible, most Mennonites, like most Dutch people, took a strong anti-German position. The persecution and annihilation of Jews, however, was carried out gradually, and the Germans were shrewd in carrying it out, so there were few open protests by the population. During those years (1940–45) a minority of the population, including Mennonites, showed themselves to be unafraid of risking their lives to rescue Jews and others who were being persecuted by the Nazi regime. In general, the attitude of the Dutch toward the persecution of Jews during the war differed little from that of several other occupied Western European nations (Denmark excluded). Formal contacts between German and Dutch Mennonites were maintained until around 1938, but the war brought about a sudden breach, which would last more than a decade after the liberation on 5 May 1945.

In the early 1940s the Netherlands had some 9 million inhabitants. Most of them were Presbyterians (Reformed) and Calvinists (almost

44 per cent of the population); the Lutherans had always been a small church (1 per cent). The census of 1930 counted 62,000 *Doopsgezinden* (0.78 per cent, children included).[2] Some 102,000 Dutch Jews, of a total of around 140,000, were murdered during the Holocaust.

Early Contacts between Mennonites and Jews

There have been many individual contacts between Mennonites and Jews in the Netherlands, ever since the seventeenth century, but there have been no specific studies about these contacts. Nor is it my aim to provide such a study here.

Until the time of the French Revolution, Mennonites, Jews, and other religious minorities were accepted and most often respected in the Netherlands yet did not have full civil rights; they were expected to be "quiet in the land" (Psalm 35:20). In principle the French Revolution made them equal to other social and religious groups. At least one Mennonite pastor, Jacob Hendrik Floh (1758–1830), was instrumental in this respect. As a member of the new parliament, the *Nationale Vergadering* (National Gathering), from 1796 to 1798, he campaigned successfully for the full equality of Jews and other citizens in the new Dutch republic: "Even though each true and sincere Jew may see his presence in the Netherlands as a temporary time of exile till his people can return to Israel, nevertheless he will be deeply grateful when our government, consisting of noble thinking patriots [*edeldenkende Patriotten*] not only accepts the deeply humiliated Jew as human [*Mensch*], but elevates him to the honorable rank of Dutch citizen."[3] Of course, Floh's remarks do call for further investigation and debate about his stance. Apparently, the "honorable rank of Dutch citizen" was the highest rank one could attain!

Yet Jews often remained barred from certain social organizations during the nineteenth century, whereas Mennonites became a respected part of the upper and middle classes. Jews were, for instance, in the beginning not allowed to join the *Maatschappij tot Nut van 't Algemeen* (Association on Behalf of the Public Welfare), founded in 1784 by the Mennonite pastor Jan Nieuwenhuijzen (Monnickendam) and his son; so in 1849 they founded their own *Maatschappij tot Nut der Israelieten* (Association on Behalf of the Welfare of the Israelites).[4]

Some Mennonite pastors in the 1920s and '30s had intensive contacts with Dutch Jews. Notably we can mention here pastor Joseph Hubert van Riemsdijk (1883–1940)[5] and Frits Kuiper (1898–1974),[6] as well as the latter's sister Johanna (1896–1956).[7] In 1936 Van Riemsdijk spoke at the centennial celebration of the synagogue in Sneek (Friesland), and at his funeral service in the Mennonite church in Sneek on

5 June 1940, four weeks after the Germans occupied the Netherlands, the chairman of the board of that synagogue, the shopkeeper Abraham Kuyt, was asked to give the closing words of the ceremony. To describe Van Riemsdijk he quoted from Proverbs 11:30: "The fruit of the righteous is a tree of life."[8] Others could be mentioned here as well, such as the pastors Willem Mesdag and Tjeerd Oeds Hylkema. The Mesdag family was instrumental in saving at least sixty Jewish children.[9] Right after *Kristallnacht* (the Night of Broken Glass, 9–10 November 1938), Hylkema visited Reverend Heinrich Grüber in Berlin; Grüber ran an office that helped Jews obtain visas in order to flee the country. He had contacts with the Protestant Refugee Committee (founded earlier in 1938) and made the Dutch Mennonite *Broederschapshuizen* (conference centres) available for Jewish and partly Christian Jewish refugees.[10]

Mennonite theology students in Amsterdam had opportunities to come into contact with Jews. That city had by far the largest Jewish community in the country, and after 1924, Jehuda Lion Palache, a distinguished Jewish scholar of the Old Testament and Hebrew language, was a professor at Amsterdam University. Like all Jewish professors, he was expelled from the university in 1941; he would be murdered in Auschwitz in October 1944.

Some Mennonites married Jews, and a few Jews became members of Mennonite congregations in the nineteenth and twentieth centuries.[11] By the 1940s some Mennonite pastors were of (partly) Jewish descent.[12]

In general, Dutch society showed, and still does, a rather open attitude toward minorities, including Jews. By the 1930s many assimilated Jewish citizens held prominent positions in society, as intellectuals (university professors), producers of culture (musicians, authors, painters), politicians (at the local and national levels, in both social democratic and liberal parties), and trade unionists. In towns and larger cities they would meet Mennonites in similar positions. Compared to the rural Mennonites in most parts of Germany and the somewhat isolated Mennonites in their Ukrainian and Russian settlements, many Dutch Mennonites had an integrated, urbanized attitude that facilitated extensive contacts with non-Mennonites.

No wonder, then, that during the Second World War several pastors and a number of lay members provided hiding places for Jews. In articles by Gerlof Homan and several others, published mainly in successive issues of the *Doopsgezinde Bijdragen*, their names and their brave acts of faith and humanity have been mentioned.[13] Unfortunately, for many of them we have no detailed records.

Yad Vashem

Since 1962, Yad Vashem has been called the World Holocaust Remembrance Center, seated in Jerusalem. The name is taken from Isaiah 56:5: "I will give, in my house and within my walls, a monument and a name ... that shall not be cut off." One of its aims is "to convey the gratitude of the State of Israel and the Jewish people to non-Jews who risked their lives to save Jews during the Holocaust."[14] One of the criteria used is, indeed, that the rescuer risked his or her life. Another criterion is the existence of testimony from those who were helped, or at least sufficient unequivocal documents to prove that they did so.

Through the testimonies collected by Yad Vashem in Jerusalem and by researchers in the Netherlands itself, useful information is available about most of those Dutch Mennonites who were honoured to be named "Righteous among the Nations." Probably some forty Dutch Mennonites from at least twenty-six families received this honour, often posthumously.[15]

Below, I try to make clear whether and to what degree their motives for risking their lives were linked to a "Mennonite" identity. Among the twenty-six family names we find four pastors and two other theologians, along with lay members. All in all so far, almost 5,800 people in the Netherlands have received the Righteous honour (and more than 27,300 worldwide), so twenty-six to forty is certainly not a spectacular number. Most probably, if one goes by percentages, members of other Christian denominations were braver and more prominent in resisting the Nazi occupiers; here I agree with Gerlof Homan.[16] However, since the Yad Vashem administration does not always mention the religious or ideological affiliation of those who have received the honour, it is impossible to ascertain whether Dutch Mennonites are overrepresented in the full list of Dutch "Righteous among the Nations." Of course, a few Dutch Mennonites may have refused this honour or may not have been nominated though they could have been, as in the case of pastor Abraham Mulder in Giethoorn. In his spacious parsonage in the remote village of Giethoorn, he hid a number of Jews throughout the war.[17]

Below I provide brief sketches of four individuals/families who have been named "Righteous among the Nations"; then I will try to draw a few conclusions.

Geesje Nieuwenhuis-Brussé

Geesje Brussé (1906–2001) was a baptized member of the Mennonite congregation of Haarlem.[18] As a child she had attended the Mennonite school there. She lived with her first husband Henk Schutte in a modest house in a working-class neighbourhood in Haarlem. The couple had no children, and their marriage was far from happy. During the mobilization before the German army occupied the Netherlands, her husband and some friends were encamped as soldiers in the province of Zeeland. One of these friends was a Jew. When the war broke out on 10 May 1940, and when two years later all Jews were arrested or had to go "underground," the friends agreed to bring the family of their Jewish comrade to safety in their homes in Haarlem. After August 1942, Geesje Nieuwenhuis (who would obtain a divorce after the war and marry Nico Nieuwenhuis) took care of the little daughter Nanette, then four years old; her parents and brother were hidden nearby. Nanette was blonde, and the neighbours and others were told she was "Netje Schutte," the child of a brother of Geesje Schutte's husband, who had been arrested because of his anti-German attitude. The little girl, as if by instinct, never asked, "Where is my mother?" but she knew exactly where her parents were hidden: across the street. Sometimes the parents could see her from a distance, playing in the yard.

Sometimes other (Jewish or otherwise) persons had to go into hiding in Geesje's house for a couple of days; then the little girl was taken to another hiding place. Often Mrs Nieuwenhuis was frightened; on one occasion a German soldier, who was about to be sent to the Western Front, wanted to hug the girl, who reminded him of his own child in the heavily bombed Ruhr area in Germany. Immediately some neighbours scolded Mrs Nieuwenhuis, calling her a *Moffenmeid* (as Dutch women who had intimate contacts with German soldiers were labelled). Little Nanette sometimes could attend Sunday School classes in a nearby Reformed church. It had been agreed that if her parents perished during the war, she would stay with Geesje Nieuwenhuis. Fortunately, she was able to reunite with her biological parents in August 1945.

The Bible text that was given to Geesje Brussé on the occasion of her baptism, John 15:8, speaks about bearing much fruit and becoming disciples of Christ. She carried this text with her throughout the war and later on. "I am grateful that our good Lord enabled me to do this," Geesje Nieuwenhuis said. "There is a God who guides our life totally. ... We have to leave to God's disposition, why the Jews have been persecuted, even though they are God's chosen people." Nanette added, in 1995, that she had very "warm feelings" about these years in hiding. She still remembered the prayers before the meal and some Christian children's hymns; these belonged to "those days." After the war, for a long time she avoided telling others she was Jewish, as if "during my whole life I have been hiding from my Jewishness." For a long time many of her memories remained "unconsciously" hidden.

Even though Nanette's contact with Mrs Nieuwenhuis was never interrupted thereafter, it would be many years before she was able to write down a witness for Yad Vashem. She felt happy that her children did not feel themselves to be "second generation" victims. Geesje Nieuwenhuis, who never had children of her own, stated during the interview, "One can help one's fellow humans. I did not live in vain."

The Roostee and Roeper Families in Arnhem

We do not know much about Johannes Roostee (1890–1976), his (second) wife Petronella Maria Geertruida Roostee-Roeper (1906–1992), her parents Dirk Roeper (1880–1955) and Petronella Koning (1877–1962), as well as his brother-in-law Dirk Roeper, Jr (1914–2011) and sister-in-law Femina Roeper-Bakker (1916–2000). Roostee's Mennonite father was born in Emden, and his Reformed (Presbyterian) mother in Amsterdam, where Johannes Roostee was born as well. Dirk Roeper, Sr, and Johannes Roostee (and eventually other family members as well) were members of the Arnhem Mennonite congregation, though probably not in leading positions. The roots of the Roepers were on the island of Texel.[19] Johannes Roostee worked several years in the army and later became a self-employed entrepreneur. He had a large house, big enough for his own family and at least three people in hiding.[20]

The Yad Vashem website states that the whole family "were religious Protestants and fiercely anti-Nazi."[21] In 1942 the Roostees took fourteen-year-old Marianne Rozendaal into their home. Two other Jews, Peter Lustig and his mother, were already hiding there. Nothing is known about them, but most probably they survived the war. Even before the war and during it as well, a handful of members of the Mennonite congregation organized themselves to help Jewish children and others who had to go into hiding. The "inspiring centre" of this group was Gerrit Veendorp, a pious teacher, who died a few months before the end of the war.[22] Eventually the Roostees joined this secretive group. The Roostees' adult children also participated in resistance activities.[23] The Roostees also made their house available for clandestine, partly illegal theatre and poetry performances. Between 1942 and 1944 these performances, by artists who had refused to sign up for the Nazi *Kultuurkamer* (Cultural Workers' Guild), were held in the homes of several reliable families. As many as fifty people attended such gatherings.[24]

The Roostees lived across from the railway station at Coehoornstraat 1, and in 1942 and 1943 Marianne Rozendaal had to witness from her window the deportation of Jews from this station. A pro-Nazi neighbour knew about Marianne's presence but never betrayed them. In their congregation, some members were pro-Nazi, but during the war they were never excluded from the Lord's Supper, according to the small commemorative volume *Een eeuw doopsgezinde gemeente* (One Century of a Mennonite Congregation).[25]

In September 1944 the Allied forces, advancing from the already liberated southern part of the country, attempted to establish a bridgehead across the Rhine at Arnhem, which would enable them to liberate the main part of the Netherlands (Operation Market Garden). The central part of the city, including the railway station near the Roostees' house, was destroyed by bombing. For some time three German soldiers were billeted in the Roostee house, which made the situation very precarious (such situations had happened in other cases as well). After the church service on 17 September 1944, the members of the Mennonite congregation were unable to leave because of the bombing and gunfire. Later that day, they had to evacuate with the entire population of the town, some 95,000 people. The Mennonite church on the Weverstraat was severely damaged around this same time, and many other churches and buildings were destroyed. Many members of the Mennonite congregation moved to around Apeldoorn (some 30 kilometres to the north), where the local congregation showed great hospitality. Others, including the Roostee family with Marianne Rozendaal, fled to Barneveld (to the northwest), and several families in that village helped Marianne hide safely there till the end of the war. Operation Market Garden failed at the cost of many lives, and not until more than nine months later, in June 1945, were the people of Arnhem able to return to their homes. Several members of the Mennonite congregation died as a result of the bombing and other hardships. At a first inspection of the Mennonite church, they even found a number of hand grenades.[26]

As far as we know, by a miracle the Roostee house was not damaged too heavily. In any case, quite soon after the war they were living there again. For many years after the war, Johannes Roostee was an active board member of the *Doopsgezinde Zendings Vereniging* (Dutch Mennonite Mission), possibly because some members of the extended Roostee family had roots in the Dutch East Indies. In November 1976 he died peacefully and unexpectedly, at the age of eighty-six, in the house where he had lived for more than forty years.[27] In 1980 the entire family received Yad Vashem recognition; a year later they attended a tree-planting ceremony in Jerusalem.

Pastor Alexander Hubertus van Drooge and His Family[28]

Alexander (San) Hubertus van Drooge (1916–1993) was the youngest son of Pastor Alexander Hubertus van Drooge (1872–1942), who served the Deventer congregation for many years and was chair of the General Mennonite Conference (Algemene Doopsgezinde Sociëteit; ADS) from 1934 to 1939. San van Drooge studied theology in Amsterdam and became a pastor in Makkum, Friesland, in 1939. His wife Eddy ter Haar had been a student at the same *Gymnasium* (high school) in Deventer. From the beginning of the war, they involved themselves in resistance activities. Eddy van Drooge said, according to her youngest daughter, whom I interviewed twice, and according to written newspaper sources: "I cannot do otherwise." To her, still so young, it was almost an adventure to thwart the Germans. Her husband saw clearly the dangers of what they were doing. For both of them, resistance was a matter of profoundly felt humanity rather than simple Christian identity. Yet pastor Van Drooge was not afraid to speak out against the Germans in his sermons – in the small village of Makkum, people knew each other sufficiently well.

Van Drooge took part in one of the three resistance groups in Makkum; however, because of his Mennonite convictions, he never wanted to involve himself in armed actions.[29] In early April 1945, just two weeks before Makkum was liberated by Canadian troops on 18 April, these groups were betrayed and their members arrested. On 7 April, six of them were cruelly executed, and at a later date a seventh as well. Eddy van Drooge told her children later on that she had turned over the dead bodies to see whether her husband was one of them. Fortunately, he was not; he would be released after a few days. Their house always had at least four and sometimes more people in hiding – Jews and others. One of them was an older man, Mr Oppenheim, who stayed with them till the end of the war.

One of the Jewish children who stayed with them for a long time was Leny Cohen.[30] She was eleven years old when she arrived in Makkum. Her family in Deventer had been befriended by Eddy van Drooge's parents, the Reformed pastor Bernard ter Haar in the village of Diepenveen. Leny's parents went into hiding, separated, not far from Makkum. Unfortunately her younger brother, who was hiding in Amsterdam, was discovered and subsequently murdered in Auschwitz.[31] Fearing he might be tortured and reveal the hiding place of his sister, Leny Cohen had to move to another family, that of another a Reformed pastor in nearby Sint Jacobi Parochie.[32] After the war she studied at the University of California–Berkeley, married, and immigrated to the United

States; her German Jewish fiancé had been able to escape there before the war, and her mother's parents had escaped there as well. Contacts with the family Van Drooge have continued to the present day.

The Van Drooges tried in vain to persuade their former school director in Deventer, Dr Louis Hillesum, who was Jewish, to hide together with his family in the Makkum parsonage. After graduating from his high school they had stayed in contact with him. Through their contacts with a (partly) Mennonite resistance group in Amsterdam (CS 6, in which the Boissevain family played an important role) and the Singel church, they planned to make this possible. Unfortunately, Dr Hillesum declined, mainly because his daughter Etty refused to go into hiding; at that time she was working for the *Joodsche Raad* (Jewish Council) and was able to travel to the deportation camp at Westerbork and back to Amsterdam; she felt that her work was necessary.[33] Later confined in Westerbork with the rest of her family, she stated in letters that she preferred to share the fate of her people. Since the 1980s, her diaries and letters have become almost as famous as *The Diary of Anne Frank*. On 7 September 1943, father and mother Hillesum, together with Etty and brother Mischa (a very gifted pianist), were transported to occupied Poland, quietly and even singing. In a brief letter, thrown out of the freight train, she wrote: "I open the Bible at an arbitrary page and find this: The Lord is my fortress. ... We shall travel three days." The whole family was murdered in Auschwitz.[34]

Like many others, the Van Drooges always harboured feelings of guilt: should they have done more to rescue victims?[35]

Geertje Pel-Groot and Her Daughters in Zaandam[36]

Geertje Pel (1889–1945) and her husband Wijbrand Pel (1889–1942) were faithful members of the Mennonite congregations in Zaandam: Wijbrand in the one west of the river Zaan, Geertje in the congregation on the east side of that river. Wijbrand Pel owned a wafer factory. They had two sons and two daughters. All of them worked at the factory. Both Geertje and Wijbrand were active in a more or less illegal working group of members of Mennonite congregations in the Zaan area, led by Cor Inja, that tried to help Jewish and Jewish Christian prisoners in the Westerbork camp, from which most Dutch Jews were transported to extermination camps like Auschwitz and Sobibor.[37] Before the war the Pel family had befriended Jewish families in nearby Amsterdam. When the time came that Jews had either to go into hiding or to report themselves to be imprisoned, the Pel family immediately agreed to take into their home the newborn baby of Betsy Swaab, daughter of Rebecca and Max Waag. Unfortunately, Wijbrand died before he could keep this promise.

But Geertje Pel did keep it, following Matthew 5:37: "Let your word be 'Yes, Yes' or 'No, No.'" So, at the end of August 1942, little baby Marion Swaab arrived in Zaandam. Her parents succeeded in fleeing to Switzerland (father Hijman Swaab) and Belgium (mother Betsy). The grandparents perished in extermination camps, together with other members of their families. In the beginning everything went well. However, a neighbour opposite their home was a notorious pro-German policeman who betrayed scores of people. On 11 March 1944, Geertje was summoned to appear at the office of the *Sicherheitsdienst* (German Security Service; SD) in Amsterdam together with the baby. This certainly would have meant the death of the baby. Geertje could have gone into hiding herself as well, but – she said – then the lives of other family members would be at risk. So she went, but right before boarding the ferry to Amsterdam, her twenty-one-year-old daughter Trijnie took the baby into safety.

Geertje was arrested in Amsterdam, then sent to the Vught concentration camp and finally to the women's camp at Ravensbrück. There she tried to comfort other women; she led Bible studies in secret and attended clandestine church services led by Corrie ten Boom.[38] Witnesses who survived the camp called her "a child of God." Geertje did not survive; weakened and ill, she died in the gas chamber of Ravensbrück around 20 February 1945. Other women had advised her to hide in one of the barracks. She refused: if she did that, then somebody else would have to die. Two months later the Ravensbrück camp was liberated by the Red Army.

The fate of Marion Swaab and her parents after the war is a sad story of its own. In any case, contact with the Pel family was lost for a long time. Time and again her parents told Marion to be grateful, because "Mother Pel" had died so she could live. That, of course, did not help a young adolescent girl. The war, in her life, is a never-ending story, she says in the documentary movie *Monumenten spreken* (Monuments Speak). Nevertheless, in the end, contact was restored, and thanks to Marion Swaab's testimony both Geertje Pel (posthumously) and her daughter Trijnie Pfann-Pel received the Yad Vashem recognition in 2013.

Conclusion

Reading and analysing the stories of the above-mentioned families (and others), it is not always clear whether they acted from explicitly expressed Mennonite convictions or out of plain humanity. Geertje

Pel clearly was motivated by her biblical faith; according to the Yad Vashem document, Johannes Roostee was a devout Christian, and Geesje Nieuwenhuis-Brussé was led by the Bible text she received at her baptism. Others, like the Van Drooge family, were moved by simple human decency.[39] Yet San van Drooge drew a line when it came to the use of weapons. Nine Treffers-Mesdag points to a certain "inner-directedness" as the basis of the Mennonite frame of mind during those years. They did stick to their convictions, "because I have been guided from within [my heart] to do so."[40]

Many Dutch Mennonites, but certainly not all, belonged to the middle and upper-middle class. This meant they had rather large homes, maintained broad social networks, and held a social-liberal attitude characterized by easy-going tolerance toward people of other convictions, including Jews, at least those who belonged to their own social class and networks. More than half of the Mennonites who received the Yad Vashem honour belonged to this part of society. Often their faith convictions were liberal as well. Most Dutch Mennonites voted for socialist or (conservative-) liberal parties, not the so-called Christian parties. Thus, the border between "Christian" and "humanistic" was never entirely clear. Geesje Nieuwenhuis certainly did not belong to the upper middle class; she lived in a rather small house in a working-class neighbourhood and was able to take Netty Jacobs into her house only because the girl was blonde. In less densely populated areas like Frisian villages, farmers living outside the villages were able to take people into hiding.

Of the four examples given above, Roostee and his children, Van Drooge, and Wijbrand Pel and his sons were involved in resistance networks, as far as we know. So were several others who received (posthumously) the same Yad Vashem honour, such as Krijn van der Helm (Leeuwarden) and his wife Johanna Cornelia Logtenberg. Van der Helm was for a time under the Nazi regime the most wanted man in the Netherlands.[41] He was killed when the Germans tried to arrest him, on 25 August 1944. Others who made use of resistance networks were pastor Willem Mesdag and his wife (Sneek)[42] and Walraven van Hall, who has been called the "banker" of the entire resistance movement in the Netherlands; after being caught in February 1945, he was executed along with others by a firing squad in Haarlem.[43]

Women were at least as active as men in the resistance network. Sometimes the women were even more courageous, perhaps since they looked more innocent. See, for instance, the attitude of Eddy van Drooge-ter Haar and Geertje Pel-Groot, but also the behaviour of An Keuning-Tichelaar, Sjoukje Mesdag-Hylkema, and the pastors Helena Cornelia Leignes Bakhoven and Johanna van der Slooten.

In most of the cases described above, there was already a direct or indirect relation between the rescuers and rescued Jews or their families. Often, however, this was not the case. The Van Drooges also provided shelter to people who were brought to them by anonymous agents of the resistance movement, some of whom were young female students. Moreover, it was safer not to know such backgrounds. And one never would talk about anything with one's own friends, neighbours, or relatives. The Van Drooges were aware that their Mennonite colleagues Mesdag (Sneek) and J.W. Sipkema (Drachten) were involved in hiding Jewish children, but they never talked about it together. Nor did the Van Drooges talk with their own brother, who was hiding people in his residence in the village of Borculo.

During the first postwar decades, people generally did not talk about their acts of heroism. Many never talked about it ever, not even to their children. Had it not been the normal attitude? In certain *gereformeerde* (Re-Reformed) circles there was a pretty hard debate during these decades about whether Jewish children who had survived the war in Christian families should be Christianized and baptized. Dutch Mennonites never had a mission aimed at converting Jews and never tried to Christianize those who had been in hiding with them. Jewish children – passing for distant relatives – may have attended church services when this was not dangerous; generally, though, Jews in hiding were unable to leave the house or even be near a window during those two or three years.

Rather often during the first postwar decades, contacts between rescued and rescuers were lost or were only infrequent, an example being the relationship between Marion Swaab and the Pel family. Everybody had his or her own way to leave the bitter years of the war behind, and all wanted to look to the future. Many Jews who survived the war migrated to Israel or the United States and tried to forget. Only since the 1990s has a culture of remembrance been revived. Of the twenty-six family names of Dutch Mennonite rescuers, only nine received Yad Vashem recognition before 1990; ten more did after the year 2000. Most often this recognition remained a private matter; their respective congregations were not informed or did not attend the ceremony. This, too, may be a sign of the general feeling that their acts of mercy during the war were just normal acts and not something in which to take pride.

NOTES

1 This chapter will appear as chapter 6 of my forthcoming book, tentatively titled *Dutch Mennonites during World War II and Its Aftermath* (Elkhart: Institute

of Mennonite Studies, 2020), and is printed here by permission of the publisher. Also, in this chapter we use the terms "Mennonites" for the proper Dutch name "Doopsgezinden" without distinction even though certain differences may exist between them.

2 Sources: www.volkstellingen.nl and Hans Knippenberg, *De Religieuze Kaart van Nederland* (Assen and Maastricht: Van Gorcum, 1992), 266–74. In 1930 – the last census before 1947 – the Roman Catholic Church accounted for some 36.4 per cent of the population and there were some 113,000 Jewish inhabitants. Due to a growing stream of Jewish refugees from Poland, Germany. and elsewhere, the number of Jews grew to 125,000 (German estimate in 1941) or 140,000 (general estimation).

3 Floh was a member of a committee of the Nationale Vergadering that dealt with the (government) salaries of Christian ministers. See S.B.J. Zilverberg, "Jacob Hendrik Floh," in *Biografisch Lexicon voor de geschiedenis van het Nederlands protestantisme*, vol. 2 (Kampen: Kok, 1983), 197; idem, "Enkele aspecten van de betrekkingen tussen Doopsgezinden en remonstranten tot aan het begin van de 19^e eeuw," *Doopsgezinde Bijdragen nieuwe reeks* (hereafter *DB*) 20 (1994): 181–94, esp. 193; Joris Oddens, "Mennistenstreken in het strijdperk. Het eerste parlement van Nederland en de mythe van de moderate middenpartij," *DB* 35–6 (2009): 337–61. Floh's plea can be found in *Dagverhaal der Handelingen van de Nationaale Vergadering*, vol. 2 (The Hague: Swart en Comp., 1796), 283–4. One more quotation from his plea: "Wie, die eenige menschelykheid bezit, die den naam van mensch niet geheel onwaardig is, keurt niet, met de diepste verontwaardiging af, een *Jood*, omdat hy *Jood* is, niet in de ruimste mate te doen deelen in de onvervreemdbare regten van den *Mensch*? – En wie herdenkt niet, onder het gevoel der treurigste aandoeningen, de herhaalde mishandelingen, het merkwaardige Volk van Israël gints en elders aangedaan door zoogenaamde vrome belyders van het Evangelie van Jesus Christus, dat algemeene menschenliefde gebied, en broederschap ademt" (Everybody who owns a form of humanity and who is worthy to be called a human being, will feel a deep indignation when a *Jew*, just because he is a *Jew*, is denied the inalienable rights of *Man*. And will not everybody commemorate with feelings of sad emotions the repeated maltreatments suffered here and elsewhere by this particular people of Israel; maltreatments committed by so-called pious adherents of the Gospel of Jesus Christ, which calls for a general love of mankind and is filled with fraternity).

4 See A.G. Hoekema, ed., *'Tot heil van Java's arme bevolking.' Een keuze uit het Dagboek (1851–1860) van Pieter Jansz, doopsgezind zendeling in Jepara, Midden-Java*, (Hilversum: Verloren, 1997), 31n6. In 1851 a branch of the Dutch Maatschappij tot Nut van't Algemeen was founded in Batavia

(now Jakarta), which allowed non-Christians, such as Muslims, to become members. At that time this was against the rules and by-laws of the *Maatschappij*, and a special committee in the Netherlands had to discuss the matter. As a result, the rules became more lenient in 1854.
5 See F.J. Hoogewoud, "'Te goed voor deze wereld.' Ds. J.H. van Riemsdijk (1883–1940) en zijn liefde voor Joden en Jodendom," *Doopsgezind Jaarboekje* 105 (2011): 36–46.
6 For more about Frits Kuiper, see Alle G. Hoekema, and Pieter Post, eds., *Frits Kuiper (1898–1974) doopsgezind theoloog* (Hilversum: Verloren, 2016). Kuiper dedicated his book *Israël en de Gojiem* (Haarlem: Tjeenk Willink, 1951) to his Jewish friend in Alkmaar, the lawyer Aäron Prins, who perished in Sobibor in 1943. One of Kuiper's friends was Cornelius Krahn, who studied in the Netherlands before the Second World War. In an interview, Krahn mentioned that friends in Germany accused him during these years of cooperating with Jews. "Cornelius Krahn – Pelgrim in Europa en Amerika," *DB* 5 (1979): 114–18 (interview by Helmut Isaak, edited by Dirk Visser).
7 Ferdinand van Melle, *Johanna E. Kuiper (1896–1956), Gewaagd leven*, PhD diss., Vrije Universiteit, Amsterdam, 2015. Johanna Kuiper had Jewish schoolfriends and always maintained cordial contacts with Jewish people. Together with her husband Reverend Klaas Abe Schipper, Johanna Kuiper was awarded posthumously the Yad Vashem recognition in 2014, because they had hidden Jewish people in their Reformed pastor's house in the hamlet of Etersheim (near Oosthuizen, province of Noord-Holland).
8 The Jewish shopkeeper Abraham Kuyt was a good friend of pastor Van Riemsdijk and had sat with him at his deathbed, a few days before Van Riemsdijk passed away: www.sporen joodslevensneek.nl/verhalen /familie-kuyt.html. He and his family survived the war, and in 1948 he became the leader of the Orthodox Jewish community in Leeuwarden.
9 Nine Treffers-Mesdag, "De pastorie in Sneek onder de bezetting. Enige persoonlijke indrukken van de positie en de houding van Doopsgezinden in de Tweede Wereldoorlog," *DB* 24 (1998): 273–80, esp. 278. Her source as to the number of children is an extensive study by Bert Jan Flim, *Omdat hun hart sprak. Geschiedenis van de georganiseerde hulp aan Joodse kinderen in Nederland, 1942–1945* (Kampen: Kok, 1996), 207–16, 319–30. On page 211 Flim writes that quite a few Jewish children were hidden in towns and villages in the area around Sneek, where Doopsgezinde congregations existed with reliable pastors; he explicitly mentions the (partly Jewish) female pastor Johanna van der Slooten in IJlst. Mesdag worked closely with a Catholic assistant priest, Gérard Jansen. In Flim's study, several other names of Dutch Doopsgezinde are mentioned, who were active in the resistance movement. The estimate of sixty to eighty children is

mentioned on page 366. Willem Mesdag and Sjoukje Mesdag-Hylkema received the Yad Vashem recognition posthumously in 1993.

10 Alle G. Hoekema, *'Bloembollen' voor Westerbork. Hulp door Zaanse en andere Doopsgezinden aan (protestants-) Joodse Duitse vluchtelingen in Nederland* (Hilversum: Verloren, 2011), 50. See also Nine Treffers-Mesdag, "De pastorie in Sneek," 273.

11 The archives of the Doopsgezinde congregation Den Haag contain a list, dated 28 August 1942, with the names of twenty Christians of Jewish descent who had ties with this congregation, as members or catechumens. It was hoped that through this list these persons could obtain a *Sperre*, which would prevent them from being deported (and murdered). In some cases this happened; others were transported to Theresienstadt and survived. Some persons on the list were deported and perished. See Alle G. Hoekema, "Doopsgezind Den Haag tijdens de Tweede Wereldoorlog," *DB* 41 (2015): 129–51. In order to obtain a *Sperre* on behalf of Doopsgezinde members of Jewish descent, the board of the Algemene Doopsgezinde Sociëteit collected such lists from all congregations and probably handed them to the German authorities. This overall list, which of course also carried a dangerous aspect, has yet to be found.

12 For instance, Else Franken-Duparc (1911–2000), who served the congregation in Blokzijl from 1942. Later she was in Indonesia with her husband, and after that she became pastor of the congregation of Rottevalle, where she founded a Christian retreat called "Heliatros." Also in Blokzijl, she and her husband hid Jewish people in their parsonage. Johanna van der Slooten (1900–1968), pastor in Hindeloopen/Koudum and after 1939 in IJlst, had a partly Jewish background. Eduard van Straten (1931–2017) had a Jewish father.

13 See Gerlof Homan, "Nederlandse Doopsgezinden in de Tweede Wereldoorlog," *DB* 21 (1995): 165–97, an extended version of an article in *Mennonite Quarterly Review* 69 (1995): 7–36.

14 Quoted from the Yad Vashem website, www.yadvashem.org/righteous /about-the-program.html.

15 An incomplete list can be found in *DB* 41 (2015): 402. Not all family members were baptized Doopsgezinde.

16 Gerlof Homan, "Nederlandse Doopsgezinden," 172: "Nederlandse Doopsgezinden leden niet meer of minder dan andere landgenoten. Ook deden ze bepaald niet meer aan verzet of gaven ze meer getuigenis van hun geloofstrouw dan andere christenen" (Dutch Mennonites suffered neither more nor less than other Dutch citizens. Also, they certainly were not more deeply involved in resistance movements nor expressed their pious faithfulness more clearly than other Christians). A similar judgment on page 192.

17 See Lies van der Zee, "'De Gemeente van Christus moet blijven het geweten der wereld.' Oorlogspreken van ds. Abraham Mulder te Giethoorn," in *DB* 41 (2015): 269–301. At least three Jews spent three years of the occupation in the Mennonite parsonage in Giethoorn. Later several other people who had to go into hiding joined them. At the end of the war eleven people were hiding in his house.
18 Most of this information has been drawn from an extensive interview with Mrs Nieuwenhuis around May 1995 conducted by F.J. Hoogewoud. This interview, partly also with Mrs Jacobs, a Jewish woman who as a child found refuge in her home, took place in the context of an oral history project carried out by the Haarlem congregation. The interview has been recorded on DVD; available in the VDGH Archives, Haarlem.
19 On the island of Texel the family name Roeper is well known, often as a Mennonite name. Elsewhere it is also a Jewish family name.
20 A photograph of their three-storey house can be found in P.R.A. van Iddekinge, *Zwarte avonden in Arnhem 1942–1944. Cultuur buiten de Kultuurkamer* (Arnhem: Historische reeks Arnhem no. 4, 1994), 58. Presently it is used as a hotel.
21 See http://www.db.yadvashem.org/righteous/family.html under Roeper Family and Roostee Family. The Yad Vashem records often do not distinguish between the many Protestant denominations.
22 See J.E. Tuininga, "Periode van strijd, ballingschap en terugkeer 1939–1946," in *Een eeuw doopsgezinde gemeente* (Arnhem: Doopsgezinde Gemeente, 1952), 40–4. Tuininga was the pastor of this congregation during the war. Veendorp had been a member of the church board between 1921 and 1933.
23 See www.roanestate.academicworks.com/donors/ina-ingwersen-family .html, about a scholarship fund, granted by Ina Roostee and her husband Johannes Ingwersen. In 1948 they had migrated to Canada and later to the United States.
24 Van Iddekinge, *Zwarte avonden in Arnhem,* passim. See esp. 98–105. Several well-known Dutch actors and poets performed in the living room of the Roostees, such as Albert van Dalsum, Martinus Nijhoff, Jan Musch, and Adriaan Roland Holst. The Kultuurkamer was a Nazi institute; all artists, authors, journalists, musicians, and so on had to belong to it in order to receive permission to work.
25 *Een eeuw doopsgezinde gemeente,* 9. "In onze kring worden niet maatschappelijke en politieke opvattingen gekoppeld aan de doopsgezinde overtuigingen. Ook in dit opzicht huldigen wij het beginsel der vrijheid" (In our circles social and political opinions are not connected with Mennonite convictions. In this respect we honour the principle of liberty).
26 Tuininga, "Periode van strijd," 44.

266   Alle G. Hoekema

27 A death notice was published in *Algemeen Doopsgezind Weekblad*, 27 November 1976.
28 I received much assistance from pastor Van Drooge's youngest daughter and other family members. See also H.R. Keuning, "In Memoriam Alexander Hubertus van Drooge," *Algemeen Doopsgezind Weekblad*, 23 October 1993; H.R. Keuning, "In Memoriam Ds. A.H. van Drooge," *Doopsgezind Jaarboekje* 88 (1994): 14–15; G.W. Haas, "In Memoriam Ds. A.H. van Drooge," unknown source (probably a local Mennonite paper in Haren, Groningen), 21 October 1993.
29 This was affirmed in Eddy van Drooge's very brief speech on the occasion of the Yad Vashem ceremony in the synagogue of the town of Hilversum, 18 March 1998. Not all Dutch Doopsgezinden refused to use arms in resistance groups. The young Hannie Schaft in Haarlem (her mother was a member of the Haarlem congregation) did use arms; it cost her her life. An Keuning-Tichelaar, wife of pastor Herman Keuning (Akkrum) carried weapons under her skirt; see Gerlof Homan, "Nederlandse Doopsgezinden," 186. Young Herman Keuning had been an assistant pastor in Makkum and stayed for a time in the house of the Van Drooges. There he became acquainted with the woman who would become his wife: An Tichelaar, the descendent of a very old Mennonite family in Makkum, well-known for its pottery factory, which still exists.
30 Leny Cohen later gave witness about the war years at a meeting in a synagogue in the United States. Her witness was recorded on DVD, Archives Family van Drooge.
31 Hans Frits Cohen, born 14 September 1932, was deported from concentration camp Westerbork to Auschwitz on 8 February 1944. Right after the war, his father, Johan Cohen, asked by means of advertisements whether anybody could give information about his fate. A few weeks later the family received the bitter news.
32 Reverend Lambertus Cannegieter and his wife Anna Coppeyne van de Coppello. See www.yadvashem.org at "Cannegieter." They also received the Yad Vashem honour.
33 See F.J. Hoogewoud, "'Ware vreugde is iets ernstigs.' Dr Louis Hillesums gedwongen afscheid van het Stedelijk Gymnasium in Deventer, 29 november 1940," in K.A.D. Smelik et. al., eds., *Etty Hillesum in weerwil van het Joodse vraagstuk* (Antwerpen and Apeldoorn: Garant, 2016), 11–40, esp. n34.
34 Etty Hillesum's complete and unabridged work has been published in the Netherlands in several editions, most recently as *Etty. De nagelaten geschriften van Etty Hillesum 1941–1943*, ed. Klaas A.D. Smelik (Amsterdam: Balans, 2008), 701. The Bible quotation is from Psalm 59:17. An English

translation appeared as *Etty: The Letters and Diaries of Etty Hillesum, 1941–1943*, ed. Klaas A.D. Smelik (Grand Rapids: W.B. Eerdmans, 2002).

35 Here we have to add that an older brother of San van Drooge, Johan Hubertus van Drooge (1911–1991), and his wife Sytske van Drooge-Stoffel, harboured Jews also. They too received the Yad Vashem recognition.

36 The life story of Geertje Pel and her family has been well-documented with much empathy by the journalist Hanneloes Pen, *Een vergeten leven. Een Zaanse vrouw, een Joodse baby en een daad van verzet* (Amsterdam: Atlas Contact, 2016). In 2013 a documentary movie about twenty-eight war monuments in the Zaan area was produced by Robert van Tellingen: *Monumenten spreken*, in which ample attention is paid to Geertje Pel-Groot. See YouTube, www.monumentenspreken.nl (no. 23). As part of my research for my book*"Bloembollen" voor Westerbork* I interviewed both daughters a number of years ago.

37 Regarding this group's work, see Hoekema, *"Bloembollen" voor Westerbork*.

38 Pen, *Een gegeven leven*, 135, 148. Corrie ten Boom (1893–1982) was the daughter of a Haarlem watchmaker. They concealed Jewish people in their home. This act of resistance and her later life have been described in the biographical book *The Hiding Place* (Washington Depot: Chosen Books, 1971). On 28 February 1944, the Gestapo entered the house (without finding the people in hiding) and arrested the father, Casper, and both daughters. Within a month, Casper died in prison. Like Geertje Pel, Betsy and Corrie were brought to Vught and finally transported to Ravensbrück. Betsy died there, but by a miracle Corrie was released at the end of December 1944. At least two other young Mennonite women perished in Ravensbrück: Sophie van Gilse from Leyden (1912–31 January 1945) and the half-Jewish Martha van Konijnenburg (Haarlem/Amsterdam), born in 1914; she died on 7 March1945, seven weeks before the camp was liberated by Russian troops. A few others survived the camp.

39 So also Willem Maillette de Buy Wenniger and his wife Miny te Winkel, according to their daughter Wies Blomjous-Maillette de Buy Wenniger, "Yad Vashem onderscheiding voor Miny te Winkel (1915–1995) en Willem Maillette de Buy Wenniger (1914–1996)," *BD* 41 (2015): 381–4.

40 Nine Treffers-Mesdag, "De pastorie in Sneek onder de bezetting. Enige persoonlijke indrukken van de positie en de houding van Doopsgezinden in de Tweede Wereldoorlog," *DB* 24 (1998): 273–80 at 280.

41 Database yadvashem.org/righteous/family.html under Helm, and Gerlof Homan, "Nederlandse Doopsgezinden," *DB* 21 (1995): 186.

42 See Treffers-Mesdag, "De pastorie in Sneek onder de bezetting," 273–80.

43 About Walraven van Hall, several articles and biographies have been written. A biopic about his life, presented in all major movie theatres, was

released on 8 March 2018. See also the documentary film *Monumenten spreken*, (no. 21). So far I have not been able to prove that he was a baptized Doopsgezinde; however, he came from a Doopsgezinde family and his sister Hester Dufour-van Hall was a Doopsgezinde pastor, who, together with her husband, also received the Yad Vashem recognition.

Chapter Ten

Identity and Complicity: The Post–Second World War Emigration of Chortitza Mennonites

ERIKA WEIDEMANN

On 8 January 1948, in Nuremberg, Presiding Justice Musmanno summoned Chortitza Mennonite Franziska Reimers to the stand as a witness in the famous Mobile Killing Squad (*Einsatzgruppen*) Trial. The defendant, Matthias Graf of Mobile Killing Squad C, was on trial for war crimes, membership in a criminal organization, and crimes against humanity. On the stand, Reimers revealed her direct involvement with the Mobile Killing Squads and the death of Jews and others targeted by the Nazis.[1]

Although not directly involved in murdering Jews, Adina Epp, another Mennonite woman from Chortitza, was complicit in the Third Reich's crimes. Epp's experiences, as recorded in her diary, revealed daily instances of collaboration with Nazi Germany.[2] While neither Epp nor Reimers is representative of all Chortitza Mennonites, these two women illustrate how degrees of complicity varied dramatically during the Holocaust.[3]

During the Second World War, the desire to survive partly influenced the complicity and choices of Chortitza Mennonites. After the war, they had to navigate a world in which their actions, or acquiescence to others' actions, haunted their ability to receive assistance from the Allied powers. The postwar immigration process clearly revealed the lasting effects of these wartime choices. In the end, however, Chortitza's Mennonites, who saw themselves as victims yet had cooperated with Nazi Germany in the Holocaust, succeeded in recharacterizing their wartime involvement.[4]

Before the War

The shifting loyalties and evolving identities of Chortitza Mennonites began not in 1945 but rather in the early twentieth century. This research, therefore, rethinks long-held transatlantic characterizations of immigration as well as pan-European conceptions of wartime migration. It highlights the global networks the Mennonite church maintained linking communities in Canada, Ukraine, and the United States with others in Mexico, Poland, and Germany.

The year 1914 marked a turning point for ethnic Germans in Russia and later the Soviet Union. The outbreak of the First World War resulted in the deportation of ethnic Germans from border areas, and in 1915 the Land Liquidation Laws laid out tsarist plans to remove the ethnic German population from Volhynia as well as lands previously granted by the Russian Crown.[5] In their efforts to avoid the consequences of land liquidation, Russian Mennonites in 1915 argued that they were Dutch rather than ethnically German.[6] The tsar's abdication in February 1917 brought an end to the land liquidation policy; however, the ensuing Civil War resulted in loss of life and goods as ethnic German villages passed back and forth between the White Army, the Red Army, and bandits like Nestor Makhno.[7] The German army's occupation of the area in 1918 brought a brief respite, but Makhno continued to terrorize the area until 1920. In 1921, a famine, partly the result of grain requisitioning, worsened the situation, and typhus followed on its heels.[8]

The 1920s were a decade of relative peace. Between 1921 and 1928, the New Economic Policy helped German villages recover economically.[9] German settlements received the status of autonomous territories. Chortitza was one of these German National Districts and thus was permitted to use the German language in schools, in courts, and in local business transactions.[10] Between 1923 and 1933, there were many German-language schools and newspapers.[11] An explanation for these more liberal policies can be found in the 1923 resolutions involving *korenizatsiia* or Soviet nationalities policy.[12] Lenin believed that extending preferential treatment to the Soviet Union's non-Russian peoples would foster equality.[13] The emphasis in this was on language, access to education, and leadership positions.[14] Historian J. Otto Pohl has argued that ethnic Germans benefited from *korenizatsiia* more than any other group.[15]

Between 1929 and 1933, however, Soviet officials implemented policies of collectivization and dekulakization in ethnic German villages.[16] This included the deportation of kulaks.[17] The number of German schools declined in 1933; then the years 1934 and 1935 saw broken contacts with Germany, increased deportations of suspect individuals, the closing of churches, and a sharp curtailing of German publications.[18] From June to November 1933 and again from December 1934 to 1935, there were official purges of ethnic Germans, who were targeted for their ethnicity and labelled as spies and saboteurs.[19] The NKVD transported Adina Epp's father to Siberia in 1934.[20] Three years later, Franziska Reimers's wealthy landowning husband Cornelius also disappeared.[21] In 1937–38 and then again in 1941–42, arrests and deportations specifically targeted ethnic Germans.[22]

During the War

The conflict between German ethnic identity and Soviet citizenship intensified after Germany invaded the Soviet Union on 22 June 1941. Viewing ethnic Germans as a suspect minority, Soviet authorities conscripted them to build defences and dig trenches and then attempted to move them eastward.[23] Franziska Reimers's story illustrates the complex situation many faced at this time. Reimers stated that on 25 August 1941, Soviet General Tchaikovsky summoned her to Soviet military headquarters in Dnepropetrovsk and gave her two options – become a Soviet spy or be sent to a Siberian Gulag. While there are valid reasons to suspect the truthfulness of Reimers's account, it is significant that after the war Reimers framed her acceptance of the NKVD assignment in terms of survival and the desire to protect her child. In September 1941, Reimers surrendered to the German army and Mathias Graf's subunit of Mobile Killing Squad C. Nazis typically shot NKVD spies; however, Reimers testified that she evaded punishment by volunteering to work for the Nazis.[24]

In September and October, Mobile Killing Squad C recorded details from multiple Jewish executions. They "cleared the country of Jews, the population shot, and the villages themselves destroyed."[25] Between June and October 1941, Mobile Killing Squad C murdered more than 51,000 people.[26] Regardless of the details Reimers left out or altered in her retelling, it is certain she was in the midst of these brutal murders in Ukraine.

Before the German army arrived in Chortitza, ethnic Germans aided the advancing German forces by remaining instead of evacuating. Ethnic German families had spent many days hiding in underground bunkers from gunfire and evacuation orders. Wagons, livestock, Soviet military equipment, and Red Army soldiers clogged the roads, and traffic slowed sharply as it crossed the Dnieper Bridge.[27] Some ethnic German families deliberately prolonged their flight by having "accidents" or breaking wagon wheels.[28]

When the German army rolled through Chortitza, ethnic Germans, like many other Soviet peoples, at first "welcomed the German soldiers enthusiastically."[29] Ethnic Germans shared information about the area with German scouts. They gladly hosted officers and supplied them with information about the terrain and the area's German population.[30] Jakob Neufeld, an ethnic German Mennonite, kept a diary of his wartime experiences. He described the German soldiers as "our rescuing angels" who "greeted us as friends."[31] On the other hand, inhabitants who failed to aid the German army would have appeared disloyal or non-German.[32]

Ethnic Germans collaborated in various ways during the Nazi occupation. Some worked for Nazi agencies – for example, Reimers was a secretary for the Department of Agriculture and Food in Dnepropetrovsk.[33] Many ethnic Germans also served as translators for the German army. In addition, some individuals turned in Ukrainians who had placed men in prison or deported them to Siberia in their role as NKVD officers. During the Nazi occupation, there were opportunities to take revenge against Soviet informers who had sent family members to the Gulag.[34] Lastly, ethnic Germans accepted clothing, furniture, and other goods that had once belonged to Jews.

Ethnic Germans also bore arms for the Reich. The occupying German forces organized *Selbstschutze* (self-defence militias) to protect against partisan attacks, murder Jews, and provide protection during later resettlement.[35] To claim that all Mennonites forsook their pacifist roots would be incorrect. That said, many Mennonite men participated in military service. Rudolf Varesko, a native of Chortitza, remembered Mennonite boys signing up for service in the German army. One of his neighbours, a boy of only sixteen, insisted on joining the front line in order to avenge his father's deportation to Siberia.[36] Karl Konrad, another villager from Chortitza, stated that although he was too young to serve, his father joined the German army, where his knowledge of both German and Russian proved useful.[37] Indeed later, upon resettlement in the Reich and after gaining German citizenship, many more men joined the German army or SS.[38] Despite the lack of choice, "most Mennonite men, full of hatred for the Soviet regime, donned a German uniform without protest, and in some cases did so quite willingly."[39] The Soviet authorities viewed all such activities as treason.

Chortitza's Mennonites knew their survival was linked to German victory and to subscribing to Nazi policy. This was not simple, however. Mennonites had to prove repeatedly that they were "German enough," first in Ukraine, then after resettlement to Germany, and often in Poland as well. The *Volksdeutsche Mittelstelle* (Ethnic German Liaison Office), an SS organization tasked with overseeing Germans living outside the Reich, registered Chortitza villagers. That office added those deemed German enough to the *Deutsche Volksliste* (Ethnic Germans List), a central registry.

Intermarriage between ethnic Germans and Ukrainians often resulted in broken families. Olga Petrikow Ross, a Ukrainian, had married into an ethnic German family from Chortitza. She and her German husband Alexander had one child before Alexander joined the German army. Olga's mother-in-law received a letter from the German authorities notifying her that Olga had been rejected from the Ethnic Germans List. The officials wrote that they were concerned about the education of the child while the father, Alexander, was away. The letter demanded that the mother-in-law take legal responsibility for the child until the father returned. Soon after, Alexander went missing in action and Olga and the child deliberately disappeared while fleeing in early 1945.[40] The stakes indeed were high for proving one's Germanness and strongly encouraged collaboration with Nazi Germany.

The Liaison Office transported Adina Epp's family and others from the Chortitza settlement by train in October 1943 to resettlement camps in occupied Poland, where they again had to prove their Germanness.[41] Individuals from Chortitza stayed mainly at two camps, Neustadt Barakenlager and Prussian Stargard Lager.[42] A group of seventy Liaison Office officials arrived at the Neustadt train station in 1944 to assess the arrivals from Chortitza and process the immigration paperwork. This special team of officials had not been in Ukraine, yet it was they who were to determine whether one was (once again) truly German. Four predetermined categories were applied when categorizing the Germanness of the arrivals.[43] The first category included Germans who were racially pure and who supported Nazism. The second was comprised of Germans who were racially pure but not committed to Nazi ideology. SS officials granted those in these first two categories the status of German citizens. The third contained those with German blood who, over the next ten years, would hopefully re-Germanize as determined by the Nazi government. The final group contained those the Nazis marked for death because of a lack of German blood or the failure to re-Germanize.[44] While these categories seem clearly defined, Liaison Office officials encountered difficulties when working in non-homogeneous ethnic areas. Officials often found that determining who was or was not ethnic German was quite difficult.[45]

The forms that Liaison Office officials filled out at the Neustadt train station during the Chortitza villagers' interview process were *Einwanderungszentralstelle* (Central Bureau for Immigration) forms, which included a certificate of citizenship. The paperwork asked a variety of questions. Questions 5, 8, and 11 inquired about ethnic Germans' commitment to ideology. Applicants had to state their citizenship and nationality and provide genealogical information, from which officials then determined whether they were 100 percent German. Questions concerning whether the applicant spoke fluent German and used German at home, and whether one's family spoke predominately in German, were almost always answered in the affirmative. Additionally, *Rasse-Kartei* (race cards) reinforced racial purity – an important component of Germanness.[46] Officials completed these forms for each ethnic German over fourteen years old. A detailed chart on one side included information on hair colour, eye colour, nose shape, height, and skull formation. These race cards might appear to be more objective than the other paperwork, but they were not. An official wrote on the card of one teenage girl: "her grandfather's brother is deaf and dumb."

Chortitzans in the resettlement camps often had the option of accepting farms originally owned by Jews or Poles. As a teacher, Adina Epp moved from school to school in occupied Poland, where she supported Nazi Germany in a variety of ways, from regularly visiting wounded soldiers in the local hospital to entertaining Nazi officers. She also agreed with Nazi ideology that Poles were racially inferior, and listened to Joseph Goebbel's speeches.[47] Her family moved to a farm in Poland. Accepting land made ethnic Germans complicit in the crimes committed against the previous owners; rejecting it could make them ideologically suspect. Some chose to risk the displeasure of the Liaison Office and remain in resettlement camps rather than indirectly participate in the murder of Jews and Poles. Inhabiting one of the 35,000 farms confiscated from the local Poles or Jews went against the conscience of some.[48]

For Jakob Neufeld, memories of their own removal from their homes would have made acceptance of such property "deeply painful." Yet he, a committed Christian who believed it was God's providence that had protected them, surmised that perhaps there was no other choice; he even commented in his diary that it would soon be time to set aside the Golden Rule that they had upheld for so long.[49] Many who settled on these farms did not deny the immorality of taking the possessions of others; fear of disobeying the Nazis simply trumped their morality, as the following account describes: "Mother was deeply concerned about who the little house and the livestock belonged to. She did not want to appropriate someone else's property, since she knew so well herself what it was like to be driven from one's house and home." Yet they accepted the land and "stopped asking dumb questions" when threatened by the Nazis.[50] Those who refused to be resettled upon learning why these farms were vacant were in effect choosing to stay confined in a resettlement camp.[51] In doing so, they were demonstrating their lack of Nazi political loyalty.[52]

Individuals who remained in the camps aided the Nazi war effort to varying degrees. Camp inhabitants near Danzig were transported to the city to work in the factories at the command of the Reich.[53] Reimers not only worked in an explosives factory frequented by the SS, but was also an informant for Mathias Graf, who asked her questions about the forced labourers working there. When the trial's cross-examiner reminded Franziska Reimers that her work in the explosives plant aided the Third Reich, she had no response.[54] Adina Epp dug tank trenches, and her father and brother were often gone on work assignments.[55] After the war, the Allied authorities viewed these actions as clear support for Nazi Germany's war aims.

After the War

The Second World War ended in May 1945. Although no longer literally caught between Nazi Germany and the Soviet Union, ethnic Germans found themselves facing the threat of repatriation to the Soviet Union. This drove many Chortitza Mennonites to argue for a non-Soviet identity and to view immigration as their only hope of avoiding a return to the Soviet Union.[56] The immigration process brought to light Chortitza Mennonite actions during the war. As they tried to avoid repatriation while navigating the complicated immigration process, government and military authorities asked probing questions about their wartime activities.

Chortitza's ethnic Germans exemplify the remaking of identity. Although historically identifying as ethnic German, in 1915 they argued that they were Dutch. In 1918, during the German occupation of Ukraine, they determined themselves to be once again German. In the 1920s, they identified as Soviet citizens. During the Nazi occupation from 1941 to 1943, they were again German. After the war, they chose a new identity – Dutch Mennonite.

They had to prove this postwar identity even as they struggled to separate themselves from their previously claimed identities. After the war, the Soviet Union still identified ethnic Germans from Chortitza as Soviet citizens. Unless individuals could prove otherwise, the implications of being a Soviet citizen involved repatriation to the Soviet Union. Repatriation often meant being sent to a labour camp, not back to one's home.[57]

During the winter of 1944–45, before the war ended, Chortitza Mennonites had fled west from Poland to avoid capture as the Red Army advanced. At war's end, Adina Epp and her family were trapped in

Berlin. Others, like Franziska Reimers, found themselves in the British Zone. To remove themselves further from the advancing Soviet Army, Chortitza Mennonites sought asylum in the recently liberated Netherlands, using Dutch identities connected to their sixteenth-century ancestors. Dutch officials and border guards at first permitted them to enter if they had Dutch-sounding last names, spoke Low German, and had Menno Passes (documents authorizing temporary entry); however, the Soviet authorities soon intervened in this. In 1946 the Soviet Union threatened to halt the return of Dutch prisoners of war if the Netherlands continued to accept Soviet Mennonites.[58]

With the Dutch borders closed, immigration overseas became the next viable option. Canada and the United States were the preferred destinations for many from Chortitza, but South America, especially Paraguay, became increasingly attractive because of its less stringent immigration laws. Immigration was the microscope through which UN organizations and immigration officials scrutinized their wartime choices.

The Mennonite Central Committee (MCC), the relief arm of the Mennonite church, headquartered in the United States, decided to intervene to help change the perception of Soviet Mennonites from ethnic German collaborators to a persecuted religious minority. MCC leaders and relief workers aided Chortitza Mennonites at each stage of the immigration process. The MCC used historical arguments and close relationships with government leaders to argue that these Mennonites were in fact Dutch and had taken German citizenship and entered military service under duress.

The first step for successful immigration was to qualify for aid as a Displaced Person (DP). DPs were individuals forcibly removed from their homes during war or citizens of an Allied country.[59] DPs received food and ration cards, lodging in UN DP camps, access to medical care, and screening for immigration. UN agencies also helped match potential immigrants with sponsors and paid for their transatlantic transportation.

Those who were not DPs were under the jurisdiction of the West German government. Allied authorities were not always sympathetic to those claiming to be DPs. In the Funk Kaserne DP camp outside Munich, the camp director gave 316 Mennonites from Ukraine an ultimatum: they must prove they were DPs or leave the camp.[60] An additional 150 Mennonites were living outside the American camp because the director would not admit them unless they were recommended by a liaison officer, military official, or consul. "Apparently people cannot go into an UNRRA camp just as they please," wrote Mennonite relief worker Peter J. Dyck in 1946.[61]

Chortitza Mennonites did not qualify as DPs because they were ethnic Germans. Although Chortitza Mennonites had been Soviet citizens prior to 1939, many were wary of touting their ties to the Soviet Union because they feared repatriation.[62] Ethnic Germans from Chortitza wanted to acquire visas to Canada or the United States and receive immigration aid from UN organizations. They did not want American or British officials to hand them over to the Soviet Union, which was a real possibility right after the war. One's citizenship and identity were thus crucial. Caught between policy on one side and Soviet aims on the other, ethnic German Mennonites turned to a third option – inventing a new identity.

DP registration forms revealed that most Mennonites claimed a religious-ethnic identity separate from other standard national identities. "Dutch Mennonite" began to appear on International Refugee Organization (IRO) forms. Comparing these claimed identities to German immigration records filled out only a few years earlier reveals the shift they were making from being 100 percent German in 1943 to denying their German heritage in 1945.

In 1947, George Warren at the US State Department asked historian Morton Royse, "a fair minded person who acts only on facts," to investigate Soviet Mennonite claims of Dutch heritage.[63] Royse argued that notwithstanding their ancestral connections to the Netherlands, these Soviet Mennonites were ethnic Germans.[64] To refute this conclusion, the MCC asked Mennonite historian Cornelius Krahn to prepare a brief. Krahn's report, "The Ethnic Origin of the Mennonites from Russia now Displaced Persons," focused on proving Mennonite similarities to the Dutch, including farming methods and Dutch last names.[65] While the IRO never officially accepted the Dutch-Mennonite connection, they allowed them to proceed as DPs.

In arguing that they were Dutch-Mennonite rather than ethnic German, Soviet Mennonites distanced themselves from their close cultural, linguistic, and relational ties to Germany. Krahn argued that Soviet Mennonites were never part of the German culture or economy; they only adopted the German language because of German church services and German-language Bibles.[66] In an attempt to strengthen their ties to the Netherlands, Chortitza Mennonites emphasized their victimization at the hands of the Soviet Union. They argued that because they had experienced persecution in Prussia and later in Russia and the Soviet Union, they remained most closely connected to the Netherlands.[67]

The argument that they were actually Dutch by national origin, or stateless, enabled many to receive DP status in a world in which ethnic Germans did not receive UN assistance. Obtaining DP status was so crucial, in fact, to the emigration process in postwar Germany that the MCC decided to separate relief operations from refugee assistance to better focus on helping their constituents qualify as DPs.[68] Refugee assistance was something their ethnic German neighbours of other faiths from Chortitza did not have the same level of access to.

Claiming their Mennonite religious identity as an ethnic identifier was convenient, and indeed significant. A 5 April 1948 brief from the MCC to George Warren argued that Mennonites' "religio-cultural" identity was separate from their ethnic German identity.[69] The only religious-ethnic group the UN officially recognized was the Jews. This was, of course, the result of the Holocaust. However, self-appointed Mennonite leader John J. Kroeker in a letter to American officer C.J. Taylor argued that "Mennonites must be classified as one of the most severely haunted and persecuted groups of people in the world. Only the Jews in Germany can be compared to them."[70] A few months later, he again wrote that because Mennonites were in a similar position to the Jews, "Mennonite" should be accepted as a national identifier or at the very least entitle them to "stateless" status.[71] Yet Mennonites had not been threatened with genocide during the war.

During the German occupation, ethnic Germans had emphasized their German identity and language; now, after the war, many Mennonites chose to be selective about their birthplaces, previous residences, and ethnic and national ties. These changes in national and ethnic identity did not go unnoticed. UN officials found that birthdates or birthplaces on IRO documents sometimes did not match Care and Maintenance 1 files that refugees had first filed when applying for aid immediately after the war.[72]

There are several explanations for the differing information on documents. Refugees most likely falsified information to avoid repatriation or to appear younger.[73] Some refugees argued that when later applying for immigration, they felt the need to tell the truth and thus different stories often emerged.[74] Yet as a group, their complicated past, which remained documented despite the chaos of war, did not make immigration easy. Adding to the confusion was the IRO's policy that it would not reinvestigate discrepancies; the DP commissioners and consul would have to decide which statements to believe.[75]

Resettlement by the Liaison Office was one aspect of this complicated past that continued to haunt Mennonites in the postwar immigration process. The IRO had stipulated in 1947 that Mennonite eligibility for DP status hinged on whether these ethnic Germans had willingly left the Soviet Union. In an IRO document now located in the National Archives in Paris titled "Mennonite Eligibility," the IRO laid out very clearly which Mennonites would be accepted as DPs. Those who were eligible included Mennonites from the Soviet Union of Dutch origin who had been "displaced into Germany" through forced labour or otherwise against their will.[76] Non-eligible Mennonites were those of ethnic German rather than Dutch origin who had "fled to Germany to avoid falling into the hands of the advancing Allied armies."[77] Therefore, if a person "left of their own free will at the time of advance of the Russian Army, availing themselves of debacle, or of German assistance, to leave their places of habitual residence," they were ineligible for DP status.[78]

Remaining in Chortitza after the German retreat in 1943 was neither a desirable choice nor a real option for Chortitzans, whom the Soviet Union viewed as traitors. While some Chortitza villagers tried to argue that they had not left Chortitza "of their own free will," the fact that they had accepted German assistance disqualified them in the eyes of the IRO agents.[79] In addition, a 1947 IRO memo concluded that there was not enough evidence to prove the group's Dutch rather than German background, which was the main prerequisite for eligibility.[80] Furthermore, wartime records held at the Berlin Document Center contained evidence that ethnic German Mennonites had aided the German war effort and participated in the Holocaust.[81]

This revitalized the argument that Chortitza's Mennonites had willingly accepted German citizenship.[82] Indeed, between 1941 and 1944, German citizenship had been widely desired by resettlers. The Third Reich had little use for those who refused German citizenship when it was offered, except as forced labourers. The records uncovered after the war in the Berlin Document Center included Central Bureau of Immigration records filled out by Liaison Office officials in 1943 conferring citizenship upon ethnic Germans. Because of this, Soviet and American authorities viewed ethnic German Mennonites as having willingly accepted German citizenship as opposed to receiving it under duress.[83]

Starvation, deportations, and restriction of freedoms in Ukraine serve as an explanation for why ethnic German Mennonites embraced the German occupation of Ukraine and subsequently German citizenship but not an excuse for contributing to the murder of Jews and others the Nazis labeled "undesirables." Adina Epp wrote in her diary on 1 February 1944 that receiving German citizenship gave her "new privileges but also new responsibilities."[84] She could not have imagined what the consequences would be after the war for accepting German citizenship and its privileges.

Yet the matter regarding German citizenship was not settled. When, in July 1949, the IRO halted the processing of Chortitza Mennonites due to questions of German citizenship, the MCC mobilized arguments that Mennonites had only accepted German citizenship under duress.[85] If the MCC could convince the IRO of this, Mennonites would remain eligible for immigration per the IRO's communiqué of 3 October 1949.[86] MCC officer C.F. Klassen travelled to Geneva to petition IRO officials there.[87] The MCC also lobbied Canadian and US government officials.[88] Ugo Carusi (the US Displaced Persons Commissioner), George Warren (US State Department), and even Major-General W.A. Wood, Jr (US IRO office), protested the ban.[89]

In response, IRO Geneva issued a statement in October 1949 regarding the eligibility of Mennonites. This communiqué acknowledged that receiving German citizenship did not automatically disqualify Mennonites from DP status since "many persons, Mennonites and others, claimed that they were ethnic Germans and used the [German immigration] scheme to escape from Russian and Communist dominated areas."[90] Furthermore, the IRO acknowledged that this was often done "under some form of duress, or as a matter of routine, or almost automatically."[91] As the Cold War heated up, the MCC's arguments became more effective. These citizenship claims were important to contest because Canada and the United States would not permit the immigration of German citizens until 1950.[92]

Although the ban was eventually removed, the MCC had to battle for Mennonites who had received visas or were in the process of receiving visas when the 1949 ban occurred in order for them to be reinstated as eligible.[93] After the first ban, Canada's Department of Mines and Resources responded to MCC officials that they would continue accepting Soviet Mennonites as they had previously. The MCC then let US officials know that Canada had committed to continuing to accept Mennonites who had been previously eligible, in the hope that Washington would change its mind.[94]

There were many successes in the story of postwar Mennonite immigration. The MCC, through the work of Peter and Elfrieda Dyck, succeeded in convincing the American military commander in Berlin to transport Adina Epp and other Russian Mennonites from Berlin to Bremerhaven; from there, they sailed to Paraguay on the *Volendam*. Thousands of others immigrated to North America. There are rumours that Franziska Reimers immigrated to Toronto, although that has yet to be confirmed.

Those who were unable to immigrate because of military service, physical disabilities, membership in a Nazi organization, or German citizenship were termed "hardcore cases." Immigration officials uncovered in German records that Mennonites had served in the German army, the *Sicherheitsdienst* (Security Service; *SD*), or the SS.[95] Service in the German military, SD, or SS made it extremely difficult to immigrate to Canada or the United States. Regarding military involvement, MCC leader C.F. Klassen claimed that no surprising information had surfaced with these findings.[96] The MCC argued that only an extremely small percentage of Soviet Mennonites had participated in German military or SS formations and that the MCC had not protested or disagreed with the IRO's decision to disqualify them from immigration.[97] On 8 August 1950, the MCC gained approval to carry out resettlement and emigration for "persons of German ethnic origin in Germany and Austria" under Section 12 of the Displaced Persons Act.[98] Thereafter, Mennonite leaders would use Section 12 to champion Mennonite cases previously rejected.[99]

Because of the evidence found in the Berlin Document Center, however, the IRO made it a rule that everyone applying for DP status would have to have their documents first checked at that office. Prior to mid-1949, immigrants left for the United States regardless of Berlin Document Center findings. However, commissioner Harry Rosenfeld halted this laxness, and this resulted in a high volume of requests as organizations and agencies submitted each potential immigrant's name.[100]

Even after the immigration battles were over, the MCC ensured that Soviet Mennonite immigration would be remembered in a particular way. In January 1953, Louise Holborn was writing the official history of the IRO.[101] George Warren alerted MCC leaders that Holborn's chapter on the MCC and Mennonites was rather unflattering.[102] The MCC's leaders responded strongly, and Warren was influential in removing that section of the book before publication.[103]

By framing Soviet Mennonites' choices during the war against a backdrop of survival, limited involvement, ignorance, and Soviet terror, the MCC successfully overcame each hurdle and helped thousands of Mennonites immigrate. The experiences of Chortitza Mennonites demonstrate the complexity of their complicity, which, while at times motivated by survival, do not lessen the horror of the crimes committed while allied with the Third Reich. Yet it was not survival alone that drove some Chortitza Mennonites to accept Jewish and Polish farms, join the German forces, and work for Nazi agencies. Proving their Germanness was an important motivation behind many of these decisions which included participation in the Holocaust. At the same time, it should be remembered that other Chortitza Mennonites chose to risk the displeasure of the Third Reich by refusing to settle on Polish or Jewish land or support Nazi war aims. Franziska Reimers and Adina Epp illustrate this group's spectrum of involvement in the

Holocaust - Chortitza Mennonites who were uniquely caught between the Soviet Union and Nazi Germany. Although successful postwar immigration was the result of effectively reinventing their identities, it also led to scrutiny and exposure of their wartime choices.

NOTES

1 Siegfried Janzen Fonds, vol. 5456. folder 2, 4844–68, Mennonite Heritage Centre (MHC), Winnipeg, Manitoba.
2 Adina Epp, *Tagebuch 1943–1945*, MHC.
3 In this study, Chortitza refers to the ethnic German Mennonite settlement often called the "Old Colony." Mennonite immigrants from West Prussia founded the settlement in 1789 at the invitation of Catherine the Great. Its villages were located along the right bank of the Dnieper in Ukraine. For an excellent women's and gender study of the experience of Russian Mennonites, see Marlene Epp's *Women without Men: Mennonite Refugees of the Second World War* (Toronto: University of Toronto Press, 2000).
4 This chapter includes Chortitza Mennonites within the term Soviet Mennonite. It uses the terms Russia and the Soviet Union to include the geographical area of Ukraine.
5 Francine Hirsch, *Empire of Nations: Ethnographic Knowledge and the Making of the Soviet Union* (Ithaca: Cornell University Press, 2005), 46; Ingeborg Fleischhauer, Benjamin Pinkus, and Edith Rogovin Frankel, *The Soviet Germans: Past and Present* (New York: St Martin's Press, 1986), 27; Ronald Grigor Suny and Terry Martin, *A State of Nations: Empire and Nation Making in the Age of Lenin and Stalin* (New York: Oxford University Press, 2002), 125–6; Adam Giesinger, *From Catherine to Khrushchev: The Story of Russia's Germans* (London: American Historical Society for Germans from Russia, 1993), 250, 251; John B. Toews, "Documents on Mennonite Life in Russia 1930–1940, Part 1 – Collectivization and the Great Terror," working paper no. 19, *American Historical Society of Germans from Russia* (December 1975): 3.
6 Abraham Friesen, *In Defense of Privilege: Russian Mennonites and the State before and during World War I* (Winnipeg: Christian Press, 2006).
7 J. Otto Pohl, *Ethnic Cleansing in the USSR, 1937–1949* (Westport: Greenwood Press, 1999), 30; Fleischhauer, Pinkus, and Frankel, *The Soviet Germans*, 29; Giesinger, *From Catherine to Khrushchev*, 253.
8 Fleischhauer, Pinkus, and Frankel, *The Soviet Germans*, 44; James E. Casteel argued that the 1932–33 famine did not target a specific group but was meant to halt resistance to collectivization. See Casteel, "Russian Germans in the Interwar National Imaginary," *Central European History* 40 (2007): 439.

Identity and Complicity 283

9 Fleischhauer, Pinkus, and Frankel, *The Soviet Germans*, 45; Toews, "Documents," 3; Peter Letkemann, "The Fates of Mennonites in the Volga-Ural Region, 1929–1941," *Journal of Mennonite Studies* 26 (March 2011): 190.
10 Giesinger, *From Catherine to Khrushchev*, 282, 283.
11 Fleischhauer, Pinkus, and Frankel, *The Soviet Germans*, 7.
12 Suny and Martin, *A State of Nations*, 74.
13 Terry Martin, *The Affirmative Action Empire* (Ithaca: Cornell University Press, 2001), 17–19.
14 Robert J. Kaiser, *The Geography of Nationalism in Russia and the USSR* (Princeton: Princeton University Press, 1994), 95, 124.
15 Pohl, *Ethnic Cleansing in the USSR*, 30. Historian Terry Martin referred to this policy as "affirmative action." Martin, *The Affirmative Action Empire*, 1. Francine Hirsch digresses slightly and argues that nationality policy "was a policy of state-sponsored evolutionism." See Hirsch, *Empire of Nations*, 103.
16 Irina Mukhina, *The Germans of the Soviet Union* (New York: Routledge, 2007), 35; Adam Giesinger, *From Catherine to Khrushchev*, 287.
17 Ibid., 287.
18 Mukhina, *The Germans of the Soviet Union*, 36–7; Fleischhauer, Pinkus, and Frankel, *The Soviet Germans*, 55, 56; Giesinger, *From Catherine to Khrushchev*, 299.
19 Toews, "Documents," 3.
20 Epp, *Tagebuch 1943–1945*, 27 October 1943, MHC.
21 Siegfried Janzen Fonds, vol. 5456, folder 2, 4845, MHC.
22 Mukhina, *The Germans of the Soviet Union*, 39; Suny and Martin, *A State of Nations*, 14; Hirsch, *Empire of Nations*, 275.
23 The rapid advance of the German Army kept many ethnic Germans west of the Dnieper safe from evacuation by Soviet forces.
24 Trials of War Criminals before the Nuremberg Military Tribunals under Control Council no. 10, vol. 4 (419). Siegfried Janzen Fonds, vol. 5456, folder 2, 4844–68, MHC.
25 Ibid., no. 10 vol. 4 (September 1941), NO-3146, 433; NO-3153, 433; NO-3154, 439.
26 Ibid., no. 10 vol. 4, NO-3155, 419.
27 N.J. Kroeker, *First Mennonite Villages in Russia 1789–1943* (Cloverdale: D.W. Friesen and Sons, 1981), 233.
28 Epp, *Women without Men*, 27.
29 Fleischhauer, Pinkus, and Frankel, *The Soviet Germans*, 73n24; Hans Werner, *Imagined Homes: Soviet German Immigrants in Two Cities* (Winnipeg: University of Manitoba Press, 2007), 29.
30 Lilly Zaft, interview with author, 13 December 2013, Hagerstown, Maryland.
31 Jacob A. Neufeld, Harvey L. Dyck, and Sarah Dyck, *Path of Thorns: Soviet Mennonite Life under Communist and Nazi Rule* (Toronto: University of Toronto Press, 2014), 218.

32 Doris L. Bergen, "The Nazi Concept of 'Volksdeutsche' and the Exacerbation of Anti-Semitism in Eastern Europe, 1939–45" *Journal of Contemporary History* 29 (1994): 574.
33 Siegfried Janzen Fonds, vol. 5456, folder 2, 4851, MHC.
34 Eric Steinhart, *The Holocaust and the Germanization of Ukraine* (New York: Cambridge University Press, 2015), 34.
35 The first appearance of the *Selbstschutz* was when German troops occupied parts of Ukraine during the First World War.
36 Rudolf Varesko, interview with author, Hagerstown, Maryland, 12 December 2013. Unfortunately, the sixteen-year-old was killed on the Eastern Front soon after enlisting.
37 Karl Konrad, email to author, 12 February 2014.
38 John C. Swanson, *The Second World War and Its Aftermath* (West Lafayette: Purdue University Press, 2008), 354, 355.
39 Epp, *Women without Men*, 49.
40 Lilly Zaft, interview with author, Mercersburg, Pennsylvania, 13 December 2013. A3342, EWZ57, R065, NARA.
41 "Berlin Correspondence 1945 June to August," MS 501, box 33, Kroeker Collection, Mennonite Library and Archives (MLA), North Newton, Kansas. John J. Kroeker in a letter to H.S. Bender, Lehman, and A. Warkentin on 27 August 1945 described his contact with Mennonite refugees in resettlement camps during the war. He stated that Mennonites "were forced" to resettle to western Poland, that they suffered greatly under Horst Hoffmeyer, and that they could not have imagined the "price they were to pay for 'freedom'" under the Nazis. Kroeker also discussed the heartache they felt to see how the Germans removed Poles to settle them on farms.
42 AA3342, EWZ58, F051, F052, F053, National Archives and Records Administration (NARA), College Park, Maryland.
43 Ahonen Pertti, "On Forced Migrations: Transnational Realities and National Narratives in Post-1945 (West) Germany," *German History* 32, no. 4 (December 2014): 605.
44 Fleischhauer, Pinkus, and Frankel, *The Soviet Germans*, 96.
45 Steinhart, *The Holocaust and the Germanization of Ukraine*, 76.
46 *Rasse-Kartei*, A3342, EWZ56, NARA.
47 Epp, *Tagebuch 1943–1945*, 12 November 1943; 20 October 1943; 8 December 1943; 27 October 1944, MHC.
48 Epp, *Women without Men*, 49; Robert Koehl, *RKFDV: German Resettlement and Population Policy 1939–1945: A History of the Reich Commission for the Strengthening of Germandom* (Cambridge, MA: Harvard University Press, 1957), 117; Lilly Zaft, interview with author, Mercersburg, Pennsylvania, 13 December 2013.

49 Neufeld, *Path of Thorns*, 300.
50 Nelly Daes, *Gone without a Trace: German-Russian Women in Exile* (Lincoln: American Society for Germans from Russia, 2001), 155.
51 Lilly Zaft, interview with author, Mercersburg, Pennsylvania, 13 December 2013.
52 Yet it is possible that their religious and apolitical leanings were the reason why they were placed in the Warthegau and not elsewhere. Maria Kreiser stated that some ethnic Germans, even though they had been given Category One status, were still placed in "the Wartheland to be 'Germanized.'" Maria Kreiser and James Gessele, *Though My Soul More Bent: Memoir of a Soviet German* (Bismarck: Germans from Russia Heritage Society, 2003), 55.
53 Lilly Zaft, interview with author, Mercersburg, Pennsylvania, 13 December 2013.
54 Siegfried Janzen Fonds, vol. 5456, folder 2, 4844–68, MHC.
55 Epp, *Tagebuch 1943–1945*, 29 October 1944; 16 December 16, 1944; 17 January 1945; 18 January 1945, MHC.
56 Ted D. Regehr, "Of Dutch or German Ancestry?: Mennonite Refugees, MCC, and the International Refugee Organization," *Journal of Mennonite Studies* 13 (1995): 7–25. General McNarney to Commander Generals of Third US Army Area, Seventh US Army Area, Berlin District, 4 January 1946, box 119, "Disposition of Mennonites," RG 260, NARA. Even Soviet Mennonites who were no longer living in a Soviet-controlled space were not guaranteed protection. Colonel Stimson and some British and American officials tried to delay or thwart repatriation attempts by following strict protocols that called for written proof of Soviet citizenship and aid to the enemy. Soviet authorities travelled to DP camps to interview Russian Mennonites they claimed were Soviet citizens. The case of Soviet Mennonites trapped in the American sector of Berlin is a well-known account of the need to remove oneself far from the reach of Soviet power. Major-General Frank A. Keating to Major General Alexander Kotikov, 21 August 1946 and 29 July 1946, box 119, "Disposition of Mennonites," RG 260, NARA. Major-General Frank A. Keating to Soviet Military Administration in Germany, 4 June 1946, box 119, "Disposition of Mennonites," RG 260, NARA.
57 Epp, *Women without Men*, 192–3.
58 Peter C. Hiebert Papers, box 12, folder 465, MS. 37, MLA.
59 MCC issued instructions on how to complete the DP Information Form. MCC created this form to provide basic information on each family; they asked for "claimed nationality" and did not inquire about wartime record. "Correspondence Jan. 1–14, 1947," folder 480, box 12, MS 37, Peter C. Hiebert Papers, MLA.

60 Peter J. Dyck to C.F. Klassen, 2 May 1946, box 12, folder 465, MS 37, Peter C. Hiebert Papers, MLA.
61 Ibid.
62 In this 16 September 1945 letter to Major Mercer of the US Welfare Division, J.J. Kroeker argued that Soviet repatriation officials were not recognizing that ethnic German Mennonites accepted German citizenship and "never were Russian." "Berlin Correspondence 1945 September to October," box 33, MS 501, J.J. Kroeker Collection, MLA. Kroeker again highlighted German naturalization and tried to convince local German authorities of it to protect additional Mennonites from repatriation. "Berlin Correspondence – undated," box 33, MS 501, J.J. Kroeker Collection, MLA.
63 William T. Snyder to Cornelius Krahn, 12 March 1948, vol. 1325, folder 956, series 3a, Canadian Mennonite Board of Colonization, Mennonite Heritage Center (MHC), Canadian Mennonite University, Winnipeg.
64 Ibid.
65 Cornelius Krahn, "The Ethnic Origin of the Mennonites from Russia Now Displaced People," vol. 1325, folder 956, series 3a, Canadian Mennonite Board of Colonization, MHC.
66 Folder 957, vol. 1325, series 3a, Canadian Mennonite Board of Colonization Collection, MHC; box 6a, folder 185, MS 37, Peter C. Hiebert Collection, MLA.
67 "Supplement to the Petition Requesting Intergovernmental Committee Assistance in the Migration of Mennonite Refugees," box 6a, folder 185, MS 37, Peter C. Hiebert Collection, MLA.
68 "Correspondence June 1–12, 1946," folder 466, box 12, MS 37, Peter C. Hiebert Collection, MLA.
69 Cornelius Krahn, "The Ethnic Origin of the Mennonites from Russia Now Displaced Persons," vol. 1325, folder 957, series 3a, Canadian Mennonite Board of Colonization Collection, MHC.
70 J.J. Kroeker to C.J. Taylor, 10 September 1945, "Berlin Correspondence 1945 Jan. to Aug.," box 33, MS 501, J.J. Kroeker Collection, MLA.
71 "Berlin Correspondence 1945 Sept. to Oct.," box 33, MS. 501, J.J. Kroeker Collection, MLA. Cornelius Krahn also argued that the Jewish people were not considered German simply because they had been culturally exposed to Germany and, therefore, neither were Mennonites German because of cultural exposure. See vol. 1325, folder 957, series 3a, Canadian Mennonite Board of Colonization Collection, MHC.
72 IRO Headquarters to G.G. Roberts, 3 May 1949, "False Documents," box 46, RG 278, NARA.
73 Some individuals felt that being younger would help them immigrate more easily. IRO Headquarters to G.G. Roberts, 3 May 1949, "False Documents," box 46, RG 278, NARA.
74 IRO Headquarters to G.G. Roberts, 3 May 1949, "False Documents," box 46, RG 278, NARA.

Identity and Complicity   287

75 Ibid.
76 Senior Assistant Director to Director, 4 February 1947, AJ/43 566, Nationales Archives, Paris, France.
77 Ibid.
78 Ibid.
79 C.F. Klassen to IRO, "Statement Concerning Mennonite Refugees," vol. 1325, folder 956, series 3a, Canadian Mennonite Board of Colonization, MHC; Senior Assistant Director to Director, 4 February 1947, AJ/43 566, Nationales Archives, Paris, France.
80 Ibid.
81 Myer Cohen to Chief Eligibility Officer, 3 October 1949, folder 957, series 3a, Canadian Mennonite Board of Colonization, MHC; A3342, EWZ 59, G019, NARA; A3342, EWZ 5440W, NARA.
82 Mennonite Central Committee (Mennonite Aid Section), box 23, RG 278, NARA. The decision by IRO to accept Soviet Mennonites who received German citizenship under duress was communicated on 3 October 1948.
83 Chief Repatriation Officer, 8 April 1946, "Disposition of Mennonites," box 119, RG 260, NARA.
84 Adina Epp, *Tagebuch 1943–1945*, 1 February 1944, MHC.
85 A.L. Jolliffe to C.F. Klassen, 31 August 1949, folder 959, vol. 1325, series 3a, Canadian Mennonite Board of Colonization, MHC; folder 958, vol. 1325, series 3a, Canadian Mennonite Board of Colonization, MHC.
86 Folder 957, vol. 1325, series 3a, Canadian Mennonite Board of Colonization, MHC.
87 C.F. Klassen to Canadian Mennonite Board of Colonization, 20 July 1949, folder 959, volume 1325, series 3a, Canadian Mennonite Board of Colonization, MHC.
88 C.F. Klassen's letter to Snyder a few days after hearing of the ban was relatively lighthearted; it focused on calling officials, waiting on the Lord, and heading to Geneva, "that familiar battle ground." See vol. 1325, folder 959, series 3a, Canadian Mennonite Board of Colonization, MHC; Snyder to Executive Committee, vol. 1325, folder 959, series 3a, Canadian Mennonite Board of Colonization, MHC; Snyder to C.F. Klassen, 2 December 1948, folder 957, vol. 1325, series 3a, Canadian Mennonite Board of Colonization. Snyder to Executive Committee, 11 August 1949, folder 959, vol. 1325, series 3a, Canadian Mennonite Board of Colonization, MHC.
89 Snyder to Executive Committee, vol. 1325, folder 959, series 3a, Canadian Mennonite Board of Colonization, MHC; W.A. Wood to Meyer Cohen, 5 August 1949; vol. 1325, folder 959, series 3a, Canadian Mennonite Board of Colonization, MHC; Hector Allard (IRO Quebec) to IRO Geneva, 10 August 1949, vol. 1325, folder 959, series 3a, Canadian Mennonite Board of Colonization, MHC; MCC to A.L. Jolliffe and Hugh L. Keenleyside, 9 August 1949, folder 959, vol. 1325, series 3a, Canadian Mennonite Board

of Colonization, MHC; W.A. Wood, Jr, to Meyer Cohen, 5 August 1949, folder 959, vol. 1325, series 3a, Canadian Mennonite Board of Colonization, MHC.
90 Myer Cohen to Chief Eligibility Officer, vol. 1325, folder 959, series 3a, Canadian Mennonite Board of Colonization, MHC.
91 Ibid.
92 On 8 August 1950, MCC gained approval to carry out resettlement and emigration for "persons of German ethnic origin in Germany and Austria" under "Section 12 of the Displaced Persons Act of 1948 as amended (P.L. 555–81st Congress)." "Mennonite Central Committee (Mennonite Aid Section)," box 23, RG 278, NARA. Thereafter, Mennonite leaders used Section 12 to champion Mennonite cases previously rejected because of German citizenship. See William M. Snyder to Edward M O'Connor, 4 April 1951, "Mennonite Central Committee (Mennonite Aid Section)," box 23, RG 278, NARA.
93 Snyder to Carusi, 10 September 19, 1949, "Mennonite Central Committee (Mennonite Aid Section)," box 23, RG 278, NARA.
94 Canada continued to accept Mennonites eligible under previous guidelines. See Snyder to Wood, 12 August 1949, "Mennonite Central Committee (Mennonite Aid Section)," box 23, RG 278, NARA.
95 Folder 463, MS 37, box 12, Peter C. Hiebert Collection, MLA; A3342 EWZ 59, G019, RG 242, frame 1752, NARA; A3342, EWZ 5440W, RG 242, NARA.
96 MCC to A.L. Jolliffe and Hugh L. Keenleyside, 9 August 1949, vol. 1325, folder 959, series 3a, Canadian Mennonite Board of Colonization, MHC.
97 Hector Allard (IRO Quebec) to IRO Geneva, 10 August 1949, vol. 1325, folder 959, series 3a, Canadian Mennonite Board of Colonization, MHC.
98 "Section 12 of the Displaced Persons Act of 1948 as amended (P.L. 555–81st Congress)," box 23, RG 278, NARA.
99 Elliott M. Shirk to Edward M. O'Connor, 4 April 1951, "Mennonite Central Committee (Mennonite Aid Section)," box 23, RG 278, NARA.
100 1 July 1948, "Disposition of Nazi Documents," box 124, RG 260, NARA. This led to a minimum of 20,000 requests per month at the BDC. The Liaison Office records alone weighed around 2.75 tons. See Myer Cohen to Chief Eligibility Officer, folder 957, vol. 1325, series 3a, Canadian Mennonite Board of Colonization, MHC.
101 Louise Holborn, *The International Refugee Organization: A Specialized Agency of the United Nations: Its History and Work, 1946–1952* (New York: Oxford University Press), 1956.
102 William T. Snyder to C.F. Klassen, 23 January 1953, folder 957, series 3a, Canadian Mennonite Board of Colonization, MHC; William T. Snyder to George Warren, 28 January 1953, folder 957, series 3a, Canadian Mennonite Board of Colonization, MHC.

103 Snyder to Klassen, 23 January 1953, folder 957, vol. 1325, series 3a, Canadian Mennonite Board of Colonization, MHC; Snyder to Warren, 28 January 1953, folder 957, vol. 1325, series 3a, Canadian Mennonite Board of Colonization, MHC; Klassen to Snyder, 28 January 1953, folder 957, vol. 1325, series 3a, Canadian Mennonite Board of Colonization, MHC.

Chapter Eleven

A Usable Past: Soviet Mennonite Memories of the Holocaust

HANS WERNER

On 22 June 1941, Hitler unleashed a massive assault on the Soviet Union, and within a few weeks German armies had arrived in the core Mennonite areas of the Chortitza Old Colony. By October 1941 the Molotschna and Chortitza colonies were both under German occupation. For those Mennonites who had been able to avoid evacuation to the east ahead of the advancing German armies, living under German authority was a tremendous relief from unrelenting Stalinist oppression. By 1941, Soviet Mennonites believed themselves to be German and were viewed as such by their German occupiers. As members of the Nazis' Aryan "master race," they were immediately raised above their Slavic neighbours, economically and socially. Despite Nazi ambivalence and later outright opposition to the resumption of Mennonite religious life, churches were reopened, and even though the highly anticipated restoration of private ownership was often not realized, Mennonites were euphoric about what had befallen them, and embraced it.

The Germans' rapid advance caused the Mennonites' Jewish neighbours to flee eastward in a desperate attempt to escape the invaders. Those who were unable to escape faced forced labour and, ultimately, death. Jews were rounded up and shot in large numbers and buried in mass graves, often in trenches dug earlier to delay the advance of German tanks. The *Einsatzgruppen* (Mobile Killing Squads) that sought them out proceeded relentlessly, so that all the remaining Jews in the Old Colony Mennonite area were exterminated in a relatively short time.[1] The rapid change in fortunes from unrelenting oppression under the Soviets to "liberation" by the Nazi invaders coloured Mennonites' views of the extermination of the Jews, both at the time and as they made sense of their memories later.

The Soviet Mennonites' encounter with the German armies, and then a short time later with occupation organizations with their more overt

Nazi ideology, was fraught with contradictions. While highly prized as examples of Germanness and always treated more favourably than their Ukrainian neighbours, Mennonites were at the same time viewed as considerably below the level of the Nazi ideal, particularly because of their sectarian religious beliefs. Moreover, their lingering pacifism was anathema to soldiers and Nazi occupation organizations. Jacob Neufeld's memoirs express these tensions thoughtfully and in depth. They convey the utter relief Mennonites felt when the German armies arrived. German soldiers were "rescuing angels," and the prospect of realizing what they had only dreamed about produced "an unimaginably glorious feeling."[2]

Neufeld writes in his memoirs that he generally welcomed the new order but acknowledges that tensions soon emerged. He notes that "our political thinking was also to be corrected," and he was pained by the preferential treatment Mennonites received compared to their Ukrainian neighbours, who faced higher grain requisitions.[3] Mennonites were disappointed in their new masters even though they were deeply indebted to and felt a connection to them. Most difficult for Mennonites to accept, according to Neufeld, was the ambivalence of the German occupiers toward the resumption of religious education. Mennonite "trust in a German willingness to support this supreme objective was grievously disappointed."[4] Instead, the Ethnic German Liaison Office staff, after "a short period of tolerance ... tried to obstruct" religious development.[5] Henry Winter, the son of the last bishop of the Chortitza church, conveyed similar disappointment in a combination personal memoir and biography of his father. He lists several factors that contributed to the slow recovery of Mennonite faith practice but concludes that the main cause was that the "Hitler government was not interested in building up the Christian church."[6] For Jacob Neufeld, the sharpest sense of being out of step with the new German order came when the gradual setbacks encountered by the German armies led to the creation of a self-defence force that included Mennonites. Neufeld recounts the creation of the *Reiterschwadron* (Mounted Squadron) that he believed to be "hardly a blessing generally and ... of questionable assistance even to the Wehrmacht."[7]

Many memoirists note their disappointment at the treatment of their Ukrainian neighbours by the Germans. Although Mennonites had always maintained a superior attitude toward their Slavic neighbours, the treatment the latter suffered at the hands of the Nazi functionaries shocked them. Jacob Neufeld notes that when the occupation organizations took over from the army, problems with the mistreatment of Ukrainians escalated. With "their inflexibility, arrogance and insolence, the officials committed so many wrongs against the Ukrainian people."⁸ Waldemar Janzen remembers the adults around him discussing the treatment of Ukrainians "with consternation and disbelief. How could the Germans antagonize their potential allies in such counterproductive ways?"⁹

Gerhard Fast was in a very different position as a member of the *Stumpp Kommando*. Fast casts himself as someone who protected Mennonite identity and worked tirelessly to foster their recovery under the Nazis. The *Stumpp Kommando* was a unit of Alfred Rosenberg's Ministry for the Occupied Eastern Territories charged with documenting the condition of Soviet Germans, including Mennonites.¹⁰ Fast travelled to Mennonite and other German-speaking villages in Ukraine to organize and assist with the filling out of extensive questionnaires about local people's ancestry and the degree to which they had preserved their German identity. The questionnaires also identified the number of Jews living among ethnic Germans and gathered statistical details of ethnic German suffering, exile, and execution under Bolshevism.¹¹

Fast mentions only briefly the points where Nazi and Mennonite values conflicted. A special agricultural emissary who visited the area reported that ethnic Germans were unwilling to work. Fast interceded on their behalf, suggesting it was due to mistreatment at the hands of agricultural supervisors, who had been seen whipping them. A week later, an accusation similar to the emissary's was aimed more directly at the inhabitants of the Mennonite village of Dolyns'ke (Osterwick). Those villagers attributed their falling behind the economic goals set for them to the hated collective farm system, the lack of food, and the severe shortage of clothing. During the same period, Fast and another expatriate Mennonite visited the office of the *Gebietskommissar* (District Commissioner), where, Fast notes, the commissioner's assistants "had nothing good to say about the Mennonites." Although Fast did not know what was meant by it, the functionary from the District Office referred to Mennonites as "white Jews," a term used in Germany by those who claimed that some Gentiles were "as bad as Jews."¹² When Fast became aware that a document was circulating in the district offices casting the "sects" in a negative light, he immediately sent a message to his superior, Karl Stumpp, warning of the measures that might eventually be taken against Mennonites.¹³

The framing of the Mennonite memories of interactions with their Nazi occupiers is best summarized by Waldemar Janzen, who suggests that "the adults around me moved from a first sense of exhilaration and liberation, which was largely confirmed by their encounters with the German Army, through two years of growing realism regarding the

Germany that they had once venerated so much."[14] Soviet Mennonites gradually developed second thoughts about their Nazi German saviours but found themselves trapped into supporting one totalitarianism, which had saved them, from another that had oppressed them. That support came at a price of knowing about, or to varying degrees becoming part of, the Holocaust.

While Mennonites have generally assumed that as a people they did not participate in the annihilation of Jews, and knew little about it, research has amply demonstrated that some people of Mennonite origin were actors in the full range of roles in the Holocaust as it unfolded in southern Ukraine. Allowing that individuals often fit into more than one category, even at the same time, Mennonites were perpetrators, collaborators, enablers, bystanders, and occasionally rescuers, and they were undeniably aware of the fate that was overtaking their Jewish neighbours.[15]

The remainder of this chapter focuses on the memories of the largest group of Mennonite actors, namely, those who likely took no direct part in atrocities but certainly had first-hand knowledge of what was happening. As the generation that experienced the Second World War fades from the stage, the number of memoirs and life writings of Mennonites who lived through these events is likely at its zenith. Many Soviet Mennonite survivors of the war migrated to Canada, or to Paraguay and then Canada, and have written their memoirs in English or German; the latter have occasionally had them translated. Migrations to Germany since the collapse of the Soviet Union have resulted in additional life writings in German. The aging of the survivors of the Second World War has fostered in them a "need to tell" their stories for succeeding generations; indeed, most these life writings are self-published, often for a family audience. How then have Mennonites constructed their memories? How have their narratives been shaped after immigration to Canada and the United States in the 1950s, or to Germany in the 1990s? And how have they given these memories meaning? Much as in their German counterparts, the most common marshalling of memories of the Nazi period casts Mennonites as victims. The waves of trauma experienced by Mennonites during the Soviet period has further complicated their memories of their brush with Germany and Nazism. In contrast to Germans, any coming to terms with their knowledge of and complicity in the Holocaust has been doubly compromised by the potency of the narrative that holds that Hitler's advance into the Soviet Union was their salvation – that Hitler saved Mennonites from Stalin.

I approach the subject as a second-generation descendant of Mennonites from the former Soviet Union who experienced the Second World

War as adults. My father fought as a soldier both for the Red Army and for the Wehrmacht (the regular German Army); my mother was a collective farm worker in the village of Dolyns'ke in the Chortitza colony when the war broke out and had personal memories that are similar to the ones you have encountered in this study.[16] Second- and third-generation descendants of those who experienced and participated in the Second World War cannot escape the trauma memories of their parents and grandparents and are forced to come to terms with their family's history. As Roger Frie suggests, as members of the second generation, we have inherited memories, "part of a traumatic past over which we have no control."[17] As a member of the second generation whose parents lived through the Soviet period and the war, seeking to understand the choices they faced and could or could not make has placed me in a chasm between two largely irreconcilable worlds.

In Germany, considerable attention has been and continues to be paid to German collective memories of the Nazi period. Academic and popular discussion has been devoted to what has come to be called *Vergangenheitsbewältigung*, the process of coming to terms with the past.[18] In the analysis of Germans' coming to terms with the Nazi past, scholars point to the period of silence that followed the collapse of Nazi Germany, when rather than confronting the Nazi past, Germans engaged in a "manic process of rebuilding."[19] Hans-Peter Söder argues, however, that Germans also developed an ever-expanding list of victims of the war that began with those who plotted Hitler's assassination and ultimately included Germany's common soldiers.[20] The 1968 student uprisings led to a change in the processing of memories of the Nazi period as second-generation Germans experienced their own loss in the sense that they came to see their parents as bystanders and perpetrators in the atrocities committed by Nazi Germany. By the 1980s, it was charged, Germans had fragmented their history: conscious and official recognition of Nazi atrocities had come to be neatly separated from the stories and memories inherited within their families.[21]

In contrast to often contested discussions in Germany about the meaning of the Nazi era and the Holocaust, Mennonite reflection on the destruction of the Jews in Ukraine has been largely muted. Mennonite affinities for Nazi ideology have appeared in studies of North and South American Mennonites, but until recently exploration of the Soviet Mennonite encounter with Nazism and the Holocaust has remained on the margins.[22] My aim is to use life writings with an eye to understanding some of the dynamics of remembering and accounting for what Mennonites in the Chortitza area knew about the killing of

A Usable Past: Soviet Mennonite Memories 295

Jews. Although themes related to the Soviet period of suffering, displacement, dispossession, and ultimately the loss of their Ukrainian homeland figure prominently in the memoirs of Soviet Mennonites, accounts of witnessing and having knowledge of Nazi atrocities make cameo appearances in almost all the life writings of those who experienced the events leading up to and during the war.[23]

When it comes to reconciling memories and finding a narrative to tell their stories, the most difficult challenge is faced by those who were adults at the time. Not surprisingly, Mennonites whose stories would have placed them among those who could be considered perpetrators or collaborators in the Holocaust, or at least to have had firsthand knowledge about the destruction of the Jews, have generally not left behind written memoirs. Also, few memoirs have been written by those who were adults at the time of these events even when they were on the bystander end of the scale. As in Germany, those who lived through the Nazi period as adults, regardless of their level of knowledge or involvement in the Holocaust, have generally been silent. In parallel with Roger Frie's analysis of German families, for Mennonites this silence has contributed to a rupture in Mennonite collective memory that has allowed for the belief that being Mennonite, and being a Nazi and a possible perpetrator or collaborator in the Holocaust, were mutually exclusive categories.

The memoir of the Mennonite minister Gerhard Fast serves as an instructive example of someone who must have known much more than his writings convey. In a 1947 issue of *Mennonite Life* and a later diary/memoir, *Das Ende von Chortitza*, published in the 1970s, Fast offers poignant recollections of the beauty of the Mennonite Old Colony region and conveys a genuine concern for Mennonite spiritual and social well-being. His only mentions of Jews are that there were 402 of them in the village of Chortitza; a note that they travelled through a Jewish village; and the reference made earlier in this chapter to a Nazi functionary who labelled Mennonites "white Jews."[24] In light of evidence that even Mennonite children were aware of what was happening to their Jewish neighbours, Fast clearly chose to focus on his mournful memories of the loss of Mennonite life and culture at the hands of the Bolsheviks, rather than on the eradication of people his Nazi superiors viewed as racially inferior.

Anna Sudermann's memoirs, also written in the 1970s but not published, feature a much more reflective view of the Nazi period. Sudermann was a teacher during the Nazi occupation and prefaces her memories of that time by noting that "the time goes back a quarter of a century. In the meantime, I have experienced a lot, have had to rethink many things. My thinking and actions of that time I now find to be dubious and imprudent." She recalls that

> it did not take long for the Jewish problem to be "solved." The more I think today about that time the guiltier I feel regarding the Jews. How confused was my judgement about how the National Socialists dealt with the Jews. We felt a great uneasiness regarding the Jews from the first day of the occupation. On the second day, we found out that the pharmacist Vogel and his wife had poisoned themselves even before Chortitza was occupied. He died, but his wife survived. ...
>
> One day we saw how the Jews, some fifty men, women and children were taken away. They were shot outside the village, including half-Jews. One mother, a Russian, apparently died together with her half-Jewish child.
>
> I am horrified to write this today.

Sudermann concludes her account holding out only the hope for forgiveness. She acknowledges it was not easy "to confess to this guilt."[25]

For those who had distanced themselves from a Mennonite or German ethnic and national identity, discussing the Holocaust came somewhat more easily. Helene (Frey) Latter was born into a Mennonite family in the Molotschna colony. As a young woman she rose in the ranks of the Soviet bureaucracy, and while critical of the blunders made by the regime, her memoir does not challenge its basic tenets. She suggests, for instance, that collectivization "was adopted out of some necessity not just because of some dictatorial government. Large landowners ... would not allow poorer people even a small corner of land for a garden."[26] Her work took her to the city of Zaporizhzhia, adjacent to the Chortitza colony. She married a Ukrainian who was "liquidated" by the Gestapo during the German occupation. Latter refers only sporadically to a Mennonite identity in her story. Except for describing her Mennonite family origins, being Mennonite seems to have been marginal to her identity as an adult. Even her connecting with the Mennonite Central Committee after the war and being sponsored to immigrate to Canada by Mennonite relatives does not figure prominently in her narrative. In Canada she married Walter Latter, a non-Mennonite, and eventually settled in Morden, right next to Mennonites, but she identified with the United Church.

In her account, Latter considers herself to be of German ethnicity, yet she almost universally refers to Nazis rather than Germans when she writes about the occupation period. While she benefited from her identity as a German, the experience of losing her husband at the hands of the Gestapo casts a shadow over her memories of the occupation and refugee experience. Latter's account of the killing of the Jews of Zaporizhzhia shows some evidence of research beyond what she experienced, but the tone of her memoir is matter-of-fact. In what seems to be a personal memory, she recalls that "they [the Jews] were obliged to wear a white armband with a yellow six-pointed star. We saw many being loaded into trucks on the pretext they would be taken to a special area for Jews. A few minutes later the rattle of machine guns echoed up from the valley below Zaporizhzhia and the trucks came back empty."[27]

Latter's narrative hints at her youthful affinity for the Soviet system and an increasing distance from Mennonite and then later even German identity. Her narrative is also coloured by the bitterness she felt over the death of her husband at the hands of the Gestapo. Her memories differ from many other narratives in that instead of considering Allied bombings and the behaviour of Soviet soldiers to be crimes, she justifies them in light of German atrocities. The rape of German women by Red Army soldiers is described as "horrible, disgusting and degrading to their own country" but is equated with German soldiers "who had behaved in like manner to Russian women." Similarly, German bombing was "repaid ... in full measure by the allies."[28]

Katharina Krüger's memoir is also written from the point of view someone who gave up both Mennonite faith and ethnic identities. Her memoir was written in 1991 at the height of the migration of ethnic Germans from the Soviet Union to Germany in the aftermath of the fall of the Berlin Wall. She was sixty-eight years old and had lived some fifteen years in Germany when she wrote down her memories. According to an analysis of her Gulag memories by Sarah Carter and Mary Hildebrandt, Krüger "lost all religious beliefs and did not convey Mennonite cultural practices and language to her son," who grew up in the Gulag.[29] She also writes from the point of view of the adjustments ethnic Germans faced during the years of their migration to Germany, where they never felt quite at home.

Krüger was a young woman of eighteen living in the Molotschna colony when their area came under German occupation in 1941. Within days of the passing of the military front, German military units were replaced by Romanian troops. She writes that "their appearance seemed unorganized, but we would soon become aware that they had specific assignments." The next day they saw the Romanian soldiers herding a crowd of people down the street. Krüger recalls:

> [I] did not want to trust my eyes, as I saw the old white-haired Jew and his wife. And there ... isn't that Sasha Reuter? The knowledge seeking

twelve-year-old boy, my most frequent visitor in the children's library, who with a wave of his hand rejected every book I offered him ... read it already! This precocious boy. Where are they taking him we asked ourselves, looking after him with concern. We would find out the same day. They were taken to the tank trench behind the town and shot.

The memory is clearly painful some fifty years later, and possibly sharpened by her own sense of not belonging in a modern Germany. Krüger embeds her memories completely in a German identity, noting that it had been her secret wish to someday see Germany, the homeland of her forefathers. Germans she encountered, whether civilian or military, assured her that they did not perform this dirty work – it was left to the Romanians. While dismayed at the hatred she saw in the killings, she is unwilling to acknowledge the lack of humanity of the German occupying forces, indicating that she believed that most found loathsome the task they were ordered to do. Strikingly, she ends her brief reflection on the killing of Jews with the simple statement that "life went on ... the rhythm of daily life resumed."[30]

The bulk of the memoir literature is written by those who were truly bystanders, largely because of the accident of age. Writers who are recalling events from their childhood face fewer moral dilemmas associated with their memories, yet they too seek to make sense of what they remember and attempt to place what they knew about into some kind of a usable understanding of what it meant.

While the Mennonite mention of the Nazis' treatment of Jews is often placed in the broader contexts of ideology, the creation of enemies during wartime, and the general horrors of war, authors struggle to give meaning to the death of innocent children and those moments when they saw evidence of, as opposed to merely hearing about, the killing of Jews. As Geoffrey Cubitt suggests, "traumatic experiences can produce a genuine and perhaps enduring crisis in the organization of biographical remembering."[31] Hearing that innocent Jewish children were being poisoned was traumatic, and recalling those memories disrupts efforts to create a coherent autobiographical narrative.

Given the young age of many of the memoirists, their knowledge of what was happening came directly from their parents or what they overheard at home and in the village. Often their most poignant recollections were about hearing of the poisoning of Jewish children. Wilhelm Janzen and his childhood friends "discussed the terrible fate of the Jews which we heard about from our parents and relatives" as they climbed the trees in the village orchard.[32] Waldemar Janzen recalls his mother telling him when he was ten or eleven that "Jewish children were being put to death" by putting "a little bit of poison ... on their lips and that they died quite painlessly."[33] Jacob Braun heard "of a Mennonite woman in a neighbouring town who had married a Jewish man. Since he was Jewish, he had fled east, leaving his wife and small child behind. When the Germans found out this child had a Jewish father, they took him from his mother and poisoned him."[34]

The writings of Mennonites who observed or had direct knowledge of the killing of Jews consistently express their horror and shock. As adults writing years later, memories of what they came to know have remained with them, but they tend to make sense of those memories on a very personal level, avoiding the larger questions of genocide. In Jacob Braun's account of joining women he was working with to go to see the trench with the bodies of Jews from their village who had been shot, he stops short because it is "too awful to describe any further details." He could not forget the scene and could not understand "how good the Germans were to us, while killing others ... but, we couldn't do anything about it."[35] Most poignantly, the death of Jewish children left Mennonites, often children themselves at the time, with only the deep emotional knowledge of something they could not forget. Once they knew, they could not "unknow." Waldemar Janzen could not understand why his mother told him about the poisoning of children. He suggests personal motives, such as her being "so shocked that she had to express it to someone," or her believing it to be better that he heard it from her rather than from others. Janzen expresses surprise that the news did not affect him more. He cannot remember "being very upset or thinking about it further," and he attributes his ambivalence to having "learned to live with countless stories ... where such things happened. ... Why should I be shocked by one more story of death?"[36]

Helena Rempel (Wiens/Franz) remembers seeing Vera, a Ukrainian woman in her village, walk by her school window holding her infant child. Vera had married a Jew and had made the difficult decision to die together with her husband and children. In Rempel's memoirs she comments that "knowing what happened to Vera made a deep impression on me to this very day."[37] Nor could adults come to terms with the death of children. In what appears to be a telling of the same story of the Russian mother, Vera, John Sawatzky cannot not shake the image of watching his children "play with childhood innocence" while "Jewish children, children as innocent as mine, were dying."[38]

The most prevalent story that Mennonites told themselves regardless of their age at the time placed the extermination of the Jews in the same category as the experience of their own people during collectivization, dekulakization, and the purges. Steve Stern's study of memory in Pinochet's Chile posits the notion of "memory as salvation."[39] Although Stern acknowledges that the idea "made his blood boil," he argues that for some Chileans the disappearances and deaths during the Pinochet regime were "contextualized ... as a modest social cost" that "had to be paid to repair the ruin" created by the Chilean Left.[40] For Soviet Mennonites, Hitler's attack on the Soviet Union became their salvation, and in the postwar period their memories fit neatly into Cold War logic that equated Stalinism with Hitlerism and that offered a way to reconcile events that would seem in a later context to be unconscionable.

Soviet Mennonite experience prior to the German occupation and the Holocaust in Ukraine differed significantly from that of Germans in Germany. For Soviet Mennonites, trauma memories began well before the German occupation. Even those who were only twelve when the German occupation began in 1941 had experienced the 1933 famine as four-year-olds; and many lost fathers and uncles during the purges of the late 1930s when they were nine and ten. In that sense their memories of the Holocaust are set in the context of traumatic memories from before and after they came to the knowledge and memory of the killing of their Jewish neighbours. In some cases these memories are constructed, as Geoffrey Cubitt puts it, to "alleviate the sense of guilt that may have attached to an earlier understanding of the same experience."[41] Broadly, their memories include or are told alongside stories that portray the Wehrmacht as innocent, and the SS and other Nazi organizations as culpable for the Holocaust, and their writings often make a case for equal judgment to be meted out to the Allies and the Soviet Union for their atrocities, such as the Gulag and the bombing of Dresden.

Otto Klassen, who was fifteen in 1942, oscillates between sympathetic memories of the plight of Jews and detailed descriptions of Stalin's atrocities and those of the Allies. His elaborate comparisons imply an equivalence between the killing of the Jews and other historical and wartime tragedies. On the one hand, he notes that his aunt conducted a Jewish choir, and he relates the story of how a woman had advised him that the German unit stationed in their village was a special SS unit whose mission was to exterminate all the Jews that had not been able to stay ahead of the advancing German army. She told him they had rounded up Jews on the Island of Chortitza, had shot them, and had forced Soviet prisoners of war to bury them. She also confided to him that she was Jewish and asked him to keep it a secret, which he did.[42]

Klassen also tells the story of Diedrich Hildebrand, an unsavoury character of Mennonite origin who was clearly a perpetrator. The account of

Hildebrand begins with his role as an NKVD collaborator who during the German occupation was accused by Mennonite women of being responsible for the arrest, exile, and execution of their husbands.[43] In Klassen's account, after the German occupation Hildebrand became a Nazi collaborator who identified Jews in Zaporizhzhia, who were then executed. While Klassen's memory of Hildebrand clearly amounts to a condemnation of his role in the destruction of Zaporizhzhia's Jewish population, the place of Hildebrand's story in Klassen's memoir serves as much to illustrate the depravity of those corrupted by communism, even if of Mennonite background. Hildebrand's role as an NKVD informer essentially places him outside the Mennonite community and transfers the burden of guilt for the Holocaust to one who had betrayed his Mennonite identity. This allows Klassen to avoid the question of Mennonite complicity.

However, Klassen also conducted considerable research and devotes a large portion of his memoirs to condemning the actions of the victors in the war. He raises a litany of comparisons: Nazi enslavement of Slavic peoples is set against Stalin's enslavement of Mennonites, the enslavement of Africans in the United States, and colonialism in general. Nazi concentration camps, he argues, were preceded by British use of them during the Boer War, while the Bolsheviks developed their own in the Gulags. The victors, Klassen concludes, have no moral right to pass judgment on an entire people.[44]

Victor Janzen, an immigrant to Canada via Paraguay, exploits the commonly held view that the Holocaust was carried out by the Nazi Party and the SS and exempts the Wehrmacht from complicity.[45] Janzen recalls their collective horror when "regardless of the kind of life they had led before, all Jews were ruthlessly brought together and shot." He notes, however, "it was wartime, human life was not worth a lot, and we had experienced enough mass murder in the last decades." He also notes that although they were shocked when they realized that Germans were capable of similar atrocities, the Holocaust was conducted by the *Einsatzkommandos* (Mobile Killing Squads) and the *Sicherheitsdienst* (Security Service; SD), not the Wehrmacht. Janzen cuts short his memories, suggesting that "about this I do not need to write more, because the topic has been dealt with enough, there have been enough documentaries and the criminals of that time are still being hunted."[46]

Peter Sawatzky, a survivor of both the war and the Gulag, conveys the sense of memory as salvation most explicitly. Sawatzky immigrated to Germany after the fall of the Berlin Wall and while on a visit to Canada in 1989 dictated his life story using only his memories. In his brother's translation, Sawatzky laments the beginning of the occupation of their area in southern Ukraine, when the Germans "started their reign by first shooting all Jews – women, children, men, and old men." Sawatzky is left only with questions about why innocent people had to die in this way.[47]

Sawatzky also explains away the Holocaust by alluding to the common argument that Bolshevism was a Jewish plot. He tells the story of a Jewish rabbi whom he overheard telling his mother, "this Hitler will punish our Jewish people for what we are doing here." A much longer section of his memoir is devoted to the atrocities committed by Stalin and his henchmen. Sawatzy refers extensively to Stuart Kahan's *The Wolf of the Kremlin*, a book written by an American journalist who claimed to be a nephew of Lazar Kaganovich, a Jewish henchman of Stalin. He concludes that "if there had been no Stalin there would have been no Hitler!"[48]

Anna Sudermann, although much more willing to engage in the question of Mennonite complicity in the Holocaust, also makes sense of Mennonite attitudes of the day in terms of the salvation offered by the arrival of the German armies. She chronicles the trauma experienced by Mennonites in the decades prior to the war. Mennonites had lived under a totalitarian regime, one without rights and justice: "we experienced dekulakization, collectivization, the mass arrest and deportation of innumerable men, but also women." In the context of their Soviet experience, the insults hurled at the National Socialists in the press only served to assure them that the Nazi Party must be good.[49] In her recollection, their country's belief that Jews had been at the forefront of Soviet economic and political life during the trauma they had experienced made plausible Hitler's contention that Jews posed a threat to Germany's security. Nazi treatment of Jews seemed excusable in that context. Sudermann acknowledges that their sense of justice had shifted.[50]

Like their German counterparts, Mennonites who experienced the Holocaust buried their memories of it in the immediate aftermath of the war. When they came to write their memoirs the knowledge of and increasing pervasiveness of the Holocaust forced them to acknowledge and, in some ways, try to resolve their own memories of what they had seen. For those whose memories were not compromised by their direct participation in the killing of their Jewish neighbours, the most accessible and least threatening memory was to recall their own sense of horror and shock at what had happened to them. While not seeking to minimize or in any way diminish the emotional trauma such memories evoked, telling the story of their sense of horror did not threaten their sense of self, nor did it invoke the negative judgment of their children.

In telling their personal memories of the Holocaust, it was often not enough for memoirists to adequately come to terms with their individual autobiographies. Narrators also sought to make sense of the autobiographical disruptions that their personal memories of the killing of Jews produced. In the context of the growing realization of the gravity of the Holocaust in the postwar period and the persistence of the Holocaust story fifty years after the events they recall, memoirists sought to place their memories in the larger context of the war, Hitler, and Stalin. To some extent this involved distancing themselves from their memories. The clearest intersection of collective and individual memories is embodied in the sense of the Germans – and Hitler – as having saved Soviet Mennonites from a godless and merciless regime bent on destroying them. Mennonites had viewed the arrival of Germans as signalling the end of arrests, executions, exile, and the constant pressure that sought to destroy both their faith and their sense of being a people. Initially the euphoria of having finally escaped Stalin's yoke and being saved by the Germans is remembered fondly and framed as justified. Yet the arrival of the Germans also brought unanticipated tensions. As the German occupation took hold, Mennonites came to realize there was a significant dark side to their saviours. Sifting through the memoirs used here suggests that the experience of being saved from Stalin made a reframing of the memory of the atrocities committed by the German occupiers almost impossible. Mennonites grasped for other narratives instead of confronting the reality of the massive scale of the Holocaust and their various levels of complicity and knowledge of its horrors in the murder of their Jewish neighbours. The collective memory that emerged equated or even elevated the trauma they had experienced at the hands of the Bolsheviks in comparison to the atrocities committed by the Germans and in some cases members of their own community. In that sense they made their own prewar Soviet experience into a Holocaust that became a usable past even after they emigrated to Western societies, where the collective memory of the destruction of the Jews continued to have widespread potency.

NOTES

1 The Jews still in Zaporizhzhia were killed in operations in November 1941 and March 1942. Likely the Jews living in or near Mennonite villages in the area were killed during the same period. "The Untold Stories: The Murder Sites of the Jews in the Occupied Territories of the Former USSR," Yad Vashem, The World Holocaust Remembrance Center, 2018, http://www.yadvashem.org/untoldstories/database/index.asp?cid=602.

2 Jacob A. Neufeld, *Path of Thorns: Soviet Mennonite Life under Communist and Nazi Rule*, trans. Harvey L. and Sara Dyck (Toronto: University of Toronto Press, 2014), 218, 219.
3 Ibid., 221–2.
4 Ibid., 226.
5 Ibid., 227.
6 Henry H. Winter, *Ein Hirte der Bedrängten. Heinrich Winter, Der Letzte Ältester von Chortitza* (Wheatley: printed by author, 1988), 80.
7 Neufeld, *Path of Thorns*, 230.
8 Ibid., 221.
9 Waldemar Janzen, *Growing Up in Turbulent Times* (Winnipeg: CMU Press, 2007), 47.
10 An analysis of the work of the Stumpp Kommando and its relationship to Nazi ideology is in Eric J. Schmalz and Samuel D. Sinner, "The Nazi Ethnographic Research of Georg Leibbrandt and Karl Stumpp in Ukraine and Its North American Legacy," in *German Scholars and Ethnic Cleansing, 1919–1945*, ed. Ingo Haar and Michael Fahlbusch (New York: Bergahn Books, 2005), 51–85.
11 For a summary and statistical analysis of the reports that were completed by the Stumpp Kommando, see Richard H. Walth, *Flotsam of World History: The Germans of Russia between Stalin and Hitler*, trans. Alexander Herzog and Michael B. Herzog (Essen: Klartext, 1996).
12 See for instance the answer provided by Nazi propagandists to answer charges that there were "white Jews" in Kurt Hilmar Eitzen, "Zehn Knüppel wider die Judenknechte," *Unser Wille und Weg* (6) 1936: 309–310. For a translation, see "Ten Responses to Jewish Lackeys," trans. Randall Bytwerk, German Propaganda Archive, Calvin College, 2004, http://research.calvin.edu/german-propaganda-archive/responses.htm. One of the counter-arguments provided was "the fact that there are so many 'white Jews' among us proves that the destructive Jewish spirit has already infected wide circles of our population."
13 Gerhard Fast, *Das Ende von Chortitza* (Winnipeg: Regehr's Printing, 1973), 45, 48.
14 Janzen, *Growing Up in Turbulent Times*, 48.
15 See for instance, Gerhard Rempel, "Mennonites and the Holocaust: From Collaboration to Perpetuation," *Mennonite Quarterly Review* 84 (October 2010): 507–49; Eric C. Steinhart, "The Chamelion of Trawniki: Jack Reimer, Soviet Volksdeutsche, and the Holocaust," *Holocaust and Genocide Studies* 23, no. 2 (2009): 239–62.
16 The stories and memories of my father are told in Hans Werner, *The Constructed Mennonite: History, Memory, and the Second World War* (Winnipeg: University of Manitoba Press, 2014). There is also one chapter on my mother's memories.

17 Roger Frie, *Not in My Family: German Memory and Responsibility after the Holocaust* (New York: Oxford University Press, 2017), 1.
18 For a discussion of the evolution of coming to terms with the past in German biographical writings, see Hans-Peter Söder, "The Politics of Memory: History, Biography, and the (Re)-Emergence of Generational Literature in Germany," *European Legacy* 14, no. 2 (2009): 177–85. A largely apologetic account of Mennonites and Nazism in Prussia is in James Peter Regier, "Mennonitische Vergangenheitsbewältigung: Prussian Mennonites, the Third Reich, and Coming to Terms with a Difficult Past," *Mennonite Life* 59, no. 1 (March 2004): n.p., https://mla.bethelks.edu/ml-archive/2004Mar/regier.php (accessed 27 November 2019).
19 Frie, *Not in My Family*, 180.
20 Söder, "The Politics of Memory," 180.
21 Frie, *Not in My Family*, 180.
22 On the Mennonites in South America, see John D. Thiesen, *Mennonite and Nazi? Attitudes among Mennonite Colonists in Latin America, 1933–1945* (Kitchener: Pandora Press, 1999). An early study of Nazi attitudes among Canadian Mennonite immigrants of the 1920s is Frank H. Epp, "An Analysis of Germanism and National Socialism in the Immigrant Newspaper of a Canadian Minority Group, the Mennonites, in the 1930s," (PhD diss., University of Minnesota, 1965). On the lack of postwar discussion of Mennonite collaboration with the Nazis in the case of the Danzig Mennonites, see Steven Schroeder, "Mennonite–Nazi Collaboration and Coming to Terms with the Past: European Mennonites and the MCC, 1945–50," *Conrad Grebel Review* 21, no. 2 (2003): 6–16. More recent scholarship has included Rempel's article cited above and Benjamin W. Goossen, *Chosen Nation: Mennonites and Germany in a Global Era* (Princeton: Princeton University Press, 2017).
23 Rempel, "Mennonites and the Holocaust," 527, 530.
24 Gerhard Fast, "Mennonites of the Ukraine under Stalin and Hitler," *Mennonite Life* 2, no. 2 (April 1947): 19; idem, *Das Ende von Chortitza*, 48.
25 Anna Sudermann, "Lebenserinnerungen von Anna Sudermann, 1893–1970," unpublished, Mennonite Heritage Archives (hereafter MHA), Winnipeg, 350–2.
26 Helene Latter, *I Do Remember* (Morden: Walter F. Latter, 1988), 23.
27 Ibid., 64.
28 Ibid., 83.
29 Sarah Carter and Mary Hildebrandt, "'Overrun and Swept Along by War': The Gulag in the Memoir of Katharina (Hildebrand) Krueger," *Journal of Mennonite Studies* 30 (2014): 238–9.
30 Katharina Krüger, *Schicksal einer Russlanddeutschen. Erlebnisbericht* (Göttingen: Graphikum Verlag, 1991), 17–18.
31 Geoffrey Cubitt, *History and Memory* (Manchester: Manchester University Press, 2007), 110.

32 Wilhelm Janzen, "A Refugee Travels from Russia through Germany over Paraguay to Canada," unpublished memoir, MHA [1987], vol. 4885, file 1.
33 Janzen, *Growing Up in Turbulent Times*, 47.
34 Jacob Braun, *Long Road to Freedom: The Riveting Story of a Young Boy Who Lived under Communism in Russia* (Winnipeg: Word Alive Press, 2011), 66.
35 Ibid., 67.
36 Janzen, *Growing Up in Turbulent Times*, 47–8.
37 Helen Rempel Wiens, "My Memoirs," *Preservings* 23 (December 2003): 116.
38 In Harry Loewen, ed., *Road to Freedom: Mennonites Escape the Land of Suffering* (Kitchener: Pandora Press, 2000), 61.
39 Steve J. Stern, *Remembering Pinochet's Chile* (Durham: Duke University Press, 2004), 30.
40 Ibid., 31.
41 Cubitt, *History and Memory*, 109.
42 Otto Klassen, *Erinnerungen aus meinem Leben* (Winnipeg: Old Oak, 2015), 36.
43 The NKVD is an acronym for the People's Commissariat for Internal Affairs, the main Soviet agency that carried out the purges. The NKVD arrested, convicted, exiled, and executed many Mennonites in the 1930s.
44 Klassen, *Erinnerungen aus meinem Leben*, 117–18.
45 For a discussion of the myth of the "clean" Wehrmacht, see Daniel Clayton, "'They were soldiers just like us...', *War, Literature and the Arts: An International Journal of the Humanities* 25 (2013): 1–27.
46 Victor Janzen, *Vom Dnjepr zum Paraguay Fluss* (Steinbach: by the author, 1995), 32. The Sicherheitsdienst was the Nazi intelligence agency.
47 Peter Sawatzky, *From Servant to Master: An Autobiography*, trans. Jacob Sawatzky (White Rock: by the author, 2007), 40.
48 Ibid., 50. American journalist Stuart Kahan published a book titled *The Wolf of the Kremlin: The First Biography of L.M. Kaganovich, the Soviet Union's Architect of Fear* (New York: William Morrow, 1987). Kaganovich was Jewish and a henchman of the Stalinist regime. Many of Kahan's claims were disputed by the remaining members of Kaganovich's family after the book was translated into Russian.
49 Sudermann, "Lebenserinnerungen von Anna Sudermann," 344.
50 Ibid., 351.

Chapter Twelve

Selective Memory: Danziger Mennonite Reflections on the Nazi Era, 1945–1950

STEVEN SCHROEDER

After 1945 the German Catholic Aid Society was responsible for meeting the needs of German Catholic expellees from Eastern Europe. When the society's leaders addressed the recent war, they attempted to, at least in some way, highlight German responsibility for the current state of suffering. In 1947, society leader Paulus Sladek claimed: "[The expellees'] suffering and fate begins with all of us ... In some way we all need to perform atonement for the sins that were begun in the name of our German people, and our atonement lies in our assistance to those who lost their homes ... and God has spared us, not because we were better, but because he wanted to give us the opportunity to become better."[1]

This admission of German responsibility for wartime misdeeds did not come naturally, or immediately. Rather, these kinds of admissions reflect part of a developing relationship between the Allied occupation personnel and the German people, in which Germans were expected to work toward making right the wartime catastrophe that the German nation had wrought on Europe. In short, the German people were being held to account for their wartime actions.

Curiously, this was not the case with the Danziger Mennonites, who had lived near Gdańsk/Danzig in the Vistula Delta before the war. While all other German citizens who wished to move forward with some autonomy under Allied occupation were forced to acknowledge the Nazi past by taking responsibility for it in some way through denazification, reparations payments, and reconciliatory work (or through submitting to Stalinization in the eastern occupation zone), Mennonites were busy transforming their wartime historical record. Their identity as pure Aryan, pro-Nazi Germans became malleable and was moulded in a way that allowed them to forget the negative aspects of the Nazi period and move forward with their lives free from this burden. The creation of a distinct, familiar Mennonite discourse made it possible for Danzigers to avoid critical reflection on their actions during the Nazi era.

This chapter posits a narrative of Danziger Mennonites' experiences and reflections during the pivotal postwar years, in the course of which they were defined as people who personally identified themselves as Mennonite, who felt connected to the Mennonite community, and, most significantly, who measured their actions in relation to that community and its dominant values and traditions. Between 1945 and 1950 the groundwork for Mennonite postwar self-understanding – and understanding of the community beyond its silo – was formed in a progression that loosely followed the cycle of grief and loss, particularly the stages of denial, bargaining, and acceptance. In the process, the Danzigers faced (and continue to face) the loss of an idealized understanding of Mennonite life in the German Reich, and loss of domicile within it.

My own family lived in the Vistula Delta, and my maternal and paternal grandparents were farmers. My great-grandfather was a preacher in the Lubieszewo/Ladekopp Mennonite church. My family had lived in this area for centuries, only moving small distances to acquire farmland. They lost everything when Red Army soldiers arrived and exacted their revenge on the German population during the winter of 1945, which is part of a broader story of grief and loss, and of suffering and trauma for the German nation. This story remains very personal on many levels – among other events, my great-grandmother died during the flight. Still, my family was part of it all: my grandfather and many other relatives served in the German military, and I remember the portraits of them in Wehrmacht uniforms that hung on my grandparents' walls. Moreover, according to the records found by Danuta Drywa, Mennonites in the area utilized slave labourers from the neighbouring Sztutowo/Stutthof concentration camp, which was part of the Nazi expansionist project.[2]

Embracing National Socialism

The gradual, centuries-old project of synthesizing traditional Mennonite values with German nationalism was essentially complete when Mennonites supported German militarism overtly in the mid-nineteenth century. Mennonites served in the German forces during the First World War, and afterward, like all Germans in the Free City of Danzig, longed to regain their "Home in the Reich." One Danziger Mennonite, a man who lived in Nowy Staw/Neuteich and who flew in the Luftwaffe during the Second World War, recalled in an interview: "We would try anything to get back into the Fatherland [after the

Versailles settlement]. Therefore, we were all in favor of organizations that went in that direction. We were politically involved as Mennonites, very much so."³ In 1939, Danziger Mennonites celebrated the incorporation of Gdańsk into the Reich.⁴ This support for Nazism coincided with the work of Mennonite preachers, elders, and deacons who simultaneously worked to "preserve the core elements of Mennonitism."⁵

This synthesis of Mennonitism and Nazism did not include denunciation of National Socialist ideology, including antisemitism. Numerous primary sources and scholarly accounts reveal that Mennonites and their non-Mennonite German neighbours shared much the same views. In an interview, a Danziger Mennonite who had served in the German military on the Eastern Front claimed that he could not understand why *they* (i.e., Germans) hated Jews, and why *they* sang hateful songs about Jews in the streets – songs he could recite easily from memory more than fifty years after the events. On cue, and unprovoked, he sang out: "Get rid of them, the entire Jewish lot, cut them out, out of our fatherland, hack off their arms and legs, then we'll be pure again!" Seemingly outraged, he exclaimed, "The kids were singing that in the street! I can't understand it."⁶

Danziger Mennonites lived near the Stutthof concentration camp; they included fifty-six Mennonite families who lived in the town of Sztutowo.⁷ They were involved in running the camp, and they utilized camp inmates as labourers on their farms. A few decades ago, Mennonite historians Horst Penner and Horst Gerlach, respectively, attempted to downplay (or ignore outright) the horrors of Stutthof and Mennonite involvement in that camp. Penner stated that "hardly anyone knew about the camp," that events at the camp were "strictly confidential," and that anyone who knew anything about the camp had been "sent to the front."⁸ Gerlach claimed that "it can be demonstrated that people of Mennonite heritage most likely did not participate in the atrocities and denunciations committed at Stutthof."⁹ Since those publications, research has revealed that Mennonites were complicit in many ways in the camps's operations. A good number of Mennonites are known to have served in the camp as guards or in other roles,¹⁰ and some of them were noted for their brutality. Furthermore, numerous Mennonites, as Gerhard Rempel put it, "exploited the available inexpensive labor provided by Stutthof prisoners"¹¹ for their farms and businesses.¹² Apparently this use of slave labour must have been widely accepted, as a preacher at the Orłowskie Pole/Orlofferfelde Mennonite church, Alfred Hinz, used Stutthof prisoners to clear about one thousand trees and to build a dam on his property.¹³ Hinz claimed that "the work was not dangerous" and that the prisoners were housed well in a clean warehouse and had "a hefty and adequate diet [and that they ate] no worse than we ate."[14]

Clearly out of line with the available evidence, Horst Penner claimed that Stutthof was "certainly different" from the other concentration camps, "where people endured the inescapable inhumanity."[15] In fact, life in Stutthof was just as horrific as in other camps in the Nazi system, and by 1944 it had an operational gas chamber.[16] Moreover, Mennonites acted just like their fellow Germans when stationed in and around the camp, as was evident in the case of one Mennonite man who was sentenced to death for his brutal actions at Stutthof.[17] Still, Penner concluded his book's section on Stutthof with these words: "Mennonites also did not escape enormous suffering."[18]

Penner and mainstream Mennonite historians tended to focus on Mennonite suffering in the war, yet the historical record shows that Mennonites were no different from their non-Mennonite German neighbours. Like all other Germans, Danziger Mennonites anticipated German victory in the war as the will of God, even while – as German historian Diether Goetz Lichdi identified as a tendency – they found it hard to admit that they had become full participants in the German war effort.[19] One interviewee claimed that even while collaborating with the Nazis and serving in the German armed forces, Danzigers had remained "*wehrlos* [defenceless, or pacifist] in their hearts."[20]

Avoidance

In a 2000 interview, a Danziger Mennonite former army captain declared boldly that Mennonites had nothing to do with the eventual fate of their community – its destruction – and that suggestions they did were seriously wrong-headed. In response to another Danziger's suggestion of this connection, the army captain stated: "I find it hard to believe that someone would be that bold, making a statement like that. ... It's absolutely unfair. ... It's just as stupid as saying that Adam and Eve are responsible for our suffering today. ... This is a sign of a lack of understanding humanity."[21]

The next sentence this interviewee uttered was all about the Soviets and western Allies' "ethnic cleansing" and inhumane attack on the German people at the end of the war. Seemingly, the brutality of this experience eclipsed the fact that the Germans had launched a total war in Europe in September 1939 in the very vicinity of the Danziger community, and with Danziger support. Instead of serious reflection on the war, many Mennonites narrowed their gaze to their own wartime suffering. As the Red Army encroached on the German settlements in Prussian territories in January 1945, one Mennonite man wrote: "It is January, 1945 – throughout the entire Reich destruction, distress and agony. Many a tired fighter asks with a shudder: 'Will our victimization come to an end soon?'"[22]

Escaping the advancing Red Army in January 1945, nearly all Danziger Mennonites made it by ship to Denmark or to locations in northern Germany, where they began life as displaced persons in DP camps, bunkers, unheated attics, pigpens, furnace rooms, and army barracks in Germany.[23] Those who remained behind were subjected to the Red Army's pillaging, rape, and murder and had to witness the destruction of their community. Others were deported on trains to work camps in the Gulag.[24]

The 210 Danzigers who survived and continued to reside in the Vistula Delta eventually came under the care of Mennonite Central Committee (MCC) workers stationed at Pelplin, Poland, after 1947. Naturally, Polish authorities wanted to rid Poland of Germans, and Danzigers, though they cherished their homeland, were eager to escape communist rule. To that end, MCC representatives applied for exit visas for them, claiming that "Mennonites are all distinctly of German race and wish to hold to their German culture."[25] The MCC succeeded in obtaining exit permits for these distinctly "German" Mennonites.[26] The majority of Danzigers were housed briefly in 1947 at the Inter-Governmental Council for Refugees (IRO) camp at Fallingsbostel in northern Germany, where MCC workers assisted in the refugee screening process, working toward their vindication, and emigration.[27]

Bargaining

Upon commencing its refugee work in Germany in 1946, MCC workers moved quickly to the bargaining stage, hoping to convince the Allied authorities that Mennonites were a distinct, peace-loving group and thus gain concessions for Mennonite DPs. In Germany's western occupation zones, the quest was the opposite of that in Poland: here, MCC workers recognized the need to prove that Mennonites were anything but German.

Unlike their German church counterparts in the Protestant Relief Work and Catholic Aid Society, the MCC was a minor player in the grand scheme of relief work in Germany. It was one of five US organizations in the umbrella organization CRALOG,[28] and, as its representatives were from abroad, it was not seen as participating in the political or educational rehabilitation of the German people, or scrutinized accordingly. In other words, the MCC did not have to perform a penitent or reconciliatory function in Germany in the same way as the relief organizations that were tied to the mainline German churches.

As a result, North American MCC workers operated freely to achieve their organization's goal, which was to get Danziger Mennonites (indeed, all Mennonites) out of harm's way. This meant different things in different contexts. To start, the MCC needed financial support from its North American Mennonite constituents, and to that end, like the Catholic Aid Society in the example above, it utilized language of German wartime misdeeds not as a tactic to gain political favour from the Allies but rather as a means to procure financial support to assist their "wayward" co-religionists. MCC staff person C.F. Klassen wrote in 1948, "for safe passage [of Mennonites] you can help out," particularly as "some of ours have, over the decades, either strayed from the community, by influencing strong but alien political-cultural currents, or by rationalist teachings of the ancient human beliefs. ... [We want to] invite them in a simple, humble, yet clear way, to examine their position before God, and to judge it correctly."[29]

However, for Danzigers, coming to terms with the Nazi past did not involve examination of this sort. Instead it centred on getting out of a difficult situation – of being DPs in Germany – which also necessitated getting out from under the designation of "German." The formerly celebrated, embraced, and favoured and privileged aspects of their identity – racial characteristics, ethnicity, and heritage – now became the very things that brought them disfavour vis-à-vis the authorities and their European neighbours. To get out of this situation, Mennonites had to be creative.

Overturning the previously held notion of serving the Fatherland to victory, Danzigers – and the Ukrainian Mennonites who were mixed among them – claimed to have been victims of the war. To circumvent the political restrictions on population transfers established by the Allied powers and the United Nations, Mennonites busily devised new strategies to claim either that they were a distinct Mennonite nationality or that Mennonites were not part of any earthly nation.[30] The schemes rekindled the traditional Mennonite notion of being "in but not of this world."

On the question of nationality and wartime activities, MCC senior operatives Peter Dyck and C.F. Klassen attempted to "dupe" (Klassen's words in 1949) the immigration officials and occupation authorities. This is seen clearly in Peter Dyck's 1946 document on Mennonite identity intended for the IRO, titled "Mennonite Refugees in Germany." Dyck stated:

Selective Memory: Danziger Mennonite Reflections 313

> The Mennonite brotherhood ... for 450 years has consistently endeavored to put into practice ... strict pacifism, not swearing of oaths ... and freedom of conscience. ... The Mennonite refugees are undoubtedly a remnant of a distinctly characterized people, a "Volk," which is neither Russian nor German. They do not greatly care what they are called, they call themselves "Mennonites" by nationality and have only one desire, to emigrate to Canada or Paraguay where they can join their relations and apply their labor to the land.[31]

In keeping with this way of thinking, Peter Dyck acknowledged that Mennonites had "bec[o]me chameleons."[32]

Moreover, bargaining for preferential treatment was evident in the attempts to equate Mennonites with Jews in terms of their persecution, chosen status before God, and unjust postwar suffering. In the process, recent events were ignored and the magnitude of Jewish suffering during and after the war was disregarded. In 1946, Peter Dyck claimed:

> Being classified as "Mennonites" would be nothing more extraordinary for these people than classifying Jews as Jews. ... To these people the concept of Mennonite is not confined to religion alone, nor does it connote a church, or church membership; it is more than that, embracing all that culture, language, tradition, and a distinct way of life implies. The only parallel of this is the classic example of the Jews, and the only difference when judging it from such a point of view lies in numbers.[33]

Additional comparisons of Mennonites and Jews were offered in these years, most poignantly in the utilization of the Exodus motif. Maria Toews, who had fled the advancing Red Army in 1945, believed that the Danziger Mennonite experience was akin to the exodus of the Israelites in the Bible: "And hell's revenge threatens us, but God led us like Israel through the sea. ... No one needs to fear anymore. Let our thanks [be known] for all Thou hast done for us; let all of us choose the narrow way that leads into the eternal Canaan!"[34]

Mennonite J.J. Thiessen, member of the Canadian Board of Colonization, and C.F. Klassen both gleaned inspiration for their work from Moses's declaration before the pharaoh, where the leader of the Israelite exodus claimed that "there shall not a hoof be left behind" – a slogan Klassen and Thiessen included in their reports to other MCC administrators.[35]

Moreover, in the book *Up from the Rubble*, Peter Dyck makes the connection between the Israelite exodus and "Operation Mennonite," during which Dyck and other MCC workers clandestinely transported 1,200 Mennonite refugees from Berlin to the British zone in 1946.[36] When asked if this was an act of God, Dyck answered: "We notice a striking resemblance here to the Red Sea crossing of the Israelites as recorded in Exodus 14: 21–30. ... In the Berlin exodus we see similar features: a people in distress cried to God for help. There was a dramatic and victorious delivery ... and everybody believed that the Lord had done it."[37]

Dyck went so far as to give the title "Exodus" to the MCC short film that depicted MCC work among European refugees. The film was shown at the State Department in Washington, D.C., on 13 November 1947, and at IRO headquarters in Geneva on 22 June 1948.

Acceptance

The acceptance stage of loss in the Danziger experience is clearly incomplete. Those outside the Mennonite community, such as the IRO officials who came across evidence detailing Mennonite involvement in "reprehensible" German units,[38] became very aware of Mennonite complicity in German war crimes. Understandably, some Mennonites think that the difficult and complex circumstances of the Nazi era have not been fully appreciated. Like some of their German neighbours, many Mennonites feel they have been misunderstood and maligned for their actions between 1933 and 1945 and have been misrepresented and condemned in both popular and scholarly historical accounts. The popular rendition of the evil nature of Nazism, according to one Danziger military veteran, is "a historical joke."[39] Another Danziger who served in the German forces stated that "people today have a completely different view of German politics because on account of the outcome of the war and the Holocaust and all this hocus pocus. ... For that matter, they form their judgements on that basis, but it wasn't that way. There was a very positive side to [National Socialist] politics."[40]

After the war, Danziger Mennonites wanted peace of mind for themselves and their community, to avoid responsibility for the German wartime crimes, and to emigrate to greener pastures. In the immediate postwar context, these interpretations of the past made sense; but they also fostered avoidance of the matter of Mennonite collusion with Nazism. Unlike their German neighbours in the mainline churches and their affiliated relief organizations, Mennonites did not acknowledge this complicity, or take responsibility for its ramifications, let alone express contrition for this troubling past.

Indeed, this volume is so late in taking up these issues (only in 2020) largely due to the avoidance, bargaining, and related Mennonite work and narratives established in the immediate postwar years. Perhaps things would be different if Mennonites had engaged these questions earlier on – if we had had a Mennonite Fritz Fischer, or had engaged in a

Selective Memory: Danziger Mennonite Reflections 315

Historikerstreit ("battle of historians") over our own history in the immediate postwar period or even in the 1980s as German historians did.

But we did not, and we have not since. Does this all matter? Maybe not in the broader scheme of things – for the vast majority of Germans and Europeans – but it should matter to *us*. Regardless of our respective religious views and practices, our cultural affinity to Mennonitism, or our last names, this is our heritage – a heritage that impacts our personhood, our engagement with the people around us, and the broader world. And if one is interested in theology, this should matter a lot, particularly for those who evangelize. Unexamined – or worse, embraced – the Mennonite encounter with Nazism remains a lingering problematic case full of injustice, particularly as Nazism harbours contempt and violence inherently. As someone of Danziger descent, I am a beneficiary of British, and Mennonite, colonial practices – in fact, though ignorant of it at the time, I purchased a house in the Fraser Valley that was built on land that was formerly the bottom of a lake – a lake that the Stó:lō people relied on for their sustenance for thousands of years. Europeans drained it and built houses and farms on the fertile land. In recent years I have begun to engage in reconciliation work with Indigenous peoples in Canada, and I can say that I did not come to this work as a result of Mennonite teaching. Some Mennonites are trailblazing in this area, but very few. In this work, truth-telling is a fundamental first step, as is the accompanying act of listening to those who have been harmed – yes, including those who have been harmed by us. In my view, a healthy way forward for us is to acknowledge that Mennonites have not only suffered harm but also caused harm. Moreover, we should address immediate issues arising from this harm, while also taking the long view of, and being committed to, reconciliatory work in relation to the colonial enterprises in which we have participated. I see the seeds of that taking place here in this volume, which is encouraging.

NOTES

1 Paulus Sladek, "*Predigt zur Förderung der caritativen Flüchtlingshilfe*," Bundesarchiv Koblenz (BAK) Z 18/101.
2 Danuta Drywa, in Wolfgang Benz und Barbara Distel, eds., *Der Ort des Terrors. Geschichte der nationalsozialistischen Konzentrationslager*, Band I: *Die Organisation des Terrors*, ed. Angelika Königseder (München: Verlag C.H. Beck, 2005), 708.
3 Interview with Danziger 1, by author, 26 July 1999.
4 Hermann Epp, "Die westpreussischen Gemeinden von 1933 bis zum Untergang," *Der Mennonit*, Januar–Februar 1948, Nr. 1–2: 12.

5 Hermann Epp, ""Die westpreussischen Gemeinden," 5.
6 Interview with Danziger 2, by author, 9 October 1999.
7 Gerhard Rempel, "Mennonites and the Holocaust: From Collaboration to Perpetration," *Mennonite Quarterly Review* 84 (October 2010): 517.
8 Horst Penner, *Die ost-und westpreussischen Mennoniten* (Kirchheimbolanden, 1987), 2:127.
9 Horst Gerlach, "Stutthof und die Mennoniten," in Diether Goetz Lichdi, *Mennoniten im Dritten Reich* (Weierhof: Mennonitischer Geschichtsverein, 1977), 248.
10 Mennonites who joined the SS and worked at Stutthof included Alfred Albrecht, Hermann Falk, Heinz Löwen, Herr Schröder, Johannes Wall, Fritz Peters, Heinrich Weins, and Kurt Janzen. Rempel, "Mennonites and the Holocaust," 517–18.
11 Rempel, "Mennonites and the Holocaust," 519.
12 Farmers included Franz Penner, Wilhelm Thiessen, Otto Froese, Herr Wiens, Herr Funk, Herr Schröder, K. Wiebe, Erich Claassen, Johann Wiebe, and Werner Klassen. Businessmen included Gerhard Epp, Heinrich Wiens, Peter Neufeld, and Eduard Reimer. Rempel, "Mennonites and the Holocaust," 520–4.
13 Rempel observed that Mennonites employed Stutthof prisoners "without any apparent moral compunction." Ibid., 519.
14 Penner, *Die ost-und westpreussischen Mennoniten*, 2:127–8.
15 Ibid., 128.
16 Rempel, "Mennonites and the Holocaust," 515.
17 Ibid., 517.
18 Penner, *Die ost-und westpreussischen Mennoniten*, 2:128.
19 Horst Gerlach recalled how, at the outset of the battle, his schoolteacher had applied the apocalyptic account in the Book of Revelation to the impending final victory of the Germans in the Second World War. Similarly, the *Gemeindeblatt der Mennoniten* began in the early 1940s to print articles with eschatological and apocalyptic overtones pointing to a German triumph. On these points, see Diether Goetz Lichdi, *Mennoniten im Dritten Reich*, 98, and interview with Horst Gerlach by author, June 2000, Heilbronn, Germany.
20 Interview with Danziger 1. Diether Goetz Lichdi claims: "The younger ones would agree with it [*Wehrlosigkeit*] and the older ones would say – we always practised it! They always practiced *Wehrlosigkeit* in their hearts." Interview with Diether Goetz Lichdi by author, 6 June 2000, Heilbronn, Germany.
21 Interview with Danziger 3, by author, 11 April 2000. Location is not included in the above interview references.
22 Klaus Toews, "Die Flucht" in Maria Foth, ed., *Lieder aus der Not* (Winnipeg: Christian Press, 1950), 29–31.

23 Emily Brunk, *Espelkamp: The MCC Shares in Community Building in a New Settlement for German Refugees* (Frankfurt am Main: MCC Press, 1950), 9.
24 See Horst Gerlach's personal account of his experience in a Siberian work camp, *Nightmare in Red* (Freeman, SD: Pine Hill Press, 1995).
25 Mennonite Church USA Archives (MCA), MCC Records, IX-19-3, file 2/32, "Basel Relief Unit, Poland, 1948," "Present Conditions of the Mennonites in Poland, 1948."
26 Letter from Jaroszuka, chief delegate of the Ministry of Recovered Territories of the Polish Republic, 25 May 1948. See, here, MCA, MCC Records, IX-19-3, file 2/32, "Basel Relief Unit, Poland, 1948"; Menno Fast's report, "A Report on Our Work among the Mennonites in Poland, April–June 1948"; and letter from Menno Fast to Siegfried Janzen, 3 September 1948. Visas were procured through Poland's Director of German Affairs, Jaroszuka, on 19 May 1948.
27 "Wie viele Mennonitenflüchtlinge in Europa?" *Der Mennonit* 4 (April 1948): 31.
28 The US members of CRALOG (Council of Relief Organizations Licensed to Operate in Germany) included the National Catholic Welfare Conference, Church World Service, Lutheran World Relief, Mennonite Central Committee, and Unitarians. Beryl McClaskey, *The History of U.S. Policy and Program in the Field of Religious Affairs under the Office of the U.S. High Commissioner of Germany* (Historical Division, Office of the Executive Secretary, Office of the US High Commissioner of Germany, 1946), 24.
29 C.F. Klassen, "Zum Geleit," *Der Mennonit*, Januar/Februar 1948, Nr. 1/2, 2.
30 William Snyder, *Mennonite Refugees: Whose Responsibility?* (Akron: MCC Press, 1948), 3.
31 MCA, MCC Records, IX-19-3, file 1/26, "Basel Relief Unit, Germany," letter from Peter Dyck to IRO officials titled "Mennonite Refugees in Germany," July 1946.
32 Robert Kreider, *Interviews with Peter J. Dyck and Elfrieda Klassen Dyck: Experiences in Mennonite Central Committee Service in Europe, 1941–1949* (Akron, Pa.: MCC, 1988), 322.
33 Dyck, "Mennonite Refugees in Germany," 3.
34 Maria Toews, "Zum Ausklang" in Foth, ed., *Lieder Aus dem Not*, 199.
35 Frank Epp, *Mennonite Exodus* (Winnipeg: D.W. Friesen and Sons, 1962), 409.
36 Peter J. Dyck, *Up from the Rubble* (Winnipeg: Herald Press, 1991), 183–205.
37 Ibid., 204–5.
38 MCC Basel, 16.1.1949, C.F. Klassen to Peter Dyck, "The Wartegau Mennonites have successfully claimed that they were forced to take German citizenship – the IRO has been duped!" See MCC 23 .7.1949, 1, Myer Cohen to Chief Eligibility Officer IRO.
39 Interview with Danziger 3.
40 Interview with Danziger 1.

Contributors

Imanuel Baumann, PhD, is coordinator for History Education at the museum "Hotel Silber," a branch of the House of History Baden-Württemberg in Stuttgart. Previously he was at Martin Luther University, Halle-Wittenberg, where he conducted research on the twentieth-century history of the Anabaptist tradition.

Doris L. Bergen is the Chancellor Rose and Ray Wolfe Professor of Holocaust Studies in the Department of History and Anne Tanenbaum Centre for Jewish Studies at the University of Toronto. Her publications include *War and Genocide: A Concise History of the Holocaust* (3rd ed., 2016), *The Sword of the Lord: Military Chaplains from the First to the Twenty-First Centuries* (edited, 2004), and *Twisted Cross: The German Christian Movement in the Third Reich* (1996).

Aileen Friesen is an assistant professor and the co-director of the Centre for Transnational Mennonite Studies at the University of Winnipeg. She is the author of a number of articles exploring the experiences of Mennonites in imperial Russia and the Soviet Union.

Alle G. Hoekema received his PhD from Leiden University. He taught at the Mennonite Seminary and at the Vrije Universiteit in Amsterdam and has written books and many articles about developments of Christian theology and Mennonite mission history in Indonesia. He has also published several articles on the theme of Dutch Mennonites and the Second World War and was a guest editor of a special issue of the *Doopsgezinde Bijdragen* on this topic in 2015.

Mark Jantzen is a professor of history at Bethel College, North Newton, Kansas. Among other publications he is the author of *Mennonite*

German Soldiers: Nation, Religion, and Family in the Prussian East, 1772–1880 (2010); he also co-edited, with John D. Thiesen, *European Mennonites and the Challenge of Modernity over Five Centuries: Contributors, Detractors, and Adapters* (2016).

James Irvin Lichti retired from Milken Community Schools in 2019. His PhD dissertation was published in 2008 as *Houses on the Sand? Pacifist Denominations in Nazi Germany*. His articles and essays have appeared in *Mennonite Life, Mennonitische Geschichtsblätter, Mennonitisches Lexikon* vol. 5, and *The Routledge History of the Holocaust*, edited by Jonathan C. Friedman.

Dmytro Myeshkov, DPhil., is a historian and archivist who studied history in Dnipro, Ukraine, and in 2005 completed doctoral work at Heinrich Heine University in Düsseldorf. After working as a researcher at universities in Düsseldorf, Leipzig, and Freiburg, since 2017 he has been a researcher at the Nordost-Institut of the University of Hamburg (Lüneburg). He is the author of *Alltag im Spiegel von Konflikten. Die Deutschen und ihre Nachbarn im nördlichen Schwarzmeergebiet und in der südwestlichen Peripherie des Zarenreiches bis zum Ersten Weltkrieg* (2020) and *Die Schwarzmeerdeutschen und ihre Welten, 1781–1871* (2008).

Colin P. Neufeldt is a professor of history at Concordia University in Edmonton, Alberta, where his research focus is the history of Mennonites in Soviet Ukraine in the 1920s and 1930s. His most recent publications include *The Public and Private Lives of Mennonite Kolkhoz Chairmen in the Khortytsia and Molochansk German National Raïony in Ukraine (1928–1934)* and "Collectivizing the *Mutter Ansiedlungen*: The Role of Mennonites in Organizing Kolkhozy in the Khortytsia and Molochansk German National Districts in Ukraine in the late 1920s and early 1930s," in *Minority Report: Mennonite Identities in Imperial Russia and Soviet Ukraine Reconsidered, 1789–1945*. Colin also practices law in Edmonton.

Arnold Neufeldt-Fast, PhD, is Associate Academic Dean and Associate Professor of Theology at Tyndale University College and Seminary, Toronto, Canada. He taught at the European Mennonite Seminary Bienenberg in Liestal, Switzerland, from 2000 to 2006.

Pieter Post is a Mennonite theologian and researcher. He earned his PhD in 2010 on the subject of the history and theology of Dutch Mennonite church songs between 1793 and 1973. Currently he is a pastor in the United Mennonite Church of Heerenveen and Tjalleberd. Recent publications include *Naar Messiaans Communisme. Frits Kuiper (1898–1974) dopers theoloog* (2014), and Alle G. Hoekema and Pieter Post, *Frits Kuiper (1898–1974) Doopsgezind Theoloog. Voordrachten en getuigenissen over Kuiper en een selectie van zijn brieven* (2016). He is preparing a biography of the Dutch Mennonite pastor Frits Kuiper.

Steven Schroeder is Teaching Chair in the Peace and Conflict Studies program and teaches in the History Department at the University of the Fraser Valley in Abbotsford, British Columbia.

John D. Thiesen has been archivist and co-director of libraries at Bethel College, North Newton, Kansas, since 1990. He has a long-standing interest in the topic of Mennonite interactions with Nazism and has several publications in this area including *Mennonite and Nazi? Attitudes among Mennonite Colonists in Latin America, 1933–1945* (1999).

Erika Weidemann holds a PhD in history from Texas A&M University in College Station, Texas. She has published in the Society for German-American Studies' *Yearbook* and has received many research grants including the Keeble Dissertation Award.

Hans Werner is a senior scholar who retired from the University of Winnipeg where he was an associate professor, teaching courses in Canadian history and Mennonite studies. He was also the Executive Director of the D.F. Plett Historical Research Foundation, Inc. and the editor of its popular journal, *Preservings*. He is the author of a number of articles and books, including his most recent book, *The Constructed Mennonite*, about the memories of his father who was Mennonite and a Red Army and German soldier in the Second World War. He has also written about the experience of Mennonite migrants from the former Soviet Union adjusting to new lives to the cities of Winnipeg in Canada and Bielefeld, Germany, in the postwar period.

Index

Adorno, Theodor, 125
Advent-Bote, 84
Akkrum, 266n29
Albrecht, Hans, 100n56
Aleksandrovsk. *See* Zaporizhzhia
Alkmaar, 160
Alliance (*Vereinigung der Deutschen Mennonitengemeinden*), 4, 78, 108, 126, 129, 142n23, 143n34, 183
Alsace, 5, 6
Althaus, Paul, 105, 118
Altmennoniten. *See* German Evangelical Baptists
Ameland, 171n57
Amish, 5
Amsterdam, 4, 28n19, 78, 157, 255, 257–9, 267n38
Anabaptists, 4, 5, 17, 73, 76, 82, 85, 88, 92n6, 97n38, 105, 130–1, 140, 154–5, 158, 162–4, 191
Andres, Kornei, 246n63
Angrick, Andrej, 53, 58
Anne Tanenbaum Centre for Jewish Studies, xii
Antamonov, 210
anthropology, 140
Antichrist, 126, 138
Antisemitism, 8, 11, 19, 22, 86–9, 104–18, 132–3, 139, 189, 232

Apeldoorn, 256
Arendt, Hannah, 126
Argentina, 235
Armenians, 50
Arnhem, 255–6
Arnold, Eberhard, 130, 144n43
Aryan Paragraph (Law for the Restoration of Professional Civil Service), 113–14, 117
Association of Behalf of the Public Welfare (*Maatschappij tot Nut van't Algemeen*), 251
Association of Behalf of the Welfare of the Israelites (*Maatschappij tot Nut der Israelieten*), 251
Auschwitz, 4, 252, 257, 258
Austria, 157
Azov, 206, 215

Baden, 6, 95n24, 104, 126
Bakhoven, Helena Cornelia Leignes, 260
Baptists, 73, 88–9, 96n31, 105, 107
Baratov, 136
Barmen Declaration, 83, 91, 98n43, 130
Barneveld, 256
Barry, Dan, 55
Barth, Karl, 85, 98n44, 118, 160

Battle of Bzura, 178
Bauman, Zygmunt, 125, 128, 132, 138
Baumann, Helmut, 119n2
Baumann, Imanuel, 21
Baumann, Thomas, 119n2
Bavaria, 6, 104, 126
Beck, von, 62
Belarus, 52
Belgium, 259
Belinsch, Moses, 61
Ben Shemen Forest, 161
Bender, Harold S., 14, 130
Berdyans'k, 54
Berg, Helene, 133
Bergen, Doris L., xi, xii, 14
Berger, 214
Berggrav (Bishop), 95n25
Berkhoff, Karel, 8, 19
Berlin, 46, 48, 51, 60, 122n25, 130, 135, 247n66, 252, 276, 280, 297, 313
Berlin Document Center, 58, 279
Bethel College, xi, 10
Biblical references: Exodus 34:7, 128; Leviticus 19:34, 123n37; Isaiah 1:15, v; Daniel 12:4, 76; Matthew 5:37, 4, 17; Matthew 25:41–45, v; Luke 10:25–27, 112; 1 Corinthians 13:9, 93n12
Bijuk-Onlar, 205
Binyamini, Hadas, xii
Black Sea, 135
Blokzijl, 264n12
Bluffton University, 155
Boer War, 301
Boer, Bouwe de, 165
Bogdanova. *See* Harms, Maria
Bonhoeffer, Dietrich, 79, 96n28
Boom, Casper ten, 267n38
Boom, Corrie ten, 259, 267n38
Borculo, 261
Bormann, Martin, 79, 95n25, 96n27

Bote, Der, 13
Branchweilerhof, 99n48
Braun, Anna, 26n8
Braun, Connie T., v, xii, 19
Braun, Jacob, 299
Braun, Peter J., 126
Braune, 213
Brazil, 69n48, 157
Breidig, Birgit, 116
Brest, 218
Brethren, 105
Brethren of the Common Life, 159
Brink, Albertina, 28n19
Brussé, Geesje Nieuwenhuis, 253–5, 260
Brussee-van der Zee, Elisabeth I. T., 22, 154–5, 167n4
Buber, Martin, 85, 101n61
Buchsweiler, Meir, 203
Bund freikirchlicher Christen, 82

California, 73
Calvinists, 250
Canada, 6, 16, 24, 35, 38, 126, 139, 177, 235, 237, 239, 265n23, 276, 280, 293, 301, 315
Canada, alternative service, 18
Canadian Mennonite Board of Colonization, 313
Canadian Minister of Citizenship and Immigration, 55
Cannegieter, Lambertus, 266n32
Carmel, New York, 54, 68n46
Carter, Sarah, 297
Carusi, Ugo, 280
Catholics, 86, 102n72, 107, 206, 215, 262n2, 263n9, 307
Cattepoel, Dirk, 111–13, 138–9, 144n45, 145n55, 151n116
Caucasus, 3, 51, 53, 59, 134, 202, 212–13, 215–16, 227n66
Center Party, 86

Index   325

Central Bureau for Immigration
  (*Einwandererzentralstelle*), 38, 235,
  238, 273, 279
Centre for Transnational Mennonite
  Studies, xii
Chełmno extermination camp, 173
Chicago, 112
Chile, 300
Chortitza Colony, xiii, 11, 24, 43, 45,
  59, 132–4, 148n80, 269–82, 290–1,
  295–6, 300
Christliche Versammlung, 82, 98n42
Christmann, Kurt, 59, 71n63
Church and Peace, 158, 167n12
Church Renewal Movement, 154–5
Civilian Public Service, 18
Clark, Ramsey, 55
Clercq, Goverta de, 159, 160
Cohen, Hans Frits, 266n31
Cohen, Johan, 266n31
Cohen, Leny, 257
Colonialism, 301
Confessing Church, 48, 81, 83, 85, 91,
  97n35, 97n36, 98n40, 98n44
Conscription. *See* Military
  conscription
Coppello, Anna Coppeyne van de,
  266n32
CRALOG, 311
Crimea, 3, 53, 59, 61, 202–6, 211–16
Crous, Ernst, 46
Cubitt, Geoffrey, 298, 300
Cultural Workers' Guild
  (*Kultuurkamer*), 255, 265n24
Czechoslovakia, 69n50
Częstochowa, 55

Dalsum, Albert van, 265n24
Danzig. *See* Gdańsk
Del', Viktor, 214
Den Haag, 264n11
Denmark, 250, 311

denominationalism, 21, 72–91
Denver, John, 13
Deutschland erwache!, 127
Deutsch-Wymyschle. *See* Nowe
  Wymyśle/Deutsch Wymyschle
Deventer, 257
Diem, Harald, 98n44
Diepenveen, 257
Dierksen, Johann Genrichovič,
  219–20
Dik, David, 246n63
Dik, Ivan Ivanovich, 55–6, 246n63
Dirks, Heinrich, 132
disabled, killing of, 11, 23, 36, 134
displaced persons, 276–81, 311–12
Displaced Persons Act, 55
Dnieper Hydroelectric Station, 230
Dnieper River, 44–6, 54, 206, 230,
  232, 239, 271
Dnipro (Dnipropetrovsk), 45, 235,
  271–2
Dniprodzerzhynsk. *See* Kamianske/
  Dniprodzerzhynsk
Dnister River, 47
Dolyns'ke/Osterwick, 37, 292, 294
Don Basin, 61, 206
Donets'k/Stalino, 52, 208, 216
Doopsgezinde Bijdragen, 252
Drachten, 261
draft. *See* military conscriptions
Dresden, 116, 300
Driedger, Erika, 143n34
Driedger, Jonas J., 87
Drooge, Alexander Hubertus van,
  257–8, 260
Drooge, Johann Hubertus van, 267n35
Drooge-Stoffel, Sytske van, 267n35
Drooge-ter Haar, Eddy van, 260,
  266n29
Drywa, Danuta, 308
Dueck, Johann. *See* Ivan Ivanovich
  Dik

Dufour-van Hall, Hester, 268n43
Dumitru, Diana, 19
Dutch Mennonite Emigration Office, 156
Dutch Mennonite Mission (*Doopsgezinde Zendings Vereniging*), 256
Dyck, A.I., 228n69
Dyck, Elfrieda, 280
Dyck, Isaak, 224n19
Dyck, Johannes, xii
Dyck, Peter J., 276, 280, 312–14

Eash, William, xi
Eastern Front Medal (*Ostmedaille*), 57–8
Ecumenical Conference on Life and Work (Oxford, 1937), 80
Ediger, Jakob, 65n14
Egides, Revekka, 233
Ehrt, Adolf, 15
Eicher, John, 14
Eichmann, Adolf, 55, 69n48
Eichmann, Eduard, 186, 188
Eicks, Jakob, 71n63
Einlage. *See* Nove Zaporizhzhia/ Kitschkas/Einlage
Einsatzgruppen. *See* mobile killing squads
Einwanderer Zentralstelle. *See* Central Bureau for Immigration
Eisenhower, Dwight, 13
Elikinson, Pavel, 241
Elspeet, 154, 157
Emden, 86, 255
England, 157
English Civil War, 75
Enns, Johann, 132
Epp, Adina, 24, 269, 271, 273–5, 279–81
Epp, David, 247n74
Epp, Frank H., 10, 65n14

Epp, Hans, 236
Epp, Johann, 134, 137
Epp, Maria, 216
Epp, Marlene, 10
Epp family, 13, 14
Erasmus, 159
Ersak, Vladimir, 238, 246n63
Eschatology, 140
Essentuki, 62
Etersheim, 263n7
Ethnic German Liaison Office (*Volksdeutsche Mittelstelle*), 136, 138, 206, 272–4, 278–9, 291
ethnic Germans, 16, 18, 20, 22, 35, 41, 52, 54, 134–5, 172, 175, 177, 179–80, 188, 191, 202–21, 229, 231, 270–1, 273, 275, 277, 292, 296–7
Ethnic Germans List (*Deutsche Volksliste*), 180, 187, 272–3
Extraordinary State Commission to Investigate German-Fascist Crimes Committed on Soviet Territory, 47

Fallingsbostel, 311
Fast, Alfred, 86
Fast, Gerhard, 46, 229, 292, 295
Fast, Ivan, 54, 237–8, 246n63, 247n66, 248n88
Fast, Jacob, 54, 237–8, 239, 246n63
Fast, Natalie Toews, 238–9, 247n73
Federal District Court, Manhattan, 55
Federation (*Verband deutscher Mennonitengemeinden*), 4, 6, 125–6
Federau, Rudolf, 208, 211–14
Fellmann, Ernst, 111
Fellmann, Walter, 97n40, 99n48, 101n66
Feodosija, 216, 224n21
Fischer, Fritz, 314
Fisher, Michael J., xii

Floh, Jacob Hendrik, 251
Florida, 51
Foerster, R., 138
Fomenko, Stephan, 238, 246n63, 247n66
Foth, Albert, 186–7
France, 6, 12, 22
Franco-Prussian War, 88
Franken-Duparc, Else, 264n12
Fransen Family Foundation, xi
Fraser Valley, 315
Fredeshiem, 154, 157
free church, 21, 72–80
freedom of conscience, 76–80
French Revolution, 5, 86, 251
Frie, Roger, 294–5
Friesen, Aileen, xii, 11, 19, 21, 23
Friesennot (movie), 16
Friesland, 171n57
Fuchs, Emil, 85, 91, 100n59, 101n60
Fuchs, Klaus, 100n59
Funk, Hilde, 109, 111
Funk Kaserne, 276

Gąbin, 172–92
Galicia, 6, 48
Galician Mennonites, 27n12
gas vans, 3, 52, 60, 71n69
gay men, 73
Gdańsk/Danzig, 3, 5, 6, 14, 16, 24, 57, 81, 88, 101n67, 106, 122n25, 126, 129, 275, 307, 308, 309
Gelderland, 154
Gemeindeblatt, 82, 129–30
genealogy, 131, 135, 139, 145n50
General Mennonite Conference (*Algemene Doopsgezinde Sociëteit*), 155–6, 158–9, 257
Geneva, 314
genocide, 4, 11, 62
Georgiyevsk, 62
Gering, Jon, xi

Gerlach, Horst, 309
German Catholic Aid Society, 307, 311–12
German Christian Movement, 48, 130, 145n49
German citizenship, 54
German Communist Party, 87
German Democratic Republic, 100n59
German Evangelical Baptists, 95n24
German Foreign Institute, 135, 137, 149n95
Gestapo, 71n63, 85, 100n57, 157, 186, 212, 240, 267n38, 296, 297
ghetto, 11, 55, 138, 173, 178, 186, 191, 233
Giethoorn, 265n17
Gilse, Sophie van, 267n38
Gingerich, Josef, 91
Glass factory massacre, 3, 39, 57–62
Glück, Theo, 107–8, 115, 119n2
Gnadenfeld, 219
Gnadental. *See* Vodiana
Goebbels, Joseph, 96n27, 133, 274
Goertz, Hans-Jürgen, 105, 119n5, 140
Goossen, Benjamin, 10, 89, 141n1, 202
Goryachevodsky, 60
Gostynin, 186, 190
Gottgläubig, 57
Göttingen, 46
Göttner, Erich, 81, 83, 106, 110–11, 122n25, 126, 127
Götz, Karl, 137–8
GPU, 43, 44, 60, 240. See also *KGB*; *NKVD*; *OGPU*; *SMERŠ*
Graf, Matthias, 269, 271, 275
Graz, Austria, 213
Great Depression, 87, 102n68
Greiser, Arthur, 88–9, 136, 150n101
Groningen, 157

Groot, Inne de, 165
Grüber, Heinrich, 252
Gulag, 44, 192, 236, 271–2, 297, 300, 301, 311
Guyana, 156

Haar, Bernard ter, 257
Haarlem, 159, 253–4, 260, 266n29, 267n38, 267n38
Hacke, Richard, 178
Halbstadt. *See* Molochans'k/Halbstadt
Halbwachs, Maurice, 17
Hall, Walraven van, 260, 267n43
Hamburg, 6
Händiges, Emil, 100n57, 126–7, 129, 138
Hannover, 239
Harder, Gerhard. *See* Luitjens, Jacob
Harder, Hans, 13, 37, 48
Harms, Maria, 205–6, 215–16, 220, 227n66
Harvey, Elizabeth, 24
Hege, Christian, 146n65
Hegewald Project, 67n29
Heidelberg, 130
Heier, Wilhelm, 181
Helm, Krijn van der, 260
Heniches'k, 214
Hesse, 98n40, 122n25
Hesston College, xi, 10
Heubuden, 126, 137
Heydrich, Reinhard, 57, 95n25
Hiersack, Karl, 236
Hilberg, Raul, 38
Hildebrand, Diedrich, 300–1
Hildebrandt, Mary, 297
Hillesum, Etty, 258
Hillesum, Louis, 258
Hillesum, Mischa, 258
Himmler, Heinrich, 8, 35, 41, 51, 57, 67n29, 79, 95n25, 136

Hindeloopen/Koudum, 264n12
Hinz, Alfred, 309
Historikerstreit, 315
Hitler, 8, 21–2, 24, 41, 44, 67n30, 72, 79–80, 87, 89, 126–7, 129, 133, 135, 136, 138, 142n17, 144n44, 153, 158, 176, 181, 183, 203, 214, 218, 250, 290, 293, 294, 300, 302–3
Hitler Youth, 35, 133, 180, 183, 187
Hochfeld, 45
Hoekema, Alle G., 17–18, 21, 23, 156, 167n3
Hoekema, Gabe B., 153, 167n3
Hoffmeyer, Horst, 208, 284n41
Holborn, Louise, 281
Holst, Adriaan Roland, 265n24
Homan, Gerlof D., 155–6, 167n5, 252–3
Honecker, Martin, 105
Hoy, Lise Rempel, 39n1
Huebert, John, 52
Hungarians, 211
Hutterites, 5, 85
Hylkema, 55
Hylkema, Cornelis Bonne, 22, 153–66
Hylkema, Govert W., 171n60
Hylkema, Tjeerd Oeds, 252

IJlst, 263n9, 264n12
Indonesia, 132, 167n3, 264n12
Ingwersen, Johannes, 265n23
Inja, Cor, 258
International Refugee Organization, 277–81, 311–12, 314
Israel/Palestine, 10, 101n61, 158
Italian fascism, 158

Jacobs, Netty, 260
Jansen, Gérard, 263n9
Jantzen, Eric, 118
Jantzen, Mark, xi, 9, 15, 118, 221
Janzen, Elizabeta Julévna, 215–16

Janzen, Heinrich, 41–2
Janzen, Jacob H., 126, 138
Janzen, Victor, 301
Janzen, Waldemar, 292, 298–9
Janzen, Wilhelm, 298
Java. See Indonesia
Jehovah's Witnesses, 90
Jewish Council (*Joodsche Raad*), 258
Jewish sources/perspectives, 23
Jewish-Mennonite intermarriage, 5, 37, 299
Jewish-Mennonite relations, 19, 42–3, 126, 134, 172–92, 201n65, 230–5, 242n10, 250–61, 295–6, 299–300
Jost, Hulda, 84

Kaganovich, Lazar, 302
Kahan, Stuart, 302
Kalinindorf, 231
Kamianske/Dniprodzerzhynsk, 45
Kansas, 14, 28n19, 39
Karaites, 50, 67n31
Kassel, 228n68
Katharinendorf, 45
Kazan, 160
Kehrer, 60
Kerch Peninsula, 53
Keuning, Herman, 266n29
Keuning-Tichelaar, An, 260, 266n29
KGB, 11, 69n50, 203. See also *GPU*; *NKVD*; *OGPU*; *SMERŠ*
Kharkiv, 208, 215–16
Khortytsya, 229–41. See also Novokhortytsya; Verkhnya Khortytsya
Kieling, 237
Kiev, 44, 49–50, 58, 221
Kipp, Michaela, 116
Kislovodsk, 3, 61–2
Kitchener-Waterloo, 38
Kitschkas. See Nove Zaporizhzhia/Kitschkas/Einlage

Kladov, I.F., 71n63
Klassen, Andrej, 227n61
Klassen, C.F., 280–1, 312–13
Klassen, Dietrich, 208
Klassen, Ivan Ivanovič, 11, 216–17, 219
Klassen, Otto, 232, 234, 300–1
Kliewer, Gustav, 177, 187
Kliewer, Julius, 245n54
Kliewer, Reinhold, 181
Kohut, Andriy, 221
Kolpanov, Boris, 238
Komsomol, 205
Königsberg, 91
Konijnenburg, Martha van, 267n38
Koning, Petronessa, 255
Konrad, Karl, 272
Konstantinovka, 214
Korff, Friedrich, 235
Korff, Tamara, 234–5
Kostenetzky, Olga, 237
Kotomtsev, I.F., 71n63
Koudum. See Hindeloopen/Koudum
Kovalevsky (Jewish family), 56
Kraemer, Gustav, 81, 125, 128–9, 138, 142n17, 144n45
Krahn, Cornelius, 66n28, 118, 130, 240, 263n6, 277
Krahn, Ivan, 246n63
Kraków, 16
Krasnodar, 52, 53, 59
Krefeld, 6, 77, 81, 94n16, 111, 125, 128–9, 138–9, 144n45
Kristallnacht, 117, 129–30, 252
Kroeger, E., 45
Kroeker, Jakob, 41
Kroeker, John J., 41–2, 55, 278
Kröger, 134
Krüger, Heinrich, 143n34
Krüger, Katharina, 297–8
Kryvyi Rih, 45–6, 213

Kuhn, Walter, 135
Kuiper, Frits, 22, 153–66, 251
Kuiper, Johanna, 263n7
Kulaks, 15, 203, 270
Kursk, 46
Kuyt, Abraham, 252, 263n8

Ladekopp, Poland. *See* Lubieszewo/Ladekopp, Poland
Ladekopp, Ukraine, 52
Langheld, Wilhelm, 71n63
Latter, Helene Frey, 233, 296–7
Latter, Walter, 296
League of German Girls, 116, 133, 180, 183
Leers, Johann von, 133
Leeuwarden, 260
Leibbrandt, Georg, 47
Leipzig, 41–2
Lemberg. *See* Lviv
Lemieux, Francois, 54
Leontev, Nikolaj, 69n50
Lepp, Olga, 245n47
Lerner, Leonid, 229
Letkemann, 213
Letkemann, Peter, 141n1
Leyden, 267n38
Lichdi, Diether Götz, 78, 105, 117, 119n5, 127, 310
Lichtenau. *See* Svitlodolyns'ke
Lichti, James Irvin, 20–2, 105–6
Lichti, Otto, 99n48
Łódź/Litzmannstadt, 41, 53, 136, 138, 150n101
Loewen, Harry, 69n48
Loewen, Royden, xii
Loganbill, Alec, xi
Logtenberg, Johanna Cornelia, 260
Lorraine, 6
Low German, 37, 276
Lower, Wendy, 8
Lubieszewo/Ladekopp, Poland, 308

Lublin, 55
Lubny, 46
Ludwigshafen, 147n74
Luftwaffe, 308
Luitjens, Jacob, 15–16, 31n47
Lumans, Valdis, 136
Lustig, Peter, 255
Lutbrandau, 137
Luther, Martin, 98n44, 140
Lutherans, 20, 28n19, 45, 83, 91, 95n25, 97n38, 98n43, 100n59, 190, 206, 215, 251
Lviv/Lemberg, 6, 48

Madagascar Plan, 138, 151n114
Magdeburg, 48
Makhno, Nestor, 237, 270
Makkum, 257, 266n29
Manitoba, 132
Mannhardt, Hermann G., 88
Marburg, 122n25
Marienthal. *See* Panfilivka
Mariupol', 54
Marpeck, Pilgram, 131
Marpeck Funk, xi
Marwell, David, 53
Marx, Karl, 163
Matčanbaeva, T.V., 212–13, 216, 226n42
Mazovia, 6, 11, 19
McKenna (judge), 55
Mecklenburg, 217
Meier, Erich, 71n63
Mein Kampf, 8, 133, 181, 237
Melitopol', 46, 52–3, 208, 212, 214, 216, 229
Melle, Friedrich Heinrich Otto, 96n31
Melnyk, Michael J., 211
Memory/myth, 17–20
Mengele, Josef, 69n48
Menno Pass, 55, 276

Menno Simons, 105, 130, 144n44
Mennonite Aid Office (*Doopsgezinde Hulp Bureau*), 157
Mennonite Brethren, 176, 183, 188–9
Mennonite Central Committee, 10, 15, 24, 55, 276, 278, 280–1, 296, 311–12, 314
Mennonite Church USA, 9, 10
Mennonite exceptionalism, 8
Mennonite Heritage Centre, 44
Mennonite identity/definitions, 8, 12–17, 18, 20, 24, 37, 72–91
Mennonite Library and Archives, xi, 10
Mennonite Life, 295
Mennonite Mission Board (*Doopsgezinde Zendingsraad*), 167n3
Mennonite origins, 4
Mennonite Peace Group (*Doopsgezind Vredesgroep*), 157
Mennonite Peace Manifesto (1936), 78
Mennonite Polish Studies Association, xi
Mennonite population statistics, 5–6
Mennonite Seminary (Amsterdam), 167n3, 167n4
Mennonite World Conference, 78, 139, 140, 155
Mennonite Youth Circular Community, 104–18
Mennonites and the Holocaust conference (2018), xi, 9
Mennonites as Dutch, 270, 275, 277, 279
Mennonites as rescuers of Jews, 3, 23, 153, 155, 157, 160
Mennonites as translators, 11, 52, 53, 213–16, 219, 240
Mennonites as war criminals, 3, 10, 11, 15, 35, 41, 51–6, 153
Mennonitische Blätter, 87, 112
Mennonitische Jugendwarte, 84

Mennonitische Rundschau, 188
Mesdag, Willem, 252, 260, 264n9
Mesdag-Hylkema, Sjoukje, 260, 264n9
Messerschmidt, Manfred, 53
Methodists, 73, 96n31, 105
Mexico, 157
Military conscription, 108–9, 177, 182
Milliman, Robert, xi
Mineralnye Vody, 3, 61–2
Ministry for the Occupied East, 292
Minlerčik, 204
Mobile Killing Squad C, 11, 24, 45, 59
Mobile Killing Squad D, 3, 45–6, 51, 53, 58–9
mobile killing squads, 16, 36, 41, 47, 52–3, 60–2, 211–12, 271, 290, 301
Modi'in, Israel, 161
Mohr, Robert, 45
Molochans'k/Halbstadt, 3, 51, 52, 57, 68n46, 133, 206, 208, 211–15, 217, 231, 236
Molotov-Ribbentrop Pact, 22
Molotschna Colony, xiii, 11, 52, 126, 132–3, 148n80, 206, 208, 215, 218–19, 232, 290, 296–7
Moltmann, Jürgen, 140
Monnickendam, 251
Morden, Manitoba, 296
Moscow, 205
Mueller, Wilhelm, 100n53
Müller, Erich, 59, 60
Munich, 122n25, 276
Münster, Hans, 71n63
Muntau. *See* Yablunivka
Musch, Jan, 265n24
Muslims, 87
Musmanno, 269
Mussert, A.A., 159
Mussolini, Benito, 168n19
Myeshkov, Dmytro, 11, 19, 21–3, 36
Mykolaiv, 59

Napoleonic Wars, 174
National Socialist Movement (Netherlands), 22, 154, 156, 158–9, 162–4, 250
National Socialist People's Welfare (*NSV*), 235
National Socialist Teachers League, 188
National Socialist Women's League (*Nationalsozialistische Frauenschaft*), 116
Nazi church-state policy, 72–91
Nazi Party, 3, 14, 57, 102n68, 116, 121n22, 127–9, 133, 150n101, 172, 187–9, 301
Neff, Christian, 84, 97n38, 98n40, 99n49
Nelyubova, Anastasia, 229
Netherlands, 5, 12, 23, 55, 126, 129, 140, 153–66, 250–61, 277
Neufeld, Jacob A., 246n57, 272, 274, 291
Neufeldt, Colin P., 11, 19, 21–2, 173
Neufeldt-Fast, Arnold, 11, 21–2, 111
Neustadt, 273
Neuteich. *See* Nowy Staw
New Economic Policy, 270
Nickel, Richard, 94n22
Nickolaidorf, 63n8
Niemöller, Martin, 85, 101n60
Nieuwenhuijzen, Jan, 251
Nieuwenhuis, Nico, 254
Nijhoff, Martinus, 265n24
Nikopol', 41, 45
NKVD, 15, 23, 203–5, 219, 221, 224n19, 227n66, 232, 270–2, 301. See also *GPU*; *KGB*; *OGPU*; *SMERŠ*
nonresistance, 5, 72, 76–80, 139, 163–4, 182–3
North Holland, 154
Norway, 95n25

Nove Zaporizhzhia/Kitschkas/Einlage, 44, 46, 206, 208, 210–11, 240, 242n10. *See also* Zaporizhzhia
Novick, Peter, 17
Novokhortytsya, 134–5. *See also* Khortytsya; Verkhnya Khortytsya
Novopyatigorsk, 60. *See also* Pyatigorsk
Novo-Zlatopol, 231
Nowe Wymyśle/Deutsch Wymyschle, 11, 19–20, 172–192
Nowy Staw/Neuteich, 308
Nuremberg Laws, 85, 114, 130, 133, 145n50, 156
Nuremberg Trials, 139, 269

Oaths, 72
Oberlander, Helmut, 14, 38, 51–3, 59
Odessa, 48, 202, 215
OGPU, 204, 219. See also *GPU*; *KGB*; *NKVD*; *SMERŠ*
Ohlendorf, Otto, 59
Oleksandrivs'k/Schönwiese, 45
Olgino, 62
Ontario, 51, 126
Oosthuizen, 263n7
Operation Market Garden, 256
Orel, 46
Orenburg, 205
Orlove/Ohrloff, 217–18, 236
Orłowskie Pole/Orlofferfelde, 309
Orthodox, 50, 230–1
Osterwick. *See* Dolyns'ke/Osterwick
Oudebildtzijl, 164–5
Overijssel, 154

Pacifism. *See* nonresistance
Palache, Jehuda Lion, 252
Palatinate, 6, 104, 122n25
Panfilivka/Marienthal, 134
Pannabecker, Rachel, xi
Panova, Maria, 221

Paraguay, 16, 69n48, 157, 276, 280, 293, 301
Paris, 278
Partisans, 41
Pauls, Minna Ratzlaff, 183–4
Pauls, Peter, 184
Pavlivka/Paulsheim, 134
Pel, Trijnie, 4
Pel, Wijbrand, 258, 260
Pel-Groot, Geertje, 3–4, 17, 258–60
Pelplin, Poland, 311
Penner, Horst, 309–10
Penner, Lydia, 166
Penner, Maria, 42
Pentecostals, 105, 120n11
People's Militia (*Volkssturm*), 192
Peters, 136
Peters, Helene, 232, 235
Pfann-Pel, Trijnie, 259
Pikloenko, Nikolaj Abramovič. *See* Dierksen, Johann Genrichovič
Pilate, 162
Pintus, Peter, 28n19
Piontkovskiy. *See* Federau, Rudolf
place names, usage of, xii
Plotha, 42
Pohl, J. Otto, 270
Pokrovsk, 228n69
Poland, partitions, 174
Poljakova. *See* Harms, Maria
positive Christianity, 21, 84, 86, 147n68
Post, Pieter, 11, 18, 21
Poznań/Posen/Wartheland, 6, 41–2, 88, 95n25, 126, 136–8, 150n102, 241
Presbyterians, 250, 255
Preussisch Stargard, 273
Prins, Aäron, 263n6
Pripet Marshes, 53
Prochnau, Daniel, 177, 187
Protestant Refugee Committee, 252
Protestant Relief Work, 311

Prussia (East, West), 104, 111, 126, 129
Prussian State Library, 46
Pryshyb/Prischib, 137
Puritans, 75
Pyatigorsk, 3, 59, 60–1, 205, 228n68. *See also* Novopyatigorsk

Quakers, 21, 73, 84–5, 90, 100n56, 100n59, 103n87, 157
Quiring, Horst, 81, 110–11, 126, 130, 138, 140, 145n49, 146n60
Quiring, Walter/Jacob, 13, 69n48

Ratzlaff, Agnes Pauls, 174
Ratzlaff, Alma, 181
Ratzlaff, David, 181
Ratzlaff, Ella, 173
Ratzlaff, Erhard, 184, 187
Ratzlaff, Erich L., 172–3, 177–8, 183, 186–8
Ratzlaff, Erich P., 201n65
Ratzlaff, Frieda, 20, 172–3, 181–2
Ratzlaff, Gustav, 174, 183–4
Ratzlaff, Leonard P., 183
Ratzlaff, Maria, 183
Ratzlaff, Peter, 20, 172–4, 181
Ratzlaff, Richard, xii
Ravensbrück, 4, 259, 267n38
Red Army, 5, 24, 42, 52, 56, 59, 62, 181, 184, 192, 210, 213, 215–17, 219, 235, 241, 259, 270–1, 275–6, 294, 297, 308, 311, 313
reformed, 98n43, 215, 250, 254–5, 257, 261
Reich Ministry for the Eastern Occupied Territories, 46
Reich Security Main Office, 60
Reichstag, 57
Reimer, Gustav, 137, 138
Reimer, Isaak I., 208, 211, 219, 221, 236

Reimer, Jack, 10, 12–13, 54–5, 68n46
Reimer, Jacob, 68n46
Reimers, Cornelius, 271
Reimers, Franziska, 24, 269, 271, 275–6, 280–1
Rempel, Alexander, 37, 44–7, 59, 71n63, 240
Rempel, Gerhard, 5, 12, 14, 20–1, 23, 35–9, 69n47, 309
Rempel, Hans, 47
Rempel, Helena, 299
Rempel, Jakob Aron, 44
Rennert, Ferdinand, 177, 187
Retzlaff, Reinhard, 71n63
Reuter, Sasha, 297
Rhönbruderhof, 85, 100n57, 157
Riemsdijk, Joseph Hubert van, 251–2
Righteous Among the Nations, 23, 234, 253
Rode, 178
Roeper, Dirk, 255
Roeper, Dirk, Jr, 255
Roeper-Bakker, Femina, 255
Roma, 3, 36, 47, 51, 179, 210–11, 216
Romanian military, 47–8, 297
Roostee, Ina, 265n23
Roostee, Johannes, 255, 260
Roostee-Roeper, Petronella Maria Geertruida, 255
Rosenberg, Alfred, 47, 79, 95n25, 292
Rosenfeld, Harry, 281
Rosental, Caucasus, 205
Rosenthal, Chortitza Colony, 45, 233
Rosenthal, Judith, 118
Ross, Alexander, 273
Ross, Olga Petrikow, 273
Rossman, 208
Rostov, 54, 61
Rotfeld, 136
Rotterdam, 157
Rottevalle, 264n12

Royse, Morton, 277
Rozendaal, Marianne, 255
Russian Civil War, 230, 236, 270
Russian Revolution, 202, 236

SA (*Sturmabteilung*), 108–9, 115, 121n22, 122n23, 138
Saint Petersburg, 236
Sanniki, 190
Sarabuz, 204
Sawatzky, John, 299
Sawatzky, Peter, 301
Schaft, Hannie, 266n29
Schindler Factory Museum, 16
Schipper, Klaas Abe, 263n7
Schlick, Friedrich, 143n42
Schmidt, Leonard, 181
Schmidt, Minna, 181
Schmidt, Paul, 96n31
Schmutz, Herbert, 111
Schnebele, Christian, 82, 97n39, 98n42, 130, 138, 143n41
Schneider, Daniel, 113
Schneider, Ferdinand, 178, 186
Schöneberg, 234
Schönwiese. *See* Oleksandrivs'k
Schoorl, 154, 157
Schowalter, Jochen, 119n2
Schowalter Foundation, xi
Schröder, Heinrich Hajo, 13, 132, 146n65
Schroeder, J.H., 39
Schroeder, Steven, 18, 20, 24, 25
Schroeder, Wilhelm, 187
Schulz, 213
Schutte, Henk, 254
SD (*Sicherheitsdienst*), 45, 51, 53, 57, 92n3, 95n25, 186, 206, 210–17, 221, 237–41, 259, 281, 301
Seenwijk, 154
self-defense units (*Selbstschutz*), 179, 206, 208, 272, 291

Selydove/Selidovka, 55–6
Sepp, A.A., 159
Sermon on the Mount, 131
Šestakovka, 216
Seventh-day Adventists, 21, 73, 84–5, 87, 99n52, 100n53, 102n70, 102n72, 105
Sharp, John, xi, 10
Shilko, Aleksandr, 233
Shoah Foundation Visual History Archive, 9
Shubert, Nikolai, 246n63, 247n66
Siberia, 45, 205, 271
Siderenko, Nikolai, 52
Sierakówek, 186
Simferopol', 58–9, 203–5, 208, 211–16, 220, 228n68
Sinti, 179. See also Roma
Sinz, Kurt, 84
Sipkema, J.W., 261
Sladek, Paulus, 307
Slooten, Johanna van der, 260, 263n9, 264n12
SMERŠ, 217, 228n69. See also GPU; KGB; NKVD; OGPU
Smith, C. Henry, 155
Sneek, 251, 260–1
Sobibor, 4, 258
Social Democrats, 86, 87, 154, 158, 163
Social Science and Humanities Research Council of Canada, xii
Söder, Hans-Peter, 294
Sohm, Rudolf, 92n8
Soviet nationalities policy, 270
Soviet prisoners of war, 36, 42, 56
Spain, 144n44
Sparrau, 219
Spat, 204, 224n19
Special Unit Russia, 48, 202, 206
Special Unit Stumpp, 135, 208, 292
Spittler, Hans, 147n74

SS (*Schutzstaffel*), 3, 13–14, 16, 35, 41, 47–8, 53–4, 57–9, 69n47, 129, 137–8, 143n34, 187, 208, 212–13, 215, 217, 234, 272, 275, 281, 300–1. *See also* Waffen-SS Division Galizien
St Catharines, Ontario, 54
Stalin, 6, 19, 24, 44, 132, 139, 218, 229, 231, 293, 300–3
Stalindorf, 231
Stalingrad, 59
Stalino. *See* Donets'k/Stalino
Steigmann-Gall, Richard, 89
Steinfeld, 236
Steinhart, Eric, 10, 202
Stern, Steve, 24, 300
St'o:lō people, 315
Stoner, Andre Gingerich, 9
Stragen, Eduard van, 264n12
Strohschneider, 61
Strübind, Andrea, 89
Stucky, Renae, xi
Stumpp, Karl, 135–6, 149n95, 237, 292. *See also* Special Unit Stumpp
Stutthof. *See* Sztutowo
Sudermann, Anna, 37, 43–4, 231, 233–4, 238–9, 247n73, 295, 296, 302
Suvorovka, 62
Svitlodolyns'ke/Lichtenau, 218
Svobody, 60
Swaab, Betsy, 258
Swaab, Hijman, 259
Swaab, Marion, 4, 259, 261
Switzerland, 259
Sztutowo/Stutthof, 5, 14, 24, 308–10

Taganrog, 52, 54
Task Force against Military Service (*Arbeidsgroep tegen de Krijgsdienst*), 154, 157–8, 169n33

Task Force of Mennonites and Kindred Spirits (*Werkgemeenschap Doopsgezinden en Geestverwanten*), 157
Tatars, 205, 212–13
Tavonius, 57
Taylor, C.J., 278
Tchaikovsky (Soviet general), 271
Tempelhof, 61–2
Terek, 62
Texel, 255
theology, 11–12, 21, 125–40, 153–66
Thiesen, John D., 10, 36–7, 69n48, 141n1
Thiessen, J.J., 313
Tierra del Fuego, 112
Timošenko, 211
Toews, Aron, 239, 247n73
Toews, H.P., 247n74
Toews, Maria Sudermann, 247n73, 313
Tokmak, 52
Tolchinski, Dmitri, 233
Tolchinski, Khaya, 233
Tolchinski, Semion, 233
Tolstoyans, 5
Toronto, 280
Transnistria, 19, 206
Trawniki, 54–5, 69n50
Treaty of Versailles, 96n29, 106, 127, 309
Treffers-Mesdag, Nine, 260
Tuininga, J.E., 265n22
Tzeyikhman, Meyir, 233
Tzeyikhman, Sara, 233

Ukraine Post, 132–4
Ukrainians, 15, 21, 23, 41, 45, 52, 58, 132, 135, 213, 219, 230–1, 233–4, 236–7, 272–3, 291–2, 296, 299
University of Toronto, xii
University of Vienna, 143n42
University of Winnipeg, xii
UNRRA, 276
Unruh, Benjamin H., 55, 127, 129, 132, 134–8, 145n50, 149n95, 151n113, 151n116
Urry, James, 10, 65n14
US Department of Justice Office of Special Investigations, 38, 41, 51, 55, 69n50

Vancouver, British Columbia, 16
Varesko, Rudolf, 272
Veendorp, Gerrit, 255, 265n22
Venda, Petr, 228n68
Verband deutscher Mennonitengemeinden. See Federation
Vereinigung der Deutschen Mennonitengemeinden. See Alliance
Vergangenheitsbewältigung, 294
Verkhnya Khortytsya, 233
Versailles. See Treaty of Versailles
Vistula Delta, 307–8, 311
Vistula River, 6
Vodiana/Gnadental, 135
Vogel, 43
Vogt, Willi, 141n1
Voigt, Karl Heinz, 90
Volendam (ship), 280
Volga, 205
Volhynia, 131, 270
Volk/völkisch, 104–18, 131–3, 138
Volkssturm. See People's Militia
Vught, 259, 267n38

Waag, Max, 259
Waag, Rebecca, 258–9
Wadden, 165, 171n57
Waffen-SS Division Galizien, 213. *See also* SS
Wannsee Conference, 47

war criminals. *See* Mennonites as war criminals
Warren, George, 277–8, 280–1
Warsaw, 55
Warthegau/Wartheland. *See* Poznań
Washington, DC, 314
Weber, Max, 74, 83, 92n8, 104
Weerafdeling (Netherlands), 162
Wegert, Reinhold, 190
Wehrmacht, 12, 24, 45–6, 59–60, 67n30, 69n47, 172, 178–9, 184, 219, 232, 291, 294, 300–1
Weidemann, Erika, 11, 18–19, 24
Weierhof, 84
Weimar Republic, 72, 76, 80, 86–8, 96n29, 101n67
Wenniger, Willem Maillette de Buy, 267n39
Wenzel, Kurt, 60, 211, 217
Werner, Hans, 5, 18, 20, 24
Westerbork, 157, 258
Westminster Confession, 75
Whip, 173, 292
White Army, 227n66, 270
Wiebe, Abraham, 219
Wiebe, Heinrich, 45, 67n31, 236–7, 239–40
Wiebe, Peter Dietrich, 41
Wiebe, Rudy, 94n16
Wieler, Joachim, 12
Wiens, A., 215
Wiens, Agnessa Korneevna, 216
Wiens, David Korneevič, 205
Wiens, E.P., 205
Wiens, Hans, 234–235
Wiens, Heinrich, 3, 4, 12, 14, 23, 30n40, 36, 39, 57–62, 71n63, 210–13, 217, 227n66
Wiens, Hermann, 57
Wiens, Jakob, 213

Wiens, Kornej Korneevič, 205, 220, 224n21
Wiens, Margaret, 39
Wiens, Suse, 234
Wiesel, Elie, 37, 140
Wiesenthal, Simon, 69n48
Wilms, Ivan, 224n19
Winkel, Miny te, 267n39
Winter, Henry, 291
Witzke, Rudolf, 181
Wohlgemuth, Heinrich, 181
Wohlgemuth, Kornelius, 181
Wohlgemuth, Lina, 181
Wolfe Chair in Holocaust Studies, xii
women, 11, 23–4, 42–3, 48, 56, 104, 116, 177, 192, 204, 210, 214, 230–1, 235–6, 254, 259–60, 269–82, 297, 299, 301–2
Wood, W.A., Jr., 280
Woodbrooke Quaker Centre, 154
World War I, 5, 15, 57, 88, 96n29, 106, 127, 169n33, 202, 219, 270, 308
Württemberg, 6, 126
Wymyśle. *See* Nowe Wymyśle/Deutsch Wymyschle

Yablunivka/Muntau, 57, 62, 211
Yad Vashem, 17, 232, 244n43, 250–61
Yakushev, L.T., 203
Yelnikov family, 234

Zaan, 157
Zaandam, Netherlands, 3, 258–9
Zaporizhzhia, 11, 23, 41–2, 44–7, 51, 54, 67n31, 203, 206, 210, 217–18, 229–41, 296–7, 301. *See also* Nove Zaporizhzhia/Kitschkas/Einlage
Zapp, Paul, 214, 228n68
Zborik, Natalya, 234
Zhytomyr, 50, 67n29
Zondagsbode, 250

www.ingramcontent.com/pod-product-compliance
Lightning Source LLC
Chambersburg PA
CBHW020351080526
44584CB00014B/982